The Boats They Sailed In

The Boats
They Sailed In

John Stephen Doherty

W. W. Norton & Company
New York   London

Published simultaneously in Canada by Penguin Books Canada Ltd,
2801 John Street, Markham, Ontario L3R 1B4
Printed in the United States of America

The text of this book is composed in Bembo, with display type set in Caslon 471.
Composition by Com-Com.
Manufacturing by The Haddon Craftsmen.
Book design by Jacques Chazaud.

Library of Congress Cataloging in Publication Data

Doherty, John Stephen.
The boats they sailed in.

1. Yachts and yachting—History. I. Title
GV812.D64   1985   797.1   85-4848
ISBN 0-393-03299-X

W. W. Norton & Company, Inc., 500 Fifth Avenue, New York, N.Y. 10110
W. W. Norton & Company Ltd., 37 Great Russell Street, London WC1B 3NU

For Ann

Contents

List of Illustrations

Simplicity and peace of mind seem to go hand-in-hand, and I've found over the years that in both sail and power the simple, slippery, mouse-powered boat has it all over the more usual over-stuffed and bejeweled boat.

... having designed some 30 million dollars' worth of yachts —many when a million was a lot of money—I can say that the simplest boats of every size were always the best and the most beloved.

—William Garden,
"Designing for Mousepower,"
Boating Magazine

The Boats They Sailed In

Preface

This is one of those books that really require a preface—a sort of town crier strolling out ahead of the text shouting, "Hear ye, hear ye, the author hereby admits and acknowledges to one and all the following about his book, that it contains. . . . "

So, I had better say something about *that*.

The choice of boats included was purely personal. The only selection control was this: I wanted to start with Slocum, include two boats from each decade (I failed in that), and end no earlier than 1980. There were twenty-four boats in the first rough selection, but the list was gradually cut back as the book progressed and early chapters ran longer than anticipated. I did not want to skimp on details, because I hope the reader will find this a "book of record," or something close to that. By that I mean that if someone finds a copy in the year 2001, he will not only take for granted the numerous craft cruising overhead but, if he's an "ancient boat" nut, will be able to find in this the spar dimensions of Pidgeon's *Islander* and similar vital trivia.

It's hard to say with assurance which came first, the boats to be included —there are hundreds to choose among—or the four themes of Simplicity, Strength, Seamanship, and Self-Sufficiency. That sounds like a classroom exercise in alliteration, but these four qualities just naturally forced themselves upon my attention during the selection process. It's probably also true —and deserves acknowledgment—that the better writers stood a better chance of having their boats included. After thirty-five years of reading cruising tales, I'm persuaded that most sailing authors are 80 percent sailor and 20 percent author. The well-told tales truly produce the sense of how it *really* is "out there" and stand out from all the rest. (They should be kept in print forever as tribute to small-boat sailors' cruising courage.)

For the professional and semiprofessional reader, I had hoped to include lines of *all* the boats, but that simply was not possible. However, I hope the reader will take special satisfaction from the isometric drawings of the hulls, which number more than I had dared hope for at the outset.

As to personal bias, I must lay claim to several: I do lean toward the heavy-displacement boat, ever since I met Gerry Trobridge and acquired his 30,000-pound circumnavigator, *White Seal*, in 1968. I also prefer the ketch rig, perhaps because that was *White Seal*'s rig, and she was the magnum opus among the boats I owned.

Another bias runs toward the *simple* approach to cruising, because I believe it's the prime—though not the only—ingredient of successful cruising. That means I fight hard to avoid convenience luxuries. I *have* been tempted, and *have* succumbed, but the 20-20 vision of hindsight has confirmed every time that luxury (complexity) leads to breakdowns, which lead to genuine inconvenience and probably unbudgeted expense. A simple but classic example: I would never install a pressure water system in my galley unless I had first fitted deep double sinks and a first-class hand or foot pump. That way, when (not if) the automatic system failed along the cruising track, my fall-back position would be the manual system, and we'd keep cruising.

Another example, which may sound like the theme of strength but is really emphasis: To me, cruising means anchoring (at least in one respect) and that means really reliable ground tackle. After owning *White Seal,* that means a heavy anchor (our working fisherman's was sixty-five pounds), a chain rode, and a windlass to handle them. These would be factored into the boat budget from the outset; and, unless I could have them—and the boat was suited to them—I would change the choice of boat.

Such matters may seem excessively precise here, but I feel they say more about the rationale behind the choice of boats in this book than would mere statements of preference.

In addition, I should note the tip of the hat I have tried to give to the backyard builder, those who *want* to build their own boats, and those who *must* if they are to go cruising. I assure them that the skipper-built boats included are regarded as having the status of any other. It seems to me that the home-built boat more forcefully emphasizes how unrelenting we must be if we want to achieve simplicity.

As for the other themes, the advice seems obvious—easy to give and hard to follow. Seamanship: Get sailing sooner, sacrifice other recreation to it, don't keep trading up to a larger boat, and make a long trial cruise before attempting an ocean. Self-Sufficiency: This one follows naturally if you can achieve Simplicity and seems to arrive on its own if you keep your boat longer—and do your own work. Strength: Well, everyone wants this quality in his or her boat, and *early* experience seems to be the surest route to achieving it.

Finally, if the reader turns the last page of this book and has strong reactions (for *or* against any boat or expressed opinion), if he finds himself rethinking his own approach to cruising, if he underlines things or adds items to his "To Do" list, and especially, if he feels he will return to the book for another reading in a couple of years, my efforts will have been amply rewarded.

Acknowledgments

A book like this, with its thousands of facts and hundreds of minor themes —sometimes crisscrossing each other like wave systems in unruly seas—can hardly be the product of a single writer. In fact, I owe a considerable debt of gratitude that extends in many directions. Thanks are due not only to the fourteen skippers whose stories make up this book (and to the fortunate circumstances that got the tales published in the first place) but to many others who provided me with commentary, technical expertise, and new information during the year I lived through the adventures of these fourteen intrepid sailors.

Before the work began, there were a number of naval architects who, over fifteen years, had a profound effect on my thinking—friendly, generous, and fascinating men, who design boats for a living and who patiently tried to reprogram my head with something beyond a mere passion for boats. Their largely unrewarded task—an obligation dumped on them by the fact that I was publishing a book each had written—was to help me see beyond the mere esthetics of a boat and try to understand from a close study of plans how it would behave at sea, what it would cost to build and maintain, what was involved in the choice among light, moderate, and heavy displacement, the significance of displacement/length and speed/-length ratios, and a half-dozen other formulae. This group includes, especially but not exclusively, Tom Colvin, Bob Beebe, Al Mason, Wink Warner, Ted Brewer, Bob Wallstrom, Bill Garden, the late Westy Farmer, and the late Jack Hanna—of *Tahiti* ketch fame, and author of considerable incisive writing on boat design. Equal thanks go to Lyle Hess for allowing me to use the plans of *Seraffyn*.

To these teachers, then, goes the credit for much of what the reader may find illuminating, interesting, or thought-provoking. As for errors, opinions regarded as cockeyed, and ideas that are off the mark, I must claim exclusive credit.

Closer to home, some special thanks are also due: to naval architect Bob Wallstrom, and Maynard Bray, technical editor of *Woodenboat* magazine, for advice on the "how" of esoteric rigs; to Lee Woas, author of *Self-Steering*

Acknowledg-ments

without a Windvane, published by my old company, Seven Seas Press, for his exhaustive experimentation with live boats and for answering the question—to my satisfaction, at least—of how Slocum got *Spray* to steer herself downwind; to John deGraff, nautical publisher extraordinaire, for many years of counsel, and guidance in finding two of the skippers in this book; to John Guzzwell, John Neal, and Lin and Larry Pardey, for providing special material for their chapters, some of which has not been published before; and especially to Captain Richard Maury, who, five decades after his cruise, labored mightily—yet with special pleasure—to produce new charts, plans, photos, and a vast store of detailed data about his beloved *Cimba.*

Finally, grateful thanks go to Eric Swenson, my editor at W. W. Norton, for his unwavering encouragement during the writing of this book, especially when I was overtaken by doubts, and for his unshakable confidence that it should be written as my impulses dictated.

Selected material in chapters 5, 8, 10, 11, 13, and 14 is reprinted from the following sources by permission of, respectively, Richard Maury (*The Saga of Cimba,* copyright © 1962 by Richard Maury), John de Graff (*My Ship Is So Small,* by Ann Davison, copyright © 1956 by Ann Davison), Peter Davies Ltd (*An Ocean to Ourselves,* by Harold LaBorde, copyright © 1962 by Harold LaBorde), Lin and Larry Pardey and Lyle Hess (*Cruising in Seraffyn,* copyright © 1976 by Lin and Larry Pardey), Patrick Stephens Ltd (*Shrimpy,* by Shane Acton, copyright © 1981 by Shane Acton), and John Neal (*The Log of the Mahina,* copyright © 1976 by John Neal).

To succeed, however, in anything at all, one should go understandingly about his work and be prepared for every emergency. I see, as I look back over my own small achievement, a kit of not too elaborate carpenter's tools and a tin clock. . . . But above all to be taken into account were some years of schooling, where I studied with diligence Neptune's laws, and these laws I tried to obey when I sailed overseas; it was worth the while.

—Joshua Slocum
Sailing Alone Around the World (1900)

Joshua Slocum

The word for him is "seamanship"; that in spite of the fact that he was almost as good a shipwright and fisherman as he was a master mariner and superb navigator. The many references to his little tin clock, used in place of a "proper" chronometer, which evoked so much incredulity and even derisive laughter in some quarters, obscured the fact that its accuracy was a minor matter to him. Slocum had long known the method of checking his "chronometer" by lunar observations, using formulae published in *Rapier's Epitome.* For many years these were also printed in the annual *Nautical Almanac,* but now they are omitted. More than any other sailor in this book, he was the consummate seaman, with thirty-five years of professional seagoing experience stowed away in his head as he set forth at the age of fifty-one to circumnavigate the earth.

We'll take a very close look at this sailor's early life, principally because we know more about him than about any other of this book's small-boat skippers. While many—if not most—readers know Slocum's *Sailing Alone around the World,* fewer will be familiar with an excellent biography of his life, *The Search for Captain Slocum,* by Walter Magnes Teller. This book, unfortunately out of print, reveals in graphic scenes why the seafaring life of a century ago was called the "era of wooden ships and iron men." The Teller book goes far beyond Slocum's to document the breadth of his seagoing experience.

Joshua Slocum was born on February 20, 1844, on North Mountain, a bleak, cold ridge in Nova Scotia that looked down on one side to the Bay of Fundy, and on the other to the farms of Annapolis Valley. Both sides of his family were seafaring people, except his father, who had the "misfortune to inherit an old clay farm" and who swallowed the anchor at an early age.

Fig. 1–1. *Joshua Slocum, in a photo that must have been taken about the time his book appeared, in a style suited to an "author" during Victoria's reign.*

When Joshua was eight, the Slocums moved to Brier Island. Here Joshua, like the other village boys, quickly became a skilled handler of any small boat on the treacherous Bay of Fundy—under oar or sail. Like most bluenoses, he never learned to swim.

When he was ten, his father removed him from school and kept him at home to help in crafting leather fishermen's boots, a job he hated but which brought in cash to feed a growing family that eventually numbered eleven children.

He was twelve when he had the inevitable run-in with his stern, authoritarian father. One day, when he was supposed to be working, he was discovered in the basement making a ship model. For this he received a beating, and the model was smashed to kindling. It's debatable which was the worse punishment. Interestingly, he bragged about his father's stern approach to child rearing and adopted it himself when he became a parent. He was a stern taskmaster to both his crews and his children, but neither cruel nor a martinet. Still, his father's beating broke the family's hold on him. He endured two more years, then ran away to sea at fourteen.

He shipped out as a cook aboard a fishing schooner, but the crew "chucked me out," he said, for lack of any culinary talent. He returned home to another thrashing but took it silently. He had a local reputation as a tough boy in a fistfight, one who could take it as well as dish it out.

At sixteen he went "foreign" for the first time, as a plain seaman from New Brunswick to Dublin, then on to Liverpool. As a foremast hand he obeyed orders at the jump, strove to please his mates and captains, and spent off-watch hours learning celestial navigation. Slocum went aboard via the hawsepipes, but he was determined to occupy a captain's cabin as quickly as brains, effort, and devotion to duty could get him there.

He next shipped out on the British ship *Tanjore* and was promoted to second mate enroute to Hong Kong. The master was a harsh man who worked his crew unmercifully under cruel conditions. Upon reaching China, Slocum sued the captain in civil court. He won the case and was awarded three months' extra wages as damages. Shipping out again to the Dutch East Indies and beyond, he came down with a tropical fever and had to be left in a hospital in Cooktown, Australia.

His next two voyages were aboard the bark *Agra,* Captain Shaw, first as second mate (age eighteen), then as chief mate (age twenty). On the first, in 1862, he was aloft during a sail change when he suddenly slipped and fell from the upper topsail yard. He would have been a dead man—and someone else the first solo circumnavigator—except that his fall was broken violently when his head and shoulder hit the main yard many feet below. This probably saved his life; but it left him with a scar as a memento for the rest of his days.

In 1865 he arrived in San Francisco and applied for American citizenship. This was not such a radical shift of national allegiance, as his ancestors had all been American, forced to emigrate to Nova Scotia after the American Revolution because of their Royalist sympathies.

Now his young career took a sharp turn, toward two other nearly equal passions—boatbuilding and fishing. With a partner, he built a 35-foot gill-net boat and went salmon fishing out of the Columbia River. Next, the two men turned to sea otter hunting for a season off Vancouver Island. But after these two brief excursions into money-making ventures, Slocum was ready to return to the sea; his apprenticeship was over.

The next time he shipped out, it was as master. Over the next twenty years, 1869–89, he was to hold eight commands, each new vessel a step up in size and grandeur; or, when a succeeding vessel was smaller, it found him as partial or full owner. Like many cruising men after him, Slocum was trading up to his ideal vessel.

Space limitations permit only a cursory glance at those two decades. The full story may be found in Teller's book *(see Bibliography).* We must remember that what follows are mere highlights, just the tip of the proverbial iceberg that constituted all he had learned about the sea and the way of ships in two decades. In sum it was thousands of facts and phenomena, observed, understood, catalogued, and tucked away for future use as a skilled practitioner of Neptune's laws. Here are the eight commands:

The first was a coasting schooner (name and size unknown), sailing between San Francisco and Seattle. This lasted only a year but gained him the title of captain. His second, the 332-ton bark *Washington,* took him to Australia, where he met and married Virginia Walker, an American girl of twenty-two. She became his wife, mother of their four children, his closest friend and his most trusted counselor. Virginia moved aboard for their honeymoon and lived aboard all his ships until the day she died. The *Washington*'s next destination was Cook's Inlet, Alaska, in quest of salmon. Anchored there, the bark was totally wrecked in an onshore gale, but Slocum and his crew built a 35-foot whaleboat, salvaged the salmon catch, and shipped it home. The owners were so impressed they gave him a new command.

Aboard the barkentine *Constitution,* in 1872, Slocum's first son, Victor, was born. Plying the route between San Francisco and Honolulu, this new command afforded Virginia Slocum a pleasant social life with the wives of other captains when the barkentine was taking on cargo in the islands. The next vessel, the full-rigged ship *B. Aymar,* was the "lying-in" place for a second son and a daughter. But in 1875, while in Manila, Slocum learned the ship had been sold.

Without a new command, he turned back to shipbuilding. He was awarded a contract for a steamship hull and, to make a profit on his low bid, set up a rough jungle shipyard on the beach at Olongapo, Luzon. With native shipwrights, he turned out the hull in twelve months. Slocum's payment was part cash and the rest in the form of a 90-ton schooner.

This fifth command (now as owner) was the *Pato* ("duck" in Spanish), and onto it he moved his growing family. Slocum sailed her 2000 miles into the North Pacific, and there, off the Russian port of Petropovlovsk, the crew caught and salted 25,000 codfish in two weeks! Then, sailing east, he sold the catch in Portland, Oregon, at a handsome profit. That, plus the proceeds from selling *Pato* in Honolulu, enabled him to purchase his sixth command —at last owner of a "proper ship."

The *Amethyst* was a full-rigged ship of 350 tons, and for two years Slocum sailed her in the Oriental lumber trade. When that trade sagged, he took any cargo he could find. It was a strenuous life, and in 1881, when Virginia gave birth to a last son, her health began to deteriorate. Slocum then sold the *Amethyst* in Hong Kong and acquired part-ownership of the *Northern Light,* which he undoubtedly imagined would be his grandest, and perhaps final, command.

Northern Light was a full-rigged ship, 220 feet overall, with three decks and a displacement of 1800 tons—over 4 million pounds! Slocum purchased the previous captain's shares, and this move put the family into truly sumptuous quarters—paneled brightwork, gilded interior carvings, gimbaled beds, separate cabins for all, bolted-down swivel chairs around a saloon table that encircled the mizzen mast under a tinted-glass skylight, oil paintings on the bulkheads, and even a library of leather-bound books. She was,

Fig. 1–2. *The full-rigged ship* Northern Light, *Slocum's grandest command, from a sketch made in 1885.*

Slocum said, "the finest American sailing ship afloat." But he had, apparently, not noted the imperfections lying beneath her exterior beauty, and the repairs she required were not the only tribulations Slocum faced aboard her.

While the ship was at anchor in New London, Connecticut, for rudder repairs, the ship's ragtag crew (with idle hands) suddenly turned vicious and refused to work. The first mate, thinking to snuff out the insurrection quickly by grabbing the ringleader, was stabbed to death. Slocum covered the remainder of the crew with a rifle while the Coast Guard station ashore was signaled. Then, with the ringleader arrested and jailed and a new mate signed on, Slocum sailed for Japan and on to Liverpool.

On that voyage, gales caused more rudder damage and he was forced into a South African port—more lost time and costly repairs. Under sail again, a plot by the second mate to kill Slocum and take over the ship was uncovered, and the mate was put in irons. Against Slocum's orders, the prisoner was kept below decks for fifty-three days, all the way to New York. When he was freed, he brought a charge of cruel treatment against Slocum, won his case and was awarded $500 in damages for "false and cruel punishment." Although Slocum was later exonerated, his reputation was under a cloud.

Trouble mounted upon trouble when the *Northern Light* was drydocked and found to need extensive repairs. The principal owners decided she was not worth the bother, so she was sold. With his share of the proceeds, Slocum went to Baltimore to purchase his final command. This was the

Aquidneck, a 326-ton bark, about the same size as the *Amethyst.* As soon as she was fitted out, Slocum found a cargo, brought the family aboard, and sailed for Pernambuco (now Recife), Brazil. Although it was a fast, uneventful passage, the unabated pace of life at sea, child bearing and rearing, had taken their toll on Virginia. Approaching Buenos Aires, she took to her bed. On July 25, 1884, Virginia Slocum died, apparently of a heart condition. It was the blackest day of Joshua Slocum's life.

In a deep despondency a few days after Virginia's funeral, Slocum carelessly put the bark hard aground on a shoal in the River Plate (Rio de la Plata). The cost of hauling her off with tugs was a devastating expense.

Slocum carried on, however, as was his nature, but seemed lost without his partner beside him. He sailed to Boston and parceled out his children among relatives (except Victor, now twelve, who remained with his father), and then made three quick passages between Baltimore and Brazil. On one voyage, damage to a valuable cargo caused by heavy weather made the venture a total loss. The tide of his fortunes was at lowest ebb.

In 1886, on a voyage home to visit his children, nineteen months after Virginia's death, he met (for the first time), courted, and married his first cousin, Henrietta Elliott, like himself an emigré from Nova Scotia. The twenty-four-year-old Hettie, like Virginia before her, moved aboard and made a cargo-carrying voyage to South America for a honeymoon cruise.

On July 23, 1887, Slocum faced his second mutiny. One night, Hettie, so frightened by the threatening manner of the crew's ringleader that she was unable to sleep, heard the crew coming aft—forbidden ground to fo'c'sle hands. She woke her husband, and he went on deck armed with a 56-caliber carbine. The mutinous crewmen dared Slocum to order them forward, and he did so without hesitation. When they went for him with knives drawn, he shot two of them, one fatally. That ended the mutiny.

Arriving in Rio de Janeiro, he had to stand trial—mandatory in Brazil after a death at sea. This caused more heavy expenses, in legal fees, housing his family ashore, and hiring a captain to sail the bark and keep her earning money. When the trial ended in an acquittal, Slocum decided to return once more to the still profitable lumber trade. But the fates were not through with him.

Early in 1888, while crossing Paranagua Bay, Brazil, with a full cargo of timber, the *Aquidneck* was caught between foul currents and gale-force winds and swept onto a shoal. While the heavy weather continued, salvage operations were impossible. The captain watched helplessly from shore for three days while his only possession, an uninsured bark, was pounded by the waves until her back was broken. He saved what he could—navigational instruments, charts, a few tools, and the family's personal effects.

To lose a ship was a captain's most dreaded misadventure, yet such mishaps were not uncommon in that era. Seemingly an *ordinary* master in routine port-to-port passages, his indominable qualities surfaced in adversity. Where another captain might have headed for the nearest U. S. Consul's office and received free passage home as a seaman in distress, Slocum, as always, turned to what he could do for himself.

What he could do was complete the construction of a 35-foot half-dory, half-sampan hull that had been started on the *Aquidneck*'s deck and saved from the wreck. He provided it with a three-masted Chinese lug rig and named it *Liberdade* in honor of the day on which the Brazilian slaves were freed. Then, with the entire family aboard, he sailed it 5000 miles to Washington, D. C.—a daring voyage whose story he later turned into a book. For Hettie, the *Liberdade* adventure was one too many—she never sailed with Slocum again. In fact, it soon became clear that their marriage had not been made in heaven. Slocum settled her on a small farm on Martha's Vineyard and visited her from time to time. They maintained a cordial if not a warm relationship, but it's clear that Slocum was always happy to turn back to the sea.

Slocum was almost at rock bottom. Upon the return to Boston, he was again forced to board his children among relatives. For over a year he sought another command under sail, without success. Offered a steamship by the White Star Line, he turned it down. He was a *sailing* man. He did odd jobs on the waterfront. For a time he worked as a shipwright in the famous McKay yard in Boston, but when they told him he had to join the union and pay a fifty-dollar fee, he quit. Slocum shrank from collective security arrangements. After two decades at sea, between ages twenty-five and forty-five, he had become the complete professional seaman, but now he could find no one who wanted his services. What that experience represented in 1890 is scarcely imaginable today.

One can imagine Slocum's state of mind between the daring voyage home of the *Liberdade* in 1888 and a dreary winter day in 1892, when he met an old friend on the Boston waterfront, Capt. Eben Pierce. As they gammed together, the retired whaling captain heard from Slocum directly —or perhaps sensed—Slocum's plight, and finally spoke the words so familiar to readers of Slocum's *Sailing Alone around the World:* "Come to Fairhaven," Captain Pierce said, "and I'll give you a ship. But," he added, "she wants some repairs." Thus Joshua Slocum acquired the *Spray,* and a new adventure was about to begin.

The *Spray*

The next day, when Slocum arrived at Fairhaven, Mass., across the Acushnet River from New Bedford, he discovered that his friend was having a bit of a joke on him. The "ship" in question was an antiquated oyster sloop that Capt. Pierce had been stuck with for seven years. It had made him the butt of many jokes himself.

The hull lay many yards from the river, propped up in a pasture. As she sat, the boat was 36'9" length overall, with a waterline of (approximately) 32 feet, a beam of 14'2", and a draft of 4 feet. The displacement, when Slocum launched her, inside ballast in place, was 24,000 pounds. It's a matter of considerable interest to follow Slocum's reconstruction of the vessel, because we're aware of what he planned to do with it, although that was a well-guarded secret from the gossipy waterfront clique in Fairhaven.

To say Slocum "rebuilt" the *Spray* is somewhat inaccurate. To most of us that suggests, at most, several major *repairs.* What Slocum actually did was build an *entirely new boat,* using the original hull principally as a "mold" to keep the shape intact in the transition from old to new.

He started by felling a pasture oak—whose wood he extolled for its great strength—and from it he shaped a new keel. Next he made a steambox and rigged a boiler for it. Now he was ready to reframe the hull. In new-boat construction he would have put molds at each station, as taken from the vessel's Body Plan, and bent around these molds a series of ribbands that formed the shape of the hull from stem to stern. Then he would have steam-bent the new frames, slipped them down *inside* the ribbands, and clamped them to the ribbands until they were dry and set. But he did not have this option because *Spray*'s original planking was still in place.

Instead, he steamed a series of white oak saplings, bent them over a log to the required curvature, and strapped them down until they were dry and set, only then slipping them down inside the existing planking, where the set curvature allowed him to clamp them to the old frames until he fastened them through the planking. It's probable that he left in all the original frames that were sound.

The new stem came next, also of pasture oak, and met with the approval of the sidewalk engineers who drifted out to the building site regularly. One of them said it was "fit to smash ice." Later, in the Indian Ocean, that stem did split a coral head in two, and "did not receive a blemish." The breasthooks were oak as well, these and other large structural timbers being shaped, after being roughed out at the mill, with broadaxe and adz.

Planking was "Georgia pine" (long-leaf yellow pine) 1½ inches thick; the butt blocks for the planking were not screwed on but were through-bolted. When the new planking was on, the hull was ceiled from keel to deck. The trapped air space had the effect of keeping the cabin cool in summer and warm in winter. (Although this benefit was not mentioned by Slocum, it was discovered by R. D. Culler when he built an exact replica of *Spray* in 1929 and lived aboard it for the next twenty-three years.)

If anyone thinks with awe of *Spray* taking on the Straits of Magellan, as well as all the world's major oceans, he should remember the new deck

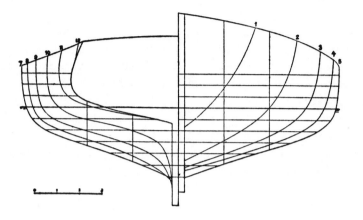

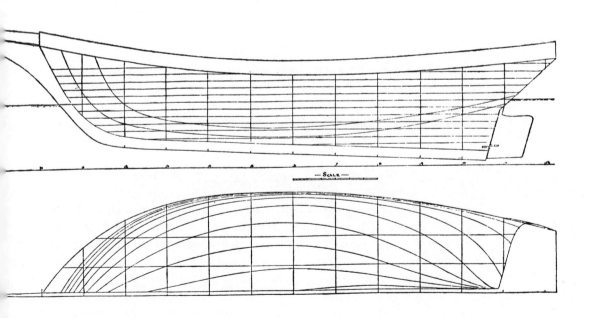

Fig. 1–3. Spray: *Body Plan and Lines Drawing.*

Slocum put in her. It started with 6″ × 6″ deck beams of oak, 36 inches center to center, and was topped with 1½-inch yellow pine planking, spiked to the beams. To visualize just how robust that is, form your fingers into a 6-inch square and then imagine its strength in solid white oak! Tom Colvin, the naval architect, builder, author, and cruising man extraordinaire, with nearly a half-century at sea, told me years ago that on a proper seagoing boat, "the decks must be at least as strong as the hull, as it's just as likely that they will take the full force of a storm wave hitting dead-on as the hull." With his shipbuilding experience, Slocum knew such things.

In this total rebuilding job—and this was a critical decision—Slocum increased the sloop's freeboard (which, since *Spray* had been a "fishing" boat, had the decks close to the water to provide easier working conditions) as follows: forward, 18 inches; amidships, 12″; aft, 14″.

There were two trunk cabins, the after one 10′ × 12′, the forward one 6′ × 6′, each rising 3 feet above the deck. The photos of *Spray* belie this height, but that's because he built new bulwarks 14 inches high, fashioned of oak stanchions sheathed with ⅞-inch white pine. (Once he got above deck level, he was careful about weight.) To prevent leaks below, he caulked each stanchion with cedar wedges on four sides, driven into the 2-inch thick covering board—lots of faying surface so the easy-swelling cedar would make up into a watertight joint. They never leaked.

The final jobs were to ship the rudder and "slap on" two coats of bottom paint and two of white-lead paint on the topsides—and *Spray* was ready for launching. He never explained how *Spray* got to the water, but when she slid in, "she sat on the water like a swan."

In all, the rebuilding job consumed thirteen months and cost Slocum $553.62—as precise a figure as we might expect from a Yankee with bluenose antecedants. To meet these costs as they arose—*some* items had to be purchased from ship chandlers—he paused in his own building efforts to work for wages on other vessels in Fairhaven harbor.

Deck Arrangement

On deck (Fig. 1–4) the layout is pretty much self-explanatory, but a few items deserve special attention. Starting from the helm, note how close the wheel is to the aft cabin. With only one aboard, Slocum didn't need deck space here, and this arrangement gave him an easy view of the compass, which was mounted behind a piece of plate glass inside the after cabin bulkhead. When steering, he was only one stride away from the companionway, enabling him to duck below quickly to glance at the chart or to grab his oilskins.

Amidships, two water casks flank the bilge pump housing. (Casks are easy to take ashore for refilling, and full ones can be lifted aboard with a

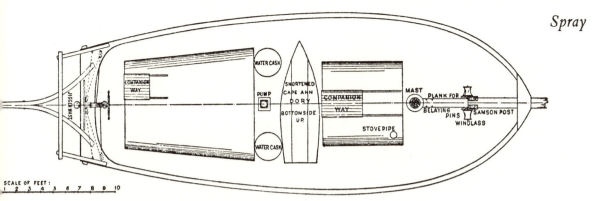

Fig. 1–4. Spray: *Deck Plan.*

halyard.) This bilge pump looks to be about 8 inches square—a size that brings up a massive gush of water with each stroke of the handle and simply dumps it on deck where it runs off under the bulwarks. This was such a standard practice Slocum probably didn't even consider through-hull fittings, although yachts may have had them in that era.

Next forward is his famous Cape Ann dory, shortened from its original length by the simple act of cutting off its stern and fitting a new transom.

The smaller forward cabin being narrower clearly provides ample foot room around the mast for working the rig without stumbling at every turn. Note, too, the plank running from the mast to the samson posts to hold the belaying pins—a simple, inexpensive system that avoided cleats on the mast. Besides, he had lived with pinrails all his days at sea.

Finally, the windlass, with its two rope gypsies. It's basically just a ratchet and cam system with nothing to go wrong, pumped by a robust oak lever (and a strong back), and provides an impressive mechanical advantage. These windlasses are still available from the Lunenburg (Nova Scotia) Foundry, with one rope gypsy and one chain wildcat, if desired. They recommend themselves to sailors with heavy boats, light pocketbooks, thick biceps, and a passion for hefty ground tackle. What Slocum carried, mind-boggling by the standards of today's "patent" anchors, were three fisherman's anchors (we now call them "yachtsman's") of 40, 100, and 180 pounds!

Before launching, *Spray*'s bilges were filled with "concrete cement," though Slocum did not specify how much. This was stanchioned down securely, since he knew the danger of shifting ballast. There was, of course, no ballast on the bottom of the keel, and this was the cause of considerable controversy after the circumnavigation. Of course, he had been sailing internally ballasted ships all his life. His brain was a computer that combined into a formula all the vital factors—stiffness of the hull shape (despite the

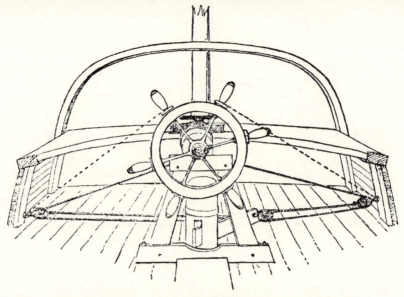

Fig. 1–5. Spray: *A sketch of the steering arrangement.*

rather shallow draft), the righting effect of the internal ballast, the weight and windage of the rig—and he reached a bottom-line answer that told him his sloop was fit for the sea and what sail adjustments would be needed to suit changing weather conditions. That he was proved right by returning successfully is perhaps too glib an answer, but he never mentioned a moment's doubt about *Spray*'s ability, and we can assume he was too good a seaman to have gone blue-water sailing in a seagoing coffin.

One notable feature on deck was the helm—cheap and strong. The sketch (Fig. 1–5) reveals that it was as simple as it was strong and foolproof. The massive rudder post came up through the deck and had a large slot cut into the head. (Note the iron band just above the slot, to prevent the turning stresses on the slot from splitting the post.) Into this slot fitted a whipstaff —just a lever arm, or tiller, facing aft. As the sketch shows, the whipstaff is moved to port and starboard, turning the rudder, by a simple arrangement of a rope running through blocks fastened to the bulwark stanchions and ending in several turns around a wooden drum that was affixed to the after side of the wheel. The beauty of this system is that with Slocum at the wheel (as we know, he wasn't there often), he merely had to glance to port and starboard to check the condition of the rope and blocks. If he spotted a bit of chafe in the nip of the rope where it passed through the blocks, it was a simple matter to move the starting point of the rope on the drum a couple of turns, thus bringing a fresh section of rope into the blocks—no different from shifting the nip of the rope on a halyard. Even if the rope didn't last a long time, it was cheap to replace.

As a final observation, *Spray* has no cockpit. That's as one would expect in an oyster sloop, whose deck was not only the crew's working platform but also the temporary storage place for the shellfish as they were brought up from the bottom. Still, one cannot imagine Slocum adding one in his rebuilding. That was a design feature for yachts, and, anyway, with bulwarks and lifelines to keep him aboard, he would not have wanted to carry the enormous weight of water the cockpit would have held, dangerously altering the trim, if *Spray* was pooped in a storm. (This passing note on cockpits is included here because the subject of cockpits in cruising boats—pro and con—will arise in several subsequent chapters.)

The Rig

Make no mistake, *Spray*'s original rig as Slocum sailed was a handful. She *was* overrigged at the start, and along the way he converted her from a sloop to a yawl, although he continued to call her a sloop (Fig. 1–6).

The boom was no less than 34 feet long at the outset, and the gaff 19 feet. The bowsprit was nearly 18 feet long (including the inboard section)

Fig. 1–6. Spray: *The Sail Plan. This shows graphically how the old oyster sloop was converted into a yawl. The solid lines show the original rig, and the dotted lines the eventual rig as converted by Slocum between Pernambuco and the Pacific side of the Straits of Magellan. Note especially that a single jib replaced the double headsails with which* Spray *started, and that the most forward sail (dotted lines) is the flying jib Slocum set on the bamboo pole he got from Mrs. Robert Louis Stevenson in Samoa.*

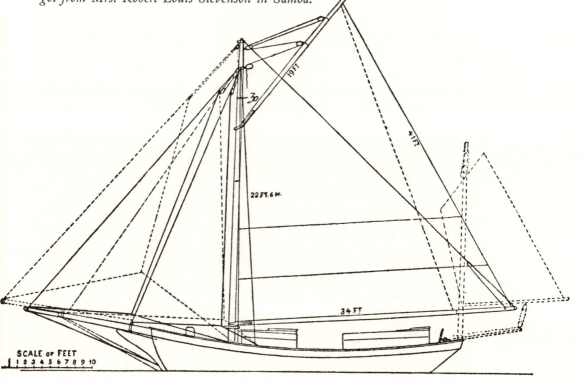

as the voyage began. Imagining the spread of sail that could be set on such a collection of spars, especially on a stormy night with driving rain and gusty winds, we shudder at the struggle it must have been to claw down armfuls of wet, flogging canvas, and we understand the Victorian expression "Pity the poor sailor on a night like this." It really was too much of a rig for a single-hander, as Slocum discovered early on. Slocum started his circumnavigation intending to sail eastabout via the Suez Canal. But at Gibraltar he was warned that Mediterranean pirates would remain a hazard to a lone sailor all the way to Suez. Heeding this advice, he changed his mind and decided to sail westabout, via Cape Horn. No sooner had he left Gibraltar than he was chased by Moorish pirates in an Arab *felucca*. He managed to outsail them and escape, but only because a freak wave that first hit *Spray* (and snapped the main boom) next struck the *felucca* and completely dismasted her. Once he was safe, Slocum fished the main boom, which had broken 4 feet outboard of the jaws, and continued his southwesterly course across the Atlantic.

Upon reaching Pernambuco, he shortened the boom once by removing the 4-foot broken piece and refitting the gaff jaws. That left the boom still 30 feet long. By now he had decided to convert to a yawl rig, so he next fitted the semicircular brace—so unique in appearance—across the stern from quarter to quarter. When he arrived in Buenos Aires, he shortened the mast by seven feet and cut five feet off the bowsprit! (He later said that he wished he had taken another foot off the bowsprit, as even shortened "it reached far enough from home.")

Some weeks later, at Port Angosto on the Pacific side of the Straits, he stepped the new mizzen mast, that spar being a "hardy spruce sapling" he had found on the beach much earlier, perhaps when he decided upon the treacherous Cape Horn route. He *knew* what that would be like. The new mizzen mast forced him to shorten the main boom *another* four feet, this time at the outboard end, and, of course, recut the mainsail a second time. With the cloths running parallel to the leech, this would not have been too difficult.

To add the mizzen mast, he attached a mast step to the vertical section of the counter stern and fitted a boomkin to form an attachment point for the sheet. Looking closely at the profile of the sail plan (Fig. 1–7) it appears that this mast is stepped on deck, but that part of the drawing is incorrect. (It's a mistake in the drawing made years later when *Spray* was hauled out in Bridgeport, Conn., and measured to produce an accurate set of plans for posterity.) The deck plan and photos in Teller's book clearly reveal that it was stepped outside the counter. In that position, the mast rested against the semicircular brace and had a single shroud to each quarter. The sail itself was a standing lug type, with a yard almost as long as the boom, and an area of about 155 square feet.

Fig. 1–7. Spray *as a yawl, from a photo taken in Australian waters.*

The mainsail spread 600 square feet of canvas. Generally, Slocum carried a single headsail, a jib of about 300 square feet. In Slocum's book, a photo of *Spray* in Australian waters bears this out, but that seems to contradict the sail plan. The answer to this is that starting out, Slocum carried two headsails, forestaysail and jib, but after shortening the bowsprit, the foretriangle was too small to achieve real sailing efficiency with two sails, so he switched to a single jib, which was easier to handle, cheaper, and more efficient, anyway.

From photos in the Teller book, it's possible to make fairly reliable "guesstimates" about *Spray*'s spar dimensions: Mainmast—a "smart New Hampshire spruce," as Slocum noted, it was at least 9 and possibly 10 inches in diameter at the height above deck where the boom jaws rested on it; it could easily have been 12 inches at the mast step. As for height, it was about 37 feet above deck. Main Boom—as noted, it started 34 feet long and ended at 26 feet; it was from 7 to 8 inches in diameter. The gaff—also as noted —was 19 feet long and about 5 to 6 inches thick. Bowsprit—it was massive, about the same diameter as the mast (except octagonal in shape), braced with a pair of shrouds and double bobstays; it started at about 18 feet overall, with 15 feet outboard, and then lost 5 feet off the outboard end; of course, there were bolt ropes to stand on while tying gaskets onto the lowered jib, and these gaskets remained permanently in place on the bowsprit. Mizzen Mast —from the photos and using the other spars to scale from, it was about 5 inches in diameter. Mizzen Boom—about 4 inches in diameter. Mizzen Yard—about 3 inches in diameter, tapering to about 2 inches at the ends. Noble spars, all.

Interestingly, the quite visible checking in the mainmast, main boom, and mizzen mast, as revealed in the Teller book photos, apparently were of no concern to Slocum. Such a condition is not particularly worrisome to those few present-day sailors who also carry solid spars without sail tracks but use hoops or lacing, because they know that such checking causes very little loss of strength. (Do not, however, try to fill them with compound to shut out the water. It will probably seep in, because of the flexing of the spar. Instead, swab down the check with boiled linseed oil, or linseed mixed with turps, 50–50, for greater penetration. The checking will give no trouble for a long time, perhaps never.) Solid spars have the virtues of being cheap at the start, cheap to replace, and available almost anywhere in the world.

As to the standing and running rigging, there was little choice for Slocum in the ship chandleries of his day. The sheets and halyards were manila, and it's unlikely that he could afford prime grade on that five-hundred-dollar budget. Some of it may even have come free, donations from waterfront friends. The number of useful gifts he received was remarkable (*see below*). For standing rigging, the choice was equally simple—galvanized —that's all there was. In photos it appears to be $\frac{5}{16}''$ or $\frac{3}{8}''$ in diameter.

Cabin and Gear

We noted that the aft cabin was 10′ × 12′. Rising three feet from the deck, this provided the 5′9½″ Slocum with more than ample headroom. We can be pretty sure of this because *Spray*'s registered depth of hold (top of keel to underside of deck) was 4′2″, so even if the cabin sole was a full foot above the top of the keel, there was 6′2″ of headroom, give or take a couple of inches. As an ex-merchant ship master, Slocum, of course, lived aft. As shown in Fig. 1–8, this cabin was simply furnished—almost stark. Although self-evident, it is worth noting that, with a 14′2″ beam (amidships), this cabin probably ranged from about 13 feet wide at the forward end to 12 feet at the after end. Although half of each bunk was under the deck, the proportions show they were quite wide, not mere sleeping shelves. The

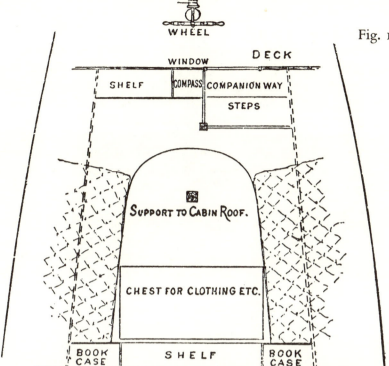

Fig. 1–8. Spray: *Cabin Plan.*

WHEEL

DECK

WINDOW

SHELF COMPASS COMPANION WAY

STEPS

SUPPORT TO CABIN ROOF.

CHEST FOR CLOTHING ETC.

BOOK CASE SHELF BOOK CASE

seaman's chest between the bunks was his simple solution to clothing storage, an arrangement he had lived with all his seagoing life.

At the forward end, the two bookshelves and the whatnot shelf between them are utter simplicity, but the charmingly rendered sketch by Thomas Fogarty (Fig. 1–9), the artist who illustrated Slocum's book, suggests a cozy home. The curved line connecting the two bunks must be the cabin sole edges, as the sloop's stern quarters would be curving upward toward the counter at this point *(see Body Plan, Fig. 1–3).*

The after end is equally simple, with a shelf to starboard, the compass on the centerline under its window, and two companionway steps. What is not clear about the companionway is revealed in a photo in the Teller book. It shows Slocum standing in the open hatch, and the threshold is at least two feet above the deck—good protection for the cabin if *Spray* were pooped while running in heavy weather. This photo also reveals that the cabin top was *not* canvased, although the companionway slide *was.* It may be that the top is double-planked with light stuff—pine or cedar—and that the lower set of seams was thus covered.

Beside the compass window and the open hatch, there was only one other source of daylight for the cabin, a single large porthole (10 or 12 inches in diameter) in the forward end of the cabin—not centered but well to starboard. The reason for this is also revealed in the Fogarty sketch—Slocum

17

Fig. 1–9. *This sketch by Fogarty shows Slocum looking particularly at home in his starboard berth in* Spray's *after cabin.*

reclining at his ease and reading in the starboard bunk (Fig. 1–9). On his left are two rifles in racks on the cabin side, and there, above his right shoulder, is the big porthole—clearly a window to read by. One other feature barely noticeable in Slocum's book, but quite clear in Teller's photos, is that the edges of *Spray*'s cabins were well radiused on the outboard corners, port and starboard, eliminating a potential source of leaks and adding a dollop of extra seaworthiness—a rounded surface instead of a right-angle joint presented to windward in heavy weather.

One final item in the after cabin: note the stanchion right in the middle (Fig. 1–8). It's not only a brace for the expanse of the cabin top but is also something to grab in the middle of a cabin over 10 feet wide. That's quite a distance to be thrown by a sudden lurch. As everyone knows, when the motion is violent, we tend to move through the cabin from handhold to handhold.

The space between the two cabins became a hold, in which Slocum stowed bulk stores: water, salt-beef, sea biscuits, etc. The forward cabin was used for cooking, which, of course, could not impinge on the "captain's quarters." So far as we know, the galley consisted of a kerosene lamp converted into a stove, and no plumbing—except possibly a bucket.

Stores and Equipment

Unfortunately, the paucity of details provided by Slocum about foods carried leaves us, at best, with a murky image of his domestic arrangements. We've already covered the built-in cabin "furnishings." Somewhere in it he carried a "well-stocked medicine chest." As for navigational instruments, he had the celebrated tin clock (it cost only him a dollar in Nova Scotia because the face was broken), a taffrail log, sextant, compass, and leadline.

As for stores, Slocum was limited by the rudimentary canning technology of his era, by its narrow range of choice, and by the slimness of his pocketbook. Generally, he sought bulk stores, protein or starch, but mainly cheap and filling, with a long "shelf life" at sea. In port he made up for missing vitamins with fresh fruit and vegetables. It's remarkable how often he received gifts of gear and food—wherever he sailed.

In Gloucester, Mass., before departure, waterfront friends gave him a barrel of "fish oil to calm the waves" and a fisherman's lantern for a riding light. Other gifts included some copper anti-fouling paint, a dip-net, a gaff, and a "pugh"—a fish prong. It was here he found the castoff Cape Ann dory and shortened it as a tender and here, too, that a lady from Boston provided the funds for "a large, two-burner lamp," which not only lighted the cabin but which, after some tinkering (probably adding sea rails), became his cooking stove. Later, at Gibraltar, he received a new jib from an admiral of the Royal Navy. Still later, an Australian yacht club commodore contributed a whole new suit of sails to *Spray*—thus proving the importance of being first at something impressive to your peers.

At Gloucester he had put aboard a quantity of salt cod contributed by waterfront friends (his chowder, he says, was famous), and at Yarmouth, Nova Scotia, his last port before the Atlantic crossing, he added butter, a barrel of potatoes, and six barrels of water. At the Azores he gorged himself on fresh bread, butter, fruits, and vegetables. In Gibraltar, where his voyage made him an instant celebrity with the English government, the Royal Navy, and the American community, a Royal Navy pinnace appeared alongside the anchored *Spray* every morning with a supply of fresh milk and vegetables—and so it went.

While today such a diet might seem like deprivation, we must remember that Slocum had eaten this way all his life, perhaps even more meagerly at sea, so he would not have thought much about it. Nor would he have bothered to list other items very likely carried, such as flour, salt, lard, corn meal, canned cream, porridge (oatmeal), tea, coffee, and sugar. These basic foods—with a dash of spices—and imagination—can produce good meals for the seagoing crew even today.

After Slocum escaped the Moorish pirates off Morocco, he sighted but bypassed the Cape Verde Islands. Somewhere in the South Atlantic he recorded a meal he especially enjoyed: fried flying fish (found on deck in the morning), hot biscuits with butter, potatoes, and coffee with cream. On the same leg of the voyage Slocum caught and butchered a sea turtle, which provided fresh meat for several days.

Forty days out of Gibraltar, he dropped anchor in the harbor of Pernambuco.

Here, again, his first thought was fresh food. He was well known in this city, and his port charges were paid by a merchant friend. He took a group of old captains for a sail one day; and he spent a good deal of time making the rig alterations mentioned earlier.

South of Rio de Janeiro, he had the most hazardous adventure of the voyage. Sailing *Spray* too close to the beach, he was driven onto a shoal. He launched his small dory and rowed out to put a kedge anchor out beyond the breakers, and it capsized in the surf just as he heaved the anchor as far as he could throw it. Unable to swim, he clung to the overturned boat for his life, and managed to work his way back through the pounding surf. Then, attaching a second anchor cable to the first—until he had out 480 feet —and heaving taut on the bitter end with the windlass, he went below and collapsed on his bunk.

When he awoke he found *Spray* lying on the shore and a small boy on horseback trying to tow his dory down the beach. The boy was astonished and disappointed by Slocum's appearance. Slocum traded a supply of ship's biscuits to the boy's family for butter, milk, and eggs. Soon after, local authorities arrived to help, but before a tug could arrive to tow *Spray* off the beach Slocum had refloated her himself at high tide and sailed on to Montevideo, Uruguay.

Once again, goods and services came his way—free docking and free repairs to his damaged keel and dory, and a gift of twenty pounds sterling from a local English shipping agent. While in this port, Slocum found an iron drum and converted it into a cooking stove, which he set up in the forward cabin. This was a big improvement over cooking on a lamp and a good source of heat in the southern latitudes.

At Buenos Aires, where he met more friends from his merchant-ship days, such as the port captain who waived port charges, Slocum took on stores (he doesn't say what) and water and headed south again—ready to battle the Straits of Magellan en route to the Pacific.

At Punta Arenas, a Chilean coaling station partway through the Straits, he paused for a rest and received more gifts—smoked venison, sea biscuits, a compass, and that unlikely but ultimately famous item, a bag of carpet tacks. His adventures in the Straits of Magellan are well known—mandatory reading for any small-boat sailor who does not already know Slocum's

book: the series of fierce gales he faced, days on end of slogging to windward, the night he spread the carpet tacks on his deck to thwart a stealthy
attack by Tierra del Fuegans (who made a yowling retreat when their bare
feet encountered the tacks), the arrival in Pacific waters on his sixth attempt
to force his way through, only to be driven back again—and then, his final
victory. All these events are the stuff of legend and must be devoured in
the original for fullest appreciation.

While resting in Port Angosto, on the Pacific side, he refitted again
(probably replacing worn running rigging) and transferred from deck to
hold several hundred pounds of lard that had floated into the cove from a
wrecked ship. Slocum knew a cash cargo when he saw one, particularly a
free one! Here, too, he completed the rig modifications—adding the mizzen
mast and sail that converted *Spray* to a yawl. From yet another friendly
captain, he got gifts of cordage and some warm flannels. Then, on his seventh
try, he reached the open Pacific.

The romantic South Seas, so alluring to so many small-boat sailors,
apparently had little attraction to Slocum, for he practically whizzed across
the Pacific, not even stopping at Tahiti! Perhaps he had had enough of remote
island ports in his earlier days, or perhaps the reason lies in Teller's persuasive
intimations that the somewhat embittered old sailor was more interested in
winning the accolades of his fellow men than in tropical sightseeing. Whatever the case, between entering the Pacific and reaching Newcastle, Australia,
he made only two stops—at Juan Fernandez Island and at Apia, Samoa, where
he had an enriching visit with Mrs. Robert Louis Stevenson. She gave him
some lengths of heavy bamboo. Those three passages consumed 72, 42, and 23
days. He arrived in Sydney on October 10, 1896.

The news of his voyage had by now preceded him, and he was greeted
as a hero—with considerable newspaper coverage of his "daring" cruise. The
commodore of a local yacht club contributed a new suit of sails to *Spray*.
After a two-month rest during which he gave some lectures and refilled his
pocketbook with the fees, Slocum was off again. He first sailed south to
Melbourne, then made a 180-degree turn and sailed north along the Great
Barrier Reef. Upon reaching Thursday Island (named by Capt. Bligh), he
turned west and headed into the Indian Ocean. (His precise route and ports
of call are listed in the next section, and *Spray*'s sailing performance in the
section following that.)

At the Keeling Cocos Islands, *Spray* was hauled up onto the beach to
have her bottom scrubbed and painted for the long haul across the remainder
of the Indian Ocean. More work may have been done, but Slocum is
frustratingly casual about details that would interest us today.

At Rodriguez Island he was given beef, sweet potatoes, and a sack of
pomegranates. At the next island, Mauritius, he got free use of the military
dock and was "thoroughly outfitted" by the local authorities. If Slocum

skimmed over such details, which would have interested small-boat sailors, it was probably because his book was written for the widest possible general audience, the best possible sale, and the highest possible royalty. It was not aimed at the waterfront community or the yachting crowd.

By the time he reached Durban and Cape Town, South Africa, his fame had spread sufficiently so that his slide lectures were in considerable demand. The fees collected in South Africa financed the rest of the voyage.

He departed Cape Town on March 26, 1898, and stopped at two islands in the South Atlantic, St. Helena and Ascension. He gave a free lecture to the lonely garrison of the former and sailed off with a large fruit cake, a basket of fruit, a bag of coffee beans—and a live goat! The goat nearly drove Slocum mad with its culinary depredations, but Slocum stoutly resisted the impulse to chuck it overboard. However, Slocum noted, the goat was "marooned" at Ascension. Here *Spray*'s captain was entertained at lunch by the island's commander and here, too, Slocum had the sloop fumigated and insisted a certificate be issued to him certifying that no other human but the captain could possibly live aboard. Only then did Slocum sail. As he neared home, he was taking no chance that anyone could charge he had "dropped off" a crew just before arrival. Solo he sailed, and the world would have no reasonable way to dispute it. (To make doubly certain, when his papers were visaed at his last Caribbean port of call, he requested that the consul make specific note of the fact that he was sailing alone.)

On May 8, 1898, *Spray* crossed her outward-bound track off the coast of Brazil and thus completed her circumnavigation, officially at least. Shortly after, Slocum met the battleship U.S.S. *Oregon* and learned that his country was at war with Spain.

After giving another lecture at Antigua, he sailed again on a course directly for Cape Hatteras, taking eight days to pass through the Doldrums, weathering a fierce tornado off the shore of Long Island, rounding Montauk Point and, on June 27, 1898, dropping anchor in Rhode Island's Newport harbor.

Slocum certainly embodies the four yardsticks chosen for measuring the cruises in this collection—strength, simplicity, self-reliance, and seamanship, perhaps more than any other sailor in the book, despite the fact that he had to translate large-ship experience into small-boat practice. Strength was everywhere evident in hull and rig, and simplicity was obvious throughout, especially in his domestic arrangements. Much of his spartan approach was dictated by the times, of course, when luxury accouterments simply weren't available. But it's not stretching the point too far to suggest that today's cruising crew might profitably take a page from Slocum's book on the value of keeping things simple.

Consider this: before you sail on a major cruise—even if you are living aboard until departure—your boat is connected to the shore by various umbilical cords, real or imagined. Once you cut these and sail off, things change, priorities shift, and attitudes alter. What is desirable and available at dockside may become troublesome and expensive to take to sea. Not only did Slocum's daring and seamanship make him the idol of cruising men who sailed in his track, but the simplicity of his approach made his feat seem possible to many whose pocketbooks were as thin as his.

Spray's Cruising Track

With fourteen cruising tales to cover, space considerations make it impractical to attempt a comprehensive summary of each voyage. And in any case, the reader is urged to seek out the original books to get the full flavor of each. But it does seem useful to provide a brief listing of where each boat went. Here is *Spray*'s route around the world:

Boston, Mass. (start) . . . Gloucester, Mass . . . Westport, Nova Scotia . . . Yarmouth, Nova Scotia . . . Fayal, Horta Island, Azores . . . Gilbraltar . . . Canary islands (sighted but bypassed) . . . Cape Verde Islands (sighted but bypassed) . . . Pernambuco (now Recife), Brazil . . . Rio de Janeiro, Brazil . . . Montevideo, Uraguay . . . Buenos Aires, Argentina . . . Falkland Islands, South Atlantic (sighted but bypassed) . . . Straits of Magellan (Cape Virgins, Cape Froward, Cape Pillar) . . . Return to Straits via Cockburn Channel . . . Same route for second attempt, weathering eight gales . . . Port Angosto (seventeen days via Pacific to) . . . Juan Fernandez Island . . . Marquesas Islands (sighted but bypassed) . . . (forty-three days from Port Angosto to) . . . American Samoa . . . Fiji Islands (sighted but bypassed) . . . (forty-two days from Samoa to) . . . Newcastle, Australia . . . Sydney . . . Melbourne . . . Devonport, Tasmania . . . north through Great Barrier Reef via Port Dennison . . . Cooktown . . . Sunday Island . . . Thursday Island (via Torres Strait and Arafura Sea to) . . . Christmas Island . . . Indian Ocean to . . . Keeling Cocos Islands . . . Rodriguez Island . . . Mauritius Island . . . Durban, South Africa . . . Cape Town . . . (via South Atlantic to) . . . St. Helena Island . . . Ascension Island . . . Grenada . . . Antigua . . . Cape Hatteras (passing offshore) . . . Montauk Point, Long Island (passed) . . . Point Judith, Rhode Island (passed) . . . Newport, Rhode Island (anchored in U.S.) . . . Fairhaven, Mass.

Sailing Performance and Notable Incidents

Regarding *Spray*'s seaworthiness and seakindliness—her ability to do what Slocum claimed—the most controversial aspect was his flat assertion that she could steer herself, hands off, for days and even weeks on end and remain on course even with the wind dead aft. Naturally, we're talking about a vessel on which Slocum did not even attempt sheet-to-tiller steering

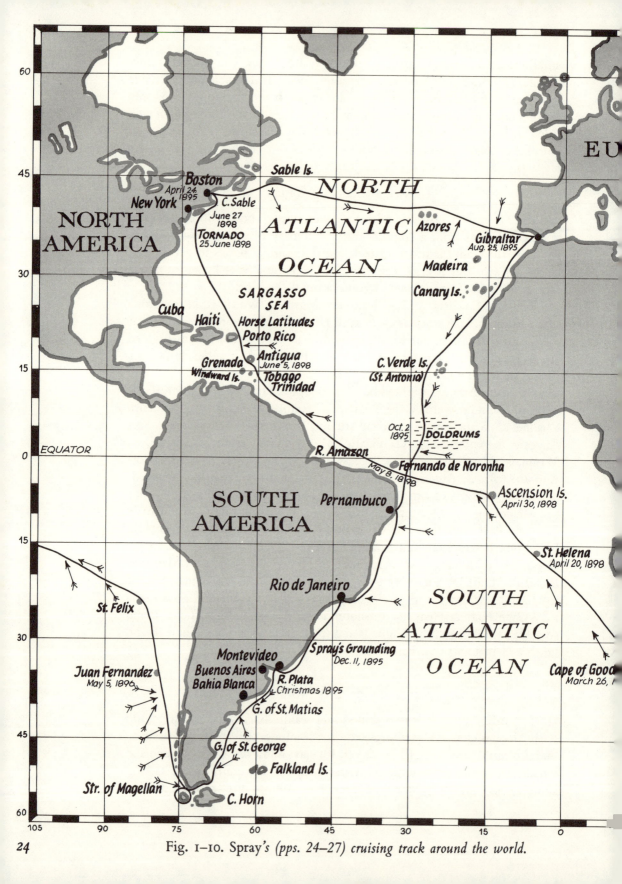

Fig. 1–10. Spray's (pps. 24–27) cruising track around the world.

24

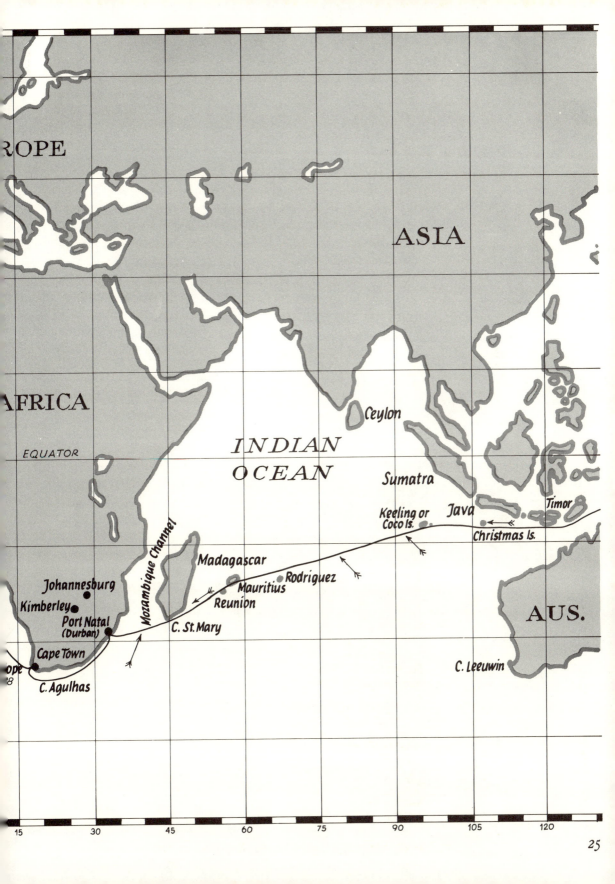

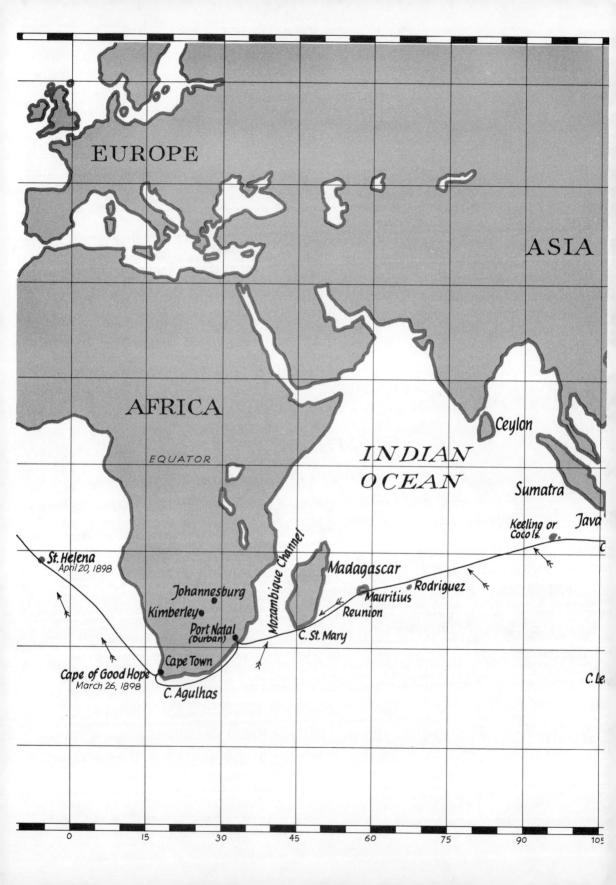

EUROPE

ASIA

AFRICA

EQUATOR

INDIAN
OCEAN

Ceylon

Sumatra

Java

Keeling or
Coco Is.

St. Helena
April 20, 1898

Madagascar

Rodriguez

Johannesburg

Mozambique Channel

Mauritius

Kimberley

Reunion

Port Natal
(Durban)

C. St. Mary

Cape Town

Cape of Good Hope
March 26, 1898

C. Agulhas

C. Le

0   15   30   45   60   75   90   105

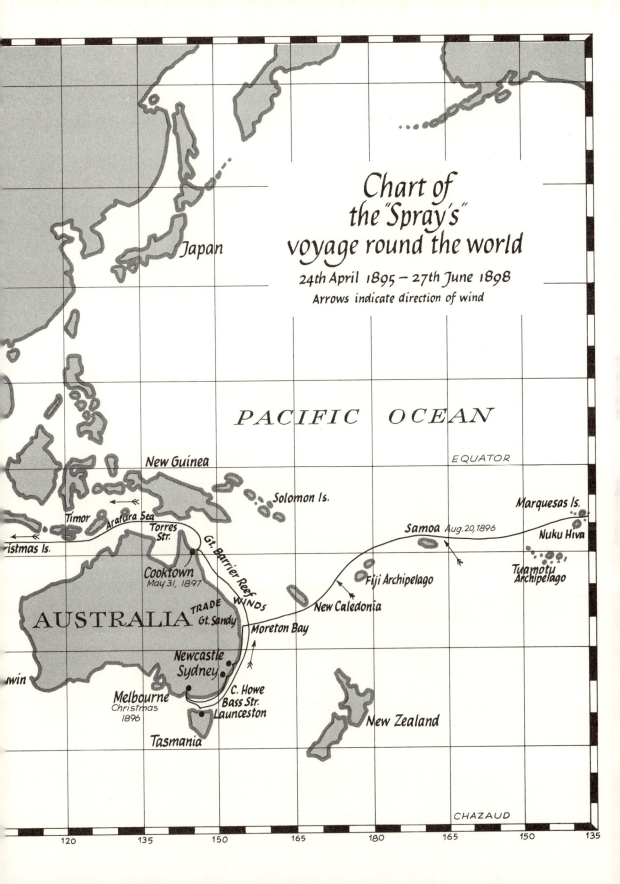

Chart of the "Spray's" voyage round the world

24th April 1895 – 27th June 1898

Arrows indicate direction of wind

Japan

PACIFIC OCEAN

EQUATOR

New Guinea

Solomon Is.

Marquesas Is.

Samoa *Aug. 20, 1896*

Nuku Hiva

Timor

Arafura Sea

Torres Str.

Gt. Barrier Reef

Tuamotu Archipelago

ristmas Is.

Cooktown
May 31, 1897

WINDS

Fiji Archipelago

AUSTRALIA

TRADE

Gt. Sandy

New Caledonia

Moreton Bay

rwin

Newcastle
Sydney

C. Howe
Bass Str.
Launceston

Melbourne
Christmas 1896

Tasmania

New Zealand

CHAZAUD

120   135   150   165   180   165   150   135

techniques—so far as we know. (These were "invented" in the 1920s and 1930s.) We'll get to this self-steering question shortly, but first, it will be useful to get a fix on just one of the essential numbers that applies to *Spray* (or any boat), one that is an absolute arbiter when discussing her sailing performance. This number applied to the original *Spray* in 1895 and would apply equally to an exact replica built in 1995 or 2095. The number is Speed/Length ratio, S/L.

This emphasis is not to discount such equally important numbers as Prismatic Coefficient, Ballast/Displacement ratio, and Sail Area/Displacement ratio, but they are put aside here for lack of space. (A Speed/Length Ratio table, S/L, is provided for each boat in this book, in the Performance section and gives us one useful way to compare any boat with any other.)

Two caveats: One, the speed figures developed and shown in the tables are for pure displacement hulls, the only type in the book except for *Trekka*'s (chapter 9), and do not apply to boats with the same waterline length, WL, but designed to achieve planing speeds, or to boats that may plane for brief periods under ideal conditions. Two, although occasional controversy still arises over this point, I have taken as gospel the widely accepted dictum that the maximum speed of a displacement vessel is 1.34 times the square root of its WL. Some naval architects contend that the top speed may be as much as 1.5 or 1.6 times the square root of the WL, but that appears to be a minority dissent to a majority report. So I will stick to 1.34, and if the reader insists on a higher number, he is free to add 1.4, 1.5, even 1.6 to the tables in this book.

The table below reveals *Spray*'s potential speed at five S/Ls, 1.0, 1.1, 1.2, 1.3, and 1.34. The right-hand column shows the number of nautical miles the boat would cover (over the bottom, ignoring current) in twenty-four hours of sailing at each S/L, if the wind remained constant and pushed the boat at that speed. (This is more explanation than many sailors need, but for those who don't yet understand this ratio, the tables provide a simple way to see why one boat did better than another on a given passage, all other factors being reasonably equal. In brief, these tables show why, ignoring major displacement and sail area differences, a longer WL = more speed = greater distance covered in a given period.)

For *Spray*'s table I've taken 32 feet as her WL, scaling off that distance from the small profile drawing in Slocum's book. The exact WL, to my knowledge, has not been published. So, 32 feet might be off 6 inches, but not as much as a foot. To make such a table for your own boat, all you need is a pocket calculator that offers the square root function. The rest is simple multiplication.

If we look at S/L 1.2, a handsome average for a full day, we see that *Spray* could make 162 NM in a twenty-four-hour period and 1134 NM in a week. Again, that's if the wind never varies and if it is blowing with a

		Spray: Speed/Length Ratio		
		(WL = 32 feet $\sqrt{32}$ = 5.66)		
S/L	$\times$ $\sqrt{WL}$	= Speed (knots)	$\times$ 24	= NM (1 day)
1.0	5.66	5.66		135.8
1.1	5.66	6.22		149.2
1.2	5.66	6.78		162.7
1.3	5.66	7.35		176.7
1.34	5.66	7.57		181.7

force to allow her to reach and hold that particular S/L ratio. Since we know Slocum had some twenty-four-hour runs in the 160 NM range, we can conclude *Spray* was a pretty good sailer in favorable conditions.

Obviously, she was no world-beater to windward. No gaff-rigged boat is—with its short luff on the mainsail and relatively short luff on the jib (because of the shorter mainmast)—since length of leading edge is a critical factor in windward efficiency. But she was no slouch, either, as we learn from Culler's *The Spray,* because her burdensome hull (24,000 lbs.) and beamy shape let her shoulder aside a chop with authority and stand up to whatever prudent sail area her skipper had aloft.

Here are a few of *Spray*'s sailing achievements:

- In early trials en route to Gloucester, *Spray* achieved 7 knots, as estimated by Slocum. I think we can trust his judgment, and that's an S/L of about 1.25, easily attainable in a fresh breeze.
- Departing Yarmouth, Nova Scotia, *Spray* did 8 knots in a fresh northwesterly while passing Cape Sable Island. That's a half knot above her top S/L of 1.34 (7.57 knots), but we can be generous about such a minor discrepancy, remembering that Slocum at the start of his voyage was finding much to praise in *Spray*.
- The next day, a "large schooner" (no hint as to size) put out of Nova Scotia, and *Spray* put her "hull down astern in five hours."
- On July 5, 1895, *Spray* again "made 8 knots, her very best work," while self-steering across the Atlantic steamer track to reach the Gulf Stream.
- On July 10, after eight days at Sea, *Spray* was 1200 nautical miles east of Cape Sable. That's an average of 150 miles per day over that period. (Henceforth, "miles" means nautical miles.)
- The passage from Cape Sable to Fayal on Horta Island in the Azores took exactly eighteen days—2600 miles at an average of 144 miles per day. Slocum achieved an S/L of nearly 1.1 for over two and a half weeks. That's sailing, since most boats average much less over a compa-

rable period. (Check this against later chapters.) Remember, here and throughout the book we're discussing cruising speeds and shorthanded crews or lone sailors.

- Leaving Fayal in a fair breeze, he sailed 90 miles overnight. He wasn't precise about the number of hours, but if it was close to twelve, he held his maximum of S/L 1.34 for half a day.
- Slocum reached Gibraltar in twenty-five days from Cape Sable (twenty-nine in all, less four days spent at Fayal). The additional sea miles from Fayal to Gibraltar actually *improved* his daily average to Fayal.

Now we turn to the great bone of contention, *Spray*'s ability to sail downwind with no one at the helm. It's not the intention to resolve that dispute here but merely to present the case as Slocum described it, suggest one way he might have achieved it, and let the reader decide for himself. First, a few items from Slocum's book:

We recall that he had shortened both mast and bowsprit in South America *before* reaching the Straits of Magellan. (And, not mentioned earlier, he had struck the sloop's topmast before departing Nova Scotia. Clearly, the topsail had been useful in coastal cruising during fair weather seasons at home, but now he was tackling the Atlantic.)

While in Montevideo, his old friend, Captain Howard of Cape Cod, was in port and Slocum took him for a sail up the River Plate to Buenos Aires. En route *Spray* had "a gale of wind, and current so much in her favor that she outdid herself." Slocum continued, "Howard sat near the binnacle and watched the compass, while the sloop held her course so steadily that one would have declared that the card was nailed fast. Not a quarter point did she deviate from her course. My old friend had owned and sailed a pilot-sloop on [that] river for many years, but this feat took the wind out of his sails at last, and he cried, 'I'll be stranded on the Chico Bank if I ever saw the like of it!' "

Now, two points the captain made about his conversion to the yawl rig at this point in the voyage. He noted that the change not only reduced the size of the mainsail, which had been more than a handful in heavy weather, but "slightly improved her steering qualities when on the wind." He added, "When the wind was aft, the jigger was not in use; invariably, it was then furled." This will not surprise most owners of ketches and yawls.

Next, his precise description when sailing off the wind: "With her boom broad off and with the wind two points on the quarter, the *Spray* sailed her truest course. It never took long to find the amount of helm, or angle of rudder required to hold her on course, and when that was found I lashed the wheel with it at that angle."

He continued: "The mainsail drove her, and the main-jib, with its sheet boused flat amidships or a little to one side or the other, added greatly to the steadying power. Then, if the wind was strong or squally I would sometimes set a flying-jib also, on a pole rigged out on the bowsprit, with the sheets hauled flat amidships, which was a safe thing to do, even in a gale of wind." (More about this below.) His final note regarding *Spray*'s performance when running: "The amount of helm required varied according to the amount of wind and its direction. These points are quickly gathered from practice."

The section on rig listed all the parts; now we should add a few of the most important "wrinkles." There were no winches at all. Where Slocum needed greater purchase for the heavier jobs, such as hauling on the mainsail's peak and throat halyards, he achieved the extra mechanical advantage by using larger blocks (more sheaves). Of course, this meant longer halyards and more "spaghetti" on the deck to coil down, but this would not have bothered Slocum greatly, and it was the price he had to pay for handling a large spread of sail alone. (Need it be added that such an approach to simplicity and economy of first cost is still completely available today to anyone responsive to its practicality?) Winches cost lots of money.

One bit of rigging insurance Slocum fitted was a "stout downhaul" on the gaff, "because without it the mainsail might not have come down when I wished to lower it in a breeze." Next, as suited a singlehander, he led all sheets aft to the helm. Finally, if the wind did not serve and Slocum was in harbor, he had—to judge by a Fogarty sketch in his book—a 12- to 14-foot sweep by which he could move his 24,000-pound hull, perhaps at a half-knot, enough to move *Spray* into a dock.

We'll note again that in Samoa, Fanny G. Stevenson gave him a couple of 60-foot bamboo trees. They must have been 6 to 8 inches thick at the butt. He used these, he noted, "for spare booms, and the butt of one made a serviceable jib-boom. . . . " That term did not mean jib *club*, as it does today, but an extension of the bowsprit to accommodate another jib, carried further forward. When does this new bamboo spar make its appearance?

One of them was used at Slocum's departure from Booby Island, off the northern tip of Australia. Once clear of the land, he rigged the bamboo on top of the bowsprit (see dotted lines in Fig. 1–6). That done, he set on it a flying jib that he had sewed up while at Juan Fernandez Island, as a spinnaker, he said, and asserted that it "pulled like a *sodger*." (This nineteenth-century slang form of the word "soldier" refers by association to a "soldier's wind," Jack Tar's contemptuous term for an easy wind, the kind loved by soldiers who feared the sea.) Well, with all these bits and pieces assembled, what did the new rig do for *Spray*? It's here that we arrive at the sloop's hands-off, downwind sailing ability. On June 25, 1897, "clear of all shoals and dangers," Slocum turned west from Thursday Island, with the wind from astern and *Spray* steering herself, and headed for the Keeling Cocos Islands. After making minor adjustments to the sheets and gaskets on the wheel, he left her alone. On the next two days, she covered 130 and 133 miles (S/L 1.0). On July 2 he sighted the island of Timor to starboard and kept sailing. On July 11 Christmas Island appeared off the starboard bow. On and on she sailed, with Slocum reading in the cabin below.

Upon sighting the Keeling Cocos, Slocum reports:

> I didn't touch the helm for, with the current and heave of the sea, the sloop found herself at the end of the run absolutely in the fairway of the channel. [That, of course, was luck, not planning.] You couldn't have beaten it in the navy! Then I trimmed her sails by the wind, took the helm and flogged her up the couple of miles or so abreast the harbor landing, where I cast anchor at 3:00 P.M., July 17, 1897, 23 days from Thursday Island. The distance run was 2700 miles as the crow flies. This would have been a fair Atlantic voyage. It was a delightful sail! During those 23 days I had not spent altogether more than three hours at the helm, including the time occupied in beating into Keeling harbor. I had just lashed the helm and let her go; whether the wind was abeam or dead aft, it was all the same: she always sailed on her course. No part of the voyage up to this point, taking it by and large, had been so finished as this.

Well, how was this passage possible?

Put simply, by setting the new, large flying jib far out at the end of the bamboo spar, Slocum moved the sail plan's center of effort a long stretch forward, putting it well ahead of the hull's center of lateral resistance. Then he sheeted the jib hard amidships so that it acted as a vane. Whenever the sloop wandered off course the jib would be struck by the wind on one side or the other and would push the sloop back on her original course.

Slocum's solution to no-gadget self-steering was propounded recently in a book I had the pleasure of editing, *Self-Steering without a Windvane* by Lee Woas, published by Seven Seas Press. In his book Woas analyzes the entire subject of making your boat's bow point where you want it to, without the use of an expensive windvane ($2000 to $4000 these days), by using a wide variety of set-ups and sails to provide the steering power, on any type of rig, and regardless of wind strength. Much of the material has been known for five decades, but it is scattered piecemeal in a half-dozen cruising tales, many of them out of print. Woas has pulled it all together in a comprehensive way, with excellent photos and drawings of every application. One of the most remarkable examples demonstrated by Woas was a 16-foot bamboo extension on the bow of a 28-foot fiber glass sloop that seems to confirm Slocum's feat in the Indian Ocean.

Despite such nonpareil qualities, it was not all beer and skittles aboard for Slocum. Chafe and failure of metal parts or wire were the same relentless enemy to him as it is to us today. In the Straits of Magellan, Slocum was flying along one day in a snowy gale, pressing hard to reach a safe anchorage in those rock-studded waters before darkness, when a fluky wind jibed the mainsail all standing. This snapped the mainsheet (which was made of cheap sisal) and caused the main boom jaws to jump off the mast. What followed was a dicey half-hour during which Slocum nearly lost his vessel, and perhaps his life, on the rocky shore to leeward.

More than a year later, on June 20, 1898, while sailing in the Caribbean on the final leg of the voyage and once again in a gale, the jibstay suddenly parted at the masthead "and fell, jib and all into the sea." With fast work, Slocum got it aboard before the jib was torn or dragged under the hull. Although he was now fifty-four, he went aloft on the wildly swaying mast and rerigged the stay—using a gun tackle—then took a reef in the jib and hoisted it again. He had reason to thank the strength of the "smart New Hampshire spruce" he had used for a mainmast, for the shrouds and the mast's husky size were the only thing that kept it standing during the time it took him to replace the jibstay. Here one wonders if the standing rigging was simply rusting out after three years of exposure, or if the wire used originally on the sloop in Fairhaven had been new or was secondhand, picked up on the waterfront as a bargain or a gift. Another natural question is whether or not, in the calm of harbors during the voyage, he regularly went aloft to inspect the masthead and all the important "stuff" that terminated there.

Once again, when Slocum was in the South Atlantic on the homeward leg, bounding along in the southeast trades, we get an excellent picture of the sloop going about her business, from the master's pen: "The *Spray* was running under single-reefed mainsail, a whole jib and a flying jib besides, set on the [Samoan] bamboo, while I was reading [below]. . . . The sloop was again doing her work smoothly, hardly rolling at all, but just leaping along among the white horses, a thousand gamboling porpoises keeping her company on all sides."

For an objective opinion, we can turn to the words of a reporter on a Durban, South Africa, newspaper, written a few weeks earlier:

> As briefly noted yesterday, the *Spray,* with a crew of one man, arrived in this port yesterday afternoon on a voyage round the world. . . . Her commander sailed his craft right up the channel past the old wharf and dropped his anchor . . . before anyone had a chance to get aboard. [His] arrival was witnessed by a large crowd. The skillful manner in which Captain Slocum steered his craft about the vessels which were occupying the waterway was a treat to witness.

Seamanship, noted earlier, was Slocum's hallmark. On June 25, 1898, bound up the Atlantic coast and still in the Gulf Stream, *Spray* was struck by a wintry nor'wester, with lightning striking the sea all about her and hailstones pelting her decks. Slocum saw clear signs to windward of even more threatening weather and quickly doused all sail. Under bare poles *Spray* was struck by a tornado, and even without a stitch of canvas aloft was hove down onto her beam ends. Slocum learned later that it had struck New York City an hour earlier and done devastating damage, wrecking buildings on shore, uprooting trees and flinging them through the air, and causing great destruction to ships moored at piers. This was the worst electrical storm he had faced and, so close to the end of his voyage, Slocum took it as a sign; he decided to bypass New York City and ran east along the Long Island coast.

He reached Montauk late that afternoon and rounded it, coming abeam of Point Judith, Rhode Island, as dusk settled. In darkness he worked his way into Narragansett Bay and, passing carefully to the shoreward side of the minefields that guarded the entrance to Newport Harbor (the war, remember), sailed *Spray* slowly into the inner harbor and dropped anchor. It was 1:00 A.M., June 27, 1898.

In three years, two months, two days, Joshua Slocum had completed the first solo circumnavigation, covering 46,000 miles, adding several pounds to his somewhat spare frame in the process, and entering his name forever in the annals of small-boat seamanship. His own words capture best his feelings at that moment: "I myself learned more seamanship, I think, aboard the *Spray* than on any other ship I ever sailed. . . . " In his book he added, "To young men contemplating a voyage I would say go." Of course he would feel that way for, as the years passed, his favorite inscription when autographing a copy of his book was, "As for myself, the wonderful sea charmed me from the first."

2. Sea Bird

If the voyage of Sea Bird *has accomplished nothing else, it has done much to prove that size has nothing to do with a vessel's seaworthiness, and that the ocean is not the malicious and merciless destroyer it is pictured to be by foolish and ignorant persons. To the weak mind all that is unfamiliar is either astonishing, horrible, or dangerous; but to the powerful mind it is intensely interesting.*

—Thomas Fleming Day
Across the Atlantic in Sea Bird (1911)

T. F. Day and Crew

*M*any older readers will instantly recognize the name of Tom Day as the founder (in 1897), editor, and publisher of *The Rudder*— America's first yachting magazine—and also as a consummate small-boat sailor. Day really practiced what he preached—cruising—to a degree hardly possible for today's busier boating editor. (Tom Day, for example, the following year made the second transatlantic crossing ever in a motorboat, taking the 38-foot *Detroit* from New York to Ireland in twenty-one days.

His crew for this voyage was two men. One was Fred Thurber, a long-time racing and cruising partner who would also make the motorboat crossing in 1912. Day says of him: "He has been with me in ocean races and as a seaman he has no superior. He does not know what fear is, he is quick, reliable, and always does his work in a skillful and intelligent way. I never knew him to lose his head even for a moment; but above all he always obeys orders, and no matter how disagreeable the situation or how uncomfortable the surroundings [he] is invariably in a good humor."

The other member of the crew was a man named Goodwin, whom Day had known for years but had never sailed with before. "He is a fine seaman," Day says, adding, "a good mechanic, and like Thurber always obeys orders. Goodwin showed great pluck in going, as he had never been in blue water in a small boat before."

The Hull

Sea Bird began as something of a design-by-committee project, whose aim, Day noted in his book, "was to produce a design to meet the demand for a small seagoing cruiser." Day worked out the general dimensions and sail plan. These data (in the form of sketches and notes, one assumes) were

Fig. 2–1. Sea Bird's *captain, Thomas Fleming Day.*

then turned over to an eminent naval architect of that era, Charles D. Mowrer—another name many oldtimers will recall. The hull was to be what Day called a "diamond-bottom type," a term that is earlier parlance for what we today call the V-bottom, but actually connotes a much shallower amount of deadrise than one finds in the Vee. Studying *Sea Bird*'s body plan (Fig. 2–2), you will see that the bottom angle, if opposed by another of the same angle, produces an elongated diamond shape.

When Mowrer had turned out a set of plans, they were handed over to the third man, L. D. "Larry" Huntington of Long Island, an experienced builder and sailer of deadrise boats. Day notes that Huntington "made several suggestions that were accepted and incorporated into the design," but he doesn't describe them. Huntington then developed the construction details and specs and built the boat.

Sea Bird had the following dimensions: LOA—25'7½"; LWL—19'; Beam—8'4"; Draft—3'8"; Displacement—not given; Ballast Keel—700 lbs.; Sail Area—365 sq. ft. (The draft of the original centerboard version was two feet, and 3'6" with the board down.) The keen-eyed reader will note a discrepancy between these dimensions and the plans (Fig. 2–2), where the four numbers under the outboard profile make an LOA of 25'9". Charge it to hasty addition by the draftsman.

Sea Bird was built in 1909, as a gaff-rigged centerboard yawl. Day says:

Why [she] was originally designed with a centerboard I don't remember, but
[I] think she was wanted some place where there was a bar harbor [harbor bar];
but I distinctly remember why we took it out and substituted a keel. The
centerboard trunk simply cut the cabin in half and made living in it anything
but pleasant.

Two seasons after her launching [in 1911] we yanked it out and rearranged
the interior, and now, except for lack of headroom she has commodious and
comfortable quarters for two. Headroom in so small a boat is impossible to
get without destroying her looks and impairing her good qualities. . . .

Day provides only a few details about the construction, merely that the
planking was 1½ inches thick and that the carlines and deck were extra
heavy. He doesn't reveal what woods were used in construction, but the
theme of strength—of special interest here—is reinforced by his remark,
"The house [trunk] shows no strain whatever and would withstand the
blows of any sea that might fall on it."

During the conversion to a keel configuration, a 700-pound ballast keel
was added, with the necessary deadwood to fair it out; no mention is made
by Tom Day of inside ballast. In his handsome book *Yacht Designs* (published by International Marine Publishing Co.), the enormously gifted naval
architect William Garden states that *Sea Bird* carried 1000 pounds of inside
ballast. I have never seen reference to this before, but if Bill says so, I'll take
it on faith as fact, as it certainly explains how *Sea Bird* could stand up to
her sail plan in reefing weather. Without it, one has visions of a yawl-rigged
cork bouncing across the Atlantic. Even with it, she must be placed in the
light-displacement category.

The Deck

The simplicity of the deck layout is apparent in the plans (Fig. 2–2).
A sweeping glance reveals no hatch or skylight—other than the main
companionway. No high marks here for safety precautions, the galley being
located aft, right next to the companionway, but a plus for achieving dryness
below—just another of the tradeoffs in cruising boat design. Today we insist
on a second exit from the cabin in the event of fire.

From forward, there is only one useful item lacking, a main boom
crutch—or better still, a boom gallows. Though the yawl is a small, the
main boom *is* relatively long, and some way to tame the boom would have
been of considerable help when reefing the main, or to keep the main boom
strapped down when sailing under storm trysail. But they didn't carry one
of these sails, which is also unusual. Perhaps Day felt that a double- or
triple-reefed main would serve that need. So, from forward, we see: a plank
bowsprit ending at a conventional samson post, with a rope-deck pipe

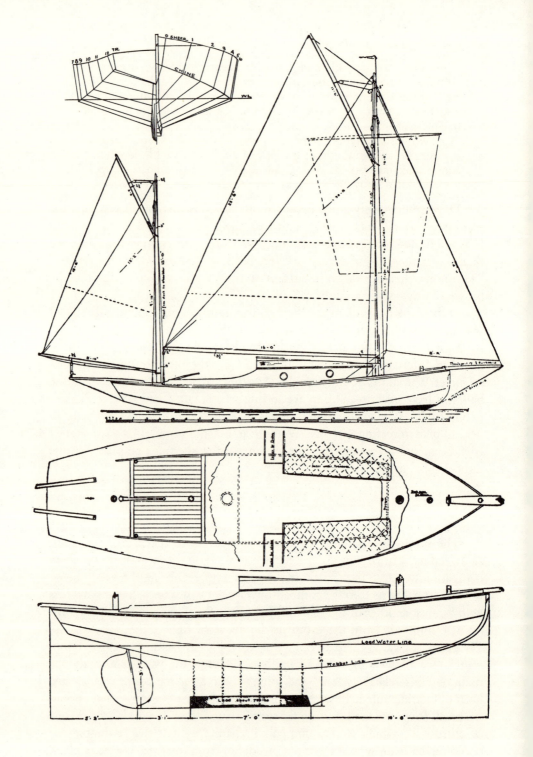

Fig. 2–2. Sea Bird: *Sail Plan, Cabin Plan, and Outboard Profile.*
(Courtesy of the *Rudder* magazine)

close-by; the trunk cabin starting just abaft the mast; the bridge deck (Day says it was 18 inches fore and aft); the companionway hatch, which appears on the plans to be on the centerline, but which was actually installed to port of the centerline; the compass under a deadlight in the bridge deck (more on compasses below); the cockpit, about 4 feet long and 4½ wide and double scuppered at the after end. These are odd dimensions for comfort as there were, apparently, no seats—an arrangement that gave rise to an even more awkward arrangement in *Sea Bird*'s big sister (*Islander,* nee *Seagoer;* see chapter 3); the rudder post, with its tiller, emerging through the counter stern just abaft the cockpit coaming; the mizzen mast; a single cleat on the centerline; and the mizzen boomkin built in the familiar keystone shape.

Unless there were slat seats, the helmsman sat on the cockpit sole, pretty wet going unless he had a kapok cushion or two under him, and steered with his feet braced against the opposite side—4'6" being a comfortable distance away for this. The small circle pecked out on the cockpit centerline must have been a fuel fill, and we know from Day's description that there were several fuel tanks jammed into the cockpit (*see engine, below*), to reduce its volume and the weight of water it would hold in the event of being pooped.

The Rig

Day dispatched the rig rather summarily in his book—barely a paragraph—probably on the then reasonable assumption that readers knew perfectly well how a yawl was rigged. A few details of note emerge from the sail plan (Fig. 2–2).

First, it *was* conventional, with a mizzen of respectable size, as befitted a yawl (or ketch) of that day, either of which was expected to sail well under jib and jigger—even beat off a lee shore when shortened down to those two sails. It is noteworthy that the mizzen had 13 square feet more area than the jib, as this is unusual for a ketch, much less a yawl. That would seem to produce a heavy weather helm, but, as we noted, Day had nothing but praise for her steering *before* the propeller aperture was cut in, and afterward, never mentioned her steering qualities in his story of the crossing.

The counter does seem drawn out a bit—considering the minimal bow overhang. Perhaps that was done to provide a longer sheeting base for the mizzen boom and add to buoyancy aft.

All the halyards are set up exactly as in the detailed description of the gaff yawl *Seagoer, Sea Bird*'s "big sister" (one-third larger), which is described in detail in chapter 3. It does not bear repetition here as, oddly enough, the details available were more precise for the later, larger boat.

Sail areas were as follows: Main—220 sq. ft.; Jib—66 sq. ft.; Mizzen—79 sq. ft.; Squaresail—80 sq. ft. As shown in the sail plan, the mizzen had

Fig. 2–3. Sea Bird *double-reefed in mid-Atlantic (from a painting by Warren Sheppard).*

one deep reef of about 4 feet; the mainsail, two sets of reef points, at about 3 and 6 feet above the boom; and the jib, none—at least none indicated.

Day notes: "She had a new suit of sails and they were well cut; the only faults were that they had battens in the leech and the reef cringles were too small. *Battens should never be put in seagoing sails* [italics added], and the maker should have known this as he had been to sea himself in a small boat." We will not find anywhere a more flat assertion of that idea than Day's. Although most contemporary cruising skippers will *assume* the presence of battens (they'll *be there* in a stock boat's sails), the idea still has merit in boats with an older, heavier rig (solid spars, gaffs) and recommends itself to owners of boats that will be out of touch with civilization for long periods, for the fewer sail repairs that will be required. This is especially true for heavy cruising sails that are roped.

Day continues: "The voyage was particularly hard on sails as we were on the one tack for 18 days, and driving hard all the time. The cloth [canvas, of course] was constantly wet, and tied for hours [reefed] when soaked; the first ten days we reefed and shook out on the average of five times a day."

The sail inventory included, besides the working rig that was bent on: three spare jibs, one extra mizzen, two squaresails, and a spinnaker. Day reports that the spinnaker was of "no use to us. The squaresail we only had a chance to use about five times, as the wind kept on the beam most of the way across; [but] when we did get a chance, it did some lively pulling." Few cruising boats carry squaresails today, a pity because it is a cheap sail to make yourself, even by hand, is simple with no trickiness such as draft, pulls like a horse, can even be kept aloft for a while when the wind is moving forward toward the beam, and is not likely to cause maddening snarls aloft—which is more than can be said for a spinnaker.

The startling item aboard *Sea Bird* was her standing rigging. Day reports, "The standing rigging was Elephant Brand *bronze* [italics mine] and couldn't be beat for strength, looks and clean qualities." Not many readers, I imagine, and that certainly includes myself, have ever heard of bronze wire, much less sailed with it. According to notes on *Sea Bird*'s full plans (more elaborate than the study plan in Fig. 2-2), this wire was ⅜ inches in diameter).

The bowsprit was 12 inches wide and 6′6″ long, of which 4′2″ was outboard. It was "slightly tapered at the outboard end and its bobstay was ¾-inch galvanized wire." Day was no piker when it came to strength.

Day continues: "She had Durkee bronze blocks and turnbuckles, and her running rigging was spun especially for her by the Columbia Rope Company. It was beautiful cordage, strong, pliant and easy on the hands." There is more than a hint here of sponsorship in kind. Durkee was for decades a respected name in marine hardware, now sadly passed into oblivion, but Columbia rope, of course, is still very much with us, after making a successful transition to synthetics. Day's remark about the running rigging being "easy on the hands" makes one wonder if this was linen line (popular with English sailors even after World War II) or just prime-quality manila.

With these few specifics, Day ends his rig description.

The Cabin

Day's book reveals virtually nothing about the cabin beyond his two remarks that the original centerboard version was annoying because its trunk cut the cabin in two and made it difficult to get from one side to the other, and that there was, naturally, no headroom. We can glean a bit more from the plans—though not much.

Between the original centerboard version (published in a *Rudder* booklet; *see chapter 3*) and the new keel version (Fig. 2-2), there is so little variation as to be unnoticeable. The two berths remained in exactly the same place, with a locker just abaft of each one. There was stowage indicated under both "transoms," and Day notes—as does the cabin plan—that the galley was aft, with lockers for food, pots and pans, and cooking utensils under the bridge deck. The stove was a kerosene-burning, two-burner Primus, which had the benefit of burning the engine fuel, and they carried one gallon of alcohol for priming it. There is no mention of a sink, but with three strapped-down water tanks of thirteen gallons each, there must have been at least a hand pump, even if dishes were washed in a bucket.

The cabin trunk was 7 feet long and 5 feet wide, with two 5-inch portholes in each side. The berths were 6′4″ long and about 2′6″ wide at the head.

As for water, a three-man crew made the bulk and weight of the required capacity a problem in a 25-footer. *Sea Bird* had two tanks under the decks outboard of the cockpit, each of thirteen gallons. To this Day added a third tank of the same capacity, strapped down forward of the mainmast. Then, at departure, he purchased twenty-four half-gallon bottles of spring water and stowed them under the cabin sole—a total of fifty-one gallons.

The Engine

Sea Bird's power plant was "a single-cylinder, 3 h.p. Knox, two-stroke, jump-spark, and the ignition Perfex," Day reports. (For more details on this type of engine, *see chapter 5, Cimba*.) It probably had the push of six horses. The prop was a 16 × 16 Columbian (another hallowed name in marine hardware). That 16-inch pitch is an instant tip-off that the Knox was slow-turning, probably an operating range of about 500 to 1500 RPM, with an ideal cruising RPM of 800–1000.

Day went to considerable lengths to find the "right" engine. He wrote to "all the builders of engines," requesting torque and fuel consumption figures, but all he got in return were evasive replies or no replies, except from the Camden-Rockland Co. This company bench-tested the Knox and provided Day with figures that, on the voyage, "came within a gallon of the actual daily performance [speed and consumption]," Day notes.

The engine was installed—for this voyage—under the bridge deck, where, Day observed, it was out "of the way but rather awkward to get at; it should have been placed one frame forward." Before going further with performance, we must deal with what—at least to some readers—will be a new wrinkle in engine types: the Knox started on gas, but ran on kerosene. (Lest such an engine be regarded as an archaic item out of a "Museum of Ancient Marine Engines," let me note that I lived with just such an engine as recently as 1968, aboard the steel ketch *White Seal,* and that this engine had carried her builder-skipper, Gerry Trobridge, around the world in a 1953–59 circumnavigation—and I don't yet consider myself an ancient mariner. Learning the trick of starting that 4-cylinder, 28-HP LeRoi was a challenge at first, then soon routine.)

Starting *Sea Bird*'s Knox required the engineer, Goodwin, to: fill with gasoline a tiny cup (less than a jigger) that was the top half of a bronze petcock let into the cylinder head; that done, open the cock, which spilled the gas down into the cylinder, and reclose the cock; then, open the salt-water intake and the gravity-feed gasoline line to the engine; next, set the spark-timing handle for slow-speed running and make sure the switch from the dry-cell battery was closed (ON position); finally, grasp the cranking handle and throw the heavy flywheel over against compression and hope there was a robust explosion on the first effort. In that event there would follow a satisfying and slowly accelerating series of explosions (a real *thump* each time), which he would speed up with the timing handle until he judged the RPMs to be "about right." Finally, after about a minute, switch over to kerosene fuel.

The Knox pushed *Sea Bird* at "3.5 knots in calm water, or 80 sea miles in 24 hours," Day reports, and this speed, according to her S/L ratio table *(see Sailing Performance)* was *below* her S/L ratio of 1.0 of 4.52 knots. Day added that the engine "is a great help going to windward; with a moderate breeze and power *Sea Bird* will make six knots when close-hauled." This is an S/L ratio of over 1.3—pressing hard up against her "hull," or maximum cruising speed of 6.06 knots.

It's clear that Day could easily have had a powering speed of 4.52 knots (S/L 1.0) with an engine of only one or two greater horsepower, if Knox made one. Indeed, it probably would not have been any great trick to push her at an S/L ratio of 1.2 (5.42 knots) with 6 to 8 HP—still not much power, especially by today's standards. Recognizing that he was facing one of those inevitable tradeoffs, Day made the conservative choice. Since his fuel capacity had *some* limit (in terms of weight of fuel carried), he preferred more miles at low speed than fewer miles at higher speed. For example, if the next larger Knox engine was 80 pounds heavier, that would have reduced the fuel capacity by 10 gallons—or 35 miles—gasoline weighing eight pounds per gallon. It's clear he only planned to power in calms, so 3.5 knots would keep the yawl moving and help to prevent the slatting about that is so hard on a rig.

With a deadline to meet—arrival in Rome by a certain date—and the extra pressure caused by a ten-day postponement of the original departure date (caused by fitting-out delays), Day ultimately took on every extra gallon of fuel *Sea Bird* would carry. (Note here that the gasoline he carried was more than half the total of kerosene carried—much more than is needed for merely starting and stopping, which are only about a minute of gasoline burned at each period of engine use. This extra gas carried was probably— an acknowledged speculation—taken because the Knox *would* develop greater horsepower when burning gasoline. (My first boat [1958], an 18-foot

Atkin keel sloop, had a one-cylinder, hand-starting Universal Fisherman that was rated at 8 horses burning gas and 5 horses using kerosene. Of course, the carburation for the two fuels is slightly different, but the point is that with the same cubic-inch displacement, these engines will produce more horses with gasoline.) Since Day carried all the extra gas outside the cabin, he apparently felt safety was not being compromised.

As the Knox was newly installed, Day had his choice of tankage capacity —within limits, as noted. First, he had fitted a thirty-gallon "seamless teel" tank under the cabin sole amidships—for kerosene. To that he added a three-gallon "auxiliary feed tank," also for kerosene, at the forward end of the cockpit; this fed the engine by gravity and was, in turn, filled from the large tank below by pressure provided by a bicycle pump. At the after end of the cockpit (both cockpit tanks were in the open and had a secondary role of reducing the volume of the cockpit well in the event of being pooped) was a five-gallon gasoline tank for starting and stopping the engine. These engines had to be *stopped* on gasoline as well as started, to burn off the residual kerosene; if any of that fuel was left in the cylinder, its flash-point, lower than gasoline's, would have made the next start-up much harder, or impossible.

Besides these permanent tanks, Day added a five-gallon can of kerosene on each side of the boat, lashed to the main shrouds, plus twenty one-gallon tanks of the same fuel lashed to the trunk cabin sides. Finally, just before departure, he added another thirty gallons of gasoline in cans that were jammed into the cockpit well so that the helmsman barely had foot room. As only one man stood watch at a time, that didn't matter.

The total of all this was: kerosene—sixty-three gallons; gasoline—thirty-five gallons. In addition, there was ten gallons of lubricating oil, but Day does not mention if they changed the lube oil during the voyage.

One other fuel note: Day reports that "we had considerable fuel trouble during the first ten days, owing to the feed pipes not being equipped with a proper filtering device. How the dirt got into the fuel is impossible to tell, but it is my timid and unbiased opinion that the mud is in the gasolene [*sic*] when you buy it but is distributed in such small particles as to be invisible. The shaking up of the particles causes them to coagulate, and then your troubles begin."

Stores and Gear

Sea Bird's captain barely gives a passing glance at these aspects of the voyage. Discussing stores, he merely notes that the yawl carried food for three men for ninety days, with only the sketchiest suggestion of what that included; among the fresh foods there were potatoes, onions, bread, oranges, lemons—just enough of these to last until they started going bad. As for another starch, rice, he has high praise and recommends that a good supply of it be carried. One other item—the only other—mentioned was a length of "sausage bologna"; this, unfortunately, was kept a bit too long (without refrigeration, of course); and, as the skipper was the last one to eat a hunk of it while going on watch, he suffered twenty-four hours of ptomaine misery.

Surprisingly, no mention was made of eggs, which keep for up to eight weeks at sea if never refrigerated before use and if the cartons are turned over every day at sea. (Other egg preservation tricks such as boiling for three seconds, or greasing the shells, are discussed later.)

As for rum and tobacco, there was only a modest amount of the former since Day was the only drinker aboard, but a good supply of the latter, as all three men smoked pipes.

Turning to gear, we noted the last-minute purchase of a "brass bilge pump" in Providence just before departure. In the bridge deck beneath a deadlight, there was a 5-inch Dirigo compass, but it was too close to the engine and showed enough deviation to make Day want another—in a more reliable location. On the last night ashore (Martha's Vineyard), Day picked up his old reliable, a 7-inch Standard Compass, and this was mounted atop the cabin on the centerline. Day says, "It had a slight deviation for the first few days, owing to being surrounded by cans [fuel lashed to the sides of the trunk, probably] but after these went overboard it was correct to a degree." After a week or so at sea the binnacle light failed and they had to lash a kerosene lantern next to the compass.

They had a taffrail log at the start, but something "took" the spinner early on and, as they had no spare, each man had to estimate and note the miles covered as he came off watch. By the end of the voyage, Day reports, the total of their day-long estimates "approached the [actual] run by about 5 to ten miles, except where we had current. . . . "

As safety measures, they ran lifelines between the fore and aft shrouds, and the man on watch, being alone, always wore a safety harness.

Not a word by Day was devoted to cooking, dishwashing, laundry (if any was done) or bathing. In light of the hard-driving, seventeen-day Atlantic crossing to the Azores, it's likely that each of them was lucky to wash his face once in a while and change his socks occasionally, so they must have reached port with seabags full of salt-encrusted, gamey sailing duds.

Cruising Track

Obviously, there's not much to discuss about a transatlantic crossing where the only port of call between Providence, Rhode Island, and the British Crown Colony of Gibraltar was a brief pause in the Azores, but

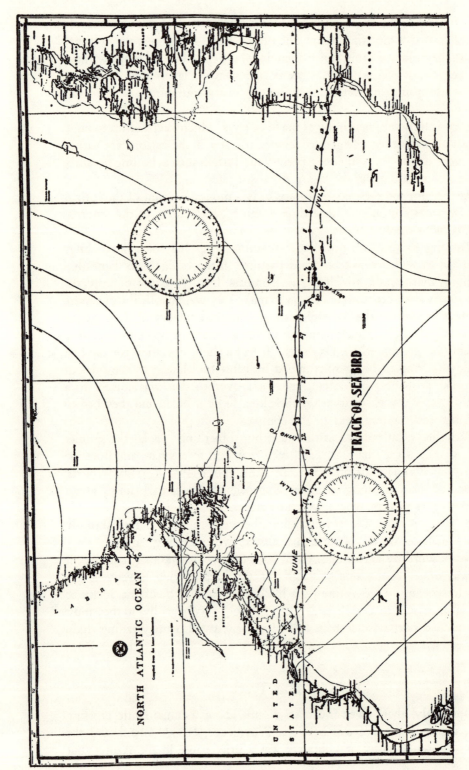

Fig. 2–4. Sea Bird's route across the Atlantic. Note that for most of the way, the yawl rode the 40th parallel of latitude.

Sea Bird's cruising track (Fig. 2–6) has a point of at least minor interest. Note the relatively even spacing between each of the noon positions plotted on the chart. Whatever Day's complaints about weather—that it was rather too much than too little—by driving his ship and crew all day, every day, he was able to achieve some pretty consistently good runs, as the performance figures in the next section reveal. In fact, some of the runs, no matter how favorable the currents or wind conditions, were quite remarkable on a 19-foot waterline.

Sailing Performance

Day had hoped to sail from Providence on June 1, 1911, in order to have fifty sailing days to reach Rome for the opening of an Italian exposition. Preparations dragged on, however, and *Sea Bird* did not leave until June 10. Of this Day says—in laughable contrast with what one might hear about such a delay these days—"It took over a month to engine, rig and fit her out, a job that ought to have been done in ten days." That certainly underscores one benefit of sailing an uncomplicated boat.

The first night out, June 10, they put in at Cottage City, Martha's Vineyard (Massachusetts), where they picked up the 7-inch compass and the extra gasoline; and then in the morning they were off. Departing Martha's Vineyard, *Sea Bird* was so heavily loaded with crew, stores for three months, and all that fuel that her freeboard was less than a foot. As Fig. 2–2 reveals, it wasn't much to begin with. So, Day decided to find out early how she would behave at sea, and drove the yawl hard out through Muskegat Channel (between the Vineyard and Nantucket Island), a place of very strong tide rips. To the pleasure of all aboard, she went through with dry decks.

For the first three days out they ran into headwinds and only logged sixty miles a day. Day's prediction that they would reach the Azores in twenty days—with the private opinion that with luck they might do it in sixteen—seemed to go by the board. Still, Day drove the crew and himself hard, holding to a four-on, eight-off watch schedule.

The next bit of bad luck was that the usually dependable westerlies eluded them. After the three days of headwinds, they had almost a week of squalls, the wind often east of south, requiring them to beat across the Gulf Stream. During one squall they couldn't throw off the halyards fast enough to lower sail, so the yawl took a heavy knockdown; but she sprang up again—a response that greatly buoyed her skipper's confidence. On June 17, Day reports, "The wind shifted to a strong southwesterly, and we headed east again and, with the whole jigger and jib, and single-reefed mainsail logged off five-and-a-half knots." Pretty good going for the 19-foot waterline.

Fig. 2–5. Sea Bird *lying ahull in a squall (from a painting by Warren Sheppard).*

On June 17 they were hitting 6 knots and at noon, the twenty-four-hour run worked out to 162 miles. (They must have been getting *some* help from current; still, it was sparkling performance *(see Speed/Length Ratio table, below).* Three hours later they were hove to in a squall, and that night they were running before a northwesterly gale, this time close-reefed, and Day says they were logging 6 to 6½ knots.

The next day's noon position worked out to a twenty-four-hour run of 183 miles. Day felt his navigation *must* be off, but a sun-sight at 1600 confirmed the noon sight. Some months later, while returning to the United States aboard the steamer *Koenig Albert* (*Sea Bird* having been shipped home as deck cargo), Day had the opportunity to read the ship's log. The steamer had passed through the same area as the yawl just two days prior to her record 183-mile run. Day discovered that the ship's navigator had logged a 48-mile favorable current for the ship's noon-to-noon run. Day interpolated this to be a 40-mile boost for *Sea Bird,* which still left a net of 143 miles made good on sailing alone. In two days, the yawl had covered 345 miles.

Such a sailing performance must be attributed, principally, to two factors: Day was a hard-driving master, and with three men standing watches the yawl could be kept driving at all times; and, second, *Sea Bird* was a really light displacement boat, with only a 700-pound ballast keel (or 1700 pounds counting the inside ballast Bill Garden says she carried) and a 19-foot waterline (or even 20-foot, loaded), so she must have been surfing or nearly so for long periods during that northwesterly gale.

Which brings us to *Sea Bird*'s numbers, as a cross-check against Day's daily mileage entries in his log, those above and those that follow. Many are right at the limit of the yawl's top speed potential, yet *Sea Bird*'s passage time to the Azores of 17 days, 16 hours, 30 minutes is, by any reckoning, outstanding.

On June 19, reality returned after the glorious days—the wind turned fluky and the yawl made only 64 miles. Later that day they weathered a series of squalls, during one of which they took another knockdown. Water poured down the companionway hatch on top of Day as he emerged on deck, soaking him and filling the cockpit, but the yawl struggled to her feet and a frigid wind died away in five minutes; shortly after, a rainbow arched across the sky ahead, the wind swung around to the northwest, and they went back up to 5 knots.

On June 22—twelve days out—Day invites the reader to "leave home for an hour and join me on *Sea Bird*" (for a taste of life at sea). The captive reader is treated to the experience of running at 5 to 6 knots before a southwest gale in a 25-foot yawl with waves "from 15 to 20 feet from trough to crest." Gradually, the wind increases and the wave heights mount until it is time to heave to. Here, Day explains his various methods of accomplishing that, depending on wind and sea conditions:

- If not blowing too hard, he heaves to under a close-reefed mainsail, "but if it is a stiff gale, then this is too much sail."
- In the latter case, he tries "a small jib and a reefed jigger . . . but no rule can be laid down; it depends on the boat, the sea and the heft of the wind."

Sea Bird: Speed/Length Ratio			
(WL: 20.5′ $\sqrt{20.5}$ = 4.52)			
(Day called the WL 20.5′, so we'll use his figure.)			
S/L $\times$ $\sqrt{\text{WL}}$	= Speed (knots)	$\times$ 24	= NM (1 day)
1.0 4.52	4.52		108.5
1.1 4.52	4.97		119.3
1.2 4.52	5.42		130.1
1.3 4.52	5.88		141.1
1.34 4.52	6.06		145.4

· Claiming that a propeller aperture tends to make a boat round up stern-to the seas, he notes that you must overcome this tendency with more sail aft, saying, "Knowing this [about *Sea Bird*] I decided to try [her] under a reefed jigger, and if [that was] not enough, add the mizzen staysail." (He did not list one of these in the sail inventory, so perhaps he used one of those three spare jibs—which usually works.)

In this same "visit" to *Sea Bird* the reader is treated to an interesting wrinkle in the endlessly debated merits of the sea anchor. (It has seemed to me in the course of reading hundreds of books over the years that the detractors outnumber the adherents by a considerable number. But I'm often impressed by the vehemence of those who defend it. They meet its greatest weakness—chafe—by a quantam leap of redundancy—such as using chain as bridle on an oversized iron hoop and, today, a nylon drogue in a diameter considerably in excess of actual strength requirement, this meticulously fitted with anti-chafe material where the rode passes over the bow.)

Day's variation on the standard hoop sea anchor came from Capt. William Andrews, who had made several voyages across the Atlantic between 1877 and 1904, sometimes with his brother, Asa, and once alone in the 15-foot sloop, *Dark Secret*. Andrews would simply stream his regular anchor off the bow (as did Fred Rebell, chapter 3, *Elaine*), and this apparently worked.

But when Day tried it, he found his anchor did not have enough "drag," perhaps because it was too heavy, so he lashed a heavy board across the arms and flukes. Then he bent on 300 feet of drogue and let it go. He reports, "It tailed out ahead as *Sea Bird* was traveling stern-first at the rate of two knots or more, and when it came to rest it was floating about two seas off and I suppose ten fathoms below the surface. It did its duty, and with her nose pointed right into the wind the little yawl rode with an easy motion and dry decks." Day links this wrinkle to our theme of simplicity with the comment: "This makes an excellent drogue, the anchor being there anyway and the board stowing in a small space." (A board would be easy to attach to a Danforth—in the open **V**—but under the plow end of the CQR it would exert a fierce pull on the lashings.)

Following that period hove to, the next moon position was only 77 miles down their track. After a short period of sailing, they had to heave to again, and this followed by running off before a squall under jib alone. Then, on June 23, after thirteen days at sea, Neptune smiled. They were across the Gulf Stream and the wind went into the southwest quadrant.

On June 24 they logged 113 miles; on the twenty-fifth, 117 miles; and the twenty-seventh, 123 miles. Then the wind swung again, east of south, and for the next seven days they were close-reaching, and all hands "had a grouch." This was rough sailing, pounding along at "five knots," the

Fig. 2–6. Sea Bird *in the Azores.*

helmsman wet most of the time. Claiming 5 knots for most of this period, Day seems to confirm that the little yawl was good for "better than 100 a day," even with unfavorable winds. *Sea Bird*'s track chart (Fig. 2–4) reveals that she ran across the 40-degree parallel pretty much as if on railroad tracks.

After the close reaching, there was another day of sailing with the sheets free, during which she again logged 123 miles. On June 28 as Day went off watch he told his relief they were within spitting distance of the Azores. They motored during a couple of calm periods that day, working further south. Then, on June 29, the islands of Corvo and Flores appeared dead ahead, one on each side of the bow.

The daily runs noted show *Sea Bird* could really foot it under favorable conditions. Day expressed disappointment in not making the crossing in seventeen or eighteen days—or, as mentioned earlier, even sixteen—and spent much time afterward studying his passage log and cruising track to determine why (more than a little hint of sailing ego here). He noted that the first three days out only netted 60 miles a day, and that we "lost about 100 miles when laid to on June 22," and concluded that the failure to meet his desired time was due to weather conditions—beyond his control. He added, "We did not loaf, for records show we reefed and shook out over fifty times in the first fifteen days." While that number is probably no record, it does resemble racing more than cruising.

Day doesn't mention use of the engine at all between the departure and that last day into the Azores. We know he had a pretty considerable amount of fuel. The "six or seven days" of close-reaching that he reported at 5 knots (120 miles per day) *might* have been power-assisted sailing, as Day had made a special point of the fact that the engine "was of great help going to windward" and "would make six knots when close hauled" *(see Engine section)*. If the yawl had made only 3 knots while close reaching (under sail alone) for six to seven days, the loss in distance over the period would have been over 50 miles a day for seven days, or 350 miles—which would have added about three more days to the passage!

On the subject of the elapsed time in the crossing, Day was not content to let the matter rest. He continues, "We beat the *Spray*'s passage from Briars [Slocum called it Briers] Island to Horta (Azores), as told in Capt. Slocum's book, but his published statement does not agree with the records, as he did not arrive at Gibraltar, according to the account kept there, until August 4th, which made him longer than 36 days out from Boston."

Day, clearly, was willing to chivvy the old master, a challenge best understood when we remember that Slocum was back from his circumnavigation only thirteen years and that his fame had not yet lifted him to the hallowed niche he enjoys today. If it's true that "no man is a hero to his family," perhaps Slocum, being personally known to so many people of Day's era, was not yet the apotheosis of sailing.

We will pass over *Sea Bird*'s four days in Horta, Azores, as it was merely a period of brief rest and overhauling the yawl's stores; and, Day remarks, "the timer on the engine, which controlled the sparking rate, [was repaired] by a very clever native mechanic." Of the remaining passage, 1200 miles to Gibraltar, we need note little because the weather was balmy and the sailing by now routine. Winds were lighter but favorable, between NNE and NNW, for the first six days. With this kind of help, *Sea Bird* strutted her stuff and reeled off daily runs of 84, 106, 118, 119, 108, and 93 miles—a total of 628 miles between July 3 and July 9—over 100 a day, on average.

On July 10 the wind became brisk and they began to log 5 knots. July 11 was cloudy and disagreeable. Just so we don't forget the everyday maritime reality of that era, that day they spotted a square-rigger, but she was too far off to speak her. On July 13 two steamers crisscrossed the yawl, and on the fourteenth, Day got a good longitude sight that put them 80 miles off the Spanish coast at "about the latitude of Cape St. Vincent." They weathered a gale that morning that lasted only six hours and, at 1700, sighted the Portuguese coast.

On July 16, at noon, *Sea Bird* was halfway between Cape St. Vincent and Cape Spartel (Africa)—about 125 miles from Gibraltar. On the seventeenth they passed Cape Spartel at 0800, picked up speed as a spanking breeze drove them along, and entered the Mediterranean at 1525. Day says, "With wind and tide *Bird* was doing eight knots, and carrying a terrific press of sail." At 1700 they rounded the last point and the Rock of Gibraltar loomed up ahead; at 1800 they ran into the harbor and picked up a mooring.

Here we end *Sea Bird*'s voyage, for, to meet his commitment to the Italian government to exhibit the yawl, Day now had the yawl slung in a steamer's davits and shipped to Italian waters, where she was launched and proceeded under her own power to Rome.

Some Cruising Aphorisms—Vintage 1911

Thomas Fleming Day was a highly regarded sailor of his time and— as one might expect from the editor of a sailing journal in the era of Teddy Roosevelt, an age of resounding American self-confidence—was not bashful about expressing his ideas. In fact, *The Rudder* had a reputation for laying it on the line right up to World War II—where opinion was concerned. This included not only Day but his successor, William F. Crosby, the naval architect turned editor, and also John G. Hanna, the contributor of a monthly column for fourteen years (until his death in 1948), who was also the designer of the famed 30-foot *Tahiti* ketch. This habit of outspoken opinion, by the founder of America's first boating magazine, has left us with a few of his fervent ideas, which he scattered through his book:

- To makers of gear intended for seagoing boats: "Make it twice as strong and twice as heavy as you think is necessary, and that adds an additional 50% weight and strength to it."
- On gales: "My long experience in small boats has taught me this: that if the boat is a good boat, when real trouble comes she is best let alone."
- More on gales: "The worst part of a gale is its tail, or to explain, a small boat is most uncomfortable when a gale has blown itself out and the sea is subsiding. . . . "
- "In a large vessel [such as a steamer] a man is on the sea, but in a small one he is *with* the sea."
- "I have always liked and praised the dead-rise type [of boat]; they are far better sea-boats than the round-bilge. This will probably be questioned by the owners of round-bilge boats, but I believe every man who had had experience with both types will agree with me. In one quality they are without question superior to the round-bilge, and that is in dry-going. I will stump any man to bring forth a round-bilge, round-sided craft of the same length as *Bird* that will equal her in dryness. Their sea qualities are due to the fact that the chime [*sic*] edge makes them have an immediate lift, so that the lifting action of the wave under any

part of the hull is instantaneous with the impact. On a round boat the fingers of the wave slip up [the topsides] for some distance before they get a lifting grip; and it is this slip that gives the sea its chance to get aboard." (It's only fair to add that in payment for this quick-lifting quality, chine boats tend to have a quicker motion, especially in light-displacement hulls, so there is, to invoke the old cliché, no free lunch.)

· On lookouts: "The best light for a small vessel at sea is a constant and active lookout. See the other fellow first and get out of his way."

· On the effect of propeller apertures on steering: "Before we cut the screw-port and put the propeller in, *Sea Bird* was one of the sweetest steering craft ever handled; in fact, under any reasonable conditions she would steer herself for hours at a time. [This, presumably, was with careful adjustment of the sheets and tiller and centerboard, and with the wind somewhere other than dead aft.] But, with the screw [prop] opening and drag of the propeller, you cannot leave the helm for an instant, except when the sail is pushing against the throw of the wheel."

Altogether, *Sea Bird* acquitted herself rather handsomely, and it is no wonder that she became such a popular design—especially with backyard boatbuilders—for the next thirty-five years.

3. *Islander*

The whole voyage was carried out with far less effort than I had anticipated. Only once did the Islander *get in a position that required assistance to get her out, and she sustained no damages that I was not able to repair with my own resources. I never arrived in port complaining of hunger or shortage of water. The* Islander *met some rough weather, but none that caused me any apprehension as to her seaworthiness.*

I am often asked about how the Islander *compares with other types of vessels. I have not had experience with other types, but I am of the opinion that I could have made the voyage in any well-found boat of the same size, but in none would it have been easier.*

—Harry Pidgeon
Around the World Single-Handed (1933)

Harry Pidgeon

Just as Slocum was a pure-bred sailor from birth, so Harry Pidgeon was a landlubber who turned himself, by hard-won experience, into a small-boat sailor of considerable accomplishment. He was the second man ever to circumnavigate alone, but while Slocum was born within sniff and sound of the sea, Pidgeon started life almost as far from it as you can get—a farm in Iowa. As he said: "I did not see salt water until I went to California, when I was eighteen. . . . So far as I know, none of my ancestors ever followed the sea."

Where Slocum set sail alone to reassemble the shattered remnants of his former station, Pidgeon went as a continuation of his adventurous life, and to see "distant places." Like Slocum, he built his own boat, and for the same reason: lack of funds to buy one. And like Slocum, he had built boats before, though not for blue-water work. We tend to think of Slocum as having been an "old man" when he sailed, but Pidgeon, at fifty-three, was two years older at departure.

Pidgeon's book, *Around the World Single-Handed,* is sparse about his early life, with only a few details about his boating background. While in California as a young man working on a ranch, he built a "canvas canoe," and a few years later he and a partner went to the Yukon to explore that still-wild territory, built themselves a quick-and-dirty skiff, and floated down the Yukon River to the sea. For a time he cruised southeastern Alaska waters in a boat he had purchased, living aboard and "making photographs along the rivers and in the mountains of that great land." Finally, on a visit

Fig. 3–1. *Harry
Pidgeon in 1926, a
year after his
circumnavigation.
(Photo:
UPI/Bettman
Archive.)*

home to Iowa, he recalled a boyhood ambition to float down the Mississippi,
so he built a flat-boat below the falls at Minneapolis and fulfilled his dream.
By the time he had reached the Gulf of Mexico, he had "resolved to see
more distant lands in a vessel of my own."

All these boating exploits had occurred in the years leading up to World
War I. Now, needing funds to build a boat, he returned to California and
took up his camera in a serious way. As he says, "I became a photographer
among the great trees of the Sierra." That he was expert in this rapidly
growing profession is attested to by the photos reproduced in his book.

By 1917 Pidgeon had found the design he wanted. It was based on an
earlier design, the famous *Sea Bird* yawl, which had been commissioned by
and built for Thomas Fleming Day, whose story we covered in chapter 2.
As a result of *Sea Bird*'s transatlantic voyage, another controversy burst forth
in the yachting press, a reverberation of the Slocum rhubarb over the
"proper size" for seagoing yachts. It would seem that the question of
size/seaworthiness was already a moot point after Slocum, but apparently

each new cruising generation produces its own clique of naysayers bent on dictating the way it should be done. Despite this, many people got the message about the once-more-revealed relationship between size and seaworthiness, and sales of *Sea Bird* plans took off like a rocket. (Many of the boats were still in boatyards when I started cruising in 1952, and I'm sure more than a few readers know of some that are still sailing.)

The design was such a success that *The Rudder* commissioned the widely respected naval architect, Frederick William Goeller, Jr., to design a new, larger version of *Sea Bird*. Thus was born *Seagoer*—at 34 feet, one-third larger. Next, a one-half larger centerboard yawl was designed, and all three versions were offered to the public in a booklet *The Rudder* sold for $2.00. It was these plans—the *Seagoer* version with a keel—that appealed to Pidgeon as the right design for his long cruise to distant lands (Fig. 3-2) and became his *Islander*.

When he had accumulated some funds from his photographic efforts, collected some hand tools, and found a rent-free site on the shore facing Los Angeles harbor, Pidgeon was ready to start building—a job that would take eighteen months.

The Hull

The *Seagoer* design that became Pidgeon's *Islander* had the following specifications: LOA—34 feet; LWL—27′6″; Beam on Deck—10′9″; Beam at WL—10′1″; Draft (unloaded)—5′; Ballast Keel—1250 lbs.; Freeboard—forward, 4′1″; least, 2′3″; aft, 2′10″; Rig Options—gaff yawl or hermaphrodite schooner; Sail Area—yawl, 635 sq. ft.; schooner, 676 sq. ft.; Engine—optional.

One missing item immediately apparent is the Displacement. This is not given by Pidgeon and is omitted on the Goeller plans. The extremely modest weight of the ballast keel, however, is a clue to one apparent fact: *Islander*, like *Sea Bird*, was an extremely light-displacement boat. Consider the following *possible* Ballast/Displacement ratios, using the 1250-pound ballast keel as the constant factor:

	B/D Ratio		Ballast Keel		Total Displ.
If	10 %	&	1250 lbs.	then	12,500 lbs.
	12½		1250 lbs.		10,938 lbs.
	15		1250 lbs.		9375 lbs.
	17½		1250 lbs.		7813 lbs.
	20		1250 lbs.		6250 lbs.

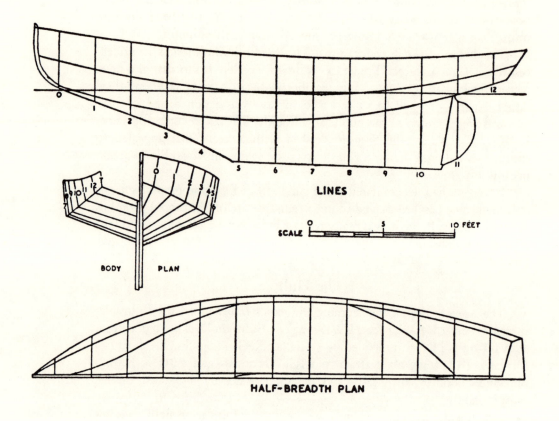

LINES

SCALE ⊢ 5 10 FEET

BODY PLAN

HALF-BREADTH PLAN

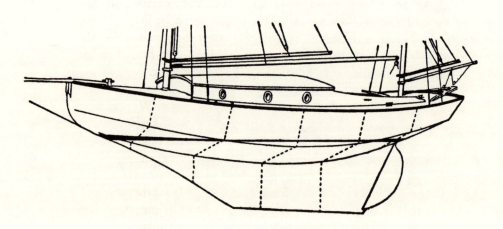

There seems to be little point in calculating any B/D ratio higher than 20 percent, as it appears virtually impossible that a 34-foot hull would have a total displacement of less than 6250 lbs. Each notch higher in B/D ratio (the ballast keel remaining constant) will *lower* the total displacement figure. *Islander*'s most likely displacement, then, would seem to be between 9375 lbs. (B/D 15 percent) and 12,500 lbs. (B/D 10 percent). (Upon reaching the Panama Canal, officials made a rough estimate that *Islander* was a five-tonner, or 11,200 lbs., and assessed Pidgeon's transit fee at that displacement. This amounts to a 12½ percent B/D ratio, confirming the preceding reasoning.)

Although it would have been standard practice in that era for Pidgeon to have had some inside ballast, there is no mention of it in Pidgeon's book or Goeller's plans. Attitudes toward inside ballast have changed markedly since those days. Then, respectable amounts of it were specified for their dampening effect on a boat's rolling and pitching motions—greater comfort at sea. The price paid for it in a boat like *Islander,* with its fin keel, is raising the Center of Gravity (CG) of the hull and thus detracting somewhat from the hull's righting moment. Just another tradeoff that must be faced when selecting a suitable hull for a long voyage.

All of this adds up to a hull that, according to Pidgeon, was easily driven in light winds but must have had a pretty "corky" motion in heavy weather. While it's true that the added buoyancy at the bilges of a hard-chine hull will dampen rolling somewhat, *Islander* was a boat for a skipper with a strong stomach.

Back to Pidgeon at his waterfront building site. As he started building, he had the aforementioned rent-free space, a nearly rain-free climate that permitted open-air building, and three small home-built boats to his credit. Perhaps most important, he was used to doing things for himself. Pidgeon and Slocum provide interesting parallels. (It's certain that Pidgeon had read Joshua's book, and he quotes from Slocum's tale with precise details in his own book.) Both men built their own boats, both had limited resources, both chose yawls, and both sailed without an engine. There, however, the similarities end, for *Spray* was as heavy as *Islander* was light.

Pidgeon notes: "The timbers for the keel were eight by twelve inches in thickness, and the largest [longest] piece was 28 feet long. When I hear anyone talking about my frail craft, I always think of those keel timbers." He shaped them with saw and adz—using hand tools throughout—and then bolted on the 1250-pound ballast keel that had been cast at a local foundry.

The wood he used was white oak for the stem and a few other strength members, but the rest of the hull was Douglas fir and Oregon pine. It is fascinating to read Pidgeon's description of the chine construction. When the heavy "chine log" was in place, let into a notch at the juncture of each

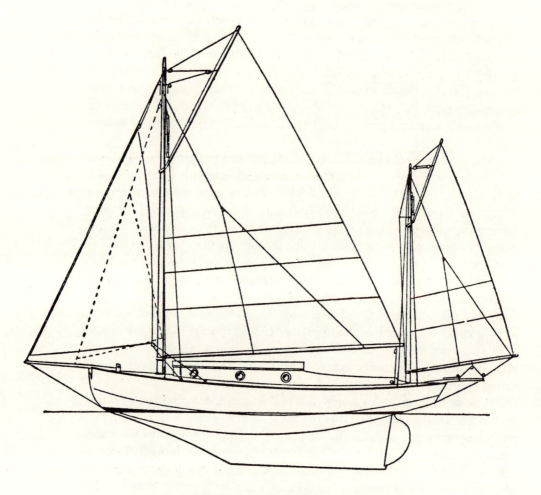

PLAN AND ELEVATION

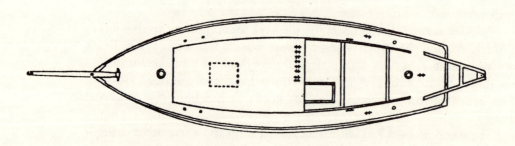

Fig. 3–3. Islander: *Sail Plan and Deck Plan.*

Fig. 3–4. *Harry Pidgeon hewing Keel timbers.*

bottom and topside frame, Pidgeon made wood templates of these bilge angles at every frame station. From the templates he cut boiler-plate gussets and bolted them on either side of the frame joints. This produced an enormously strong chine.

This wrinkle clearly impressed some boatbuilder about forty years ago, who must have read Pidgeon's book, because he duplicated these chine reinforcements exactly in building a replica of *Islander*. I came upon this boat in the early 1960s at a boatyard in Glen Cove, Long Island. It was owned by a family of five who were working together to remedy the ravages of age. Their big job was to replace several planks. (Boatyard neighbors being irrepressibly curious about one another's boats, we were soon swapping tools and exchanging fitting-out tips, and I quickly became absorbed in their project.) When I peered into the gaping slot created by the removal of a plank directly above the chine in the cockpit area, I discovered the familiar boiler-plate gussets spanning each frame corner. They were quarter-inch steel with quarter-inch bolts and, although badly rusted, still had enormous strength. The sight produced an eerie sense of *déjà vu,* like staring into *Islander* herself.

Consider this: to get those chine logs in place (Pidgeon called them "bilge strakes," but terminology changes), which were 2½ inches thick and 7 inches wide in the middle, tapering to 6 inches at the ends, Pidgeon—

61

working alone—had to bend these pieces (not counting the fore-and-aft curvature) 20 inches *on edge*. He did it without the aid of a steambox.

With the hull framing complete, Pidgeon turned to the planking. All the planks above the chine were of single length, for strength, appearance, and to avoid the risk of rot to which butt blocks are prone. Tribute to his skill came from a local shipwright, who said, "I know how we would put on those planks in the shop, where we have a steambox and plenty of help, but how you got them on I can't see." Pidgeon admitted they were the hardest part of the job but added: " . . . when it comes to blocking up and driving wedges, they could not have beaten me in the boat shop. Those planks had to come to place or break. That they would break was what I feared, but they did not. . . . "

When the planking was fitted, he laid the deck and covered it with canvas. Each side of the trunk cabin was a single piece, continuous with the cockpit coamings, and there were three portholes in each side. For power, Pidgeon had only the sails. He observed: "She was adapted to the use of auxiliary power, but for many reasons, mostly financial, I did not install a motor. However, the real sport is to make the elements take one where he wants to go; and then, a motor never functions properly when left alone with me."

Deck Layout

Islander's deck was simple and uncluttered. Pidgeon gave no details in his description of building the yawl, but a few emerge later in the book. The bowsprit extended 6′6″ outboard of the stem, and the inboard end terminated at a samson post. Although the photos do not reveal it, Pidgeon wrote that there was a windlass just abaft the samson post. We also know from the text that he had at least two anchors and chain for each, but we don't know the sizes. There is no hatch in the foredeck, sure evidence that Pidgeon stowed his ground tackle there. (It would have been too much trouble to keep it in the forepeak and carry it through the cabin every time he needed it.) A confirmation of his use of chain for an anchor rode is found in several photos of the yawl in remote harbors, in which the rode is hanging straight down from the stem—highly suggestive of chain.

Returning to the foredeck, the mast passes through it just forward of the cabin. The deck plan (Fig. 3-3) shows a dotted rectangle in the cabin top—probably a skylight, with that shape—but Pidgeon did not build one, as the photos confirm. At the after end of the cabin trunk there is a line of cleats on the starboard side of the companionway hatch, good practice for a singlehander—all lines leading aft to the cockpit.

Goeller's deck plan reveals an unusual feature: the companionway hatch is located right in the bridge deck. In the first place, this bridge deck, 4 feet

Fig. 3–5. Islander *in frame. The five beams that formed the bridge deck are visible just aft of amidships.*

in its fore-and-aft dimension, is quite long by any standard. The Goeller plans calls for the companionway to be cut *into* it, to port of the centerline —perhaps to avoid cutting into the cabin top beams? If so, it's done at the expense of doing the same thing to the bridge deck beams—a questionable tradeoff, as the bridge deck, just aft of amidships, is the ideal spot in the hull to achieve massive athwartships strength. And, if you cut the hatch in the bridge deck, you then have to build up sides for it—a rickety lash-up at best. Pidgeon just ignored this design feature and put his hatch in the cabin roof, on the centerline. As the photo of *Islander* in frame reveals (Fig. 3–5), there are five beams in the bridge deck (clearly visible, as their radius is different from those fore and aft of them). Since the five frames are on 1-foot centers, the net length is 4 feet.)

Next, the cockpit itself. It's a simple foot-well, 4 feet long, 6 feet wide forward and tapering to 4 feet wide at the after end. Using some "quick and dirty" numbers, and one assumption, let's see what that volume would hold in weight, if the yawl were pooped and the cockpit filled. The length is 4 feet, the average width is 5 feet, and the (assumed) depth is 2 feet. Thus $4 \times 5 \times 2 = 40$. Since a cubic foot of water weighs 62 pounds, we get $40 \times 62 = 2480$ pounds if the cockpit is filled, plus the weight of Pidgeon.

That's more than a long ton of water, not an encouraging prospect in heavy weather, yet he never mentions it as worrisome.

What's more, the cockpit's shape is odd. It doesn't look comfortable because it's too wide, without a place to sit or to brace your feet when the yawl heeled. However, Pidgeon must have altered this, too, for his book contains a photo of the yawl sailing off Catalina Island in California. In it, someone is at the tiller, leaning on the cockpit coaming in an attitude that suggests a seat is under him. Perhaps, then, he built locker seats on both sides and reduced the cockpit volume. To drain the cockpit, there were scuppers at the after end, port and starboard.

If all this about the cockpit size and seats sounds like much ado about nothing, it's discussed at length because as noted earlier the subject of cockpits—to have or not to have—comes under close scrutiny (for seagoing boats) several more times later on.

We've noted that *Islander* was tiller-steered, and just abaft the rudder head the mizzen mast passes through the deck. Astern of that we see the familiar keystone-shaped boomkin extending off the counter stern, essential to anchor the mizzen sheet, and a handy place to stand when reefing that sail.

And last, though not really part of the deck but always carried on it at sea, there was a 9-foot lapstrake "tender," built by Pidgeon, and carried upside-down on deck, leaning against the cabin. Lapstrake dinghy construction is not the hallmark of the novice builder.

The Rig

Here again we must discover most details by inspection of plans and photos, and by the few additional facts Pidgeon provides. First, *Islander* was gaff-rigged on both masts, fairly common practice for yawls and ketches right up through the 1920s. While it's true that a gaff mizzen offers more area than a Marconi when reaching and running, on these points of sailing the mizzen often blankets the main and spoils its drive, so most skippers lower it then. Besides that, despite the fact that most mizzens are cut absolutely flat, they're pretty much useless when beating. They're handy at anchor, however, when hoisted to keep the boat heading into the wind, as a place to attach the after end of the cockpit cover, and they permit setting a mizzen staysail; but, Pidgeon didn't carry such a sail.

The sail areas for the working rig (to an impressive precision), which totaled 634.30 sq. ft., were as follows: Jib—119.38 sq. ft.; Mainsail—394.31 sq. ft.; Mizzen—120.6 sq. ft. In addition, the dotted line on the sail plan shows a storm jib of 70 sq. ft. If we study the sail plan (Fig. 3-3), we see that the mainmast is so far forward it reminds one of the mast position on the Friendship sloop. One benefit of this is that it keeps the mast out of the accommodation, which is otherwise a real obstacle to going forward in that era of thick, solid sticks. On the other hand, that mast position makes it clear why *Islander* needed a bowsprit—to achieve a fore-triangle large enough to set a jib of adequate power for tacking, and to balance the mizzen. But, what a price: a main boom 23 feet long and a gaff 15 feet long.

Many seagoing sailors of Pidgeon's era (and right up to World War II) have expressed the opinion that the maximum sail area one man could handle alone was 400–500 square feet; a few, like my friend Tom Colvin, go as high as 600 square feet. Most sailors today would probably put the limit at 350–450 square feet; at that, they would be thinking of a Marconi sail, not one with a gaff, and, since the arrival of dacron, of a total weight considerably lighter than the same area in canvas. It appears that what might raise eyebrows today was commonplace to both Goeller and Pidgeon—and to Slocum, too, for that matter, considering the size and heft of his original mainsail and spars.

Islander's sails were canvas, of course, and like *Spray*'s were sewn with narrow cloths in vertical seams—to prevent a tear from running all the way across the sail. The leech was cut straight—no roach at all—and there were no battens. Pidgeon had his sailmaker put in the three sets of reef points specified by Goeller, but where the sail plan shows a topping lift *and* lazyjacks, Pidgeon did without the latter, a curious omission for a single-handed sailor. To live with lazyjacks is to love them—especially if your mainsail is large.

The spar dimensions on *Islander* were light by *Spray*'s standards, but then so was the displacement. *Islander*'s mast heights, deck to shoulder: Mainmast—28 feet; Mizzen mast—20 feet. As for the spar diameters, they're just over half of *Spray*'s: *Mainmast*—5¾ inches at the deck, 5¼ inches at the boom gaff jaws, and 3¼ inches at the shoulder; *Main boom*—4 inches in the middle, tapering to 3 inches at theoutboard end and 2¾ inches at the gooseneck; *Main gaff*—2½ inches at the jaws, 3½ inches in the middle, and 2¾ inches at the outboard end; *Mizzen mast*—4½ inches at the deck, 3½ inches at the gaff jaws, and 2¾ inches at the mizzen shoulder; *Mizzen boom*—3 inches in the middle, tapering to 2 inches at each end; *Mizzen gaff*—2 inches at the jaws, 2½ inches in the middle, and 2⅛ inches at the outboard end. (*Note:* what is termed "middle" here is actually a point about three-quarters of the way along these spars from their pivot points, the point of greatest stress.)

As for the bowsprit, the plans show it as a plank-type, sprung down a bit, with a wire bobstay ending in a turnbuckle. Pidgeon changed this to a round bowsprit, used chain for a bobstay, and added bowsprit shrouds. (He was wise, I think. While I am generally reluctant to inject personal experiences into this book, it's worth an exception on a point like this.) Having cruised a gaff-rigged (on the main) cruising ketch for eight years, I simply can't see how anyone could tuck a reef into a jib, or muzzle it in stops, without having a bowsprit shroud to sit on while bracing his feet against the bobstay. I would hate to tackle this job while clinging to the jibstay with one hand and working with the other. Pidgeon relates an incident in which, during a gale, he had to lie flat on the deck with half of his body stretched out on the bowsprit to drag down the jib and put stops on it—a decidedly risky job without bowsprit shrouds.

Turning to the standing rig, Pidgeon tells us nothing about its size. In *The Rudder* plans booklet, the 25-foot *Sea Bird* calls for ⅜-inch galvanized wire throughout. But those plans were overseen by Day, who was not a naval architect. He probably specified what experience suggested was "about right." As to *Seagoer,* Goeller says nothing about any aspect of the rig. My own estimate is that ¼-inch wire would have been fully adequate for *Sea Bird,* and ⅜-inch for *Islander*—with the extra ⅛ inch added only by worriers and overdoers like Day (and myself).

Each mast had three shrouds on each side, each shroud ending in a turnbuckle at deck level and this attached to the hull by a husky chainplate. Pidgeon did not fit ratlines, a surprising omission, as they are very useful, even for a singlehander. There is no evidence of running backstays, probably because a fairly robust mainmast was strong enough to resist bending under the pull of a jib of only 120 square feet. As with the bowsprit, the mizzen boomkin stay is chain.

The running rigging echoes the Slocum approach—manila rope, no winches, but with extra blocks added to the halyards to provide the necessary mechanical advantage to manage the pulley-hauley without undue strain. All the halyards and sheets, as noted, ended at cleats within reach of the helmsman. Fortunately, the photos in Pidgeon's book are sharp enough to delineate the halyard arrangements:

Jib Halyard—Starts with a becket block hanging from a masthead strop. The halyard starts at the becket, runs down through a block shackled to the jib head, up again and through the becket block, then down to cabin-top level, where it passes through a fairlead block and aft to its cabin-top cleat.

Jib Sheets—There are two blocks shackled into the clew. Each sheet (P & S) starts at a padeye or eye-bolt on deck just abaft the after main shroud. The sheet runs from this up through one jib-clew block, back down to the deck and through a swivel block, thence aft to a cleat on the outside of the cockpit coaming.

Main Peak Halyard—Starts at the gaff peak, passes through a block hanging from the masthead, passes back through a block on the thickest part of the gaff, forward again through a block on the mast, down to the cabin top, and aft through a fairlead block.

Main Throat Halyard—Starts at the becket on a single block attached to the main gaff jaws, runs up and is rove through a double block hanging from a strop hanging just below the peak halyard blocks, passes down and through the single block at the gaff jaws, back up through the double block, down to the cabin top, thence aft through its fairlead block.

This simple arrangement was, for a boat this size, well proved in the inshore fishing boats for a century or more, and is still a good one today. The throat halyard is the "heavier" hauling job, so if the gaff or sail (or both) are too heavy, or if the crew is smaller or older, it's simple enough to make *both* of these blocks doubles, put the one with the becket at the opposite position from the description above, start the halyard at that becket, and thus gain one added factor of mechanical advantage, from 3:1 to 4:1. The fairlead blocks at cabintop level are only for the singlehanded convenience of leading all lines aft. They don't add mechanical advantage; in fact, they reduce it a bit by adding friction.

Main Sheet—This is something of a mystery. Goeller shows a double-ended mainsheet, with cleats on both side decks outside the cockpit coamings. Though this system is somewhat rare today, some sailors still swear by it because it allows the helmsman to trim the mainsheet on either side of the cockpit. As the name indicates, the sheet is free on both ends. To set one up, starting, say, on the starboard side, make sure the line is very long. A length of line is laid on deck, say five feet beyond the starboard cleat. The other end runs aft, passes through a swivel block mounted on deck (directly opposite the rudder post), passes up through one sheave of a double block hanging from the main boom (a few inches inboard of the end), then down through a single block mounted on deck directly below it on the centerline, up again and through the other sheave of the double block, then down and across to the swivel block on the port side, thence forward to its portside deck cleat.

The required length of this sheet is determined by cleating down one end (say the starboard, with a three-foot bitter end), reeving the line through the blocks, as above, then pushing the boom out to port, allowing the line to run through the blocks until the boom reaches a point about one foot short of the port after main shroud. Then, leaving a three-foot bitter end on that side, cut it off; and, of course, whip the ends.

Caution: The prudent skipper will do one more thing. He will install a bulls-eye (through-bolted) on each side deck, between the cleat and the swivel block, run the sheet through it, and put a stopper knot near the end of the sheet. Thus if the sheet is someday jerked out of his hand while he's trimming it, by a gust hitting the mainsail, the boom will not fly out on the opposite side and hit the shroud, possibly breaking the boom, but will come up short when the stopper knot reaches the bulls-eye—still quite a strain on the boom, but not as bad as the first case. A foot or more of sheet extending beyond the stopper knot will facilitate grabbing the end of the sheet to haul it in and cleat it down again.

Apparently Pidgeon didn't care for this arrangement, for it appears—from the photos—that he adopted a more conventional approach. We can't pin down precisely all the moving parts, but it *appears* that he mounted a pair of double blocks, one on the boom's end, the other directly below it on deck. One of them had a becket (as in the *alternate* main throat halyard arrangement, above). After reeving the sheet through all four sheaves, producing a 4:1 advantage, the bitter end of Pidgeon's mainsheet ended at a cleat close to the lower double block.

It's surprising that neither Slocum nor Pidgeon employed a mainsheet horse (traveler). Perhaps these were more of a "yachting" vogue in Slocum's day (although pinky schooners of the northeast had them), but one wonders why Pidgeon didn't fit one, especially for its contribution to sailing performance—keeping the mainsail flatter by holding down the main boom when the sheets were eased. This is especially true with a gaff sail. With the mainsheet anchored to a single point on the boat's centerline, as you ease the sheets on, say, a broad reach, the boom rises, the leech rises, and the gaff sags off even further to leeward, and much driving power at the top of the sail is lost. Perhaps the horse—one additional bit of hardware and expense—was something Pidgeon felt he could, or had to, dispense with.

Mizzen Sheet—A simple lead: from the end of the boom, down through a single block on the boomkin, up through a single block in the middle of the boom, down through another single block on the boomkin, and then forward to its cleat just abaft the mizzen mast.

Mizzen Halyards (throat and peak)—Same as mainmast.

For a boom crutch, Pidgeon had a scissors-type, a second-rate method of keeping the main boom tamed and one that has been roundly condemned by many long-distance voyagers. The benefits of a permanent, stoutly constructed boom gallows are many: 1) really solid support for the main boom when reefing; 2) an excellent hand-hold in rough weather (as is the boom itself, when strapped down in it); 3) a good back brace—tied to it, if necessary—when taking sights; 4) a convenient place to fasten the after end of a cockpit awning; and 5) a fine "stanchion" for lashing deck "cargo." Many of the sailors later in this book, as, for instance, Edward Allcard in chapter 6, would not go to sea without one.

The Cabin

The Goeller plans for *Seagoer* contain no accommodation plan at all. Pidgeon gave only a brief description, barely enough for us to visualize the cabin: "The cabin was twelve feet long, arranged with a berth on either side and spaces for drawers and a *wood-burning stove* [italics mine]. Under the deck between the house and the cockpit was a good space where supplies for a long voyage could be stored." Well, we can see the stovepipe poking up out of the cabin, so we know it was on the port side. It's more than a bit mind-boggling to visualize Pidgeon cooking on such a stove all the way around the world, especially since most of his track was in humid, tropical waters—but it's true. However, he does remark that he did *some* cooking on an "oil stove," so we may assume it was a Primus. There was no mention of a sink, but Pidgeon said that his water capacity was 100 gallons. On some of his longer passages he carried extra water in containers, but, keeping to his ration of one-half gallon a day, he never needed it.

Somewhere along the way he made two semicircular sheet-metal rain guards that fitted, open-side down, into the top of his portholes, allowing him to leave the ports open when he went ashore, to keep the cabin cool without admitting the tropical rain that fell every day. This wrinkle still works today, even with screens in place, and is cheap. When a mosquito invasion struck the Fijis, Pidgeon made screens for the hatches and portholes.

However fuzzy the impression of how he lived aboard, gained mostly by inference from odd remarks, there's little doubt Pidgeon's life-style was on the lean side of spartan. But with his background of roughing it in the outdoors, this did not bother him. His was truly a sightseeing voyage, as his long layovers in many ports attest (see below), and he was willing to pay the price by living cheaply; he really had no other choice.

Stores and Equipment

Like Slocum, Pidgeon economized on food. Years of camping had taught him what was simple, cheap, and long-lasting. His bulk stores were kept in moisture-proof containers (we don't know what kind), and they included: peas, beans, rice, dried fruit, bacon, sugar, wheat, and cornmeal; in cans he had salmon, milk, and fruit; and for fresh foods he carried potatoes, onions, and a few other vegetables. He makes no mention of such things as tea, coffee, salt, pepper, or spices—perhaps too obvious to list? In port, like Slocum, he immediately sought fresh fruits and vegetables. The only meal eaten at sea that he mentions was an echo of Slocum: ". . . vegetable soup, rice, flying fish and toast."

Here's a quick summary of foods he got (mostly as gifts) in ports around the world, all of which one could find today, though probably only at native markets, and for cash: Nukuhiva, Marquesas—breadfruit, bananas, coconuts and eggs; Bora Bora, Society Islands—coconuts and bananas; Vila, New Hebrides—yams and oranges; Rennell Island, Torres Strait—corn, sweet potatoes, and pumpkins; Koepang, Dutch Timor (now Indonesia)—fruit and vegetables at the native market and sugar (made from the juice of palm trees); Christmas Island, off Australia—various "supplies" donated by the local island manager; Keeling Cocos Islands, Indian Ocean—many "gifts from the kind people"; Saldanha Bay, South Africa—meals sent to him during his stranding, plus a gift of £7 sterling; Ascension Island, South Atlantic—vegetables and bananas; Port of Spain, Trinidad—oranges and other stores for his Caribbean crossing; Balboa, Canal Zone—stores for his final passage to Los Angeles, plus firewood and water.

All this tropical produce sounds romantic and domestically—if not nutritionally—out of tune with today's expectations. As an approach in the 1980s, however, it still commends itself to those who have more time than money and who have an open-ended schedule rather than having to cross an ocean, say, on a summer sabbatical. Pidgeon's circumnavigation, made with so little cash, is difficult to imagine today. Even then, it raised eyebrows. Along his cruising track, Pidgeon met E. W. Scripps, founder of the great newspaper chain, who was cruising the world. (This was at Thursday Island, in the Torres Strait.) Scripps invited Pidgeon aboard his yacht for dinner and pumped the lone skipper with many questions during the visit. Although Pidgeon was evasive in his answers—the proud but penniless sailor vs. the millionaire yachtsman—Scripps concluded at the end of the evening that Pidgeon was living on fifty cents a day.

Still, there had to be *some* money, as Pidgeon paused to work on his yawl no fewer than twenty times during the voyage. Whatever the charms of wood cruising boats, and there are many, low maintenance is not one of them. How did Harry Pidgeon earn money? With his camera, of course. His excellent photographs were easily converted to lantern slides, and with them he copied Slocum's trick of giving illustrated lectures about his voyage, usually by local request. The first was at Suva in the Fijis. This was repeated at Mauritius Island in the Indian Ocean, and it continued with several lectures each in Durban and Cape Town, ending with a final performance at St. Helena. Pidgeon's talks were warmly received, and his lecture fees from South Africa covered his expenses for the remainder of the voyage.

To close out Pidgeon's skimpy equipment list, there was fishing gear that he used extensively—though not with great success—to supplement dry stores. He had a long sweep for moving about harbors in calms—another echo of Slocum. And, when he was almost all the way around the world, on the Pacific side of the Panama Canal, his original cast-iron stove was rusted out, so he replaced it.

For celestial navigation his equipment is another repeat of Slocum, except for better timepieces: " . . . two compasses, a sextant, parallel rulers, dividers, a taffrail log and two watches, one for Greenwich Mean Time and one for local time." A generation after Slocum, things had changed hardly at all. (We can assume Pidgeon had a lead-line.) With this list today, especially if the watches were of the quartz type, the contemporary skipper could repeat Pidgeon's voyage. Alternatively, a good radio receiver like the Zenith TransOceanic, which will provide timeticks on short-wave station

WWV, would enable one to maintain precise time with less accurate timepieces.

A final item, interesting because of today's natural-food craze, was a small hand mill, which he used to grind his bulk foods.

Refitting and Repairs

Pidgeon spent long spans of time in most of the island groups where he put in, satisfying his curiosity about the "South Seas." As a result, his wood hull, anchored for weeks on end in tropical waters, often developed a heavily fouled bottom. Beside applying anti-fouling paint to protect his hull against teredo, normal wear-and-tear and mischance led to considerable maintenance work.

On his first, trial voyage, solo to Hawaii, the jib halyard parted and he had to go up the mast in heavy weather to replace it, a brutal and exhausting job—not to mention dangerous, especially for a novice sailor so early in a voyage. In Honolulu he did a scrub and paint job on the bottom, completely renewed the running rigging, and "made a temporary sea anchor out of some boards." After returning to California (with a crew of one), Pidgeon decided to make the long voyage, and that required major preparations.

He made a new sea anchor of canvas, received gifts of a larger compass and a taffrail log, and purchased the volume of sailing directions and charts for three island groups of the South Pacific. Then, with time to spare before his projected sailing date, and with extra canvas on board, he hand-sewed a complete suit of new sails.

At Nukuhiva, in the Marquesas, he beached *Islander* for a bottom scrub and paint job. During a long stay in the Society Islands (after departing Tahiti), he paused in Bora Bora to repair his sails and rigging. As he left Samoa, a jibe in a sudden squall snapped the main boom in two, and Pidgeon (like Slocum) had to "fish" it while at sea; at Suva in the Fiji Islands, he made a new one. When his topping lift parted during a gale near New Guinea, now wiser, he waited for calm weather before going aloft to replace it. In New Guinea waters too, the stock of his anchor was broken; he had a new one made and fitted at a local machine shop.

During a squall in Torres Strait, the strop holding the main gaff block to the gooseneck parted, and the mainsail sagged slowly down onto the cabin top. It was a pretty dicey situation for several minutes, until he got the gaff under control. He kept sailing under jib and jigger until the next day, when he anchored in the lee of an island and replaced the strop. A few days later, at Price of Wales Island, he beached the yawl for another scrub and paint job. While there, he made repairs on the deadwood and rudder, which had been slightly damaged during a grounding, and repaired his old suit of sails.

At Rodriguez Island, halfway across the Indian Ocean, the local harbor pilot, obeying local regulations, anchored *Islander* with two anchors and managed to hook both of them firmly under the transocean telegraph cable stretched across the harbor floor. When it was time to leave, Pidgeon worked for hours but could not free them, so he had to cut his chain rodes and abandon both anchors. At Mauritius Island, the proceeds of one slide lecture more than bought two new anchors. There, too, the harbormaster gave *Islander* a free haul-out so Pidgeon could do yet another scrub and paint job.

At Durban, South Africa, Pidgeon replaced all his standing rigging with new, heavier galvanized wire. En route to Cape Town, this roundly cursed stretch produced a gale that gave him the roughest ocean conditions of the entire circumnavigation. His storm jib was split in two, and when he tried out his homemade sea anchor it was a failure. With no headsail available for heaving to, Pidgeon was thrown about violently until he could restitch the storm jib and reset it. (Most sailors report similar heavy going in the passage between these two South African ports.)

The two most difficult repair jobs of the entire voyage came near the end of it. After the stranding on the South African coast *(see below),* he sailed

Fig. 3–6. Islander *on launching day, eighteen months after Pidgeon laid her keel.*

back to Cape Town, had the yawl hauled, and in three days of work replaced a large section of deadwood that had been torn off and, apparently, replaced the lowest pintle and gudgeon on the rudder. That major repair was matched by the one he did later in Trinidad following a collision with a steamer off the Brazilian coast (see below). There, he made an entirely new bowsprit out of a baulk of tropical hardwood, then replaced the headstay, the mizzen gooseneck, and the mizzen shrouds. Then, apparently anxious to sail back into Los Angeles in shipshape and Bristol fashion, he rove all new running rigging and painted the entire boat.

After crossing the Caribbean and transiting the Panama Canal (the measurement fee was $5.00 and the canal toll $3.75), Pidgeon did his final refit for the passage to California and home. That included tiding out for a final scrub and paint on the beach at Balboa, purchase of the new cooking stove, and bending on the suit of sails he had sewn before departure. It's well he did all this, plus taking on the extra firewood, water, and stores mentioned above, because this final leg took eighty-five days.

If my count is accurate, Pidgeon did eight scrub-paint jobs during his circumnavigation, a good bit of work, it's true, but necessary for a wood hull in tropical waters. Probably the anti-fouling paint of Pidgeon's time was only a rudimentary copper formulation, a simple exfoliating type, compared to the more toxic and adhering types available today; this would explain the frequency of doing that job.

Sailing Performance and Notable Incidents

After launching (Fig. 3-6), *Islander* made a trial voyage to Hawaii, taking twenty-six days outbound—a bit slow for 2,400 miles (92 miles a day), but the novice skipper was probably being cautious. It was his practice to lower the main and mizzen before going below for the night, and to allow the yawl to carry on under jib alone until dawn. On the return voyage, Pidgeon took forty-two days, which is not bad for a passage dominated by windward work.

Because of his long descriptions of sightseeing, Pidgeon provides only skimpy details about handling *Islander* at sea, except for a dozen or so brief remarks about reefing or lowering the mainsail in heavy weather. These comments seem aimed at the general reader rather than cruising sailors, who made up a really small audience for a cruise book in those days. Perhaps that's why Pidgeon's tale did not appear until 1933, eight years after his return.

Of course, getting enough food and sleep to remain mentally alert to make seamanlike decisions is the constant challenge to the singlehander. The questions seem endless: Should I keep driving on in this fair wind? Is it time to reef? If I don't reef now and the wind builds, how tough will it be to round up and do it later? Can I make harbor before darkness, or should I heave to and wait until morning? Am I so tired and hungry now that I should reduce sail and go below to eat and rest, so that if this gale worsens I'll have the strength and will power to do what's needed later?

Pidgeon appears to have taken chances. His yawl would heave to, yet he often carried on with full working rig while he was sleeping below, even in narrow waters. Here are some of his risky near-misses:

While in Suva, Fiji, he was warned of an approaching hurricane and advised to take shelter in a protected cove across the harbor. He sailed over at dusk, without a chart or local knowledge, and ran onto a reef. Although he quickly put out an anchor with his tender, the tide was falling so fast he was too late to kedge off, so he had to wait, stranded at a steep angle, through a complete change of tide. This was nerve-wracking as night came on, rain began to fall, and the wind started to rise. When high tide finally returned, he was able to haul *Islander* off the reef with his windlass but then found that his anchor was inextricably fouled on the bottom. He buoyed the chain and slipped it, and reached the recommended cove in blustery darkness. Fortunately, the hurricane veered off during the night.

While still at Suva, Pidgeon went ashore one evening to have dinner with new friends. When he returned to the harbor near midnight, an offshore gale was blowing, and *Islander* was gone. He roused his friends and they went out to search in a power launch, but in the darkness the danger of running onto the reef was too great, so they turned back.

Then, Pidgeon remarks, "With the first streaks of dawn we were off again. Far out we found the *Islander* anchored to a reef. The chain was laid out across the reef, and she was swinging to it in the quiet water under the lee. How she could have got by the reef without striking, I could not see. . . . When we hauled in the anchor we found the stock broken out. We concluded that the stock had caught on some obstruction when it was put down at the anchorage, preventing the anchor from biting into the bottom. The stock must have snapped off under the strain of the fierce gusts that swept over the harbor in the early part of the night, and *Islander* drifted away in the darkness with her broken anchor until it caught in the jagged coral. . . . I had had a bad night, but it all ended well." Luck sailed with him.

Later, in New Guinea waters, he was approaching Port Moresby as the sun was setting and had no chart of local waters. He hove to on the offshore tack and went below to fix a meal, intending to keep an offing until sunrise. Suddenly, he felt a dreaded grinding under his feet as his keel began dragging on a coral reef. He rushed up on deck to find frothy breakers all around him. By luck, the water over the reef was just slightly less than Islander's draft, so "I was able to wear her around and head off. She grated a few more times, then I saw the white coral going out from under, and she was soon in deep water . . . I had lost my appetite for supper, and I stood offshore all night long." Another close one.

After leaving Port Moresby, headed west again, Pidgeon ran into a gale. Sailing through scattered coral islands, he found shelter in a bay and anchored near a native ketch. Here's what happened next, in his words:

> The water seemed shallow, but the native skipper of the ketch said there was a fathom and a half. Being tired and sleepy, I turned into my berth. I was awakened when the keel began pounding on the bottom. The tide had fallen, and the swell coming in through the entrance was dropping my boat on the hard ground with a heavy jar. The crew of the ketch had gone ashore. I got the anchor up and put on sail, but the yawl was too hard on the bottom to come about and drifted off to leeward, thumping the ground with every swell. Several times the rudder struck with such violence that I thought it would be driven up through the boat. After bumping along for about 200 yards we went off into deeper water, when I anchored and went off to sleep again.

One would like to think he hove the lead first.

His final two close escapes occurred in the South Atlantic. The first was a few days after departing Cape Town (Fig. 3–7) for the first time. Still sailing close to the South African coast, he was sleeping below with all working sail set, when the wind changed and *Islander* was swept ashore. The yawl landed on a sandy beach perhaps a half-mile long, the only stretch of shoreline free of offshore reefs and onshore rocks for miles in either direction. Fortunately, help was at hand. After eight days ashore, a tug hauled *Islander* into deep water, and Pidgeon sailed her back to Cape Town, where he repaired her.

The final incident, at least, was *not* Pidgeon's fault. North of the equator off the Brazilian coast, Pidgeon was asleep below—well offshore, this time —when *Islander* was approached by a passing steamer whose captain took the yawl to be a derelict. The steamer drew close so the captain could determine if there were survivors aboard. Pidgeon rushed on deck to find the ship looming over him, so close to his windward side that the yawl lost steerage way. Caught by the surging waves, *Islander* was flung against the steel side of the steamer in a crunching collision. Only by screaming up at the steamer's bridge was Pidgeon finally able to get the ship to pull away. Then he turned to survey the damage. The mizzen gooseneck was broken, the mizzen shrouds were parted on one side, the bowsprit had snapped off short, taking with it the jibstay and leaving nothing up forward to support the mast. Under lively conditions Pidgeon managed to jury rig a temporary jibstay to the stump of the bowsprit, but that permitted him to use only his storm jib, and he had to leave more permanent repairs until he reached his next port, Trinidad.

As for speed under sail, Pidgeon made only one reference to it in the entire book, saying he once sailed 70 nautical miles overnight. Assuming that

Fig. 3–7. Islander *sailing in Table Bay, Cape Town, South Africa.*

was twelve hours, he could achieve a 140-mile day, just over an S/L ratio of 1.1. It seems likely that he often bettered that (say 6 knots) at least for short periods. Otherwise, we must turn to the Speed/Distance table for *Islander* to see her potential under various wind conditions:

Islander: Speed/Length Ratio			
(WL = 27′ 6″ $\sqrt{27.5}$ = 5.24)			
S/L $\times$ $\sqrt{WL}$ =	Speed (knots)	$\times$ 24 =	NM (1 day)
1.0	5.24	5.24	127.5
1.1	5.24	5.76	138.2
1.2	5.24	6.29	150.9
1.3	5.24	6.81	163.4
1.34	5.24	7.02	168.5

Other than the one speed reference by Pidgeon, we must rely on a mixed bag of indicators to form any impression of how *Islander* behaved at sea. She could be hove to under storm jib and reefed mizzen and, Pidgeon says, " . . . be more comfortable than when riding to the sea anchor." (The sea anchor he made simply did not work.) Her motion was wicked under rough conditions in which a heavy displacement boat would have had a slow, steady roll. On the shakedown cruise to Hawaii, Pidgeon remarked: " . . . the motion . . . did not interfere with my working ship or standing watch at the tiller, [but] it was very different when I went below and attempted to solve a problem in mathematics. The very first time I opened the tables and started to work a time-sight something began to gyrate in my head, and I realized I was not immune to seasickness."

On his departure for the world voyage, Pidgeon bypassed Hawaii and sailed nonstop to the Marquesas Islands in forty-two days. This passage is very close to 4200 miles, so his average of 100 sea miles a day was respectable, considering *Islander*'s waterline length (27′6″) and lack of any self-steering method to ease steering duties. As his circumnavigation progressed and his confidence grew, Pidgeon gradually fell into the habit of leaving up working sail when he slept, which produced the close calls mentioned above. Although he generally hove to when approaching land at night and entered in daylight, the few times he neglected this rule nearly cost him his boat.

As for self-steering qualities, *Islander* easily went to windward with helm unattended, which is not surprising for a boat with a long, straight keel. But she also steered herself when running, according to Pidgeon, although he didn't make much of it in his book. While in Cape Town he took a friend on a cruise along the coast. As Pidgeon described it:

> Mr. Tubb was a very keen sailing man, so I gave him an opportunity to see what he could do with the *Islander,* but on the run to Saldanha Bay there was a surprise coming to him. When night came we shortened sail a bit, lashed the tiller and went below to have a hot dinner, and then turned into our berths for a few hours' sleep. As there were no lights of any description around the entrance to Saldanha Bay, it was necessary to keep a good course if we were to find it in the night. Consequently, Mr. Tubb went frequently on deck to look at the compass, and expressed himself as *amazed to find the boat running steadily on before the wind* [italics added].

This is as remarkable, in its lesser way, as the same feat by Slocum's *Spray,* and the wonder is that Pidgeon did not make more of it. It is virtually certain that he was carrying a copy of Slocum's book and would surely have been impressed enough by *Spray*'s downwind sailing ability to have noted the same quality in his *Islander.* We *know* he had *Sailing Alone Around the World* aboard, because at Thursday Island he makes specific reference to Slocum passing through Torres Strait in June 1897. Later, at St. Helena in the South Atlantic, he met the very man who gave the goat to Slocum twenty-six years earlier.

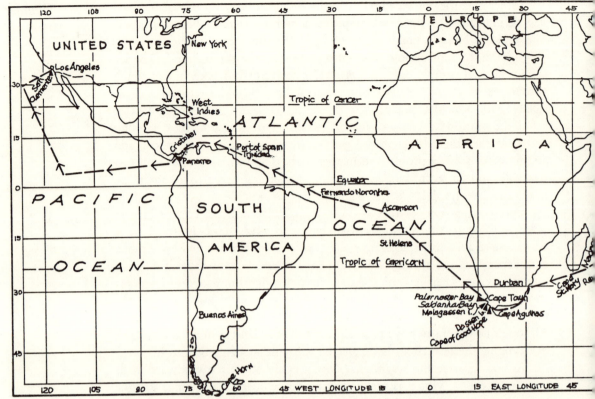

Fig. 3–8. Islander's *route around the world*. (Chart courtesy of National Geographic magazine)

Cruising Track

Interestingly, Pidgeon visited only half as many islands and ports as Slocum but spent about twice as much time in each of them—or more. Of course, Pidgeon had the easier route as, departing from Los Angeles, he crossed the Pacific, Indian, and Atlantic oceans first and then had the Panama Canal route open to him for the final leg home, whereas Slocum took the Cape Horn route. Here are Pidgeon's ports of call:

Los Angeles . . . Takaroa, Marquesas Islands . . . Tahiti, Moorea and Bora Bora, Society Islands . . . American Samoa . . . Fiji Islands (several stops) . . . New Hebrides Islands (several stops) . . . New Guinea (several stops) . . . Thursday Island . . . Christmas Island . . . Direction Island, Keeling Cocos Islands . . . Rodriguez Island . . . Mauritius Island . . . Durban, South Africa . . . Cape Town, South Africa . . . Northwest Bay, South Africa (where he was washed ashore) . . . St. Helena Island . . . Ascension Island . . . Port

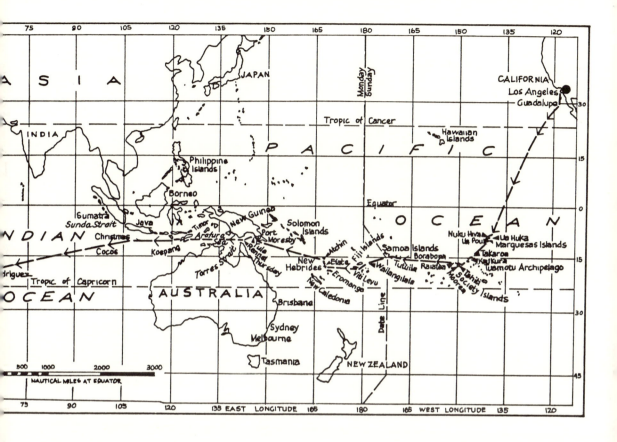

of Spain, Trinidad . . . Cristobal, Canal Zone . . . Panama Canal . . . Balboa,
Canal Zone . . . Los Angeles, California.

From the Canal Zone to Los Angeles, Pidgeon made an eighty-five-day
nonstop run, running low on food to a degree that forced him to become
a serious fisherman, and facing the hardest passage of his entire voyage—
the fight to gain westing so he could sail north to find the tradewinds that
would carry him back into the California coast. With so much windward
work at the outset, the motion of his light-displacement yawl was unremit-
tingly the worst he had faced, but he plugged on.

On October 30, 1925, he "drifted under the lee of Catalina Island." The
next morning he caught a westerly breeze and ghosted into Los Angeles
Harbor. By noon his sails were furled at the end of the second solo circumnavigation in history, consuming three years, eleven months, and thirteen
days.

In his own words, "My voyage was not taken for the joy of sailing alone. It was my way of seeing some interesting parts of the world. . . . I avoided adventure as much as possible. Just the same, any landsman who builds his own vessel and sails it alone around the world will meet with some adventures, so I shall offer no apology for my own voyage. Those days were the freest and happiest of my life. The *Islander* is seaworthy as ever, and the future may find her sailing over seas as beautiful as did the past."

And so it did. Harry Pidgeon circumnavigated again in 1932–37, starting at age sixty-four. As if that were not enough, he tried again *after* World War II (in 1947, I believe), this time with a wife. But this attempt was one too many: *Islander* was wrecked on a reef in the New Hebrides, though without injury to her crew.

Two and a half times around the world was not a bad record for the farm boy from Iowa.

I made the preparations for my voyage with considerable care; but of course I could not anticipate every little trouble that might crop up. Spray splashed on my canvas hood, for instance; and I soon found it was not so waterproof as I had hoped. In fact, everything under it got saturated. Three days out I discovered my mandolin was so soaked with water that it had fallen to pieces—and I had to throw it over the side. My bedding and blankets also were soaking wet, and sleeping in them became a nightmare. It was nearly a week before a day came fine enough to enable me to dry the bedding a little, and to put another coat of waterproof dressing on the hood.

—Fred Rebell
Escape to the Sea (1939)

Fred Rebell

*A*mong the sailors in this book, Fred Rebell surely ranks as the most desperate, and also as the unhappiest. He did not sail for adventure, for the joy of cruising, or to visit exotic islands. Rather, his voyage across the Pacific in an 18-foot open centerboard sloop was just the latest in a series of "escapes" from intolerable personal circumstances. Each one was a quest: for freedom, for love, for roots. His Pacific voyage had an added motivation: to flee a scene of previous misery and failure.

Fred Rebell was not his real name but one he coined for himself—a new identity for a new life. He was born in 1886, in Latvia on the Baltic Sea, his native land then ruled by czarist Russia. As an impressionable college student, he read an antiwar novel and became convinced he must flee his homeland rather than face conscription into the czar's army. Thus his first escape.

He slipped across the border into Germany but found the land of Kaiser Wilhelm as militaristic as Russia. After much aimless wandering he arrived in Hamburg, a stateless man without papers. There he bought a seaman's passport for the equivalent of fifty cents. With some deft alterations, he became Fred Rebell. After serving as a stoker in steamships for a couple of years, and being denied entry to England by the king's immigration authorities, in 1907 he decided that Australia might fulfill his dream of a new homeland and a new beginning.

He stowed away on a ship, turned himself in when it was well out to sea, and worked out his passage in the engine room. Arriving in Australia, he settled on a government land grant in the western part of the country

Fig. 4–1. *Fred Rebell trying out his homemade sextant before
departure from Sydney, Australia.*

and tried farming. Failing at that, he became a lumberman—a job paying
high wages. Two years later, with money in the bank, his thoughts turned
to marriage. He advertised for a wife in Latvian newspapers, and eventually
a country girl named Lonie accepted his proposal; Rebell sent her a steamship ticket.

Fate, alas, was not yet on his side. World War I had begun, and by the
time Rebell's "intended" arrived, by a long, circuitous route, she had a
tearful tale to tell. During her long voyage, she told Rebell, she had fallen
under the charms of a ship's captain—at least for one brief, romantic
moment—and now . . . now, she reported tearfully, she was very much
enceinte.

Rebell felt betrayed. He considered sending her home, but his loneliness
overcame his bitterness and in time he relented, forgave her, and married
her. If this much of his tale sounds like a Victorian soap opera, half bathos,
half comedy, the plot turns even worse. After the birth of her child, Lonie
soon revealed that she had not escaped a life of drudgery on a Latvian farm
for more of the same in the Australian outback. Worse, she developed a
wandering eye when any of the local swains were about. After twelve
miserable years, their marriage broke up.

Rebell moved to Perth to start life anew, becoming a carpenter. At a
local dance, he lost his heart once again, this time to a charmer named Elaine.
He pursued her passionately for months and finally proposed marriage, but

she spurned him. Rebell fled to Sydney (Fig. 4–1)—just in time for the stock market crash of October 1929 and the start of the Great Depression. Unable to find work, Rebell went on the dole; his life was at rock bottom. What to do? And then, an idea—emigrate to America, where he might finally find the freedom and happiness he sought. But how? He was virtually penniless. Desperate, he decided to cross the Pacific in his own small boat. Working two jobs at once at one-fifth of standard wages for nearly a year, he agonizingly saved some money; then he went looking for a boat.

Hull and Deck

What he found was an 18-foot daysailer, of the type Australians used for sailing in Sydney harbor. It was wood, of course, of lapstrake construction. Its dimensions: LOA—18′; LWL—17′; Beam—6′6″ (or 7′0″); Draft—1′6″. The LOA and draft are correct, as provided by Rebell; the LWL and beam are approximations made from photos in his book. This daysailer, which for some curious reason he named *Elaine,* after the second woman to break his heart, had a plumb transom stern with a robust outside rudder and tiller steering (Fig. 4–2).

Rebell knew he was risking his life to attempt a Pacific crossing to Los Angeles in an open sloop, but he felt he had no choice. With only £100 in his pocket (about $500 in those days), he paid £25 for the sloop ($125); the remainder of his capital had to provide everything else he would need.

To start with, *Elaine* was not a bad example of the general type. She had a foredeck, rather wide side decks, higher than average coamings and an after deck about 4 feet long fitted with a lazarette hatch. This stowage area suggests that its forward end had a bulkhead running right across the boat, for if the same space was reachable from the cockpit, no hatch would have been needed. The cockpit coaming was about 4 inches high, except in the stern, where it was at least 8 inches high; Rebell had to reach over it to grasp the tiller. Finally, the cockpit could not have been self-bailing.

Rebell's improvements included doubling the number of frames and "fixing an outside keel." As for the new frames, *Elaine* had a round bottom, so they could have been steam-bent "sister" frames or, possibly, since he had been a carpenter, sawn frames. The new keel might have been cast iron and slotted for the centerboard but more likely was just a heavier centerboard —perhaps with a bit of weight introduced into it. In his tale, Rebell is a bit vague about some details.

Up forward there was a bowsprit, extending outboard about 4′6″, perhaps a bit more. On the starboard side deck, amidships, there was an oarlock. Like Slocum and Pidgeon, Rebell used a long oar to move the boat in calms.

Fig. 4–2. *Fred Rebell in* Elaine's *cockpit, on her mooring.*

The Rig

Elaine was a gaff-rigged sloop, the rig proportions being characteristic of daysailers of that era; that is, the mast was not very lofty, but with the boom extending about 3 feet off the stern, and the bowsprit, the sail plan was well spread out fore and aft. The mast appears to be just about as tall as the hull is long—18 feet or, at most, 20 feet (Fig. 4–3). And, like Slocum's *Spray,* the boom is very nearly as long as the boat. The gaff, also impressive, is 12 to 14 feet in length. One other improvement was interesting. Rebell increased the size of the mainsail. As his sails were cut vertically, in the fashion of the day, a photo in his book reveals that he added two panels of canvas to the leech. This, of course, was cut straight, without roach or battens. The jib, so white in the same photo that it suggests a new sail, was loose-footed and was hanked to a single headstay that ran to the masthead. In area, the jib appears to be about one-third of the mainsail. The main was about 150 square feet (perhaps 175) and the jib about 50 square feet (possibly as much as 60 or 65). Rebell doesn't reveal the sail area.

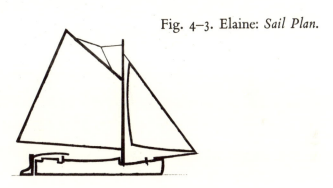

Fig. 4–3. Elaine: *Sail Plan.*

With the main boom overhanging the stern, there could be no standing backstay. So, to counteract the mast-bending effect of the jib in strong winds, there was a chainplate on the hull amidships, clearly intended for a running backstay. Running backstays are archaic today but were common enough then, even in so small a boat. Finally, there were *two* bobstays and a pair of shrouds on each side of the mast. It appears that jib halyard and main throat and peak halyards all ended at the base of the mast, so Rebell had to go forward around his "canvas cabin" to raise and lower the sails. Not the safest arrangement, but at least he had decent decks to work on (Fig. 4–4).

Fig. 4–4. Elaine *under sail in Sydney harbor.*

The mainsheet's lower block rode on a horse, the first traveler we've encountered. As for the jib, its fairly modest area suggests only a single-part sheet, rove through some sort of fairlead—block or bullseye—running aft to the helm. Finally, *Elaine* had one of those damnable scissor-type boom crutches. That invention of the devil is hardly better than holding the boom between the topping lift and main sheet but was probably considered adequate for a harbor day sailer then as now. A boom gallows would have added weight and windage up high and might have appeared as a bit of blue-water pretension on a sloop designed for protected waters.

The "Cabin"

Since there was no cabin, we can only guess at layout of the shelter into which Rebell crawled when he had to eat or sleep. It seems likely *Elaine* had simple seats to port and starboard, and, considering the expanse of deck, that's about all. To create some sort of shelter from the elements, Rebell bent four or five bows across the cockpit from port to starboard, then stretched a piece of canvas over them, fastening its lower edges to the coamings. One photo shows the cockpit cover as light canvas, and another, later photo shows a second, darker canvas tarp on top of it, suggesting he tried to control the leaks by doubling up the canvas.

Under its dubious protection, if there were slatted seats, Rebell probably used one for sleeping, perhaps with a kapok mattress (a common type then) and the other for cooking. As for a head and sink, a reasonable guess is that he used a couple of buckets.

Stores and Equipment

Living in such an enclosure, Rebell needed innovative ideas to protect his food and equipment. He estimated that the voyage would last a year or more, but he only had funds for a six-month supply of food. So, in selecting stores, he followed the examples of Slocum and Pidgeon: flour, rice, wheat, pearl-barley, peas, beans, semolina, sugar, rolled oats, powdered skim milk, and cocoa. He carried thirty gallons of water in tins and drums that he lined with asphalt. Although this sounds awful, the water remained cool enough to keep the tar hard. Rebell reports that this prevented the containers from rusting. Other food items included dried fruit, potatoes, onions, lime juice, olive oil, treacle, and yeast. All the dried foods were stored, rather ingeniously, in one-gallon galvanized cans, the kind with a screw-top used to hold kerosene that, until a decade or so ago, could be seen in any hardware store—until plastic jerri-jugs came along.

For cooking, he carried a kerosene-burning Primus stove, everyone's first choice in those days. As for other day-to-day impedimenta, he noted that he carried a flashlight, his carpentry tools, paint, pitch (tar), odd pieces of wood for repairs, nails, and a collection of might-be-useful odds and ends. Obviously he also had blankets, cooking utensils, and the like. Rebell's really ingenious preparations came when he faced the task of acquiring navigation instruments—with empty pockets. He solved this by making his own.

First, of course, came a sextant. He made this (Fig. 4–5), as he described it,

> with several pieces of hoop iron, a Boy Scout telescope [price, one shilling], an old hack-saw blade and a stainless steel table-knife. I broke pieces off the table knife to make the mirrors. They had to be ground optically flat, which I accomplished by melting a lump of bitumen onto them for finger-grips, and by rubbing them across emery cloth laid on a piece of plate glass. I used three grades of emery cloth—coarse, medium and fine—and finally I gave the steel a mirror finish by rubbing it on a damp cloth covered with jewelers rouge.
>
> The hacksaw blade, of course, was for the degree scale. I chose it because of its regularly cut teeth, and because I could bend it into an arc. I so chose the radius of the arc that two teeth made one degree. I took the temper out of the blade so that I should be able to reshape the teeth, and for a tangent screw I took an ordinary wood screw that would engage nicely with the [blade]. This way, I could read half-degrees of the arc straight off the teeth of the [blade]. But half a degree of latitude represents thirty nautical miles, and you need far greater accuracy than that. So I enlarged the head of the screw, and subdivided its circumference by sixty. Thus I was able to read to minute of arc off the screw-head itself, each minute corresponding to *one* nautical mile only.

Just this item was remarkable enough, but there was more.

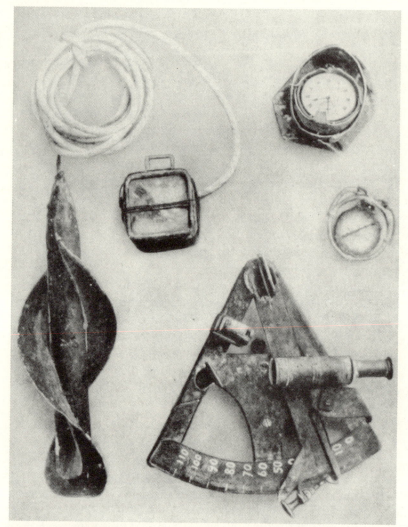

Fig. 4–5. *Rebell's homemade instruments: "patent" log* (left), *gimbaled "chronometer" and compass* (top right), *and sextant* (bottom right).

"The next thing I needed was a chronometer. Well, I could not make a chronometer; but I bought two cheap watches [each a check on the other] for a few shillings. I slung them in gimbals [which he made], so that the motion of the boat should not affect them." This was a remarkable solution for keeping time because it was simple *and* practical, but Rebell was not through yet. He reports:

Next came the taff-rail log. . . . I made my spinner from a bit of broom-stick, to which I set aluminum blades at such an angle that the spinner would turn once for every twelve inches of passage through the water. For the indicator I adapted a little clock, gearing it down so that every minute on its face should mean one mile of distance sailed. When I tried this log out, I found there was a slip of twenty percent. But an error in a nautical instrument does not matter, provided it is constant and you know it. You can allow for it. And until the . . . little clock corroded with the sea air and water, this taff-rail log served me well.

Knowing nothing of seamanship, he read a how-to-sail book in the Sydney library and then practiced in Sydney Harbor. As for celestial navigation, he bought a seventy-year-old manual on the subject and taught himself along the way. He could not afford charts, either, so he traced them out of a library atlas! This turned out to be a somewhat unreliable solution, as the atlas was so old its maps did not include some islands—discovered after the atlas was published—that lay along his cruising track.

His final hurdle was "ship's papers" and some form of personal identification. The American consul had discouraged him from attempting to emigrate to the United States because of strict immigration quotas, but Rebell could not be deterred by minor matters. He looked the consul in the eye and advised him he *would* sail, *would* reach America, and *would* be admitted to that country.

What Fred Rebell did is really not so surprising, considering his lifetime attitude—forced upon him, really—toward ideas of national sovereignty and the traditional sanctity of the borders between countries. He made his own (Fig. 4–6). Not only that, but he had the temerity to offer it to the authorities at Christmas Island and Honolulu—and in both places his home-made passport was visaed!

Cruising Track

In sailing more than 9000 miles across the Pacific, from Sydney to Los Angeles, in a year and a week (December 31, 1931, to January 8, 1933), Rebell adopted an island-hopping plan. His longest passage was 2200 miles; his shortest, 700 miles. Here's how those passages ran:

Sydney to Kermadec Islands	1500 NM
Kermadec to Suva, Fiji Islands	1100
Fiji Islands to Apia, British Samoa	800
British Samoa to Danger Island	700
Danger I. to Jarvis Island	1150
Jarvis I. to Christmas I. to Honolulu	1300
Honolulu to Los Angeles	2200
	8750
Actual Sailing Distance, Hawaii-Los Angeles (add)	800
	9550 NM

Refitting and Repairs

Rebell's work on *Elaine* during his voyage creates an exaggerated picture of usual wood-boat maintenance, perhaps unfavorably so for today's would-be voyager; but it's a distorted picture. Rebell's sailing was all in tropical waters, where weed and barnacle foul a bottom at an accelerated pace. Even in the five months of nonsailing the effect of on an idle hull was very nearly the same, perhaps even greater, than if Rebell had sailed with few stops. To keep the sloop's bottom clean and the hull in shape, he did the following maintenance, at the following places:

Yanutha Island, Fiji Islands—Scraped barnacles and weed off bottom while afloat in the island's lagoon.

Suva, Fiji Islands—Did a major refit after four months at sea to remedy some pre-voyage jobs neglected due to his hasty departure. This included repairing a cracked plank, rigging new standing and running rigging, and repainting the boat. In addition, he received as gifts from new friends a compass, a barometer, a full set of charts, a used mainsail, and a newly built centerboard to replace the one that had fallen apart *(see below)*. As he noted, "*Elaine* was now a finer boat than when I had left Sydney."

Apia, British Samoa—Hauled the sloop out on the beach for a scrub and a coat of antifouling paint.

A job at sea—Near the equator, Rebell realized he had been taking big risks each time he went forward to muzzle the jib in heavy weather, with no hand-hold but the bowsprit or the jibstay. He rigged a downhaul on the jib so he could handle that job from the cockpit.

Christmas Island (between Samoa and Hawaii)—The local copra plantation manager had his native crew haul *Elaine* onto the beach for a free scrub and paint job.

Honolulu—Rebell doesn't mention any work done here. (His six weeks in Honolulu were filled with sightseeing.) However, just before departure, he did "overhaul" his remaining food stores for the final 2200-mile passage to California.

Sailing Performance

Departing Sydney just a jump ahead of the tax collectors, who were still dunning him for back taxes on his long-sold farm, Rebell slipped away from his mooring on a light southerly, on December 31, 1931. Being ashore while other men celebrated New Year's Eve with their sweethearts was not for him.

Reaching Sydney harbor, he shot the sun with his homemade sextant and found that his fix—checking against visible landmarks—was accurate to within two to three nautical miles. As he neared the open sea, *Elaine* was hit by a severe squall and Rebell began to doubt the wisdom of his hasty departure as he struggled to haul down his mainsail. But moments later a small dinghy scudded past him, its two-man crew reveling in the swift sailing. That recharged his courage and he kept sailing. At sea that night, he reduced sail, lashed the tiller, and went "below" for six hours of sleep.

The second day, gusty winds kicked up heavy spray that soaked his "cabintop" and quickly revealed it was a long chalk from waterproof. The leaks were so bad that by the third day his mandolin had fallen apart; he chucked the pieces overboard.

Sailing east across the Tasman Sea toward Auckland, New Zealand, he laid out a route that would allow an island-hopping voyage all the way to the Hawaiian Islands. This cautious approach was dictated by his lingering uncertainty about the ultimate seaworthiness of *Elaine,* an anticipated need for frequent rest, and the hope that short runs between ports might permit him to wait out bad weather in sheltered harbors.

Elaine was struck by a real gale on this leg of the voyage but weathered it successfully. For several hours Rebell lay to a sea anchor, until the bridle chafed through. Still, after many hours at the helm, Rebell realized his sloop was more seaworthy than he had believed, and he felt a new surge of confidence in her. During the final hours of the gale, however, the sloop developed a heavy leak that had Rebell frantic until he traced it to the bow planking. It had him bailing every hour, but when the wind died and the seas moderated, he went over the side with a handful of pitch and forced it into the gap in the lapstrake planking. He was lucky; that single effort stopped the leak completely.

Rebell was four weeks at sea without a landfall—although he always knew *generally* where he was—when he sighted a cluster of low tropical islands lying ahead. He knew what they were—the Kermadec group, northeast of New Zealand—but he also knew they were not on his chart tracing, because they had not been in the ancient atlas from which he had made the tracing; so, he sailed around them. By the fifth week out, still moseying northward at 2 or 3 knots, Rebell had lost his fear of the sea and gained a new confidence in *Elaine.* One miserable, if not dangerous, mishap was that the can that held his kerosene rusted through, leaked into the bilges, and spread a thin patina of that smelly fuel over everything.

In his fifth week, too, first one and then the other of his two watches succumbed to the damp salt air and stopped. Such was Rebell's ingenuity, however, that he took one of them apart, analyzed the problem as a broken end on the mainspring, and found a way to bend a new hook onto it so it would again engage the proper gear and run. Rebell's years of poverty had produced an unusually innovative mind.

On the fortieth day, he sighted the Fiji Islands, but before he could close with the land, he had to ride out another gale. At last he reached shelter at Yamutha Island and came to anchor in a coral lagoon. When he hauled up the centerboard, he found half of it gone—broken off. He filled his water cans at a nearby village and later that day sailed thirty-five miles to the capital, Suva, arriving two months out from Sydney.

Here he remained for two weeks, resting and sightseeing. On his first day in Suva, he was interviewed by the editor of the *Fiji Times* and, overnight, became an island celebrity. After doing a major refit mentioned above, he sailed again on April 20, 1932.

With over 250 scattered islands in the Fiji group (and after nearly running onto a reef on his first night out), Rebell changed to daylight sailing only. But reefs were not the only danger. Floating tree trunks were a constant hazard, so that once in this area and twice more on the voyage the sloop slammed into one and snapped the bobstay. While still in the Fijis Rebell stopped at Naitamba Island. After his two weeks at a dock in Suva, the sloop's topside planking had opened up under the tropical sun. It leaked badly for many days after, making conditions miserable "below decks."

What it was like, sailing day after day in an open boat, is captured in two comments by Rebell's about the need for constant vigilance and the difficulty of his sailing track:

> But a few days later a squall stole up on me so unexpectedly that the boat heeled over before I could get in sail, and was in danger of swamping. That, indeed, is the worst feature of ocean sailing in an open boat; a man can never be wholly at ease. Day or night, asleep or awake, you must be on the *qui vive,* ready to jump at a moment's notice when some sudden emergency arises. . . . If it had not been for this one thing, perhaps I should have enjoyed my sailing more keenly than I did.

A little further along, he continued:

> Anyone who has read accounts of single-handed voyages will have noticed that for the most part these voyages were from east to west. This is not accidental: it is to take advantage of the prevailing winds, which, especially in the tropics, blow in that direction. My voyage, on the other hand, was to the eastward as well as northward: hence the little progress I often made; for I was generally battling against headwinds.

Considering the preponderance of windward work he faced, this is a good point to consider *Elaine*'s performance potential, under *good* sailing conditions, by looking at her numbers.

Anyone who for twenty-four hours *averages,* say, a Speed/Length ratio of 1.1—which seems low—has had a pretty good sailing day. To make the point another way—so as to emphasize the importance of this S/L ratio factor in a boat's sailing performance—let's imagine this: Fred Rebell, with his 17-foot waterline, achieves an S/L ratio of 1.1 (4.53 knots) for a full twenty-four-hour day. On the same day Harry Pidgeon with his 27'6" WL only manages to sustain the lower S/L ratio of 1.0, yet that's 5.24 knots.

		Elaine: Speed/Length Ratio			
		(WL = 17′ (est.) $\sqrt{17}$ = 4.12)			
S/L	×	$\sqrt{\text{WL}}$ =	Speed (knots)	× 24 =	NM (1 day)
1.0		4.12	4.12		98.9
1.1		4.12	4.53		108.7
1.2		4.12	4.94		118.6
1.3		4.12	5.36		128.6
1.34		4.12	5.52		132.5

Truly, Rebell had a better sailing day, even though he only covered 108.7 miles to Pidgeon's 127.5. The reason is that, using S/L ratio as a yardstick when comparing two boats of different WLs, we are comparing apples and apples. If we merely note that Pidgeon's boat, with the longer waterline, covered more sea miles during the period, that's comparing apples and oranges.

So if Rebell achieved S/L 1.1 for a whole day (which he never or rarely did, incidentally), he was having a whiz-bang day. That's because if you introduce into such a seemingly modest expectation the *least* variation—a foul current, a few hours of calm, a brief squall that forces a sail reduction, or a few hours hove to—it's easy to see how the dream of a 100+-mile day would go aglimmering.

On May 24, 1932, Rebell and *Elaine* reached Apia. He remained there for five weeks; like Pidgeon, he visited the home of Robert Louis Stevenson and worked on his sloop. When he sailed again on June 25, he found the southeast trades at last and began to make smarter progress toward the equator and Jarvis Island. Unfortunately, salt air had by then completely stopped both of his watches, and he was unable to obtain longitude. So, he adopted the approach of the ancient navigators: he sailed north to the island's latitude, then ran down his easting until he raised the land.

(Minor events of Slocum's and Pidgeon's voyages were repeated: flying fish "on deck" many mornings, which were fried for breakfast; a bout with ptomaine poisoning when he ate leftover fish and rice for breakfast; a method of baking bread in a frying pan on his primus stove, using a bit of oil to keep the dough from sticking.)

As he approached Jarvis, Rebell abruptly decided to bypass the island, perhaps because he was uncertain of his longitude and feared he might fetch its outlying reefs in darkness. Instead, he shaped a new course for Christmas Island, and reached it without navigation difficulties on August 14. Here he

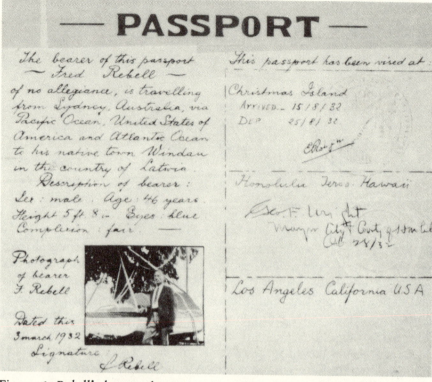

— **PASSPORT** —

The bearer of this passport
— Fred Rebell —
of no allegiance, is travelling
from Sydney, Australia, via
Pacific Ocean, United States of
America and Atlantic Ocean
to his native town Windau
in the country of Latvia.
    Description of bearer:
Sex: male. Age: 46 years.
Height 5 ft. 8 — Eyes: blue
Complexion: fair. —

Photograph
of bearer
F. Rebell

Dated this
3 march 1932
    Signature
        F. Rebell

This passport has been visaed at:

Christmas Island
Arrived:— 15/8/32
Dep   25/8/32

Honolulu Terro. Hawaii

Los Angeles California USA

Fig. 4–6. *Rebell's homemade passport, visaed at Christmas Island and
Honolulu, Territory of Hawaii.*

was royally entertained by the French manager of the island's copra plantation. Here is where Rebell made his own passport (Fig. 4–6) and had it
visaed by the manager, Paul Rougier, who also provided the free maintenance to the lone skipper, described above. When Rebell sailed again on
August 25, he discovered that his homemade taffrail log was so rusted it was
inoperable. But by now he had become proficient at estimating his sloop's
speed. His estimates of sea miles sailed were confirmed by accurate ETAs.
Now his course was due north, 1300 miles to the Hawaiian Islands. This
landfall did not concern him greatly, because his modest sailing speed
virtually guaranteed he would sight the islands' high mountains long before
he could run ashore. By shortening sail at night and reducing the sloop's
speed to about 2 knots or so, he would only cover about twenty-four miles
during darkness; the mountains would be visible from farther off than that.
    He reached Honolulu on September 20—twenty-six days out from
Christmas Island—for an average of only fifty miles a day over this passage.
That's 2.08 knots, an S/L ratio of about 0.5, and slow going indeed.

Hawaii was a major milestone for Rebell, as Australia had been for Slocum and South Africa for Pidgeon. He was interviewed by reporters, and by the morning editions he was a celebrity. Sightseeing tourists flocked to the waterfront to gawk at *Elaine* and ask the usual lubberly questions. The waterfront boat dwellers, however, immediately adopted Rebell and took up a collection to pay his charges by the port doctor and his quarantine expenses. This instant fame led him to imitate Slocum and Pidgeon: he gave lectures on his voyage at more than a dozen schools and colleges.

The time, remember, was the pit of the Great Depression; in Honolulu, pineapples were selling at six for five cents! Rebell could have stayed on and lived in that tropical climate for next to nothing, but he was determined to sail on. The United States remained his passionately pursued goal. On November 3 he sailed again while a crowd of sixty on the dock waved farewell. The last leg of his Pacific voyage began.

Eight days out, Rebell spoke a U. S. Army transport heading for the islands and got his position. He appreciated the gesture but noted, "[This] . . . was of little use to me so early in the passage; it is toward the end . . . that you really want to know where you are." Then he repeated his general approach to sailing: "Moreover, with so wide an objective as the American coast, I was not sailing any particular compass course—just edging along, to the north and east, as the wind suited."

As he began to gain some northing, the weather became noticeably cooler, and he cut up a blanket to make two heavy wool shirts. Spray often soaked him and he developed chilblains, the worst of this in his feet—which remained bare throughout the voyage.

On December 10—one month out—he was struck by a northeast gale that steadily mounted in fury, swung around the southeast, then backed again to the northeast. Forced to lower all sail, Rebell fought to keep the sloop headed into the wind by putting over his sea anchor, but this did not work well, he noted, because his centerboard was located rather far aft in the hull and the sloop tended to pivot on that point, causing the bow to be blown off to leeward. Obviously, he had the board down—somewhat surprising, because most sailors feel that in such conditions a small boat behaves better and is safer with the least draft possible: if you have a board, haul it up.

The larger boat, this theory holds, with its deeper draft, heftier construction, and heavier ballast keel, may be able to take the pounding while lying hove to. But the small boat cannot and does better to adapt the technique of the seasoned pugilist who rolls with the punches—giving way to the shock of the oncoming waves by sliding off to leeward rather than absorbing the shock force of each wave. Rebell hinted that some righting moment was provided by the centerboard, but what can it be? An iron shoe? Some lead let into the lower corner? Whatever it was, he was counting on it to help keep the sloop on her feet. His exact reason for lowering the board in such conditions was, as the King of Siam said to Anna, " . . . a puzzlement."

When the sea anchor proved inadequate to keep the sloop's head up, Rebell hauled it in, triple-reefed the main, and hoisted it. This did a better job—provided he was at the helm—of keeping the sloop angling into the seas. But occasional cross-seas struck the boat, sending sheets of spray over the hull and soaking the skipper and everything below. Rebell had to bail every few minutes. The wind mounted in intensity and he steered for many hours on end. Occasionally, whenever the gale slackened, he was able to duck under the canvas cover for food or a short nap.

On December 13, the third day of the storm, a rogue wave hit the hull broadside, throwing her onto her beam ends. *Elaine* was within a whisker of going all the way over, when she stopped and rolled back to an even keel. Rebell said, "Thanks to the heavy centerboard, however, she righted herself." (Perhaps the board was cast iron and the puzzlement is solved?) Rebell crawled into the open cockpit and discovered that both rudder pintles were bent and the tiller was broken off short. He couldn't worry about those problems then, however, as the sloop was half full of water. He bailed steadily for hours. When the hull was finally empty and buoyant again, he looked further and found that the sea anchor was gone—the bridle chafed through again. This was the new one received as a gift in Honolulu.

He decided he would not survive the mounting storm without one, so he hauled the centerboard up out of its trunk, fastened two ropes to it, and heaved it over the bow. It was not as good as the real one, slewing from side to side and causing the boat to lurch erratically, but it worked after a fashion and kept the bow generally into the wind. But now the sloop showed a marked tendency to capsize as the shrieking wind continued to rise. Rebell felt that if one more cross-wave hit her, the sloop would go over and not stop. The former agnostic began to pray and then crawled under the canvas—exhausted—to await his fate, and apparently fell asleep.

When he awakened at 0800 December 14, the wind was gone—not even a hint of breeze remaining. Rebell was convinced it was his prayers that did it. He tapped his barometer and the needle twitched upward: the gale was over.

After a long struggle, he managed to get the centerboard on deck, drag it aft, and ease it back into its trunk. Then he raised canvas and began sailing again. Though he didn't know it, the climactic event of his voyage was behind him. He would face more heavy weather and a few frightening moments, but nothing to match the gale just ended.

On December 17 he sighted "a motorship" and then a mailboat, both, he reckoned from his chart, on the San Francisco–Panama steamer track, and this helped to confirm his position. On December 25 a northerly gale struck, and Rebell was forced to heave to under a triple-reefed mainsail, the

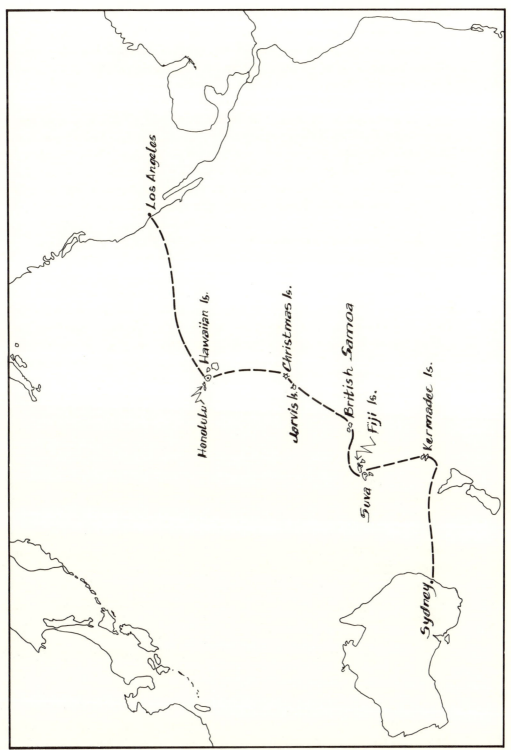

Fig. 4–7. *Elaine's* sailing track across the Pacific.

97

weather again driving him far south of his course. This gale and some lesser squalls hounded him for several days, during which the newly repaired tiller broke again and had to be repaired. His original mainsail was now ripped to shreds, so he bent on the used one, the gift presented at Suva.

Once again he needed a sea anchor. Unable to face a repeat performance with the heavy and unwieldy centerboard, he juryrigged one of crossed oars to which he lashed an old jib. This lash-up lasted only a few hours and then disintegrated. Next, Rebell put his anchor in a canvas bag, and put this over the bow. That, too, worked for a while, until the anchor flukes tore through the canvas and the anchor dropped almost straight down and no longer had any effect on the bow. Once more he prayed and, once more, after an anxious night, dawn and calm arrived together. By afternoon he had picked up a nice following breeze and raised all sail.

Elaine was making good time and recovering much of the northing lost in the two gales. The perfect sailing breeze blew for three days. Then, on New Year's Eve, 1932, another gale struck and continued into the first day of 1933. It blew out his storm jib but did not reach the ferocity of the previous two; below in his canvas cabin, Rebell restitched the storm jib and prayed. Once again, by the morning of January 2, the storm was over and was replaced by a spanking breeze from astern.

On course again he was loathe to lose any of such a favorable breeze by sleeping, yet he found that " . . . with the wind, my boat was hard to keep on her course. She yawed and showed a tendency to gybe." It was a predictable dilemma on that point of sailing, but what could he do about it? He took a page from Slocum's book. (We know he had read the old Yankee's tale, because he quotes Slocum in the early pages of his own book.) So, in his own words, "To keep her sailing steady, I rigged an extension to the bowsprit and set a spare jib [on it] spinnaker fashion." More than a half-century ago another lone sailor had learned the trick of pushing the center of effort of his sail plan so far out in front of the hull's point of lateral resistance that the boat had no choice but to follow its elongated nose and sail itself even with the wind astern. It begins to appear this is another sailing wrinkle that has been forgotten in the span of a generation.

The fair breeze held all the way to the California coast. On January 3 Rebell sighted seagulls and later that day picked up St. Nicholas Island, which lies about eighty miles southwest of San Pedro, California. With this island as a fixed point on his chart, Rebell was able to work his navigation backward and determine that his watches were now one hour and twenty-seven minutes off the correct time; but it no longer mattered, because he knew where he was.

For three days, he lay becalmed between Catalina Island and San Pedro. Finally, on January 7, a light zephyr arrived, and on it *Elaine* ghosted into the harbor, where Rebell picked up an unused mooring near Cabrillo Beach. The voyage was over.

A year and a week had passed since his departure from Sydney. Of that time, he had been seven months at sea, sailing well over 9000 miles. He had weathered a dozen gales and he reported, had only about as many days of dead calm. Upon arrival, he still had aboard a four-month supply of food and a two-month ration of water. Fred Rebell had paid $125 for his sloop and had spent only another $100 for all other expenses—in a year of cruising.

If we multiply his expenditures by five—or even *ten*—to raise his figure to today's inflated equivalent, it would be difficult, probably impossible, to match his achievement. He might well have entitled his book *Across the Pacific on a Pittance*. We shall not see such days again.

Sad to relate, his homemade passport was not at all impressive to U. S. Immigration authorities, and his travails with them—further embittering him against authority—dragged on for many months. But one notable highlight of his stay in California was his meeting with Harry Pidgeon (Fig. 4–7), a brief encounter that seems to stitch together so many of these

Fig. 4–8. *Fred Rebell* (right), *with Harry Pidgeon, at San Pedro, California, after both singlehanded sailors had made their voyages.* (*Photo by Stanley Wheeler,* Los Angeles Herald and Express). Courtesy of the Hearst Collection

early voyages into a common tapestry and reveals how small the ocean-cruising fraternity was in that era.

Rebell's final words in his book put his economical ocean crossing in perspective: "Should I ever go on another such voyage I would choose a decked-in boat, bigger and more comfortable than *Elaine*. And yet she served me faithfully. . . . "

We saw her first from the top of the cliff. She turned at her chains to every attack of wind, swaying, airy, and buoyant as though cut of fragile porcelain on the sea below. She was a two-masted schooner almost as small as they go, almost as stalwart, and, for all the evidence of wood and metal, failing to appear entirely material—an illusion she carried unto the end. . . . Far down, at the foot of the cliff, came the unmistakeable sound of a dory being hove into the water. We began to descend; we were going to board that craft.

—Richard Maury
The Saga of Cimba (1939)

AUTHOR'S NOTE: One of the pleasures of writing this book, beyond rereading the stories with an attentive eye to those ideas that might improve cruising for us all, came with a serendipitous discovery—in this case, untapped material that wonderfully expanded the story of one of the cruises. Such was the case with *Cimba,* whose skipper, Richard Maury, produced one of the best-written cruising tales of this century.

In an age of so much cruising activity—sailors, boats, passages, and books—the *Saga of Cimba* has real literary merit, besides being a whacking good sea tale. (The reader is urged to track it down; *see bibliography*.) The book not only relates the story of a schooner voyage to the South Pacific but captures, as few others do, the *magic* of being at sea in a small boat, especially so in an age—the 1930s—when a sea voyage in a small boat was not a common event.

As this voyage took place fifty years ago, I assumed—quite mistakenly, it developed—that Maury had long since sailed off to that Great Cruising Ground In The Sky. But a phone call to John de Graff, who has published Maury's book twice in the past thirteen years, revealed that the author is still very much alive and living in California.

An exchange of letters produced even better news—that Richard Maury would be delighted to provide additional data to flesh out the special concerns of this book's theme.

So, this chapter is the richer for the extensive commentary he has provided, for photos and plans not published since he wrote a series of articles for *The Rudder* over a half-century ago, for new drawings of *Cimba*—the most accurate ever, he says—that he generously made for his chapter in this book, and for a new track chart of *Cimba's* route to the South Pacific.

Fig. 5–1. *Richard
Maury about the time
of the cruise.*

Richard Maury and Crew

Maury was born in 1910, at St. David's, Bermuda, of an American father and a British mother, and thus possessed dual citizenship. He attended grammar schools in both Bermuda and Bayside, New York, until he was twelve, when a childhood illness ended for good his formal education. At sixteen, returning health allowed him to take on a great and irresistible challenge—to sail before-the-mast in America's last cargo-carrying full-rigger, the famous old *Tusitala,* often called by the old salts who served aboard her "the workhouse of the North Atlantic." He served in this 1700-ton three-master from the late spring of 1927 until her final lay-up at Baltimore early in 1928.

Next, fired by an ambition to join the first Byrd Expedition to the South Pole, he worked his way by freighter to New Zealand, there only to learn that neither the supply ship nor the flagship—the bark-rigged auxiliary *City of New York*—had the slightest need for a seventeen-year-old volunteer, however enthusiastic he might be.

Returning to San Francisco in the steamship *Golden Bear,* Maury spent the following year knocking about the Pacific as ordinary seaman aboard the low-powered freighters of the era, finally returning home to the U.S.

East Coast in the tanker *Leo,* there to try his hand at shore employment, mainly office work, until setting forth in the *Cimba* in 1933.

Following the *Cimba* cruise, he was ashore until World War II, when he enlisted in the British Merchant Navy. During this service, he was injured, hospitalized, and—after Pearl Harbor—transferred to the U. S. Merchant Marine. He saw action both in the South Pacific and the North Atlantic convoys. Simply by studying at sea, in four years' time Maury advanced himself from able seaman to Master Mariner, when he held an unlimited license, qualifying him to command steamships of any tonnage upon any ocean. Liking the profession immensely, he stayed on after the war, enjoying a full, active, and colorful seafaring life. This continued until 1978, when he retired ashore, in good health and with an undiminished love and affection for the sea and her ships.

The skipper of *Cimba* and author of the book, *The Saga of Cimba,* was twenty-three at the start of the cruise in 1933, a dream he had nurtured for six years.

Maury's original mate—one, sadly, destined not to make the voyage— was Carrol Huddleston (Fig. 5–2), newly returned from the jungles of Central America, where he had been working as a civil engineer. Like Maury, his dream of a voyage to tropical seas was a longtime quest— thirteen years. They met, discovered their shared ambition, joined forces, and went searching for a boat.

Nothing they found in the Connecticut boatyards along Long Island Sound seemed quite right—since they had a schooner in mind from the start.

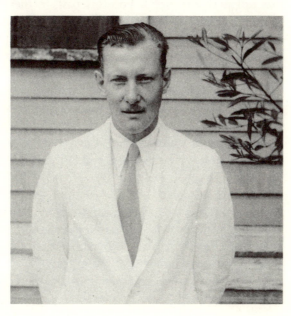

Fig. 5–2. *Carroll H. Huddleston, who was in at the beginning but, tragically, did not make the voyage aboard* Cimba.

The few boats they did find were beyond their means. Then, from George Stadel, a naval architect of Stamford, Conn., himself a designer of handsome cruising vessels, they learned of a Nova Scotia fishing schooner that was up for sale. Studying a photo of her, they agreed she "looked right" and seemed worth an inspection trip trip to Nova Scotia for a closer look. By steamer from New York to Yarmouth, by rail to Mahone Bay and by local taxi to nearby Indian Harbor, they traveled down east. There, on a bluff overlooking the harbor, they got their first view of the schooner—which inspired the eloquent paragraph that opens this chapter.

It was September 6, 1933, and they felt they had found *the* vessel. Her name was *Wassoc,* the name-board half-hidden under the raking counter, but locally she was referred to as "White 'Un," and she was, by local reputation, the fastest boat around. At her fisherman-owner's invitation, they took her for a trial sail to the next harbor and back. That convinced them she could really sail; it only remained to haul her out for a survey to make certain she was sound.

The following day the schooner came out of the water—hauled by a dozen men heaving on a two-part tackle—bouncing on her bilge strakes up a corduroy ramp of logs and onto the sandy foreshore. This rough handling was unspoken comment on her reputation for sound construction. She passed Maury and Huddleston's survey, and on September 8, payment and a bill of sale changed hands.

After the extensive modifications at Indian Harbor *(see details on Hull, Deck, and Rig, below),* and now renamed *Cimba*—after a Scottish clipper in the Australian wool trade that was much revered by Maury—the schooner was sailed to Stamford. For this passage there was a third man aboard, Warren Heisler, a local sailor of sterling seagoing reputation. When *Cimba* reached her permanent hailing port, Heisler returned to Nova Scotia, and the final fitting-out began. In the midst of this work, just a few weeks later, Maury and Huddleston received shocking news.

Warren Heisler, their cheerful, willing, and supremely competent shipmate, had gone missing on October 26 while aboard a fishing schooner at sea. The news was a pointed reminder of the sea's benign indifference even toward superior seamanship, a reality they would soon be facing. The days of preparation were slipping by so fast they were already facing a "late fall departure."

But for Richard Maury, an even greater shock lay just ahead. As October merged into November 1933, the last few jobs were tackled with mounting urgency. Maury was sleeping at home ashore, but Huddleston had chosen to live aboard. On November 5, during a vicious sleet storm that swept Stamford Harbor with raw, gusty winds, Carrol Huddleston somehow went overboard—there was no clue as to how, or what he was doing when it happened—and he was lost.

Fig. 5–3. *Russell "Dombey" Dickinson* (left), *who replaced Huddleston, and Richard Maury, at Coast Guard Pier 6, New York City, just before departure.* (Photo: UPI/Bettman Archive)

Such a sobering, second tragedy would have been taken by some as a warning, even an omen, and indeed, several of Maury's friends pressed him hard not to sail until spring. But when you're twenty-three and convinced of your immortality—that illusion preempted by youth—even such a setback is shouldered aside by bolder surges of unshakable confidence. To postpone the voyage was, somehow, a tacit admission you feared the sea. So, after a sobering pause, you go on. On top of this youthful reaction there was a more practical one: Maury did not really have enough money to sit around for six months and wait for spring.

A few weeks later—November 25—a new mate appeared. He was Russell "Dombey" Dickinson, who had apprenticed in sail, worked his way up to officer rank in steamships, and now was serving as "skeleton-skipper" of a windjammer permanently moored at Rye Beach, New York. He was another who had carried the dream of a long cruise. By November 29 Dickinson had signed on and they had sailed *Cimba* to Pier 6 in New York City (Fig. 5–3).

The Hull

The schooner's hull shape was clearly revealed on the shore at Indian Harbor. Maury noted that "the slight apple bows gave way at the waterline to a fine-cut entrance beneath; that the bilges were hard, while the run, noticeably fine, and forming only concave lines, extended an unusual distance forward." His reaction to the hull's sweet lines is a tribute to the builder's talent. Maury continued: "It was incredible that Vernon Langille [her builder] had designed the *White 'Un* without so much as drawing, a line on paper, or even whittling a model for a pattern. He had merely tacked together eight molds, or life-sized cross-sections, guaging them, one after another, by eye, before immediately starting to build."

The result was a schooner (ultimately) of five tons with the following dimensions: LOA—35′; LWL—26′; Beam—9′6″; Draft—3′3″ as they found her and 5′ at departure. As purchased, *Cimba*'s ballast was 800 pounds of beach stones in the bilges. Except for a small cuddy forward, she was completely open all the way aft to the helm. Still, she was, in Maury and Huddleston's view, as beautiful and strongly built an example of a "Nova Scotia harbor schooner" as they had ever seen. However, she was not ready for a long voyage, so modifications began.

The masts were unstepped and all the rigging stripped off. The cuddy was ripped out, and two new cabins were built in its place. The step-down between them (Figs. 5–4 and 5–5) was not uncommon then and was required by their decision to have a 'midship watertight bulkhead. This bulkhead conferred enormous strength on the middle of the hull and separated the two cabins. It was bolted to a massive timber that ran across the hull, which in turn was fastened to the topsides with heavy, through-bolted knees. This beam served as the mainmast partners.

An important addition was the casting and fitting of a 2000-pound iron ballast keel, with the necessary deadwood to fair the keel line—the beach rocks remaining temporarily in place as inside ballast. The original rudder was left in place.

Although the cabin tops were fitted with handrails located rather close to the centerline so that a man using them going forward kept his own center of gravity well inboard, the tops themselves were left uncovered. As Maury noted, " . . . their smooth, utterly flawless surface appeared canvased." (The wood must have been white pine or Northern white cedar, either of which, if even damp, swells to a joint tight as a drum—a Nova Scotia feature reminiscent of *Spray*.)

Six weeks passed at Indian Harbor with *Cimba* undergoing the major part of her metamorphosis. Then the schooner was sailed to Stamford. Here, the fitting out continued at Schofield's boatyard through October and into

Fig. 5–4. Cimba, *at St. Georges, Bermuda—bow view* and Fig. 5–5.—*stern view.* (Photos courtesy Eugene L. Smith)

November, including purchase of a folding canvas dinghy and the replacement of the beach stones by 1000 pounds of internal ballast in iron pigs—securely battened down.

The Deck

In the photo of *Cimba* at Bermuda (Fig. 5–5) we get a fine quartering view of the deck layout. This photo and Fig. 5–11, taken at the seawall in Tahiti, reveal several features worth noting.

- The low but sturdy boom gallows, each notch leathered to prevent chafe —the first of this item we've seen so far.
- The heavy rubrail, stem to stern.
- The deep bulwarks, 7 inches high, with nine scuppers of good size, to throw off a deckload of water quickly.
- The break in the cabin line, providing a somewhat easier entry into the forward companionway, and better footing when handling the main halyards.
- The engine exhaust pipe, just forward of the running backstay.
- The position of the cabintop handrails, mentioned earlier.
- The lightboards and kerosene running lights on the foremast shrouds, port and starboard.
- The "wingsail" boom (*see Rig below*) lashed between the foreward and main shrouds, where they served as a handrail when not in use.
- The raised deck forward, about 7 inches above the main deck level (to the top of the bulwarks); the jib traveler is under Dickenson's foot; one of two foredeck grabrails is visible to port of the furled jib.
- Turning aft again, the highly unusual cockpit (Fig. 5–5). Maury called this a "steering well," perhaps a better term. The sketch reveals its distinctive shape, as wide as the after cabin, very deep, but only two feet long in its fore-and-aft dimension. It was *not* self-bailing and had a drain in the sole that let water run into the bilges. Generally, Maury reports, they kept this drain plugged and bailed out the well by hand whenever necessary—which was rarely. Maury is convinced this cockpit saved his life in the capsize en route to Bermuda. It certainly is one extreme in the spectrum of cockpit types, very conservative, possibly even a type unto itself in that it makes no concession whatever to passenger comfort when daysailing. There was a narrow seat on each side, with a foot-rail opposite to brace against when steering was hard in heavy weather.
- Finally, just abaft the cockpit, the tiller, and just beneath it, the curved tiller comb. The tiller extension handle, when slipped onto the tiller, brought the handle right into the cockpit and gave the helmsman greatly increased leverage when the steering was hard.

As for the comb, such a device was common in Maury's time but is rare today. It's still a handy device, even if only used a few seconds while you duck below to check the chart, and is quicker to use than tiller gaskets. With many slots in the comb for the bronze stud fastened to the underside of the tiller, this item permits fine-tuning the rudder angle.

In the after face of the steering well a watertight door led to the lazarette, which held paint and spare halyards; to port and starboard of the steering well, there were small lockers right at the helmsman's back. One held the kerosene running lights; the other was for "strops, reef earrings, sail gaskets, small stuff (short lengths of line), a marlin spike, an extra knife, the logline, fog horn, etc." At the after end of the cabin top and on the centerline, the compass was mounted under a deadlight.

The Rig

When *Cimba*'s rig was removed at Indian Harbor, none of it went back but was replaced with new solid spruce spars and new standing rigging of ⅜-inch galvanized wire. No turnbuckles here, but deadeyes and lanyards, anchored to the hull by heavy galvanized chainplates, *outside* the planking —the preferred location for strength if not esthetics, and one much less likely to cause leaks below than today's frequently seen inboard location.

Before departure from Stamford *Cimba* received a gift of a genoa from an R boat, which was recut to make a fisherman's staysail; about the same time, a used storm trysail found its way aboard (Fig. 5–6).

In Bermuda, after the horrendous passage and the capsizing *(see below)*, the gaff main was recut into a Marconi sail, and one cloth was removed from the leech to "bring the sail entirely inboard," as Maury reported in his book. His recent comment on this change expands on that decision:

> *Cimba,* with her pronounced overhangs fore and aft, and finely molded hull, was always extremely lively, even in the most moderate ocean conditions. There was ever the rolling, pitching, and general commotion of a vessel highly responsive to wave and weather—*unusually* responsive. She was always on the move—possessed, as it were, by a restless energy all her own. She never slept out there; she and lethargy were strangers.
>
> All this being so, I was rather fearful that her exaggerated motion, particularly when humming along off the wind, might cause her high-peaked main boom to get out of control and cause a gybe, perhaps even to rip the mainsail —our driving sail. In our opinion, we could convert the main into a jib-headed one without any loss of speed. We guessed right about this.
>
> We never regretted the change, but we would not have done the same thing to the foresail. There would have been too little left of this already none-too-large sail.
>
> The recutting job was done by a skilled Bermuda sailmaker named Fred Brangman. I wish I could remember what he charged us—it was modest— but the figure escapes me. Suffice it to say the job took great skill to make

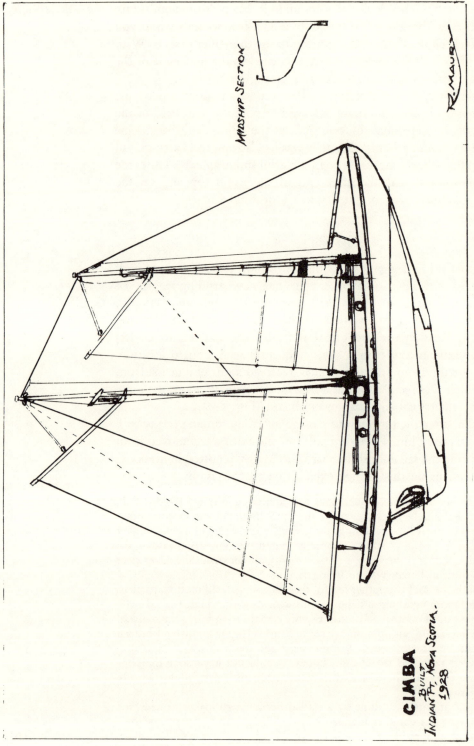

MIDSHIP SECTION

CIMBA
BUILT
INDIAN PT, NOVA SCOTIA.
1928

R. MAURY

Fig. 5–6. Cimba: Sail Plan. This drawing of the schooner was done in 1984, fifty years after the cruise began. Maury notes that he put in the reef points, but not the reef bands, that the dotted lines on the mainsail indicates how it was recut in Bermuda, that the mainsail and foresail were laced to their gaffs and booms (but the lacing is not shown), and that the luffs of these two sails were on mast hoops but that these, too, are not shown—all these omissions in the interest of clarity. Finally, he remarks, "It gives me a strange feeling to view the results. For the first time in my life I've made what I consider a faithful resemblance to the old schooner."

over a gaff-rigged sail in this manner, but Brangman . . . knew what he was doing. The new mainsail set and drew perfectly. The schooner seemed much more snug and sound aloft thereafter, her rather remarkable turn of speed undiminished.

At Bermuda, *Cimba*'s crew tried out the spinnaker that had been acquired back in Stamford, while sailing in these balmy "local" waters, but it was rarely hoisted at sea. As Maury explains: "The spinnaker, from an old R boat, was rarely successful and seldom used. It soon gave way to a pair of what I called 'wingsails,' borrowing from an old term. They, too, were a *form* of spinnaker, but were small in area. Though they, too, set on poles, the poles were short and the sails were manageable."

The jib was club-footed so that to come about, the helmsman only had to cast off the windward backstay before putting the helm over, as the three working sails were self-tending.

The Cabin

As Maury reported in his book, "The after cabin was smaller [shorter], and was separated from the main [forward] cabin by an amidships bulkhead. This cabin [Fig. 5–7] was entered from a companionway to port, directly from the steering well. Below there was an ancient engine [see below]."

Forward of the engine and strapped to both the athwartships bulkhead and the mainmast partners beam were two thirty-gallon water tanks, each filled from inside the cabin—no vents to the desk. They were fitted with small bronze spigots to prevent wasting water; and, they were not piped to the forward cabin, so cans of water were carried forward as needed. (On longer ocean runs, a fifteen-gallon water keg was carried on deck, bringing the total to seventy-five gallons.) The space between these water tanks and the engine, right across the ship, was used for the stowage of bulk stores, so that small amounts of food were transferred forward from time to time.

The forward cabin was entered by its own companionway hatch, to starboard, directly from the well-deck. In this cabin (Fig. 5–7) there were "two coffin-like bunks, each six feet long and about eighteen inches wide." Outboard of each bunk was a deep food bin for canned goods.

Forward of the port bunk—still in place from the schooner's original cuddy—was a cast-iron coal- or wood-burning stove—almost a twin of the U.S. Shipmate—this Canadian model being named "Fisherman." It was manufactured then and is still available today from the Lunenburg Foundry in the Nova Scotia city of that name. The stove had a top that was 19 inches by 13 inches, with a small oven next to the firebox and searails around the cooking surface.

"It was bolted down, of course," Maury says in a recent letter, "and . . . required that a Charley Noble project through the cabin top at least two feet [for it to draw well]." The stovepipe, emerging from the port forward corner of the cabin, "was just beyond the swinging arc of the foreboom, even when the foresheet was payed out to the full."

There was no galley in any real sense. Aside from a well-fiddled shelf above the stove that held the pots and pans, and the catch-all shelf forward of the stove, there was no counter, no sink, no locker, no drawer. The cook sat where he could—usually on his bunk—and prepared the meal on a chopping board on his lap. His total galley gear was a couple of pots and pans on the stove, a few utensils hanging from hooks, a can of fresh water, and a bucket for dirty dishes.

Maury expanded recently on his book's description of the day-to-day routines in the forward cabin: " . . . simplicity ruled throughout *Cimba*. I have mentioned the absence of a cabin table [dictated by lack of space]; the only seats below were the bunks. No head at all. No radio. No sink, of course. For that matter, no headroom below—4'8" maximum—and Dickinson and I were both six-footers. But you know, I have absolutely no recollection of being uncomfortable as a result of any of the above."

For a chart table, Maury reports today, there was "a mere board secured to the after end of the starboard bunk by hinges. When raised, it blocked the companionway ladder, so it was usually kept in the down position. All writing I did on my lap."

When *Cimba* reached Schofield's, the work continued at a breakneck pace through late October and into November. Minor concessions to comfort were made: a root berth was added forward, whose canvas could be rolled up and stowed against the side of the hull; a signal bell was fitted in the main cabin with a long bell rope that snaked through the hull to the steering well, so the helmsman could signal the off-watch man without leaving the tiller; a new hatch for light and ventilation was installed in the main cabin top; and a kerosene lamp was mounted in the forward cabin.

Stores and Gear

Cimba sailed off to distant islands on principles then widely embraced —the four themes of this book—ideas probably absorbed by cruising skippers of that day from Slocum, Day, and Pidgeon, and by their own years at sea. *Cimba* exhibited each of them to a remarkable degree. Thirty-eight years after *Spray*, twenty-two after *Sea Bird*, and twelve after *Islander* (omitting *Elaine*, because Rebell's economies were imposed by abject poverty), *Cimba*'s stores, in 1933, reflect remarkably little change from these earlier voyagers. Maury's recent comment on this is both amusing and instructive: "Simplicity prevailed. Russell Dickinson and I, both out of the Merchant Marine, automatically looked on sea fare to be at best nutritious and at worst merely nonpoisonous. But fancy it was not. The merchant ships of our day were said to feed *almost* as well as the average jail."

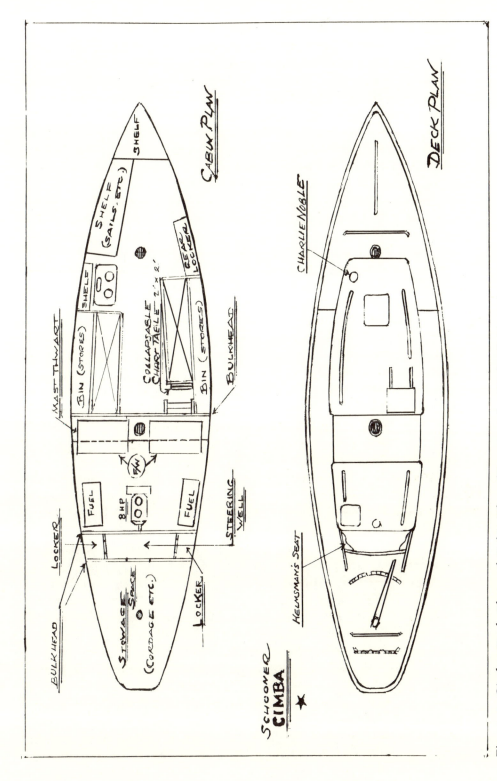

CABIN PLAN

SHELF

SHELF (SAILS ETC.)

SHELF

GEAR LOCKER

MAST THWART

SHELF

BIN (STORES)

COLLAPSABLE SHORT TABLE 2'x 2'

BIN (STORES)

BULKHEAD

FW

FUEL

8 HP

FUEL

STEERING WELL

LOCKER

BULKHEAD

STOWAGE SPACE (CORDAGE ETC.)

LOCKER

SCHOONER
CIMBA
★

DECK PLAN

CHARLIE NOBLE

HELMSMAN'S SEAT

Fig. 5-7. Cimba: *Deck Plan and Cabin Plan.* (Drawings by Richard Maury)

Staples included ship's biscuit—also called, he notes, "pantiles" or "hardtack"—cans of bully beef, salmon, sardines, other meats, and baked beans. There was a small keg of salt pork, and vegetables included potatoes, onions, and carrots. Of dried foods *Cimba* carried flour, pancake mix, peas, rice, coffee, tea—and Rose's Lime Juice. There being no icebox, there were no beer or soft drinks, and no hard liquor, either.

Along the voyage track, especially in the Pacific, they were able to buy tinned New Zealand butter, which of course keeps without refrigeration. (I found some of this in the native market at Nassau in the Bahamas twenty years ago, but the crew was disappointed by its granular texture. Later, in Miami, I reported this to world-cruising friends who had loaded up with it in New Zealand; they said ours was the only such complaint they had ever heard and urged us to try it again. I would do so; however, margarine, stored in the cool bilges, has pretty much supplanted butter at sea.)

In a recent remark about provisioning, Maury added, "I gave this minimum thought. This could scarcely be called sound planning, and at times amounted to an almost lordly indifference—such as often seems to go with the buoyant optimism of youth."

At Stamford, more items went aboard: a set of international signal flags, spare canvas, sail twine and needles and a leather palm, rope in various lengths and diameters, extra blocks, marline, paint and brushes; white lead, tar and oakum (for calking); a watch tackle and a gun tackle. These last are rarely seen today but on *Cimba* were a practical necessity for, as Maury says, " . . . setting up lanyards and deadeyes to our shrouds." We tend to forget today, that these were first slack, then taut in alternately dry and wet conditions. For the navigation department: a sextant, a well-rated chronometer, binoculars, a U.S. Navy star guide, parallel rules, pilot books for all intended sailing areas, and a "vast" collection of charts. For self-defense, in an era when most cruising boats carried weapons (unlike today, when it's a risky idea), they had a Winchester .30-30 repeating rifle, a 12-gauge shotgun, and a .38-caliber revolver. Enroute to Bermuda, one of the most useful items aboard, particularly in light of their late departure, was an extra-heavy watch coat contributed by a friend, which was worn by each man in turn at the helm.

As for ground tackle, *Cimba* had two fisherman anchors, of 55 and 75 pounds, each with a 50-fathom rode of 1-inch diameter manila. With the heavy anchors she carried, the recommended scope with a *chain* rode is 3 to 1 and, say, 5 to 1 with a *rope* rode; so *Cimba*'s 300-foot rode enabled her to anchor in a 60 depth *or,* with a much more acute rode angle to the bottom —and thus more safely—in depths up to 30 feet. It should be added, however, that the superiority of the fisherman's anchor in rock or coral-studded bottoms is offset by the vulnerability of manila rodes in such holding ground. In coral waters they shackled a couple of fathoms of chain to the anchor to provide chafe protection. As for the work of raising the hook back up to the deck, that was accomplished with muscle power.

Cimba had a standard ship chandler's sea anchor, but it failed the first time they used it—a victim of the enormous strains on it, which tore the canvas right out of the bolt ropes, and bent the steel hoop backward. Maury notes in a recent letter, "We were not the first to discover that the run-of-the-mill contraptions . . . sold were absolutely inadequate against the great forces at play in truly heavy weather." After losing another one in a storm, this time when the cable chafed through in the bow chocks, Maury remarks that they were "obliged to make one of our own. It was sturdy enough to take us through a hurricane such as we had encountered earlier."

At Bermuda, the schooner was hauled out and the bottom given a coat of bitumastic (a tar derivative) followed by two coats of copper paint. As noted earlier, the mainsail was recut, fresh grass was cut, dried, and stuffed into their mattress covers, a load of cedar was taken on as cooking fuel, another kerosene lamp was added in the forward cabin, and an old tarp was sewn up into a sun awning. Here, too, they purchased a second anchor (the heavier one), and, finally, they loaded stores: 50 pounds of hardtack, 100 pounds of canned corned beef, canned milk, pancake flour, lime juice, emergency lifeboat rations, onions/carrots/potatoes, Marmite (a beef-flavored English spread), Bovril (beef bouillion), tea, and cocoa.

At Balboa, facing long Pacific passages, they took on their last load of stores: flour, corn meal, tinned beef, canned milk, onions, more ship's biscuit, canned potatoes, and several jars of marmalade. Bacon, eggs, butter, and coffee were considered unnecessary luxuries, but they did purchase 1000 rounds of ammunition for the Winchester, and the kerosene Primus stove that would replace the wood-burner in the tropics. For maintenance, they bought tallow (lubricating blocks and standing rigging), white lead (painting), fish oil (calming seas), more canvas (patching sails), and marline (100 uses). When they sailed from Panama on July 5, 1933, the freeboard amidships was 11 inches! Say what they will about sparkling performance, light-displacement advocates cannot escape the reality of the increased displacement of their boats when loaded for long voyages.

The Engine

In her original configuration, *Cimba* had been fitted with an "ancient" 8-HP, two-cylinder, two-cycle, make-and-break gas engine. Of the two companies then making such engines in Canada, Acadia and the Lunenburg Foundry, *Cimba*'s came from the latter and carried the model name "Atlantic."

Almost everyone who has ever fired up one of these simple, heavy, powerful engines agrees that its horsepower rating was but a pale indication of the real torque produced at the prop. The general consensus seems to be that if you double the nominal horsepower rating, you are close to the real output. *Cimba*'s top speed with the engine full-out was 5.5 knots.

One of the special virtues of a two-cycle engine, especially on a long voyage where engine mechanics are a thousand miles apart, is the design philosophy behind their original conception. The engine was made for fisherman who might live in an outport many miles from the factory and who installed *and* maintained it himself. So, each was sold truly *complete:* engine, gas tank, piping, shaft, prop, stern bearing, through-hull fitting, hold-down bolts—even a tool kit. Offered only in a hand-starting version, it gives you a choice of ignito or jump-spark ignition—the first producing its own spark as in today's smaller outboards, the second requiring a battery to provide the spark, usually a dry cell.

The original design concept was a power plant that could be almost totally broken down for owner maintenance. That included removing the cylinder head to decarbonize the parts fouled by the gas-oil mixture, required at regular intervals—a time-consuming job yet not difficult. But most impressive were the removable inspection plates in the sides of the sump below the block, which—the bearings being of the split-type—made it possible for a fisherman to remove replace worn-out bearings himself. Such an approach depended on a reliable parts inventory (deliveries of which were usually made by coastal boat) and upon virtually no "tricky" annual design changes just for the sake of "change." The Lunenburg parts catalogue today—you order by number from several exploded-view assembly drawings—looks like the same one they have been using for five decades, a refreshing example of unchanging standardization. This is the design philosophy that underlies the Folkboat and the Volkswagen—awfully attractive to the thin pocketbook.

Despite the knuckle-busting proclivities of these hand-starting brutes (and wrist-breaking tendencies, too, if you didn't pull your hand back quickly enough after throwing the heavy flywheel over against compression), the 8-HP Atlantic in *Cimba* was probably a pretty good choice as she sailed in 1933. Maury's remark to the contrary *(see below)* was valid more because of indifferent maintenance or, perhaps, lack of parts, than from basic unreliability.

Sailing Performance

While *Cimba* is among the early boats in this collection, she ranks among the very best performers, despite the fact that she is the only schooner (a good and popular rig, but one rarely chosen for long-distance, tradewind cruises). Despite her reduced rig, she appears not to have lost any speed afterward. In fact, her rather light displacement probably enabled her to stand up better to the shortened rig: a hull with a mere eleven inches of freeboard adds nothing to performance while dragging lanyards and dead-eyes through the water.

That light displacement, however, was a distinct advantage in light winds. Five tons by Maury's estimate, she was 5 × 2240 (long tons) = 11,200 pounds displacement (approximately), of which 2000 pounds was on the keel and 1000 pounds inside. That's a Ballast/Displacement ratio of 27 percent—a bit low by comparison with most blue-water boats today—with a beam of only 9′6″ (I say *only* because many of today's 35-footers might easily have two feet more beam). But that narrow beam certainly contributed to her being easily driven, particularly when heeled. With nine feet of overhangs, her 26-foot LWL might actually increased to 30 or 31 feet. So, let's turn to her numbers here, before discussing her performance as supplied by Maury from the ship's log.

Cimba: Speed/Length Ratio				
(WL = 26′ $\sqrt{26}$ = 5.1)				
S/L ×	$\sqrt{WL}$ =	Speed (knots) ×	24 =	NM (1 day)
1.0	5.1	5.10 (5.50)		122.4 (132.0)
1.1	5.1	5.61 (6.05)		134.6 (145.2)
1.2	5.1	6.12 (6.60)		146.9 (158.4)
1.3	5.1	6.63 (7.15)		159.1 (171.6)
1.34	5.1	6.83 (7.37)		163.9 (176.9)

In the case of *Cimba,* there's a departure from the usual numbers provided, the addition of a *second set*—speed and twenty-four-hour run—*based on a 30-foot waterline;* these are shown in parentheses following the figures for the 26-foot datum waterline. This is useful in *Cimba*'s case because she often sailed on a functionally longer waterline. Also, they clarify the performance figures from Maury's log.

At departure from Sandy Hook, New Jersey (they had sailed there from Pier 6 for a night at anchor before entering the Atlantic), at noon on November 30, 1933, Maury and Dickinson, both twenty-three, knew the sea conditions they might be facing and could only hope for a fast passage to Bermuda, to gain the balmier, friendlier waters of more southerly latitudes.

In the first twelve hours, catching a brisk westerly, *Cimba* reeled off 101 miles. This was confirmed by a star sight taken by Maury near midnight. They were "averaging 8.4 knots over this period," as Maury noted. He continued, "She was making better than nine knots when I went below (at the change of watch)." But he was quite sure she was "in for a dusting."

Fig. 5–8. *Noontime crowds from New York City's Wall Street area crowd around Pier 6 to inspect* Cimba *and talk to Maury and Dickinson about their impending "cruise around the world," to quote the caption under the Acme Newsphoto that was printed in the New York Herald Tribune. (Photo: UPI/Bettman Archive)*

She was. Within two hours they were being buffeted by a full gale, and *Cimba* was hove to under sea anchor and storm trysail—and remained that way for twenty-two hours. Then, after a few hours of brisk sailing, gale no. 2 hit them, and they hove to again. It was not until December 4 that they got under way again. A day later, gale no. 3 struck, and this time they lay to the sea anchor for thirty-three hours—when the hawser to the sea anchor chafed through, in spite of being heavily wrapped with canvas at the bows. In haste and working in violent motion, they jury-rigged a substitute sea anchor out of an extra spar, a spare sail and a 50-pound pig of iron from the internal ballast. The motion made this a herculean task, as the northward-flowing Gulf Stream was being rubbed raw by the northwesterly gale.

Some hours later they lost this second sea anchor but managed to calm the seas rolling up from astern by putting over the windward side (on a line) a can of Stockholm tar they had punctured with a small hole. The oily base of this tar had the effect of calming the seas—a reasonably good substitute for fish oil. That worked for several hours until a vagrant wave picked up the can and threw it aboard, covering the decks, the cockpit, and the helmsman with the slippery black stickum. In their first ninety-six hours at sea (after the first half-day) they had made little real progress toward Bermuda.

Space does not permit a complete description of *Cimba*'s early trials in this late autumn passage, and, in fairness to the reader's enjoyment of the original story, just a few details must serve to capture the essence of the schooner's first passage:

In all, she weathered eight gales: no. 5 reached force 11 on the Beaufort Scale and capsized her 180°; this dumped the contents of the stove firebox onto the cabin overhead and set it afire; the rest of the cabin looked like a beef stew of jumbled articles that had been flung out of every corner; still upside down, the schooner's keel was hit by another wave, and the hull slowly righted itself, *without damage to the rig!* The waves reared up astern, and the arduous work at the tiller became so exhausting that their usual six-hour watches were reduced to a single hour—all that a man at the helm could tolerate; gale no. 6 carried winds of 80 knots, and no. 8 went to force 9, forcing them to heave to again, this time for 130 hours.

During all this they were driven far south of Bermuda and had to beat their way back. When they finally reached the island (Fig. 5–9), two weeks out of New York City, they discovered they had been given up for lost. The same series of gales had sunk, in their immediate area, a 45-foot schooner, a 65-foot ketch, and a large four-masted schooner.

Strength from *Cimba*'s excellent construction, light displacement (which had permitted the schooner to recoil from the heaviest blows of the storm), and good seamanship, it seems, were critical to her survival during and after the capsize.

Fig. 5–9. Cimba *sailing in Bermuda waters, before the recutting of the mainsail.*

The pleasures of Bermuda and the need to complete voyage preparations in a port with adequate supplies kept the two men on the island (where Maury had relatives) until March 17, 1934. They next sailed for Grand Turk Island, 600 miles off at the southern end of the Bahamas. As they left, Maury made an estimate to his shipmate that henceforth *Cimba* would average 140 miles a day, given anything near decent sailing weather, but he conceded that breaking into the 150s or 160s would depend on nearly perfect wind conditions for sustained periods.

One day out Maury jotted in the log what was a fairly typical meal at sea: boiled tongue (canned), boiled potatoes, sea biscuits, and tea. In the first two days they covered 207 miles, not bad (a 100-mile day certainly is respectable for *any* cruising hull with a waterline under 30 feet), but still far from Maury's expectations. On the third day they were overtaken by a northwest gale that reached force 7 before it abated, and they sailed on under reduced canvas. Then *Cimba* picked up the northwest trades and really began to move. On the seventh day out they covered 140 miles. The next day, in gusty conditions and under only main and jib, the schooner tore off 198 miles! They reached Grand Turk certain that they had a fast little ship, indeed.

After a few days' rest, they sailed again, on a run to Kingston, Jamaica, that took three and a half days, though Maury recorded no daily mileages.

At this island, after some bothersome red tape with customs officials, a bit of sightseeing, and a victory against a much larger boat in an informal race sponsored by the Royal Jamaica Yacht Club, Maury and Dickinson were off again.

The passage to Colon, Panama Canal zone, took five days, Caribbean winds usually being favorable for that passage. Maury found this port to be a cul de sac for cruising dreams. Sailing there from both sides of the North Atlantic, many skippers discovered that once through the Panama Canal "there was no turning back." Once on the Pacific side, they faced three daunting alternatives: a westward circumnavigation, an ocean crossing by the tradewind route and a return to North America via the North Pacific, or a horrendous beat up the Central American coast (we recall Pidgeon's eighty-five-day passage) to the California coast. In response to the challenge, many of the boats simply dawdled—and rotted—in Panama.

For *Cimba* the canal transit fee was ten dollars, and she passed from the Atlantic to the Pacific in one long day under her own power. In Balboa (Fig. 5–10) Maury and Dickinson beached her (a considerable tidal range

Fig. 5–10. Cimba *careened at Balboa, Canal Zone, for a scrub and paint job to her bottom, just prior to departure for the Galapagos.*

there makes this easy) for a scrub and paint, a job they did in one long day, although they finished daubing on bottom paint by lantern light. They also rove all new running rigging, acquired the aforementioned fifteen-gallon water keg for the long passages ahead, and took on victuals *(see Stores and Gear).*

Cimba's next port of call, the Galapagos Islands—lay 800 miles to the southwest, but rather than sail there directly, Maury laid out a route that took them south along the Colombian and Ecuadoran coasts to the horse latitudes, then west to the islands; this increased the total distance to 1400 miles.

At the start, they had the usual weather conditions of this passage—as reported by so many skippers—fluky winds followed by dead calms followed by squalls—a seaman's basic training in quick sail changing. Erratic weather netted them only 120 miles in the first four days. Nearing Ecuador, they got an hour—a single hour!—of sailing at 7.5 knots, but on the seventh day the wind steadied and they covered 120 miles.

Twelve days out they met the Humboldt Current, crossed the equator (with the man on watch bundled up against a curious chill for those latitudes), and on the sixteenth day, having sailed the 1400 miles, arrived at Post Office Bay on Charles Island. After a few days of hiking the hills of this lofty island, they sailed on, 117 miles in one day to Tagus Cove on Albemarle Island, where they spent a few more days exploring. (The fuller story and the people they met are a fascinating part of the original book.) Then they were off for the Marquesas, nearly 3000 miles distant.

From conversations with other sailors and from books, the best time Maury and Dickinson had heard for this passage was twenty-three days, an accomplishment by a large vessel (Maury didn't name it). They accepted this as a challenge and decided to race against that elapsed time. They hoped at least to come close to twenty-three days—in the unlikely event that they could beat it.

Hoisting a now-standard, "everyday" rig of main, wing-sail, and jib, they immediately ran into several days of fluky winds, which seemed to doom their chances from the start. Then, an abrupt turnaround. They picked up the southeast trades and began to reel off the miles: four days of 147, 158, 170, and 141—an average of 154, impressively above Maury's hoped-for 140. Gradually, they increased their watches in this tropical weather to twelve hours at a stretch; or, more precisely, each man had eighteen hours on watch and six off one day, and the opposite in the next twenty-four hours.

Their best sailing speeds, they discovered, were achieved in the first five hours after dawn, and the same span after sundown. (Breakfast usually consisted of strong tea and a handful of ship's biscuit, with or without marmalade. A typical lunch was canned salmon, ship's biscuit, and limeade with sugar.) *Cimba* often reached 8 knots for several hours on end during these days. In the second week they were on a broad reach that covered 141 miles one day and 170 miles two days later. Coming off watch, the man just relieved would find a typical supper waiting for him of canned beef stew, sea biscuits, canned pineapple, and hot cocoa; he would gulp it down quickly and tumble into his box-berth—a no-frills tropical cruise.

For a few days they had a cluster of 125-miles days in fluky winds, and then the trades returned, giving them 141, 167, 148, 146, 149, 148—an average of 149.8 for the six days. Then, in the final stage, to the Marquesas, they reeled off a new sequence: 169, 151, 147, 147, and 146—averaging 152 for five days.

On the nineteenth day out, Ua Huka in the Marquesas hove into view and ended *Cimba*'s race against the "best time" passage of twenty-three days. They passed by this island and sailed on to the better-known Nuku Hiva, where they anchored in Tai-o-hae Bay. Here they spent a week, resting and absorbing their first taste of Polynesian life—native dancing, tribal feasts, and new friends.

In the nineteen days, as Maury wrote, Cimba had "averaged 6.4 knots or 150 miles a day. . . . " That's 2850 miles, and if we add the mileage of one more "average" day, we get 3000 miles in twenty days—well ahead of the best-time record they had competed against.

Fig. 5–11. Cimba *moored to the seawall in downtown Papeete, Tahiti, with an anchor off the bow to keep her in place within the row of yachts and local boats. The pipe projecting over the starboard rail is the engine exhaust.*

From the point of view of our Speed/Length ratio yardstick, *Cimba's* passage is even more impressive: the schooner averaged an S/L ratio of better than 1.25, all day, every day, for two and a half weeks! Again, at 150 miles a day, the ten miles over Maury's estimate of 140 netted an extra 190 miles upon arrival at the Marquesas, thus reducing the duration of the passage by one and a quarter days. Modern rigs would be hard-put to better *Cimba's* achievement.

After a week at Nuku Hiva, *Cimba* sailed on, covering 273 miles in the first two days, carefully passing through the Tuamotu (native for "dangerous") Archipelago, and arriving at Papeete, Tahiti—a passage of about 700 miles—in a few hours over seven days. Here Maury and Dickinson remained for six months (Fig. 5–11), living ashore, refitting *Cimba,* waiting out the hurricane season, and even appearing as extras in a Hollywood South Seas movie—which provided funds for new gear.

Here, too, we must leave *Cimba,* as most of her remaining voyage was island hopping—the longest passage 1000 miles to Samoa—with much sight-seeing in each tropical port, until her eventual stranding on a reef off Suva, Fiji, her salvage despite great damage, and the ultimate loss of ownership by Maury (Dickinson having returned home to marry) by a tangle of diplomatic and financial red tape, snarled and resnarled by the pettiness of island bureaucrats.

The final few months of the voyage (Fig. 5–12), with its many major and minor adventures, are better left to the imagination and the color of Maury's original book. For the record, however, here are *Cimba's* calling ports: New York City. . .Sandy Hook, New Jersey. . .Bermuda. . .Grand Turk Island. . .Jamaica, B.W.I.. . .San Blas Islands. . .Colon, Canal Zone . . .Panama Canal. . .Balboa, Canal Zone. . .Las Perlas Islands.. . .Galapagos Islands. . .Nuku Hiva, Marquesas Islands. . .Tahiti-Raiatea-Bora Bora-Maupiti, Society Islands. . .Mopelia Atoll (Lord Howe Island), Scilly Group . . .Tau Island and Pago Pago, American Samoa. . .Apia, British Samoa . . .Suva, Fiji Islands. . .Kanduvu Island, Fiji. . .Great Suva Reef (wrecked).

Afterthoughts on *Cimba's* Cruise

Here, briefly, are some reflections on the voyage that remain vivid to Richard Maury fifty years later.

- "If I had it to do over I would not tackle the North Atlantic in winter, especially in a vessel with only a 26-foot waterline.
- "I would make certain I had a reliable engine. The failure of our engine caused our final downfall.
- "What we did *right,* and which remains so today, was to stick to our conviction that all gear and equipment should be just a little stronger than need be.

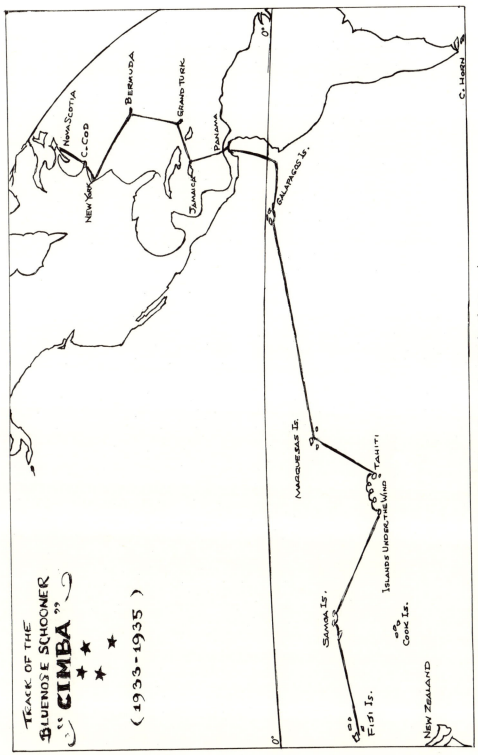

Fig. 5-12. Cimba's track to the South Pacific. (Chart drawn by Richard Maury)

125

- "All things being equal, cruise with no more than the minimum number of hands needed to sail your vessel, this to insure maximum efficiency and comfort. Two seems the perfect ship's company—one on deck at all times, one below. It insures ample privacy; total lack of privacy is a form of misfortune bordering on barbarism—as I see it. But then again, I've sailed in crowded fo'c'sles and been perfectly content. Sailors are adaptable characters.
- "The steering well was a great success because you could steer standing up with never a risk of going overboard.
- "A makeshift craft will not do. Long-voyage crews are influenced above all by the temperament of the boat they sail, adjusting themselves to her living spirit. . . . At any rate, once off soundings, the sea can make or break the spirit of any venture by making or breaking the spirit of the crew.

"The craft herself must also be an adventurer in the real sense—a living spirit. And that spirit is more vital than vague, emanating in a good craft directly from the integral spirit of her designer; a symbol revealing his science but, more important, his art, and even before these his ideals, loyalties, faiths. And there is nothing mystical here, merely a hint that the craft chosen be approved by the heart as well as the mind; that she be designed by one who goes beyond to the feel of ships, striving to find truth in his creation; not by one who is a scientist only. . . . "

6. Temptress

All types of boats have cruised the world, but it is generally agreed that for deep-sea cruising it is better to have a hull with [a] long . . . keel . . . for ease of steering, heaving to, and self-steering. Short overhangs, good beam and a moderate draft will provide some of the characteristics required, and the construction should be STRONG. Bad luck alone can put one ashore, and it is the heavily built craft that usually gets away with it.

I also tend to favour the type of stern which allows the rudder to be slung outboard where it can easily be got at.

Experience with nearly all rigs has brought me to the conclusion that the ketch rig is best for off-soundings work, [with] two headsails. With such a rig it is possible for one man, without leaving the cockpit, to reduce sail by rolling up the jib and lowering the mizzen.

Regarding the actual length of the boat, it is merely a matter of what accommodation is required. Seaworthiness has nothing to do with size.

—Edward C. Allcard
   Single-Handed Passage (1950)

AUTHOR'S NOTE: The reader who likes to pore over the illustrations before he starts reading will notice that although in the quote above Edward C. Allcard espouses a ketch rig and an outboard rudder, his yawl *Temptress* has neither—nor "moderate" draft, for that matter. She was, however, the closest he could find to his ideal in postwar England. Later, he was to find one much better-suited to his long-range cruising plans *(see below)*.

Despite some shortcomings in *Temptress* (too much draft, too small a sail area for its displacement), she had a few superior features for an ocean-cruising boat. Taken as a team, this skipper and his boat come as close, it seems to me, to being the ideal personification of Seamanship, Simplicity, Strength, and Self-Sufficiency as any other in the book, and this despite a slow transatlantic passage, which was largely the result of sailing only half of each day. What's more, as a writer, Allcard comes across as totally forthright in his description of "how it is out there." Next, Allcard writes well—a benediction in itself—in an era when many cruising authors are 80 percent sailor and 20 percent writer. His sterling writing qualities are simplicity, brevity and clarity, as he tells us what he did about problems. We "see" and understand his voyage.

Although much of his advice is rooted in a technology now thirty years old, it seems to me that any particular piece of gear or clever wrinkle can be easily accomplished with a contemporary equivalent. Allcard's ideas age well.

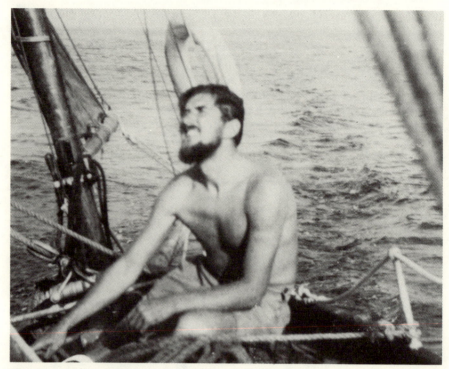

Fig. 6–1. *Edward Allcard at the helm of* Temptress.

Edward C. Allcard

*A*llcard was a naval architect (whether professional or amateur is not clear—but he was knowledgeable) who appears to have been well educated; I take his wry humor as a sign of that. He was probably well-off, too, although not rolling in pounds, shillings, and pence. He is as reticent about personal matters as most of his countrymen but makes occasional references to a mother and father who seem to provide a home base; they, along with a number of friends in the yachting and boatbuilding fields, constituted a reasonably good logistical base.

Exploring the world's oceans in his own boat, sailing alone, seems to have been Allcard's almost mystical quest, undertaken with the dedication of an ascetic heading into the desert to find ultimate truth. At the same time, however, he is easy going, unhurried in his cruising pace, experienced in sailing since boyhood, a veteran of the Royal Navy in World War II, resolute of character, unpretentious, and, though a bit reserved, able to make friends easily and enjoy foreign ports. Finally, with his spare frame, he seems to have had little need for fancy foods—except for the occasional dinner out—and to have gotten along on the simplest fare—whether by preference, or for economy, or both. In a later vessel, the 35-foot *Sea Wanderer,* he raced across the Atlantic on a one-dollar bet—which pretty well sums it up his love of cruising.

The Hull

By any standard, *Temptress* (built in 1910 and thirty-eight years old when Allcard sailed) was a *heavy* yawl. She had sat out World War II in a boatyard and, in fact, had not been in the water for ten years when he bought her in 1948 for $4000. Her displacement was 28,000 pounds, of which 8000 was in her cast-iron ballast keel. (Her original keel, of lead, had been requisitioned by the British government during World War I.) Allcard says, "She has a slightly rounded bow and a pretty canoe stern, with a deepish forefoot and a long, straight keel to make for steadiness at the helm. They built well in those days. Planking is of 1-inch-thick pitch pine, copper fastened on grown oak frames, and my pride and joy is her scrubbed teak decks, 1½ inches thick." He could have mentioned that all the planks were full length, without butt blocks (this from his second book).

Specifications of the yawl were as follows: LOA—34'; LWL—31'6"; Beam—10'4"; Draft—6'8"; Displacement—28,000 lbs.; Ballast Keel—8000 lbs.; Sail Area—600 sq. ft. She is only one of two canoe stern vessel in this book. Her ballast/displacement ratio was 28.5 percent.

Studying her Lines drawings (Fig. 6–2), the first such guide to hull shape we've had thus far (because Allcard took off the lines himself and didn't mind providing them, because it was not his design), we can see in the bottom view that *Temptress* has a fine entrance—which is also apparent in the Body Plan. The hollow in her bow sections is quite clear. This easy entrance is partially a result of her modest beam of 10'4". While most U. S. cruising boats of today carry a beam about one-third of the LOA, British boats, especially in 1910, were more likely to have a beam closer to one-third of the LWL. In the case of *Temptress,* her 10'4" beam, tripled, comes to 31 feet—a bit less than her LWL of 31'6". For Americans puzzled by the disparity of design approach between U. S. and British naval architects toward the "proper" amount of beam, it's not just differing esthetics. Rather, the comparative narrowness of British boats derives from economic considerations, which led to the plank-on-edge type of boat (long, narrow, and deep) that is often called "typically British."

More than two centuries ago, the method adopted in England for computing port charges and customs duty was based on the vessel's tonnage. ("Ton" is the modern version of the old English word "tun," which means "cask"; thus tonnage—or tunnage—was originally the vessel's cask capacity.) Considering England's lack of vineyards and fondness for the wines of

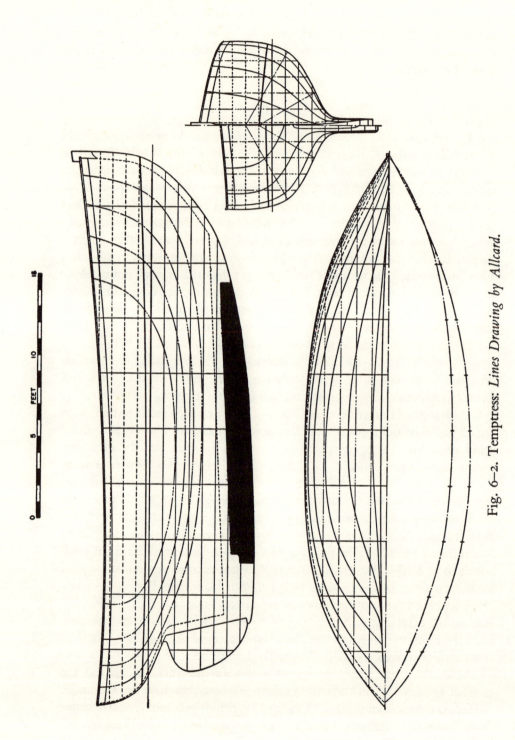

Fig. 6–2. Temptress: Lines Drawing by Allcard.

FEET

0   5   10   15

France and the Iberian Peninsula, it's small wonder we say "tonnage" today rather than "crateage" or "boxage."

Since it was a practical impossibility to unload every vessel upon arrival at an English port of entry to measure exact hull capacity, a formula was developed using dimensions obtainable from *outside* the hull. These were length, breadth, and depth. (This last is depth of hold, the distance from the top of the keel to the underside of the deck beams; there was always someplace, even in a full hold, where you could thrust a measurement stick to get this dimension.) Once obtained, these three figures were combined arithmetically to produce a sum that became the vessel's tonnage, the fixed multiplier of its port charges forever.

This apparently simple solution was not long in force before the all-too-human game of How-to-Pay-Less-to-the-Ruddy-Government discovered a potential loophole in the formula: the beam measurement was not taken at full value. So, even a small arithmetic reduction of this measurement in a new boat resulted in a geometric reduction of the final tonnage figure. What followed inevitably, with passing time, was a succession of new boats sliding down the ways with less and less beam. The trend just naturally carried over into yachts. This is borne out by older copies of *Lloyd's Register,* which list boats such as a 40-foot cutter with a 6-foot beam!

Returning now to Allcard and his yawl, her modest beam to American standards is nevertheless substantial by English 1910 standards—probably because she was a yacht and not subject to port charges. But her draft of 6′8″ is something of a wonder. While a cruising boat should have enough draft to give her a grip on the water—lateral plane—to beat off a lee shore, it seems to us today that 5 feet, perhaps 6, should be adequate for that. (Entering many remote harbors and coasting along shorelines, it's a comfort to sail just outside the one-fathom line on the chart, and 18 inches less draft would have made many more remote harbors available to *Temptress* for anchoring.) Still, generally the skipper must take his boat as he finds it— the trade offs again—so long as critical requirements are satisfied: strength, the preferred rig, adequate accommodations. Besides, deep draft is not really a vice, only a drawback. You always know about it, so you sail and anchor accordingly.

The Deck

The first thing you notice about *Temptress*'s deck (Fig. 6–3) is its truly seagoing layout: plenty of foot room forward for working headsails and ground tackle; a cabin trunk kept short by its starting abaft the mainmast; wide side decks made possible because the depth of hull provided full sitting head room over the saloon settees; a trunk cabin nevertheless long enough to carry an 8′6″ dinghy on top of it; a bridge deck for strength amidships;

a companionway hatch to the cabin on the starboard side, with a high threshold to keep out water; and finally, a small, snug cockpit aft, with a low shelter across its forward end.

Clearly this cockpit was designed with one dominant idea: safety and protection for the helmsman at sea. Of course, it was self-bailing and scuppered and, in one way, is reminiscent of *Cimba*'s cockpit—both having been designed with seagoing use paramount, and the devil take all other considerations. While some might object to the limited seating space in the cockpit—woebetide a third crewman—Allcard knew he was sailing alone, and the benefits of the tiny doghouse, although open-ended aft, more than outweighed the lack of seating. This shelter allowed Allcard to keep both handy and dry a chart, binoculars, and other necessary impedimenta of the sailing day. In coastwise sailing it would have been nearly impossible for him to dash below to check a chart on the saloon table and return to the helm before the yawl had wandered off course or run aground while sailing a narrow channel. As for keeping a chart dry in an open cockpit—even keeping it aboard—forget it; so, for a solo sailor this arrangement was nearly ideal.

There are several interrelated features on the foredeck that are unusual.

1. The bowsprit is off-center to port, eliminating cutting into the strength of the stemhead.

2. This placed the anchor roller on the starboard side of the bowsprit, which kept the lead of the anchor rode (chain) on the centerline.

3. This, in turn, required the windlass to be fitted just to port of the centerline for a fair lead from it to the roller.

4. The location for the windlass "pushed" the forehatch to starboard of the centerline, thus leaving the king plank in a single length.

5. Finally, the pair of samson posts at the inboard end of the bowsprit provided a second, strong and handy place for docking lines.

Moving aft we see a small cowl vent in the deck just to port of the mainmast, a skylight and handrails atop the trunk, the dinghy in chocks on the port side of the trunk (with just enough room to slip past it when going below), and, at the forward end of the cockpit shelter, a permanent main boom gallows frame. Note, too, the large compass mounted atop the shelter. A somewhat hazy photo in Allcard's book shows it to be a grid-type, with a card about 8 inches in diameter. It's housed in a simple binnacle, just a box with hinged cover that closes over it in heavy weather and, even when closed, allowed Allcard to see the card through a small window in the after side of the cover.

To starboard of the cockpit is the bilge-pump housing with its screw-top deck cover, a type quite popular in British boats, with quite a large pumping capacity *(more on that below)*. Finally, dead aft, the tiller—nothing exceptional there—the mainsheet horse (or traveler), the mizzen mast, the 6-foot-

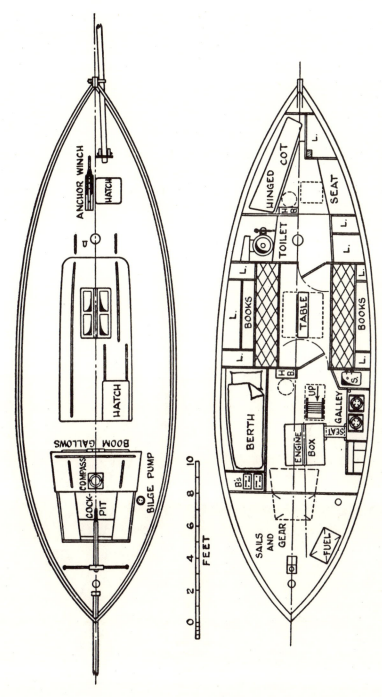

ANCHOR WINCH

HATCH

BOOM GALLOWS

COMPASS

COCK-PIT

BILGE PUMP

HATCH

HINGED COT

SEAT

TOILET

H B

L

L

BOOKS

L

L

L

TABLE

BOOKS

L

L

H B

S.

BERTH

UP

GALLEY

SEAT

ENGINE BOX

B's

SAILS AND GEAR

FUEL

FEET

0 2 4 6 8 10

Fig. 6–3. Temptress: *Deck Plan & Cabin Plan. Water tanks of 25 gallons each are located under the saloon settees.*

133

long boomkin, the lifelines, and low stanchions (about 1 foot high).

Taken together, this deck gives an impression of simplicity, strength, and safety. A close, critical view might insist that only two portholes in each side of the trunk (there were none in the foreward end) and only one mushroom vent in the deck foretells poor ventilation below, but the skylight would materially increase air flow, and the two hatches, when open in fair weather, would help considerably.

The Rig

First off, the yawl rig on *Temptress* seems to have unusual proportions —just from the look of her large mainsail. In fact, of the total sail area of 600 square feet, the mainsail represents 62.5 percent and the three other sails 37.5 percent. I'm surprised by the modest area of sail carried by *Temptress*.

Fig. 6–4. Temptress: *Sail Plan*.

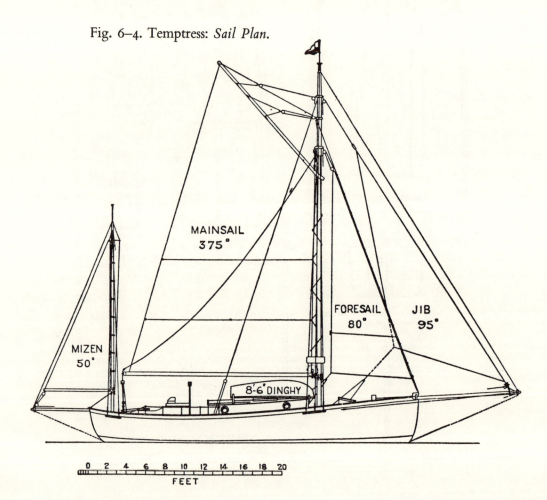

My own 30,000-lb. ketch carried 693. sq. ft., and I always considered her under-rigged. A cruising boat's working rig *should be* designed to propel the boat at hull speed in winds of about 20 knots, so that most of the work is lowering or reefing sails, then raising or shaking-out, rather than changing sails back and forth. The exceptions, of course, are a storm trysail in really heavy weather and a drifter in light.

Starting from aft, we see a mizzen, almost certainly kept small to avoid depressing the stern in heavy winds, since a canoe stern has limited buoyancy, whatever its merits in heavy following seas. Next forward, the afore-mentioned mainsail (Fig. 6–4). Its main boom was 19 feet long, quite a handful, though not as awesome as Slocum's 34-foot boom (as long as *Temptress* herself), or Pidgeon's 23-foot boom. As shown in the Sail Plan, it carried two sets of reef points. Forward again, two headsails, neither of which has any overlap, yet the forestaysail was not self-tending on a boom; if both were, it would have eliminated handling two sheets when coming about. Allcard reports, "My only light-weather sail was a huge reaching staysail [area not given] which is hoisted on the working sail halyards after snapping it onto the forestay." Well, the forestay being its hanking point, it couldn't have been what we would call huge today, particularly as this stay was the shorter of the two up forward; therefore, the luff could not have been very long. As a guess, let's say it was double the size of the forestaysail, or 160 sq. ft.

The sail areas were as follows: Main—375 sq. ft.; Jib—95 sq. ft.; Fore-staysail—80 sq. ft.; Mizzen—50 sq. ft. With 600 sq. ft. in her working rig, *Temptress* was 34 sq. ft. shy of *Islander*'s total, yet Pidgeon's yawl displaced 16,000 pounds less! Whatever else this may signify, it surely explains the daily runs recorded by Allcard.

Most of the notable features of the rig can be seen right on the Sail Plan (Fig. 6–4). For example, Allcard had "three strings to his bow" up forward to insure that the mainmast would remain standing: the headstay, the wire in the luff of the roller-furling jib, and the forestaysail stay to the stemhead. The mainmast had three shrouds on each side, the mizzen mast two, and there were running backstays.

There's been a tendency in recent years, as running backstays disappear, to regard them as a devil's invention to keep sailors hopping. (Casting off the windward one was the first thing Allcard would do when tacking, before tending two sets of headsail sheets, then setting up the *new* windward backstay.) The danger of them, goes the argument, is breaking the main boom against one in an unexpected gybe. These objections have some validity but are ultimately outweighed in a gaff rig by the mast's absolute need of some force to counteract the forward-bending effect of three sails. In windward work especially, the headsails,—which, being short, lack lead-ing edge—must have taut luffs, or performance will be unacceptably poor. Lastly, running backstays are not in use all the time; when they are, the new working one can be set up after all sails are trimmed and the boat is driving on the new tack.

Now, to some particulars:

Mizzen—The foot ran on sail track, but the luff was on mast hoops, because Allcard believed that sooner or later slides jam in their tracks when trying to lower sail with the wind abaft the beam—which is sometimes required. The mizzen mast has a permanent backstay leading to the outboard end of the 6-foot boomkin, this being braced by a bobstay and two shrouds to the rails. Finally—and it is rather unusual—this mast, though carrying only 50 square feet of sail, has a jumper strut and stay at its head, mostly to balance the pull of the permanent backstay.

Main—The foot and luff were attached in the same manner as the mizzen. (Here we might leap ahead and note that in his next boat, Allcard changed his mind on one point: he retained the mast hoops but eliminated the boom tracks and replaced them with lashings—a further simplification, as he felt lashings almost never fail. And, lashings are much cheaper than track.)

At departure, there was no topping lift for the main boom, and no permanent boom gallows, but these were added en route or at Gibraltar for the Atlantic passage. The mainsail had two lines of reef points, at 4'6" and 10'6" above the foot. This sail was new and made, Allcard says, "of almost too-heavy canvas." It was tanned and mildew-proofed. Heavy-duty bronze roller reefing gear was fitted to the main boom.

Forestaysail—This sail, as noted, did not overlap the mainsail but nevertheless had no boom, so was not self-tending; it had one line of reef points, 4 feet above the foot. An older sail, it was in only "reasonable" shape. It had two-part sheets, running through fairleads aft to the helm. The block for the sheets hung from a pendant that was attached to the sail's clew. *(See explanation below, in Jib.)*

Jib—This was set flying inside the headstay on a ⅜-inch stainless wire in the luff and was fitted with roller-furling gear of robust model (probably by Wyckham-Martin, a popular type with British yachtsmen). This was an essential item, as the bowsprit extended 10'3" outboard. Like the forestaysail, the jib had two-part sheets, running through blocks that hung from the sail clew on pendants, thence aft through fairleads to the helm. This sail, too, was "in shaky condition" at departure, and Allcard could only hope both heasails would survive crossing the Bay of Biscay to Gibraltar.

As for a storm trysail, Allcard says, "I do not like messing about shifting to a storm trysail in a gale of wind, and consider that [this sail] should merely be used as a spare mainsail if the (mainsail) is . . . unbent for some reason." Today, many a cruising sailor sets up his storm trysail on its own track alongside the mainsail track (or uses a switch-over onto the mainsail track somewhere *above* the clustered slides of the lowered mainsail), and leaves the tryail on deck, permanently bagged or in stops and ready for instant hoisting.

Regarding headsails, Allcard had fixed ideas: "I like a moderate-sized jib that can be left up in all weathers. The single-hander has better things to do than mess about changing jibs. The forestaysail is permanently hanked to the forestay, which comes down to the stemhead, and has one deep reef in it, with two cringles at the reef [band] to facilitate the reduction of sail and allow for an extra line to be used [as sheets] instead of the [regular] sheets when hove to in a gale." (This avoided shifting the regular sheets upward.)

The bobstays for bowsprit and boomkin were heavy chain, and both carried a pair of wire shrouds led to chainplates on the topsides. In order to widen the shroud base for both masts on a hull only 10′4″ in beam, channels were fitted to the topsides to port and starboard of each mast. The shrouds led to turnbuckles, and these to chainplates that ran outside the channels, gaining 8 to 10 inches of extra spread, in total. (It is the general consensus, I believe, that the minimum adequate shroud-mast angle is 15 degrees to provide proper staying strength.) The shrouds and stays were attached to the masts by robust bands, strongly clamped on with bolts at the appropriate heights. Allcard also had strong feelings against drilling holes in the mast. When he made a new mainmast in Gibraltar, he bragged that there were only two holes in it.

As for the halyard leads, they are very close to those for *Islander* (chapter 3), and Allcard's Sail Plan (Fig. 6–4) shows all the parts pretty clearly.

The same can be said of the sheets, with one minor difference between *Temptress*'s and *Islander*'s. The jib and forestaysail sheets, having blocks attached to their clews for a 2:1 mechanical advantage (no winches on *Temptress*), were not shackled directly onto the clews but hung at the end of pendants, which in turn hung from the clews. The jib's pendant was 5 feet long, the forestaysail's 1 foot long. This arrangement seemed puzzling at first. Why not just shackle the blocks directly to the sails, which only adds a few feet to the length of the sheets and is simpler? I finally concluded that it improved the set of the sails when the sheets were eased on any point of sailing from a beam reach to a dead run. These pendants kept the lead of the sheets lined up with the miter line of each sail, allowing the sail to hold its best shape when rap-full of wind, and prevented a *downward* pull that would strain it and spoil its set. This was so because with the pendants, the fixed starting point of the sheet on deck was further aft than it could be without them—sort of an ideal midpoint between the furthest points aft and forward one might choose. The pendants, however, were not so long as to prevent the two sails from being bowsed down hard for windward work.

The Cabin

Here is a layout that appears ideally suited to the comfort and efficiency of the singlehanded voyager. It just *looks* like a proper home afloat for the long-term live-aboard sailor. Allcard's berth and the galley flank the companionway ladder, and we can see him living in this snug one-quarter of his ship for days on end. The prime advantage of this arrangement is not visible in the Cabin Plan itself (Fig. 6–3): It is that the sleeping, cooking, and eating were done in that part of the ship with the least motion. That is not to be regarded lightly, especially when one will be at sea for weeks on end—as Allcard anticipated—and when that benefit is still enjoyed in open anchorages exposed to the surge of the sea. The layout derives from that small cockpit, which is placed so far aft. A longer cockpit would have shoved the sea berth and galley forward, much closer to amidships, and, in fact, would have altered the entire Cabin Plan. But these two items are just the major benefits.

In addition, the engine-starting batteries were boxed at one end of his berth, handy for servicing; a small, folding hand basin was fitted right next to the berth; and, across the way, the cook had a really snug seat tucked in between the engine box and the stove flat. Being able to sit rather than stand while cooking—provided the cook has everything within arm's reach—must be experienced to be fully appreciated. (I cruised with this arrangement —a galley seat on a swivel—and it was wonderful. The sole even had a rail to hook your feet under if the boat lurched while both hands were occupied. Obviously, cooking while standing has proved itself workable today, but the simple fact is that, despite vast improvements in galley design in recent years, few designers feel they can "spend" enough space to permit a galley seat. *Temptress*'s galley was 6 feet long, so it was possible.)

The rest of the galley is self-explanatory: two kerosene Primus stoves hung in gimbals on the stove flat, with dish racks aft of them, and, forward, a stainless steel sink with fresh- and salt-water hand pumps. Even if Allcard were standing in the galley when the boat lurched, his back would come up against the companionway ladder before he was thrown far enough to suffer injury. Another unusual aspect of *Temptress* is that although she was built in 1910, and had what looks like a paid hand's berth in the forepeak, the galley was aft.

The main saloon amidships is a typically British layout, with doors either end for privacy (further suggesting the presence of a paid hand forward) and the standard arrangement of settee berths flanking a drop-leaf table, with lockers and bookshelves outboard. Allcard carried seventy books, one of which was Slocum's other book, *The Voyage of the Liberdade*.

Next forward is an arrangement often seen today: a head compartment (which he used as a sail locker at sea) opposite hanging lockers. The forepeak, though small, has a pipe berth, its own folding basin, a seat for pulling on one's sea boots, a locker for the hand's duds (if it wasn't jammed with bo'sun's gear), and, overhead, a hatch for ventilation—and a source of private leaks for the poor soul who lives there.

All the way aft we see no sign of a lazarette hatch (there's really no space for one in that tiny triangle), so we must assume Allcard could reach the stowage areas aft by crawling past the engine box on either side. Or, the small athwartships seat in the cockpit—it scales to only one foot fore and aft—may have been hinged (there's a line in the deck plan suggesting that) to give at least arm-reaching access below.

The water capacity was sixty-two gallons—a twenty-five-gallon galvanized tank under each settee, plus a dozen one-gallon cans stowed in odd corners. Allcard considered this amount "enough for 120 days."

The Engine

Allcard wraps up his description of the engine succinctly. It was a gasoline-kerosene engine (we've met this type already), "which would propel the boat at four knots in still water," and, he adds, " . . . it had a large generator driven off the flywheel to charge a heavy-duty battery of 12 volts." (The Cabin Plan shows two batteries—take your pick.) This engine, truly an auxiliary to the sails, was used principally for giving Allcard electric lights below, a practical necessity in tropical climates, though he noted that even such low horsepower was adequate for powering up rivers too narrow to sail. It was boxed as shown in the Cabin Plan, with two hinged flaps on top and removable sides for routine maintenance access, and it was totally removable for major work.

Temptress had two kerosene tanks (though only one is shown in the plans), and with extra cans, the total fuel capacity came to twenty-four gallons. The 7-HP engine, Allcard calculated, gave him a range under power of 250 miles. But for just charging the batteries, that much fuel lasted all the way to New York.

A small tank of gasoline (capacity not given) for starting and stopping the engine was fitted in the cockpit, under the shelter, where possible spillage would be handled by the scuppers.

The Profile/Sail Plan (Fig. 6–4) does not show the yawl's underbody, so some readers who have not noticed the odd angle of the propeller shaft in the Cabin Plan will be surprised to learn that the propeller—a folding type—was a quarter installation, emerging on the starboard side of the rudder. This was not unusual in either British or American auxiliaries of forty to fifty years ago. In many cases engines were added years after the boat was built, so there was no space in the sternpost to cut a propeller aperture. Further, as early engines were usually regarded only as "necessary evils" and not worth any pampering, a quarter installation with a folding prop often seemed adequate. This approach either dismissed—or had to tolerate—the much greater vulnerability of the prop to floating debris and the almost total lack of control moving sternward under power.

Fitting-out, Stores, and Gear

After ten years ashore in a boatyard (1938–48), *Temptress* was dried out and badly in need of complete refurbishing. Unfortunately, Allcard had time only for the essentials before departing England in the late summer of 1948. In fact, even sailing in August, he was miserably cold for the first few days out. Here in the United States we tend to forget—or don't realize—that the most southerly tip of England (Lizard Head in Cornwall) lies at 50 degrees north latitude, whereas New York City, considered to be in the chilly U.S. Northeast, rides the 41-degree north parallel and shares this latitude with Madrid.

Planning a total refit at Gibraltar before attempting the Atlantic, Allcard only had the boatyard where he found *Temptress* install a new set of galvanized keel bolts—on the sound enough notion that he would not sleep well nights with thoughts of the keel dropping off running through his head. Then he had a thorough overhaul done of the engine. The rest would have to wait.

The navigation lights were kerosene burning, but Allcard also carried a battery-powered 360-degree light that he switched on at night in crowded waters.

He carried a short-wave radio receiver for weather reports and time-ticks from station WWV but had no transmitter or any other electronic device except electric lights in the cabin. For "emergency" lighting *Temptress* had gimbaled kerosene lamps in the saloon.

His bilge pump, located just outside the starboard cockpit coaming, was something special. As Allcard himself describes it:

> This was no mean pump. To begin with, the diameter of the barrel was four-and-a-quarter inches so one could put one's hand down to clear the bottom valve should it become clogged. But then it never did foul, for I had made several major modifications [to it]. These . . . surely would have shocked [its] original designer. It had been converted into "the perfect pump" at the cost of fourpence! The whole of the natty brass bottom-valve assembly had been ruthlessly torn out with hammer, cold chisel and hacksaw, and replaced with a [round] block of wood with an adequate hole in it covered by an oiled leather flap, thus making it into a pump so powerful that it once brought up a bolt! A child could use it, shifting half a gallon at each stroke, and . . . it was no labour to pump out . . . twenty-five gallons of water. . . .

Allcard didn't describe his anchors, but one photo of the foredeck (unfortunately too poor to reproduce) shows at least one fisherman's anchor —in the 60- to 75-pound range—and a length of heavy chain that looks to be ⅜ or ½ inches in diameter. Allcard considered heavy anchors with chain the only acceptable ground tackle.

One really unusual feature is the counter-weighted "swing table" in the saloon. We hardly ever hear of them anymore, but they were once fairly commonplace—at least in English boats. Although they perform like gimbaled lamps, such tables can be locked in any position. The obvious objection is that eating on the windward side is fine—even if you're hunched over —but on the leeward side your chin would be permanently in your soup, which is fine for some but a dubious benefit for the bearded, like Allcard.

For navigation, Allcard carried a barometer, sextant, the aforementioned radio receiver, a patent log, and an Omega watch by which he kept time for his longitude.

Forced to put into La Coruna, Spain, en route to Gibraltar, he spent a few days putting things in order: dismantling and cleaning the engine, making new fenders, mending his two headsails, and repairing other small damage. Then he "sneaked" ashore and replenished his stores at a village shop.

He gives no details about the food he carried, but we know he had porridge, because he sometimes ate it twice a day—easy to prepare, of course, in rough going. He also reports buying rice, bread, and butter in Lisbon.

At Gibraltar, after a few days of rest, Allcard was ready to tackle fitting-out again. The first item on his list was a new mast, as he had completely lost confidence in the old one on the southward passage. He started by importing a 50-foot Corsican pine from England that arrived as deck cargo and was lowered into the water and towed across the harbor by Allcard in a little motorboat—to avoid customs. It weighed half a ton!

This great baulk of timber was lifted out and rolled on a hand trolley to the yacht club shed. There, for the next few weeks, Allcard slaved away to extract a mast from it. In places it was 1½ inches in diameter greater than the old one. First by chipping away with a small Spanish adz, then "with over two-thousand strokes of my plane," he brought it down to final dimensions of 41′6″ long and 7⅞″ in greatest diameter. Then, after days and days of hand-sanding, he slushed it down with 1½ gallons of linseed oil, replaced all the hardware—and it was done. The unstepping of the old and the stepping of the new was a major event in Gibraltar's Torpedo Camber one day in April 1949.

About this time, *Temptress* was moved across the harbor to a Spanish boatyard in Algeciras, where she was hauled out for a scrub-and-paint job on the bottom. A bit of rot aft was fixed by cutting it out and fitting a

Dutchman, and some iron work on the sternpost was strengthened by welding. Sailing back to Gibraltar, Allcard found the repainted bottom added half a knot to *Temptress*'s speed.

In the meantime, two new headsails made by Ratsey had arrived from England. They were hand-sewn throughout and of flax, with the cloths running parallel to the leech and no battens, and they were tanned with Allcard's favorite mildew-proofing compound, Kanvo, about which he says that it also prevents chafe, since it always remains slightly greasy.

The last item on his work list was fitting a permanent boom gallows for the main boom at the forward end of the cockpit shelter. Then, after a day cruise across the Mediterranean, as a "thank you" to about a dozen English friends who had made his stay a pleasant one for seven months, and with stores for 100 days aboard, Allcard and *Temptress* were ready for the Atlantic.

Sailing Performance

When Allcard sailed from Falmouth, England, on August 27, 1948, bound for Gibraltar, his yawl, as noted, was just barely ready for sea. His plan, and hope, was to sneak across the Bay of Biscay before the onset of the autumn gales that sweep the North Atlantic. It was not to be. *Temptress* ran into a gale almost immediately and lay hove to for sixty hours. At the end of the gale, when Allcard wanted to power out of the violent slop, he found his engine full of sea water—he had forgotten to close the exhaust seacock. This forced him to alter course for La Coruna, Spain, to overhaul the engine before it was ruined—a two-day layover at anchor.

Sailing again, *Temptress* reeled off a fifty-six-mile passage to an almost deserted anchorage in Camarinas Bay, where Allcard found that the day's rough sailing had again filled his engine with salt water. Once more he disassembled it and cleaned it out, then proceeded down the Spanish coast to a third overnight anchorage, at Muros Bay.

After that, following his usual practice of heaving to for meals and sleep, and spending between twelve and sixteen hours at the held each day, Allcard recorded daily mileages over the next six days of 53, 77, 43, 45, 30, and 15 —an average of 43 per day. He was not pushing himself, now that he was in balmier waters, but still, compared to the performances of Slocum and Day in these same general waters, Allcard's *very* modest runs must be attributed in part to his yawl's heavy displacement and only half-days of sailing.

Perhaps this tradeoff is the most significant one we shall encounter in this collection of voyages—that of light versus heavy displacement. It might also be expressed as (relative) comfort in heavy weather versus high performance in most conditions; or, load-carrying ability versus minimal accommodations and gear. Perhaps the cutting edge between these two types is determined by the skipper's approach to cruising: the desire to live aboard in comfort at sea on an unhurried cruising timetable versus a passion for optimum sailing performance and fast passages. We'll see differing approaches to this throughout the rest of the book.

On the passage from Spain to Portugal, Allcard had two more problems: somewhere up forward the hull sprang a leak, and as Allcard was unable to find it, he had to pump the bilges every day; then, slatting about in a calm, the boom-end fitting that held the lower ends of the topping lifts snapped, flinging the main boom to leeward and snapping the mainsheet. What followed was one of those hairy half-hours that most cruising sailors have experienced, until he got the main boom back aboard, a new sheet rove, and the yawl sailing under control again.

Forced to sail cautiously through increasingly crowded waters as he neared the Mediterranean, with steamer tracks converging on it from south, west, and north, Allcard nevertheless brought *Temptress* into Gibraltar on October 8, 1948. Here he remained until May 1949, doing the work just described.

When *Temptress* sailed from Gibraltar on May 21, 1949, his plan was to sail nonstop to New York, along a track that would loop far to the south —to 22 degrees north latitude—and then curve upward in a northwesterly direction to his destination. This had not been attempted in twenty-six years —to his knowledge—since the French circumnavigator, Alain Gerbault, had sailed the route in 1923—taking 109 days to reach the same port. Allcard expected to reach New York City in 80 days or less.

Because *Temptress* was without a self-steering system (Allcard did not even attempt sheet-to-tiller steering), we will not encounter any exceptional runs on his voyage. In fact, most days he recorded well under 100 miles. His own estimate is a clue: By estimating 80 days to cover a rhumb-line distance of 3000 miles—but an actual sailing distance of about 5000 miles —he was anticipating a daily average of only 62.5 miles. So, we will not try to cover the voyage in detail—space limitations, again—but must make do with a synopsis, picking up such details as dovetail with our major themes.

Worthy of note by anyone contemplating this passage *(see Track Chart)* is that it makes maximum use of natural sailing advantages along the route: the northeast trades at the start, the westward-flowing north equatorial current in the middle section, and the northward help of the Gulf Stream in the final leg. These are the considerations the cruising sailor values more highly than a shorter distance.

On the first day, *Temptress* got a running start from Gibraltar on an easterly wind that sent her swiftly toward the Pillars of Hercules and the

Atlantic beyond. By noon that day—May 21, 1949—Allcard was in a gale, under reduced sail but still moving. Late that afternoon he was abreast of Tangier, Morocco; and, well before dusk the yawl was bounding along in Atlantic waters.

A bowl of hot porridge started each sailing day for Allcard—it is ever thus with English sailors, it seems—and going on deck, the strength of his new mast was comforting to him as he contemplated the tradewinds ahead. Conditions remained variable for several days—calms alternating with gusty winds. This required much reefing and shaking out, jobs that drew Allcard's praise for the convenience of the new permanent boom gallows. Heavy northwesterlies gave *Temptress* a beam reach and much violent rolling, so that Allcard was thrown about even when in his bunk; he called the conditions "vile," as over his head heavy water went coursing across the deck.

By the sixth day Allcard, now adjusted to the motion, notes, "I did not seem to mind the weather and continued to knock off seventy miles or so a day under the headsails without even the helm lashed."

At the end of the first week, the wind went into the north and the seas moderated. May 28, Allcard records, "was the first day of reasonable sailing conditions since leaving Gibraltar," so that he was able to take a sponge bath, comb his hair, air the yawl, and eat a proper meal at the saloon table. It appears that a gin taken before lunch and/or supper was a barometer of his morale.

In the second week, conditions turned ideal—the reality finally matching his mental picture of a tradewind run. So the days passed, *Temptress* rolling along and Allcard turning on his short-wave radio for a few hours each evening to listen to music from the BBC and to catch the time ticks he needed to rate his watch.

After a few more days, the violent motion of the first two weeks had put great strain on the rig. "The main shrouds," he says, "were hanging in bights." He briefly considered putting into the Canaries to adjust the rigging but decided that if he could find a calm spot in the lee of one of the islands, he would pause only long enough to do the work, and then continue his nonstop voyage. When he sighted the high land of Palma, he powered close to shore (also charging his batteries) and drifted for a few hours while he went aloft to free a burgee halyard that "had jammed various blocks." Then he set up the rigging again, pumped the bilges, and cleaned his stoves. By dusk, sweaty, tired, and dirty, he went over the side for a quick swim. In the morning he refastened a section of bulwark that was coming adrift, then raised sail again.

Now, with the first 850 miles of the crossing in her wake, *Temptress* was entering the "serious" part of the voyage. But that night, sailing under headsails toward the southwest, Allcard was awakened by a great cacophony

Fig. 6–5. Temptress *sailing in the Tagus River, Portugal.*

overhead. Rushing up on deck stark naked, he found that the wind had shifted and *Temptress* was rushing straight back toward Palma! He got her turned around in the midst of a black squall, dashed below to dress and don oilskins, and returned to the deck only to find the yawl lying in a dead calm! Through the night, squall followed squall as he hunched over the tiller. Once the boat was pooped by a great wave that exploded over him and filled the cockpit. He was alarmed to discover how long it took for the cockpit to empty through the two one-inch scuppers—a surprisingly skimpy arrangement for a deep-sea boat. After sixteen hours at the helm, *Temptress* could be left to sail herself under headsails, and Allcard crawled below to sleep.

By the start of the third week at sea, Allcard was beyond the Canaries and past the 1000-mile mark of the crossing. Tramping along at speeds between 4½ and 6 knots, Allcard found that both the Portuguese and true northeast trades varied in strength from hour to hour, and "it was, therefore, not possible to lash the helm with the mainsail up for any length of time." So, he was a prisoner of the helm every day, remarking that "A ten-hour trick was normal and, on [a] sunny day, we reeled off close-on fifty miles in that period." His comment about Slocum's *Spray,* which could sail itself under full mainsail with the wind aft, is tinged with more than a touch of envy. Of course, he *knew* about tradewind rigs (twin staysails or the like), but he had been unable to afford such a rig before departure.

Fig. 6–6. *Edward Allcard taking a sight at sea.*

By June 7 *Temptress* was one-quarter of the way across. (Fig. 6–6). That was the seventeenth day, and seventeen times four (one-quarter) would have given Allcard a landfall at New York in sixty-eight days. But that was not to be—and he knew it—because he still had to pass through the horse latitudes, which would certainly slow him down. (The horse latitudes get their name from the early Spanish Conquistadors en route to the Americas, who, running short of food and waters when becalmed in these regions, were forced to throw their dead and dying horses overboard.)

After weathering another calm, the climate turned tropical and Allcard found his first flying fish on deck one morning. On a typical day in this period he put 43 miles in his wake in ten and a half hours. We can call that 4.3 knots and, by extension, calculate a 24-hour run at that speed (if the wind held steady) as 103.2 miles. That's a Speed/Length ratio of under 0.8. Someone (whose name I can't recall) did extensive research on dozens of long blue-water voyages and developed data showing cruising boats do well to average an S/L of 1.1 across an ocean, despite top hull speed of 1.34. For *Temptress,* S/L 1.1 is 6.17 knots, and Allcard hardly ever recorded that speed in his log. (At 6.17 knots, he would cover, in 24 hours, 148 miles.) So this is a good point to look at the yawl's numbers. We will add the three S/Ls that precede the usual starting point of S/L 1.0:

		Temptress: Speed/Length Ratio			
		(WL = 31′ 6″ $\sqrt{31.5}$ = 5.61)			
S/L	× $\sqrt{WL}$	= Speed (knots)	× 24	= NM (1 day)	
0.7	5.61	3.93		94.3	
0.8	5.61	4.49		107.8	
0.9	5.61	5.05		121.2	
1.0	5.61	5.61		134.6	
1.1	5.61	6.17		148.1	
1.2	5.61	6.73		161.5	
1.3	5.61	7.29		175.0	
1.34	5.61	7.51		180.2	

When we observe that the yawl's mileage potential at S/L 1.1 is 148 miles, and match that against many of Allcard's log entries showing only two-thirds or even one-half of that, we are confronting a slow crossing indeed. Many skippers today would consider *Temptress* a "slug" and no pleasure to sail. Well, how are we to understand this torpid pace on an impressively long waterline—for a 34-footer—of 31′6″? (The LWL is 92.5 percent of the LOA.) Allcard doesn't address the question at all, so we must dig for answers in the few facts we know.

First, 28,000 pounds was very heavy displacement for a 34-footer; second, with 600 square feet of sail, she seems underrigged—at least another 100 square feet seems indicated; third, Allcard could not keep her moving twenty-four hours a day, because he had no self-steering system; fourth, as Allcard notes, tradewinds are not that consistent in their power; fifth, although she was anti-fouled just before departure from Gibraltar, by the second half of this eighty-day voyage she had developed considerable bottom growth—clearly, the toxicity of 1949 paints did not nearly match today's; sixth, the summer of 1949 might have had more variable tradewinds than "normal;" seventh, Allcard was admittedly at the helm only about ten or so hours a day. Is there any substantiation for all this?

Well, if we use the average S/L of 1.1 cited above and credit *Temptress* with 10 hours at that ratio, and the other 14 each day at, say, S/L 1.0, we get: (10 × 6.17) or 61.7 N.M. *plus* (14 × 5.61) or 78.5 NM, which equals 140 NM per day. He's nowhere near that, so let's try again.

If we lower each S/L one notch, to 1.0 and 0.9, we still get 126.8 NM. We're still not close to actual performance, as the yawl's best noon-to-noon run was only 94 miles! The only precise figures Allcard provides are four, nonconsecutive weekly mileage totals, given here with the daily average in parentheses after each one: 522 NM (74.6), 472 NM (67.4), 475 NM (67.8), and 225 NM (32.1). The last figure was for a week spent in the horse latitudes. The conclusion is inescapable that *Temptress* was a slow boat, though it would be interesting to see Allcard's passage figures with a steering vane and/or a twin-stay sail rig. At the end of this chapter, we'll see what Allcard did about all this.

Returning now to *Temptress* in her fourth week, Allcard was prompted to experiment with his rig—showing he was aware of how slow he was sailing—so he dragged out his brand-new storm trysail (which had come with the boat), to see if it would add speed in conditions too rough for the whole mainsail. Unfolding it on deck, he was shocked to find that "It had a foot as long as the main boom, little hoist and the tack was a right angle. Hopeless." (It was a small Marconi mainsail in shape.) After several attempts he finally got it aloft" . . . as a sort of square sail [except that it was triangular], forward of the mast, upside down and hoisted on the staysail halyards." This attempt lasted only a day, as the next dawn provided perfect weather for the full working rig.

Later that week he marked the halfway point across by turning over his ocean chart and beginning to plot his daily positions on the "eastern" side of the chart's crease. On June 13 his position was 24°19′N., 31°43′W. He had only to drop down another two degrees before turning eastward.

On the twenty-third day out—June 14—Allcard ate the last of his fresh onions. The next day winds were variable and the heat intense, often 94°F. on deck, and 80°F. or more below. Several times a day Allcard took a plunge in the ocean. On June 16 he was in a flat calm. After loafing on deck for several hours, he got a charge of ambition and did several chores: modified the generator bracket on the engine and adjusted the belt; stripped down the head pump and made and fitted a new gasket; did engine maintenance; replaced the gland packing on a water pipe leading to a galley pump; filled the stoves with kerosene; and renewed "worn parts of the rigging." Later he ran the engine to charge the batteries and installed a standpipe (loop) in the engine exhaust so that sea water could no longer flood the engine.

In the fifth week, he passed the true halfway point in mileage. Then a new problem appeared, a leak he was not able to trace, which required pumping every day or so for the rest of the voyage. Another frustration was that the new jib, received in Gibraltar, had finally stretched to its final shape, and now its clew overlapped the forestaysail stay, causing it to chafe every time Allcard tacked. In frustration he asked rhetorically, "Why is it that sailmakers never allow enough for stretch, yet riggers nearly always cut the rigging short?" What was worse, the new jib rolled up unevenly with the furling gear because too small a luff wire had been installed.

That day Allcard's latitude was 23°26.9'N., and the day after, *Temptress* dropped south of the twenty-third parallel (Fig. 6–7). On June 22 the trades strengthened, and she covered fifty miles in under ten hours, but on the twenty-fourth it was back to a flat calms, the yawl slatting about in broiling heat.

In the sixth week, Allcard recalled that he had planned to declare each Sunday a "day off," for rest and chores, but he had not done that. Now he started, and spent this sixth Sunday as follows: trimmed his beard and cut his hair; took a sea-water bath; laundered his "pillow case, towel and drying-up cloths"; cleaned and filled the stoves, pumped the bilges; scrubbed the teak decks; and cleaned and oiled his guns (first mention that he carried any). Then he shot the sun at noon and loafed till supper.

The week was now marked by stronger trades, good progress, plus a special event—the sighting of the steamer *Jagiello*. Allcard hastily hoisted the signal flags that requested he be reported to Lloyd's of London. In a few hours (he learned weeks later) his father received a telegram that he had been sighted, safe at sea after thirty-eight days. In the next two days blustery conditions found him sailing under the storm trysail again. The week ended with *Temptress* in a markedly different position—Barbuda in the Leewards lay only 550 miles off his port beam.

Here Allcard makes an interesting comment about the French circum-navigator Alain Gerbault. Twenty-six years earlier, while on the same meridian of longitude, Gerbault complained bitterly (in his book) about the disappearance of the tradewinds. Allcard notes that his longitude may have been the same as Gerbault's, but his latitude wasn't. *Temptress* was 360 miles farther south, getting plenty of tradewind push. He adds that Gerbault had only himself to blame, because all data and records show that the winds do not hold so far north." That's a point worth remembering by anyone planning an east-to-west passage from Europe. The literature of small-boat crossings (and many OSTAR races) echoes with this same complaint by almost all who—probably trying to shorten the route—turned east before sailing far enough south. So ended Allcard's sixth week. (Fig. 6–7).

In the seventh week Allcard got several days of "storybook tradewind weather and knocked off 475 miles without any excitements." Now he was on the northwesterly component of his track, already above 24°N. and still climbing the latitude ladder. On July 10, fifty days out, he checked his water supply and found he had used only half of it. "The sails were in good condition and the hull and gear were standing up pretty well," he notes, "although there was plenty of attention needed. However, I planned to give her a thorough overhaul in the calm area, only a few days away."

A pair of black squalls now passed over the yawl to port and starboard, touching her with nothing but a few gusts of wind but reminding Allcard that the hurricane season was fast approaching—though he felt reasonably safe for the remainder of July. His chart position showed he was only 1250 miles from New York. The long weeks of tropical sun baking the yawl had opened up the seams of the teak deck, and leaks now soaked his berth below, so he slept for a time in the forepeak berth.

On July 13 Allcard had his closest call of the voyage. He was at the helm when he noticed that the mainsail luff was somewhat slack, so he went forward to give a good heave on the throat halyard. As he did, the halyard, rotted by the sun and salt spray, snapped, and a block flew down out of the rigging and struck him above his left eye—knocking him out and flattening him on the portside deck just as *Temptress* rolled to starboard. If the timing of this "incident" (as he calls it) had been a few seconds earlier or later, he would have been "shot over the side [, and] one can imagine the thoughts of a lone mariner on seeing his boat sail away as he struggles in the water and the sharks turn in to investigate."

With no more than a bad headache and an impressive bruise, he went up the mast that afternoon to reeve a new throat halyard, returning to the deck with "more bruises and grazes. . . . " He continues, "The next day, in order to prevent any further untoward incidents, there was the most difficult job of re-reeving a new peak halyard. One end had to be shackled aloft, while I stood on the cross-trees. A line round my body and the mast prevented me from being flicked off, since the boat frisked among the waves. While at this job I discovered to my alarm that the [steel] clamp fittings were slipping down the shrinking mast [obviously the cause of the mainsail luff going slack] and one would shortly be grinding into the eye-splices of the main shrouds."

For two days winds were so heavy that Allcard did not dare raise the main, but sailed under jib only at night, and jib and jigger during the day. On the eighth day after the broken halyard, July 21, he finally was able to go up the mast and tighten the bands. It was a bruising, exhausting job that took over an hour. Each band had to be raised five inches—with all blocks and halyards hanging on it. Clinging to the mast and shrouds with his thighs and feet—he needed both hands to use a wrench in each—left his blood running down the shrouds and down his thighs where they were pinched between the mast and his bo'sun's chair. He lowered himself at last and fell exhausted into his bunk. Later in the day, remarkably recovered, he removed the engine's cylinder head and decarbonized it. Allcard was not one to allow discomfort or pain to lead to slackness in the maintenance department. As the week ended, the wind died and Allcard knew he had reached the horse latitudes. In spite of that *Temptress* had sailed from 27°N. to 30°N.

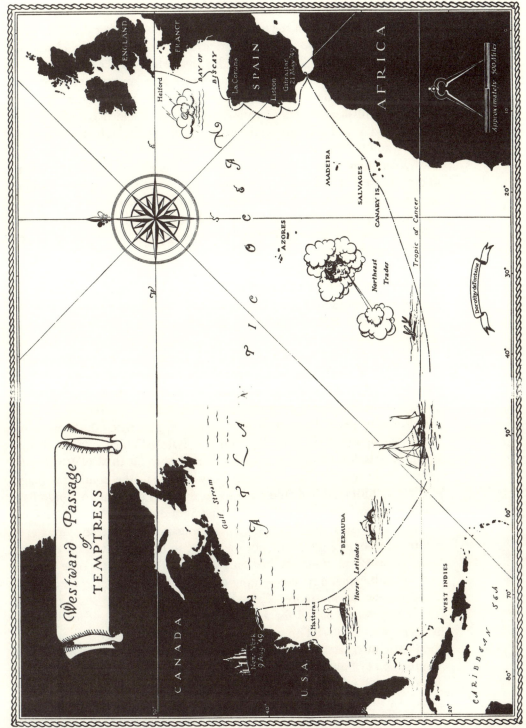

Fig. 6-7. Temptress's sailing track across the Atlantic.

151

The first three days of the ninth week, "*Temptress* lay becalmed on white oily swells," so Allcard powered for seven hours one day to charge the batteries. During this period he saw his first whale of the voyage.

Sliding into the tenth week, a moderate gale kept the yawl jogging along under reduced canvas for half a day. The chart revealed that *Temptress* was now abreast of North Carolina. As the week ended on July 30, the seventieth day out, Allcard realized he would reach port the following week.

Closer to the United States coast now, he caught some of the prevailing southwesterlies of summer, and it "provided one of the best days of sailing of the voyage." For the first time in months, *Temptress* was heeling to starboard! But this final week also brought many squalls and thunderstorms, as any summer sailor on this coast knows well, with much rolling up and rolling down of the mainsail.

At this point, Allcard had discovered that *Temptress*'s bottom was badly fouled by long weed trailing astern, and the whole week netted only 225 miles. Oddly enough, it also produced the best day's run of 94 miles. That's an S/L ratio of only 0.7—a sobering figure to represent the "best" of eighty sailing days.

Below decks Allcard suffered under a humid heat that often reached above 90°F., normal summer temperatures now intensified by the Gulf Stream. Pitching to windward in a gale for three days under headsails with bar-taut sheets, *Temptress* nevertheless covered nearly 300 miles. At the gale's end, Allcard plotted his position as 100 miles off the coast, equidistant from Sandy Hook and Long Island's Montauk Point. Which one to choose? While he was pondering, a wind-shift from SW to W to WNW made the decision for him: "It was no longer possible to lay the course for Sandy Hook." So Montauk it would have to be, 87 miles off, and he would have to sail westward the length of Long Island Sound to reach New York City.

The wind died and darkness fell, accompanied by a steady drizzle, so Allcard started the engine and motored through the night well off the Long Island coast. By midnight he had only 40 miles to go. At 0200 he was still in the steamer lanes now converging on New York harbor, so he powered 6 miles closer to the shore. Then, he stopped the engine and—the calm continuing—went below for a two-hour nap. At dawn he found himself in a heavy fog, still with no wind, so he motored for another six hours, until noon, August 6. But the fog persisted (I can hear the Long Islanders and Southern New Englanders who sail these waters chuckling empathetically). Allcard heard a fog horn in the distance but he could see no land. He sounded with the lead—30 fathoms. Six miles further, another sounding—20 fathoms. Onward again—now 14 fathoms, but no end to the fog. Finally . . . a buoy! And then land.

Moving in cautiously, he identified it as the shore of Block Island. Dead tired, and reluctant to face officialdom so soon after seventy-six days at sea, he anchored off the beach (outside Great Salt Pond) and went below to sleep.

On August 9, 1949, having sailed over 100 miles westward in the maddeningly light winds of August that Long Island Sound sailors know so well (he did not dare use his engine, because he was down to a couple of gallons of fuel), Allcard dropped anchor off the shore of City Island, New York, exactly eighty days out of Gibraltar. Slow as it was, his voyage merits at least grudging respect for its skipper's seamanship and toughness in the face of an awesome challenge.

Allcard's Aphorisms

At the end of his book, Edward C. Allcard appended fifty bits of practical advice for deep-water cruising that he entitled "Deep-Sea Sense." While the technology underlying cruising boats has changed radically since 1948, the sea has not. Most of these aphorisms, if treated as principles rather than literal suggestions, still make sense. Here are a baker's dozen plus two out of the fifty:

1. Have your sails made with vertical cut, cloths running parallel to the leech (and no battens). 2. If you can afford roller reefing, fit it—but use a heavy pattern. 3. Have at least 60 fathoms of stout anchor chain, and mark it. 4. Don't use "yachty" fittings—they are only good for Long Island Sound. 5. Have extra stout rigging screws (turnbuckles) on the shrouds. 6. The mast and rudder should never fail. 7. Don't have a big cockpit—deck it in. 8. Assume one day the boat will be temporarily submerged by the sea. 9. Have two nonchoke bilge pumps, one at the helm, the other below. 10. Two deep sinks are best for the galley, but fit nonchoke waste pumps—gravity outlets are of no use in a heeled sailing boat. 11. Arrange it so the cook can chock himself in and can administer with both hands in a seaway. 12. Don't catch gadgetitis—Simplicity is best. 13. Fit a wide boom gallows, not the flimsy crutch usually fitted. 14. It is better to lose twelve inches off the foot of the mainsail than to have a dinghy on the side deck. 15. Finally, trust all men. Yea, even princes. Then cut the cards yourself. *Caveat emptor!*

Postscript

During his six months in the United States, Allcard wrote his book (and magazine articles for both sides of the Atlantic), submitted to radio interviews (an Atlantic crossing was still newsworthy in those days), and refitted *Temptress.* He also bought a derelict 35-foot yawl (with a *sound* hull) and stored it in the backyard of an American friend. Next, he sailed *Temptress* back to England via Casablanca and Spain—in seventy-six days—and wrote a book on that voyage *(see Bibliography.)* He returned to the United States and converted the "derelict" into his "ideal" ketch at Howland's Boatyard in Pandanaram, Massachusetts. In changing boats he: gained a reduction in draft from 6′8″ to 5′4″; switched rig from gaff yawl to Marconi ketch, this time with a twin staysail rig for the tradewinds; tolerated the new boat's counter stern (because that's the way she was built); got a displacement reduction of 1.5 tons, from 28,000 to 24,600 pounds; sailed the new boat, *Sea Wanderer,* back to England in seventy-six days; and, finally, tore out the old interior and replaced it with one identical to the familiar one in *Temptress.*

He headed out on another blue-water voyage in 1957, first to Gibraltar, where he left the ketch for several months to return home and earn money for further voyaging, returned to Gibraltar in May, 1958, sailed to Tangier, Morocco, and then went on to Las Palmas in the Canaries. Here he met Peter Tangvald—who was to become a circumnavigator in the next few years— and they agreed to race across the Atlantic to Antigua on a one-dollar bet! (Tangvald won, but his yawl was nine feet longer overall.)

After chartering his ketch for three years in the West Indies (where he befriended Harold LaBorde—chapter 10), Allcard continued his world voyage, sailing in November 1961 from the Caribbean on a wide-looping non stop passage of 6000 miles—first northeast, then southeast past the Cape Verde Islands, then south, and finally, southwest to Montevideo, Uruguay —in 100 sailing days. Here, resting and refitting on the banks of the Rio de la Plata, he wrote his third book, *Voyage Alone* (his second was *Temptress Returns; see Bibliography*).

Sea Wanderer 's next challenge was Cape Horn.

With a particular sense of guilt, as if committing an act of desecration, we removed the dinghy, which had become almost a permanent feature of the boat, so long had it been there. We unscrewed the cockpit coamings, then forced ourselves to bore holes in the deck. We ripped up the canvas deck covering and, most irrevocable of all, sawed a great slit right across the wide, clear foredeck. We paused to stare at the results of this first dire deed in horror; then, we turned desperately to hacking and rending in a fit of frenzy. We stood back after an hour to gaze upon a murdered Nova Espero.*

She was opened up so that looking down on her, a tiny triangle of foredeck and the small original aft deck was all that was left of to remind us that she had, but a short hour ago, been a complete and beautiful little sailing boat. Her hull was exposed, so that the pathetic little ribs gleamed in the sun like the remains of some lovely animal.

No man on earth ever gets nearer to heaven than the enthusiastic boat-builder!

—Stanley Smith and Charles Violet
The Wind Calls the Tune (1952)

AUTHOR'S NOTE: Although *Nova Espero* (Latin for "new hope"), like *Temptress* in the previous chapter, is an English boat completing a westward crossing of the Atlantic in the early 1950s, in many ways the two voyages could hardly be more different. Both yachts were yawls, but there the similarities end. *Nova Espero* was only 20 feet overall in length yet had a crew of two; she carried no fresh water; and, though she consumed 110 days in the crossing, in some ways she performed more respectably than *Temptress*. The comparisons are interesting. And, it's my feeling that younger readers may find in this tale—about a truly tiny ship—their own new hope for an economical boat suitable for crossing great oceans.

Stanley Smith and Charles Violet

There is a brief before-the-beginning story worth reporting before launching into *Nova Espero*'s voyage covered here. Some readers may consider her first voyage no more than a dangerous stunt and may even regard her second Atlantic crossing as not much better. But she made both safely, and it's hard to argue with success, except that some will mutter she was just lucky she didn't go down. Here, especially, the crew's seamanship was the special ingredient; the size of the ship was not the controlling factor. The smallness was dictated by necessity: it was go cheap or not go at all, and the crews of both voyages were young men consumed by an ambition to cross an ocean in their own boat.

Fig. 7–1. *Stanley Smith* (left) *and Charles Violet aboard* Nova Espero, *at City Island, New York.* (Photo: UPI/Bettman Archive.)

In 1949 Stanley Smith and his brother, Colin, who had collaborated on *Nova Espero*'s design during the war years, took a liner to Nova Scotia. There, in a rented basement, they built the 20-foot hull, rigged her as a sloop, and sailed her across the Atlantic, from Dartmouth, Nova Scotia, to Dartmouth, England. Because of the need for extreme economy, the little sloop did not have a cabin, merely a long, open cockpit with coamings all around;

it was not self-bailing. To provide *some* protection from the elements, they built a 7-foot pram dinghy of plywood, its sheer contoured to fit over the coamings that ran around the edges of the cockpit. Under this "shelter" (6′ long and 4′ wide, with headroom of 3′6″), the off-watch man slept on the floorboards on the bottom of the boat.

Despite the extreme discomfort endured by the Smith brothers—being dry was the exception—they crossed the Atlantic in forty-four days in that summer of 1949 and received tumultuous welcomes both at Dartmouth and at their home port of Yarmouth. Following that voyage, in early 1950 *Nova Espero* was shipped *back* to Nova Scotia as deck cargo by Charles Violet, a friend of both brothers, who attempted a second Atlantic crossing. Unluckily, when he was 500 miles out, he suffered severe burns in a flare-up of his Primus stove and was forced to return to Nova Scotia. So, once again the sloop and Violet crossed the Atlantic eastward on the deck of a freighter, arriving in Liverpool in late 1950.

Soon after, Smith and Violet sat down to talk. "I immediately broached the subject on my mind," Smith says, "a second crossing of the Atlantic in the *Nova*. Without a moment's hesitation he agreed, and thus was started the greatest adventure of our lives."

Stanley Smith was raised in, on, and around boats, as his father owned a boatyard and built boats in his yard at Yarmouth on the Isle of Wight. Smith was the kind of boy who could sail a boat before he could ride a bike. Charles Violet had a similar background, having spent all his early years "messing about in boats." Beyond this shared grounding in seamanship, of course, Smith had one Atlantic crossing behind him in this boat, and he knew her behavior characteristics at sea in all weathers.

The Hull

The yawl's basic dimensions were these: LOA—20′; LWL—16′; Beam—6′3″; Draft—2′10″; Displacement—1 ton (2240 lbs.); Ballast Keel—800 lbs.; Sail Area—200 sq. ft.)

A glance at *Nova Espero*'s plans (Fig. 7–2) quickly reveals one dominant characteristic: she has, despite her size, a very buoyant hull. This is especially clear in the Body Plan, which shows "plump" sections at both bow and stern and a midship section that is almost pure English dinghy in shape. Here's Smith on that subject:

> In the design a fairly full fore-section was aimed at in order to help carry the water supply forward of the living space [they carried water on the first voyage, which was of much shorter duration], and to lift the boat quickly when bucking the last sharp curl of a big sea. An easy, rather flat run under water was designed to give the boat a seagull-like sit "on" instead of "in" the water, and to allow her to plane forward on "white water." A long fin keel, not too deep, with the weight distributed along a considerable length was

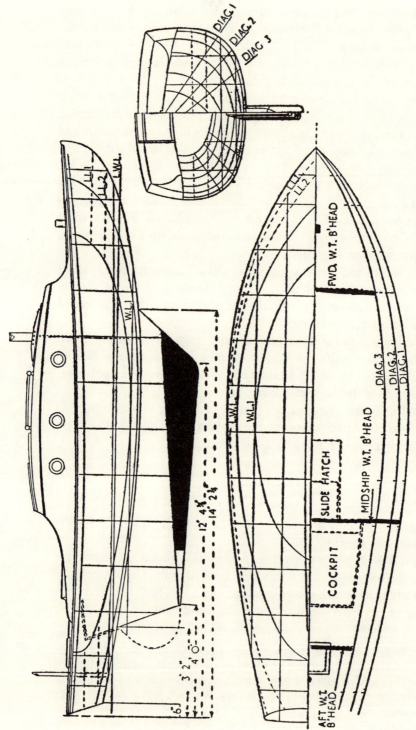

Fig. 7-2. Nova Espero: Lines, Outboard Profile, and Body Plan.

designed to give additional longitudinal strength, to ease the violence when pitching and to provide a long plane of lateral resistance to reduce any tendency toward restless wandering off course. . . .

In construction, the hull was lapstrake planked for reasons Smith explains:

> We adopted clincher construction because of its great strength from weight, each "land" [plank overlap, copper riveted at close intervals] representing an unbroken . . . stringer. It also provides a partial interruption to the swish of water in the bilge and, very important, curbs the persistent film of water which runs up over a smooth topside [a point that, we recall, preoccupied T. F. Day in chapter 2], catches in the breeze and rains down upon all on deck.

For this second Transatlantic, much longer in miles (to sail in favorable wind systems), Smith and Violet knew they needed a major modification. Smith explains: "This time we needed a real cabin, otherwise we should bear the risk of being unable to stand the prolonged exposure. The cabin was constructed with three main purposes in mind—reserve buoyancy [the raised deck providing more of this than would a trunk cabin], comfort with utility, and strength." The raised deck is, of course, stronger than a traditional trunk cabin.

This alteration started in the early spring of 1951, beginning with the drastic first step described in the opening quote of this chapter. With that much done in only part of an afternoon, they immediately turned to the

Fig. 7–3. Nova Espero: *Sail Plan.*

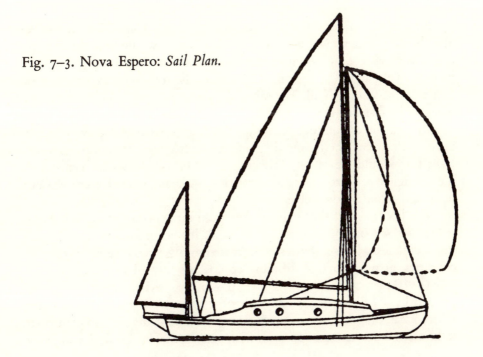

slower, more complex job of rebuilding her. First, they removed the cast-iron ballast keel. Then they shanghaied a group of boatyard onlookers and, with this collective manpower, levered and pushed the hull into a shed. While they worked on the cabin, Smith's father cut 100 pounds of iron off the ballast keel to compensate for the new weight being added.

In the following weeks they completed the following jobs: built three new watertight bulkheads (see Figs. 7–2 and 7–4); fitted a row of American elm "frame extensions" amidships for about 8 feet along each side of the hull; built a laminated plywood frame (⅞ inches thick) as part of the new cabintop beams, which would take the thrust of the mast so they could step it on deck (this beam started at the keel on both sides, curved up both sides of the hull, then arched across, matching the curve of the new cabintop beams); fitted mahogany cabin sides and a ⅜-inch plywood cabin top that was glued and screwed onto the beams; fitted three fixed portlights in each cabin side with Perspex (plastic) dead lights, framed with stainless finishing rings; built a main companionway hatch that was hinged to open, there not being enough length to fit a sliding hatch.

The isometric drawing (Fig. 7–4) clearly shows the watertight bulkheads, both cockpit coamings, the helmsman's seat, the method of stepping both masts, and the plywood frame to support the mast step. Note the cutaway forefoot for quick responsiveness when coming about.

The Deck

Nova Espero's deck is about as simple as they come. To achieve an all-inboard rig, there was no bowsprit. Few sailors would want to lean out over the bow to drag down a soggy job in a gusty wind, especially on a boat as lively at sea as this one. Otherwise, the foredeck has a stout little samson post, and that's all. The raised deck section—eight inches above the sheer line—has no openings but the main hatch. With minimal cabin ventilation, the discomfort of smuggy air below when the crew was shut up in a blow must be balanced against the better protection against heavy leaks that would create even greater misery below. It would seem that a well-designed and strong Dorade ventilator—already in use for two decades or more—would have helped.

The cockpit will shock many American sailors—as mentioned above, it was not self-bailing. On the other hand, it's not uncommon in English yacht design tradition. Here is another design divergence between the two countries, growing out of differing approaches toward safety at sea.

The American anticipates the possibility—eventuality?—of being pooped by a following sea and wants the water confined to the cockpit, where it can drain out the scuppers. He doesn't want any of it to get below, so he often buttresses this approach with a substantial bridge deck and, when he's most cautious, has the main hatch threshold built higher than the side decks. That such a self-bailing cockpit may cause him to sit even higher above the level of the sea, subject to more motion and exposure, does not —if he considers it at all—concern him greatly. This is mostly an outgrowth of "that's the way it's always been."

The Briton, on the other hand, considers it initially safer to be tucked well down in the boat and considers exposure, the exhaustion caused by greater motion, and the chance of being thrown right out of the boat to be greater dangers. (Today, fiber glass auxiliaries are pretty uniformly built with self-bailing cockpits on both sides of the Atlantic, but the contrasting views seem nevertheless interesting—particularly for the minority that might build, or have built, a small cruising boat.) If you want to sit well down in the boat, and the boat is a mini-cruiser, you must do without the self-bailing feature.

Look at the isometric drawing (Fig. 7–4) again, and visualize the difference of motion the helmsman would experience sitting on the deck beside the cockpit well (which is where he would be if the sole were raised to make the cockpit were self-bailing). Then consider the reduced motion and greater protection if he were snugly perched on the athwartship seat shown, well down in the boat. If being soaked with spray and tossed about leads to the hypothermia and exhaustion that cause mistakes of judgment, a case can be made for the British approach. To keep a balanced view— if this assertion is reasonable for the smaller boat—it's much less applicable as the boat reaches 35 feet LOA and has moderate to heavy displacement. Finally, it's worth a leap ahead (to Sailing Performance) to note that neither man considered this cockpit worrisome or noted that the yawl took on any endangering amount of water from astern. Perhaps that's because a heavy canvas cover could be fitted over the cockpit coamings in really violent weather. Worth noting, too, is that the after deck was 4 feet long—to keep crew weight well forward of the transom.

There is one other point to be made. It is the Briton's feeling that if a self-bailing small boat is pooped, perhaps the *worst* place to have that enormous weight of water is in the stern. Why? Because before the water can be drained by the scuppers, the boat, now sluggish from loss of buoyancy and slow to answer the helm, may be vulnerable to having the next comber crash aboard, and the next, until she sustains enough damage to be over-whelmed.

However, if the cockpit sole drains into the bilges, the weight, being quickly distributed along the entire length of the keel, and lower down than in the full-cockpit instance, will let the boat remain on her designed water-line and keep sailing reasonably well. This gives the crew time to pump it out, while retaining maneuverability enough to change the point of sailing or round up to heave to.

To clench the rove that holds this argument together, *Nova Espero* was capsized 170 degrees on this voyage and did not, obviously, fill up and sink. This approach to cockpits may not suit the summer auxiliary that sits unattended on a mooring all week—though a simple boom tent will keep out rain—but it deserves some consideration when planning the small cruising auxiliary. (Eliminating the cost of cockpit construction saves a considerable amount, while removing most of the risk of dry rot and substantially increasing stowage space aft.)

The Rig

The first thing worth noting about *Nova Espero*'s Sail Plan is that she is not gaff-rigged but is a sliding gunter-rigged yawl. This "variation" of the gaff rig is a rarity to most U. S. sailors but has much to recommend it: 1. It permits the yard (not gaff) to be peaked almost as high as a Marconi mainsail but requires a much shorter mainmast, a distinct advantage in heavy weather when windage aloft is so undesirable. 2. When you reef the mainsail, you "reef the mainmast" at the same time, and when you lower the mainsail entirely, you further reduce the height of the rig. 3. The halyard arrangements are utterly simple. 4. The windward performance is superior to that of the standard gaff rig.

It is inexpensive to install, with its solid spars and minimal standing and running rigging. In spite of the yard, the weight aloft is not excessive. In fact, *Nova Espero*'s mainmast is only 18 feet tall, and its mizzen only 10 feet high. In Fig. 7–1 you can see that the copper chafe band on the mast is only about 8 feet above the deck, if we assume that Smith, at left, is about 6 feet tall. With one reef tucked into the main, the bottom of the yard is only 4 or 5 feet above the deck, and its peak is just barely above the main truck. While this reduces windage aloft, it also shortens the amount of leading edge of the mainsail luff when going to windward. Somewhat compensating for this, the yard is peaked so high that the head of the mainsail functioned—to a marked degree—as a luff.

Smith notes that the total sail area of the working rig (Fig. 7–3) was 200 sq. ft. but doesn't break it into components. So, with a glance at the Sail Plan for general proportions, and applying the sailor's pseudoscientific principle of "that looks about right," lets approximate them this way: Mainsail—130 sq. ft.; Jib—40 sq. ft.; Mizzen—30 sq. ft.

In addition, *Nova Espero* carried: light balloon spinnaker, small storm trysail, large storm trysail, and "tiny" storm jib. This latter and the large trysail were heavy flax; the other extra sails were of cotton canvas. Smith notes that they rarely set the large storm trysail because they considered it "to be a bit too close to the area of the reefed main to be useful as an

alternative," which echoes Allcard's sentiments about the sensible size for a Remove *Nova Espero*
storm trysail. Why carry an extra sail you won't use on a small boat when
weight and stowage space are so critical? The pleasure they experienced
when their new sails arrived is captured by Smith:

> While these alterations [the new cabin] were in progress, suitable sails
> were being cut by the best-known sailmaker in the world [presumably Rat-
> sey]. He gave much helpful advice, and many practical ideas were developed
> to make them strong enough for the punishment they were likely to receive.
> When the sails arrived, they were a sheer delight. A close examination revealed
> a masterpiece of needle-work, rope-work and wiring, and when they were
> hoisted they swelled out into a near-perfect set. They had been sent for
> colouring, anti-mildew treatment, and water-proofing. We found this process-
> ing a tremendous asset. The colouring toned down to a very lovely shade after
> a little exposure and, when we arrived at our destination, there was no trace
> of mildew. The waterproofing also proved a greater advantage than might first
> appear, for heavy, soggy sails can be difficult to handle. . . .
> The sails were made of strong Egyptian cotton with the seams on the main
> and mizzen running up and down, so that a tear in a panel would only go
> from seam to seam instead of right across the sail, as would happen with
> horizontal seams. The luff wires were stainless steel. There was only a single
> deep reef [he obviously means the mainsail only as the mizzen is too small to
> be reefed]. After all, when the wind increases a small boat can't dally with
> halfway measures. Battens hamper the rapid handling of sails, so these were
> eliminated. A high foot for the [jib] was provided to avoid the danger of the
> sail being burst by a heavy sea.
> Main and mizzen are laced to their booms.
> We kept the rigging as simple as possible with sheaves and [blocks] large
> enough for the [sheets and halyards] to slip through easily. We had the halyards
> leading [through fairleads] to jam cleats aft on the cabin-top, [so] the main
> and jib could be lowered in a matter of seconds from the cockpit—very useful
> in squalls!

The standing rigging consisted of a single jibstay to the stemhead, a pair
of shrouds on each side of the mainmast, and for the mizzen single shrouds
to port and starboard. Lanyards and deadeyes instead of turnbuckles were
chosen as cheaper and less troublesome.

The running rigging is comparably simple. The main and mizzen halyards ran over masthead sheaves to cleats at the base of each mast. The jib
halyard was rove through a single block hung from the masthead.

The sheets, too, were the simplest setup possible. Since the jib overlapped
the mast, it had to have twin jib sheets, each running through its own fairlead
on the raised deck to a jam cleat on the after end of the cabintop. (These
are visible in Fig. 7–1.) In this size boat—with this size jib—jam cleats make
sense because the strain on them is hardly great enough to cause them to
fail. And, it's vital to be able to cast off a sheet in a hurry when a gust hits
you and your boat displaces only a ton.

All we can tell about the main and mizzen sheet arrangements is what we can deduce from the Sail Plan. It's pretty evident that the mainsheet starts at the end of the boom, runs through a block on deck, then through a block on the boom—about a foot inboard of the end (to spread the load), then down to its cleat near the helm—possibly a jam cleat there, too. The mizzen sheet, which controls a mere handkerchief of a sail, appears to start at the end of the boom and run down through a swivel block on the boomkin, thence forward to its cleat—again, handy to the helmsman.

One of the cleverest ideas aboard *Nova Espero* was that every single piece of wire rigging was made the same length, thus making all of them interchangeable. In addition, they carried one extra length of the same size wire, to replace any one that broke. This idea is worth emulating by any small-boat sailor.

The alert reader will have noticed we've omitted the most unusual part of the rig—how to raise the mainsail. It's been left to last because it's the only rig of its type in the book and not very familiar to most U.S. sailors.

First, the yard is usually hoisted with one (or sometimes two) halyards. We don't know the arrangement aboard *Nova Espero* because Smith and Violet didn't describe it, perhaps because they felt English readers are completely familiar with the rig. With a small mainsail, only one "string" to pull is preferable: simpler is better.

The peak halyard is attached to the "yard" about two-thirds of the way up from its heel. Hauled aloft, the yard rises until the attachment point of the halyard comes "double-blocked" against the masthead sheave through which it runs—at which point it is virtually parallel with the mast. Now, something must hold the lower end tight against the mast or the upper end of the yard will cant to leeward on a beam reach, putting a severe strain on the middle of the luff.

We don't know how the lower end of the yard was handled aboard *Nova Espero,* but there are two methods: one, curved jaws that curl around the mast on the lower end of the yard when it's in the raised position; or, two, a second (or "throat") halyard that is attached to the lower end of the yard, runs around the mast, through a sheave in the heel of the yard, and down to its own cleat. Hauled taut when the yard is aloft, it locks the heel of the yard against the mast.

Finally, special mention is due the high praise both men gave the mizzen, for its sailing benefit in general, but more essentially as being absolutely mandatory for heaving to safely. This developed from the boat's failure to do so on its first crossing as a sloop. Apparently, the cutaway keel forward allowed the bow to be blown off to leeward more powerfully than a sea anchor lying to windward could counteract. When the Smith brothers (the crew of that first voyage) tried streaming the drogue off the stern, heavy seas broke into the cockpit and flowed into the cabin. During this voyage, Charles Violet had been experimenting with the addition of a small mizzen (to another boat) and found that, thus yawl-rigged, the boat answered all requirements. "She would weathercock head to seas and, under mizzen and foresail [jib], she would sail well without anybody at the tiller. So clearly a mizzen was needed for the new voyage."

En Route to the Azores, their rudder became detached at the lower end and became inoperative—lying athwartship and jammed against the bottom. Were it not for the use of the sea anchor with the mizzen raised—until the weather eased—they felt they might have been overwhelmed by the sea. On this occasion, the weather being so terrible, they took the bitter end of the mizzen halyard, led it forward, and cleated it down at the base of the mainmast. It served as a mizzen forestay and eased their minds about the heavy strain on the mast.

Occasionally during the crossing, just to catch up on lost sleep, they hove to under mizzen alone (without bothering to haul the jib aweather), and this system, too, kept the boat lying comfortably.

In a final remark on the mizzen, they write: "The second [voyage] has proved to our satisfaction, at least, that a mizzen is a tremendous asset."

As for their spinnaker, they used it at least seven times, so it can be considered a "regular" passage-making sail; of course, on a 20-foot yawl, it must have been quite a small spinnaker (area not given) and no real challenge to a two-man crew.

The Cabin

The isometric drawing (done by Smith) shows, even better than a Cabin Plan could, what the little yawl's interior looked like. In such a small cabin, the utterly simple layout was undoubtedly the only practical choice.

Starting from forward, there was the forepeak (with its watertight door), in which they stowed their large tins of what is labeled "sea biscuits." What happened when water got into this compartment is explained below.

Next aft, there are bunks to port and starboard, each 6'6" long, with bins beneath. Abaft these bunks, there is a countertop on each side—again with stowage beneath. The port side one is designated the galley, the starboard side the "navigation table."

Moving to the cockpit, we recall that it is flanked, fore and aft, by watertight bulkheads. That insured that any sea water that did enter could be bailed (or pumped) out by the man at the helm. I suspect that the jumble of gear at the bottom of the cockpit is more representational than actual. The same, I think, can be said of the helmsman's seat, which appears to be nothing more than a wide board running athwartships.

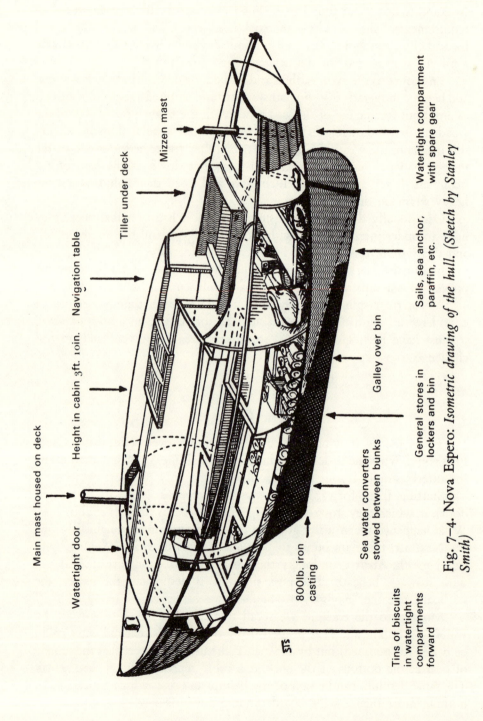

Main mast housed on deck

Watertight door

Height in cabin 3ft. 10in.

Navigation table

Tiller under deck

Mizzen mast

800lb. iron casting

Sea water converters stowed between bunks

General stores in lockers and bin

Galley over bin

Sails, sea anchor, paraffin, etc.

Watertight compartment with spare gear

Tins of biscuits in watertight compartments forward

STS

Fig. 7–4. Nova Espero: *Isometric drawing of the hull. (Sketch by Stanley Smith)*

Dead aft was the lazarette, kept watertight by a hatch that could be dogged down; in this compartment they stowed lighter gear, not often needed, to maintain the stern buoyancy.

Stores and Gear

Two men spending one hundred-plus days crossing the Atlantic adds up to considerable weight and bulk of food. Using the most commonly quoted figure of 2½ pounds of food per man, per day, they faced a payload of 500 pounds aboard *Nova Espero*—one-quarter of the entire displacement. First let's look at the variety they carried, then see how they managed weight.

Smith's isometric drawing—obviously made before departure—shows "sea biscuits" in the forepeak, whereas they actually carried Ryvita—a hard, biscuitlike "bread," not then but today widely sold in the United States. It was light and, sealed in tins up forward, insured that the bow remained buoyant—matching the loading of the stern.

The remainder of their stores were more or less "standard" for the period, though there's greater variety here than in either *Temptress* or *Cimba:* butter and peanut butter, baked beans, luncheon meat, stews, steak and kidney pudding, ham, bacon, sausage, pemmican, canned fruits and vegetables, cheese, chocolate, Marmite, porridge, dehydrated potatoes, and dried soup mixes.

At the Azores they purchased wine, a stem of bananas, two wheels of cheese, fruit preserves, and honey.

It's interesting to note that all the stores fitted into the lockers shown in the drawing, with no loose items lying about. Though small, the hull was commodious.

The real problem, of course, was water. (The daily water requirement for two men is twice the weight of food needed.) How to carry enough of it to sustain life healthfully for two men over an anticipated voyage of 100 days?

Generally, both U. S. and British sailors use the same rule of thumb: one-half gallon a day per man, for cooking, washing, and drinking. This usually allows a splash or two for washing every few days. For the Briton, that's a few gulps more to drink, as the imperial gallon is three-quarters of a pint greater than the U. S. gallon. Working with the 10-pound weight of the U. S. gallon—just because it's an easy round number—we get a requirement of 10 pounds of water per day for two men, or 1000 pounds of water for 100 days. Obviously, this is impossible in a one-ton boat already loaded with 500 pounds of food and, say, 300 pounds of crew. What to do? (Before providing the answer, a quick aside: *Nova Espero,* at her designed displacement, is basically a one-man boat for ocean crossing.

The solution was to *make* water every day. *Nova Espero* carried patented "sea water de-salting kits," produced by England's Permutit Company. The company provided enough of these kits, gratis, for the crossing. Smith describes the procedure:

> The making of fresh water from the sea was usually done in the afternoon. We would get out eight of the rubber bags, (each of) which had a filter and stoppered rubber tube at the bottom. Into each bag we would put half a pint of sea water and then add a block of four cubes. [This was the combination of chemicals developed by the Permutit scientists.] According to instructions, the bags, after being sealed at the top, should then have been occasionally shaken. We tied them in the rigging and they got all the shaking they needed. Half an hour later we pressed the finished product from each bag into a bottle. This produced half a gallon and lasted us twenty-four hours.

So, they got along on half the standard ration.

As for gear and equipment, this is another voyage for which only the skimpiest details were provided.

The port-side galley, to judge by the isometric drawing, had no sink, so we can only guess that dishes were washed in a bucket—probably out in the cockpit. The water for cooking and drinking was probably poured right out of the "collecting" bottle" as needed.

The description of the galley stove calls it a "Burmos" and, while there may be such an animal (I've been reading the English yachting magazines for years and never have seen one advertised), this brand name is another puzzler. One suspects a typographical error somewhere in the publishing process converted "Primus" to "Burmos." In any case, it burned "paraffin" (kerosene), as did the single gimbaled lamp down in the cabin. The stove was in gimbals and mounted on the after end of the cabin above the galley flat. On the subject of cooking, Smith asserts that a pressure cooker is a "must," for saving fuel, reducing cooking time, and lowering temperature in the cabin.

Galley gear was the irreducible minimum: a couple of saucepans, one frying pan, two each of plates, bowl, cups, and a knife-fork-spoon set for each—although Smith notes that they rarely used any utensil beyond a spoon, except when cutting meat. All cooking and eating gear was "washed up over the side." It's difficult to visualize any simpler approach, as befitted so small a boat with such limited space for extras.

Departing England, they both wore water- and wind-proof coveralls and wool duffle coats—and still they were cold for several days out—a repeat of Allcard's experience on departing England.

For navigation, they had a chronometer, sextant, barometer, radio receiver, charts for the Azores and a large-scale one of the Atlantic. But apparently they carried no patent or log or binoculars. Their twenty-four-hour runs apparently were calculated by measuring from one daily plot to the next and scaling off from the edge of the chart.

They set sail without an anchor (to save weight) but purchased one later in Nova Scotia—*see below*. A sea anchor figured strongly in their plans and was used constantly in the crossing. This was always used in tandem with the mizzen when they hove to. Smith described their self-designed sea anchor (which could be made by any small-boat sailor) as follows:

> The mouth of ours was 27 inches in diameter, with the canvas sewn double thickness around an iron hoop formed of [a] 5/8-inch galvanized rod [or bar]; a further double thickness of canvas was folded over the hoop and laced through eyelets in the drogue about three inches [below] the mouth. The length of the bag was 30 inches and ended in a small opening three inches in diameter. It was made in segments [presumably four pieces] with 1½-inch manila rope running down its length. (The English designate rope sizes by circumference; this one is ¾-inch manila.) The four-part bridle was also of [the same size].

In lieu of a hard dinghy—which they couldn't carry in any case—they had an inflatable one that came with short paddles that could be attached to the hands. Their medicine chest was simple but adequate: gauze bandage and the Ace type (for sprains), salve for salt-water sores, penicillin (today's various mycins were not yet developed), aspirin, sleeping tablets, "stay-awake" pills, splints, adhesive tape, vitamin pills, a laxative, and "digestive" tablets. According to Smith, they needed only the last item—from overeating!

As for an engine—inboard or outboard—there was none.

Refit and Repairs

We've covered the major structural alterations to the yawl, but there were jobs waiting to be done right up to the last minute before departure.

They still had not spliced the new, heavier galvanized wire meant to replace the original rigging—so they spent the last four days doing this and installing it. Then, just before sailing, they stepped the new mizzen mast. When they tried the new working rig, they got a shock. The arc of the main boom as it swung across caused it to hit the mizzen mast. So, they hurriedly cut four inches off the boom and reset the boom lacing and clew lashing. At Dartmouth, their official departure port, they topped up their supply of kerosene and alcohol for the stove and cabin lamp.

En route to the Azores—and still 400 miles out—their rudder came adrift at the lower end, and they were unable to steer at all. This lasted for three days while they jury-rigged a new one. First, they installed two large screw-eyes in the counter stern. This job was done with one man hanging over the stern—his head more in than out of the water—to drill the pilot holes and screw in the eyes, while the other man crouched in the cockpit and hung onto his legs to keep him from going overboard. Then, they ransacked the boat for suitable materials to build a new rudder—and finally found a mixed bag of pieces that would serve. Smith's father (a boatbuilder, remember) had been unhappy with the decision to step the mast on deck, despite the addition of the heavy plywood beam under the new raised deck. He had made a stanchion of pitch pine three feet long, three inches wide and two inches thick and insisted they take it along as an emergency mast strut, to brace the raised deck if it showed signs of flexing or cracking. Now it came into play as a new rudder post, with two locker tops forming the blade and other odd pieces nailed on as a tiller. This contraption they hung on the screw-eyes using "various shackles and nails [as] pintles."

It worked, but unfortunately not for long. Only a little over a day later, rough seas and heavy motion caused the new rudder to come adrift. (What they did next is reported in the section on Sailing Performance.)

At the port of Horta, on the island of Fayal in the Azores, *Nova Espero* was lifted out of the water by crane and placed on a dock where the regular rudder was repaired by re-welding the broken heel fitting that held the lower end of the rudder post. It's curious that they should have suffered this one gear failure, one that Allcard spoke about so firmly in his *Deep-Sea Sense* ("The rudder and the mast should never fail"), as Allcard was a special hero of Smith and Violet's for his voyage to America and return to England in *Temptress* during the three years prior to their voyage.

At Las Palmas, the sea anchor was sent off to a local sailmaker to be reinforced and resewn in several places; meanwhile, Smith and Violet scrubbed and painted the bottom and recaulked the seam between the new cabin side and the hull, which had "worked" enough on the voyage down to cause leaks.

During the entire voyage they had no failure of rigging or major problem with sail chafe because every day one of them circled the entire boat—a brief but athletic inspection tour—to check for chafe and remedy it.

Sailing Performance

In a departure from the usual format for this section, an approach chosen because this tiny yawl seems to accentuate some aspects of ocean voyaging and makes others irrelevant (particularly because it was two men in a cockleshell), let's begin with a few points stressed by both men. There are other small-boat voyages in this book, yet all but one were singlehanded; it is the second crew member who raises the specter of trouble, just as it takes two sticks rubbed together to produce the friction that causes heat and, sometimes, fire.

Personal Behavior. From the outset they understood that living in such a cramped space absolutely demanded the utmost in self-control from each.

To achieve harmony each agreed never to swear at each other—or the boat
—but no holds were barred regarding the sea around them.

Mood. For the first few days out, not yet having their sea legs—a tough acquisition in a 20-footer—and feeling faintly seasick, they "suffered a few queasy qualms of wretchedness." Some days later, when the reality of what they had undertaken really hit home, with each man facing twelve hours a day at the helm, they were taken aback. At this point, bound for the Azores, they complained, "We think that the motion—continuous, noisy and infinitely maddening since we had not yet got used to it—contributed much to our early despondency."

As the summer drew on and the Caribbean hurricane season approached, they both felt under pressure to keep *Nova Espero* sailing hard and so avoid the ultimate storm they might not survive. Their two other greatest fears were going overboard or an illness striking one of them thousands of miles from help.

This pressure was felt most strongly during the four weeks sailing *to* the Azores. As they noted at the time: "Squalls, variable winds, a succession of gales and grey skies deepen our ever-growing sense of despondency. Everything that came seemed to frustrate us: tiny accidents, the occasional bruising we got when thrown off balance by an extra-heavy sea, an extra gallon or two of spray down our backs, a broken fingernail when reefing; water in the lamp, the stubbing of a bare toe. The way we reacted to these little annoyances showed clearly that our nerves were very highly strung. There was a strong tendency to get annoyed with some little act or remark of the other man. We became terribly tired, for although off watch for . . . twelve hours in every twenty-four, much of our off-watch time was spent doing daily chores—cooking, cleaning and converting sea water." (*For an even stronger version of this malaise see chapter 8,* Felicity Ann.)

That's the dark side of conditions aboard *Nova Espero.* But there was a bright side, too:

> Yet there is a strange, though very real comfort in a little boat at sea. When the weather is bad one can imagine the sort of tasks confronting the crew on larger boats. A large spread of canvas calls for so much extra labour. Reefing is an operation on a large scale by comparison, and takes longer. When we were called from . . . a nice warm bunk to assist in reducing sail, it was usually a matter of minutes only before all was snug once more. It was nice to dash shivering below again, and leap into the warmth of blankets. Sometimes we felt so good about this that we would light the stove and make a hot drink to pass out to the poor wretch outside. For several hours after, however, there was such an unbearable light of virtue suffusing the atmosphere of the cabin that we later preferred to forego the pleasures of this saintly behavior.

Beyond the Azores, and well settled into their sea routine, their mood took a fanciful turn. In mid-July (1951) they began to develop a feeling they were not alone at sea but were accompanied by the presence—the spirit—of Joshua Slocum, a hero to them as he was to so many small-boat sailors. Smith wrote in his log: "We both feel honoured with the kindness and fatherly interest of Joshua Slocum. We draw no conclusion from this. We just feel it is so, and are grateful. We do our best to act like true seaman and be efficient because there is a very definite desire to please the Old Man and merit his interest and sympathy."

The sense of "not being alone" was a repetition of the experience shared by the two Smith brothers during *Nova Espero*'s first Atlantic crossing, and it closely parallels the almost eerie experience Slocum himself had—not mentioned in the chapter on him, incidentally—that he was accompanied by the pilot of the *Pinta,* the third ship in Columbus's fleet. This is a vast subject in itself *within* the topic of ocean cruising. The experiences of extrasensory perceptions have consumed many years of research by Dr. David Lewis, one of five entrants in the first, 1960 OSTAR race, a renowned blue-water sailor and author of several excellent cruising books. Lack of space is the censor to this fascinating aspect of ocean cruising.

An outgrowth of these experiences was a growing affection for the yawl by both men. As she carried them onward across the sea their feelings deepened:

> Whenever we discussed the little boat we did so with a strange mixture of the practical and the sentimental, in which perhaps the latter predominated. She became almost a person when she rose magnificently from trough to crest of awkward seas. She did not do so because her buoyancy was sufficient to avoid the danger of being overwhelmed; she did so because she had the spirit in her to live despite the seas. When she sailed on course without attention for several days on end she did so because she thought we needed rest, not because she had a long keel and the right shape and rig to do so. She became a personality to us and as such we treated her with similar respect. Even during the severest buffetings . . . we never swore at the boat or her antics. As we have said before, it was the sea, wind, and sky at which we directed our invective.

Indeed, there is no really adequate way to describe the empathetic relationship between skipper and boat, especially after the boat has carried the skipper safely on the sea.

Motion at Sea. This aspect of any voyage, symbiotically linked with comfort, was especially important to Smith and Violet in the tiny yawl, and they made several comments about it:

> It might be thought that an oily calm spells peace. Unfortunately, this is seldom the case at sea, for only very, very rarely is the surface *really* undisturbed. Almost always there is a certain amount of undulating activity lifting and lowering the most glassy-looking sea. Consequently, although a big ship would not be affected, a small vessel lifts and drops, rolls and pitches. The

lifting and lowering and even the pitching go almost unnoticed, but the rolling takes toll of one's nerves when there is no wind to fill the sails and stop the crashing and slamming of the gear aloft.

And again, in a gale, memories of the *sounds* that seemed to accompany motion:

How miserable and small we felt, as we watched the seas climb higher and higher and heard the restless whine of the wind in the rigging; a mournful whistle as we wallowed in a trough, rising to a scream as we breasted the summit of the sea. . . . We could hardly hear each other speak inside the cabin and the clatter of loose cans in the bilge, a reward for our lazy lack of method when taking out supplies, irritated us beyond measure.

Still later, in the same gale:

The *Nova Espero* is not bothered by such seas [forty footers]. It is the "little ones" on the big one's backs that throw her viciously in all directions. Also, the occasional breaking top buried her, often completely, under boiling "white water." Some curled over and fell sheer on us from great heights, with tremendous blows which worried us in spite of the great care we [had taken] with the structure of the cabin. Heavier blows came later, however, and examination at the end of the voyage revealed no signs of weakness anywhere.

How easy it is to overmatch a small boat in heavy weather is revealed in a comment made by Smith in a moderate gale. They were sailing with one deep reef in the main when a sudden gust knocked them down so that the man below was looking at solid green water outside the fixed portlights.

Fig. 7–5. *A sketch by Stanley Smith of the yawl in heavy weather.*

Nearing Nova Scotia on the final leg, they were sailing under spinnaker one afternoon when the pole suddenly exploded in two places at once (it was bamboo). Quickly they lowered it and just a few minutes later they took a 90-degree knockdown—and had to wrestle the mainsail down horizontally with the decks nearly vertical. For *Nova Espero* and similarly small boats, the wind forces and sea conditions described in the Beaufort Scale probably have the effect of being at least one notch higher.

Storm Tactics. Smith and Violet had a fairly standard routine they followed in deteriorating conditions: The sequence went as follows: 1) Wind rises at start of a gale; 2) Lower main, reef it and raise it again; 3) Wind increases and large waves form; 4) Lower main and hoist *small* storm trysail; 5) More wind comes and waves start breaking; 6) Lower trysail and try to sail under jib and jigger; 7) If this is impossible, lower jib and heave to under mizzen and sea anchor. One other point about that tiny mizzen: it was too small to reef, so it was left up at all times, either sailing or when lying to sea anchor.

At least ten times during the voyage the yawl was forced to heave to, with the two men jammed into their bunks trying to get some rest and the

Fig. 7–6. *Chart: The departure from England.*

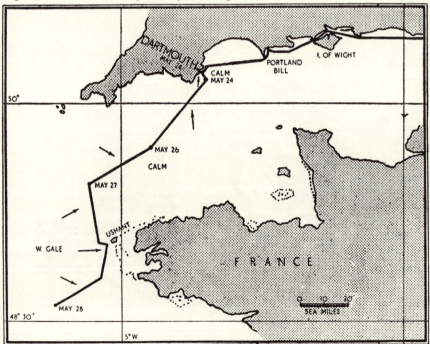

hatch closed tight against the wind and spray. Several times this happened in conditions in which even slightly larger boats could have kept sailing.

The Capsize. One June 12, the nineteenth day out from England and bound for the Azores, they were overtaken by a gale that slowly mounted in intensity and continued into June 13. On that day, as noted above, the rudder broke, and they hove to in the usual way. Lying in their bunks they discussed what they might—or could—do to solve the steering problem—as wind and wave mounted. They had to *shout* to hear each other. In Smith's words:

> Suddenly, in a weird hush, we heard a slight warning hiss high above the boat. The cabin darkened.
>
> The sequence of events during the next few moments will forever remain unknown to us. We remember only a fantastic roar and a deafening, stunning *bang*.
>
> Charles was hurled out of his bunk on the port side into the cabin roof opposite, together with the radio and a mass of loose clothing, cans and bedding.
>
> Everything went dark as night, and water seemed to fill the cabin.
>
> We remember thinking only, "This must be the end," when we found ourselves in a heap on the starboard berth.
>
> A second later, with a loud sucking noise and another tremendous *bang*, we saw light again. We watched the water fall down from the cabin roof, drenching everything. We heard it swilling about heavily from side to side. The little boat had righted and resumed the old familiar dance on the surface of the sea.
>
> Slowly we sorted ourselves out and in stupified amazement, shaking violently with shock, scrambled out into the open cockpit.
>
> We imagined everything, mast, sails, and gear, would certainly be gone, and we could hardly believe our eyes when we saw everything dripping, but in place.

As Smith and Violet reconstructed it, the breaking top of a vast wave had curled over them—causing the mometary darkness—and then carried them all the way over until the mast was pointing vertically down—or nearly so. They also had the feeling that they lay that way for several seconds in the swash of the collapsed wave, and that this caused so much water to be forced into the cabin; that if they had gone all the way around in a 360-degree circle, instead of rolling *back* along the capsizing arc, they would have been upside down a shorter time and far less water would have entered.

It's probably futile to try to draw precise conclusions—or dependable rules for avoidance—from this, our second capsize in seven boats studied. We can only note that a capsize, probably the second-most dreaded event after fire at sea, appears *not* to be the "certain death" event many of us assume it might be. Balancing this remark, however, is the reality that we usually don't learn the cause of disappearance when the occasional yacht goes missing. Ultimate disaster from capsizing *may* be higher than we think.

Steering with the Sails. After the rudder broke and was rebuilt, the second one broke, and the capsize occurred, *Nova Espero* was still 400 miles from the Azores. So once again the two men put their heads together and came up with a solution—steering by trimming the sails. They didn't describe just where the winds originated, or how they trimmed the sails, but it's certain the mizzen figured strongly in the various combinations, as it would serve as the "steerer." When they were only 130 miles out from Horta, they managed to repair the jury-rigged rudder again, and it held up for the rest of the way.

Watch System. Unlike most boat crews of two or more, Smith and Violet did not dog the watches so that each man went on duty at a constantly changing hour. Instead, they set a watch list at the start and stuck with it:

2400–0200:	Smith	1000–1400:	Smith
0200–0400:	Violet	1400–1800:	Violet
0400–0600:	Smith	1800–2000:	Smith
0600–1000:	Violet	2000–2400:	Violet

Although this arrangement gave each of them the same hours of darkness on watch every night, it did not bother either man. In fact, both men seemed to settle into the system and "although always wishing [the hours of darkness] were not so long, [we] did not find cause for complaint on this count."

Meals at Sea. In spite of the reasonably varied list of foods taken, as listed above, their meals were not of the caliber to set a gourmet salivating. In fact, this voyage, six years after World War II, shows remarkably little advancement over the menus of the previous six voyages. Here are some typical meals:

Breakfast: Porridge with sweetened (canned) milk (cooked in a mixture of sea water and Permutit water), with tea or Nescafé and two Ryvita biscuits each, spread with tinned butter and Marmite.

Lunch: Spaghetti (canned) in tomato sauce, Ryvita, and tea.

Dinner (three days running): July 8—Ham, potatoes, and carrots; July 9—Ham, potatoes, and beans; July 10—Ham, potatoes, and peas.

'Nuff said?

Speed under Sail. It's unfortunate that Smith and Violet, the latter serving as navigator, didn't provide more examples of their daily runs. With her buoyant hull and light displacement, in spite of her short waterline, *Nova Espero* would have—I believe—shown more days of over 100 nautical miles than we have in her meager record. As it is, we have only six daily runs of known mileage by which to judge.

Before listing them, let's first take a look at the yawl's basic numbers, so the reader can better see what sort of Speed/Length ratios she was achieving:

Nova Espero: Speed/Length Ratio (WL = 16′ (15′ 11″) $\sqrt{16}$ = 4.0)			
S/L $\times$	$\sqrt{\text{WL}}$ =	Speed (knots) $\times$ 24 =	NM (1 day)
1.0	4.0	4.0	96.0
1.1	4.0	4.4	105.6
1.2	4.0	4.8	115.2
1.3	4.0	5.2	124.8
1.34	4.0	5.4	128.6

Before the "official" departure, *Nova Espero* had been exhibited at a boat show in London. On the cruise from there to her departure port, Dartmouth, she reeled off one 100+-mile day along England's south coast. As we can see in the above table, that's an S/L ratio of about 1.1—not bad going. After departing, rough weather kept the two men reefing and heaving to on many of the twenty-nine days of sailing to the Azores, but one day, south of France, they did get ideal conditions. On May 24 they covered 110 miles, noon to noon. After that they had the broken rudder, etc., and not until they were beyond the Azores—July 25, 1951—did they catch a

Fig. 7–7. *Chart: Arrival at the Azores.*

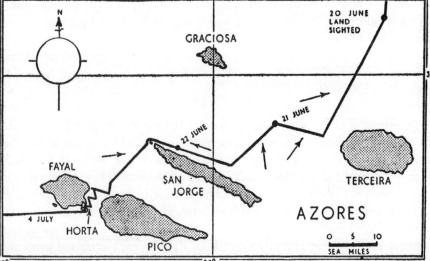

true tradewind condition and log 125 NM in twenty-four hours. That was the best day's run of the voyage and a remarkable S/L ratio of 1.3 for twenty-four hours.

At the other end of the performance scale, sailing in the doldrums—and in calms generally—produced such unimpressive figures as 12 and 50 miles on two different days, and even 56 miles in forty-eight hours! In the final stage of the voyage, nearing Nova Scotia *(see below),* the yawl ticked off two days of 78 and 110 miles. These, unfortunately, are the only daily runs we have.

Cruising Track. The hard—or unlucky—part of *Nova Espero*'s voyage was the first twenty-nine days—to the Azores. Once the broken rudder was repaired at Las Palmas—nothing else serious happened—Smith and Violet *still* felt they must divert to Nova Scotia. This decision was made halfway between Horta and New York—about 1000 miles from each. One day, sailing at a large angle of heel, one of them glanced over the side at the bottom. To his horror, he saw hundreds of goose barnacles trailing off into the water, firmly attached to the fresh anti-fouling paint—applied at Horta at a price that had shocked them. This explained their increasingly slow progress in the previous two weeks and called for another conference. On a boat with limited speed potential at best, and with at least 1000 miles to go, they now realistically faced being at sea when the hurricane season arrived. Another consideration was that they were representing the 1951 "Festival of Britain," a national promotion of post war British products (token samples of which they were carrying aboard), and they were due in New York City in time to deliver these products for the "fall season" in the large department stores. Speed—the best possible—was essential.

So they decided to divert to Nova Scotia, only 700 miles off, reasoning: "This would bring the prevailing winds on our beam and give us a faster passage for the rest of the way. . . . Once there, we could clean off the underside, recoat with anti-fouling and continue down the Gulf of Maine, through the Cape Cod Canal, Buzzards Bay [and Long Island Sound to New York]."

Cruising Track. After sailing from Dartmouth, England, to Horta, Fayal, Azores, *Nova Espero* crossed the Atlantic on about latitude 38°N. That strikes one—from previous voyages examined here—as *much* too far north, as they were well above Bermuda's latitude all the way. They did not discuss this, or the possibility that they might have made better speed further south, and thus shortened the duration although increasing the miles, had they done so. At 50°W. longitude, they turned northwest and made for Nova Scotia, arriving at Shelburne. Here they tided out for a bottom scrub and paint and bought a fisherman's anchor for the coastal sailing to follow. They coast-

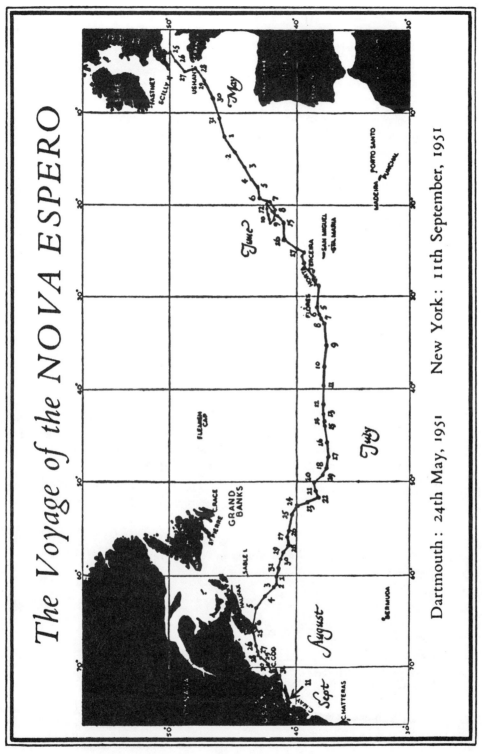

The Voyage of the NOVA ESPERO

Dartmouth: 24th May, 1951   New York: 11th September, 1951

Fig. 7–8. *Chart: Nova Espero's track across the Atlantic.*

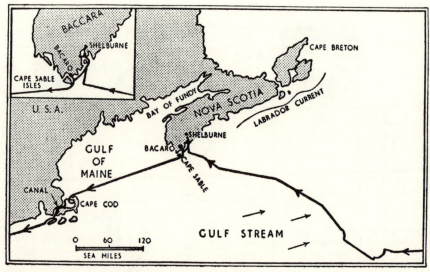

Fig. 7–9. *Chart: Northwest to Nova Scotia.*

hopped to Baccaro, N. S., and then crossed the Gulf of Maine direct to Provincetown, Mass., where they got a tow through the Cape Cod Canal. The final sail to City Island, New York, was made with overnight stops at anchor at Cuttyhunk Island, Mass., then, in Connecticut, Duck Island Roads, Guilford, Milford, Southport, the Norwalk Islands, across the sound to Lloyd's Neck Harbor on the Long Island side and, finally, arrival at City Island on September 11, 1951—110 days out of England.

Fig. 7–10. *Chart: Long Island Sound to New York City.*

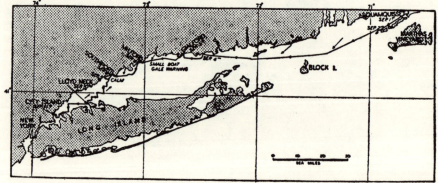

Afterthoughts

Among the cruising wrinkles the two men included in the appendices to their book, these few points bear repeating:

- Without the Permutit desalting kits they would have been unable to make the voyage—the necessary weight of water being beyond the capacity of the one-ton yawl.
- The mizzen, too, was an absolute necessity, if only for use in heavy weather; this was so despite the general rule of thumb that the smaller the boat, the less cut-up the sail plan should be.
- The sea anchor was also indispensable, as the yawl was too small (and light) to adopt any other storm tactic but the one they used—heaving to with sea anchor off the bow and mizzen raised.
- Small boats, with their slow speed, tend to mislead the navigator as regards how much the boat is being set to leeward by foul currents. Allow for more than your estimate.
- Because of the water weight saved, they were able to carry rations for two men for 120 days—stowed out of sight.
- Carry charts for land areas you will be passing; you may not plan to stop, but may have to, and making an entrance without a chart is not worth the cost to your nerves.

8. Felicity Ann

> The only way to live is to have a dream green and growing in your
> life; anything else is just existing and a waste of breath. My dreams
> don't run [along] mink coat and diamond lines—not that I have
> anything against mink coats and diamonds, but they aren't much use
> on an island or in an airplane, or on a boat, and those are the sort of
> lines my dreams run along. Adventure, some people call it, or romance,
> or when they are really frustrated, escapism. If anyone asked me and
> I was unguarded enough to reply, I would call it the pursuit of beauty
> or truth, and if I was honest I would admit it was largely curiosity,
> the urge to find out the why, the what and the how at first hand, without
> simply taking someone else's word for it.
>
> —Ann Davison
> *My Ship Is So Small* (1956)

AUTHOR'S NOTE: From the beginning, Ann Davison and her sloop *Felicity Ann* had
to be in this book. I'm sure that today, mid-1984, it would be easy to compile a
list of female seafarers who have achieved spectacularly dramatic feats at sea. That
list is now respectably long. But Ann Davison was the first woman to sail solo
across the Atlantic, and that first, it seems to me, looms higher than many other
feats that may have been more difficult, because they followed in her wake.

Beyond the general challenge of such a cruise—and we have just explored two
such efforts so we know what it is like—she had to break through the psychological
barrier that the world, and she, had serious doubts she could do it. Her feat bears
a close resemblance to other first-time-ever challenges—climbing Everest, sailing
around the world nonstop, landing on the moon. Once one woman has done it,
it becomes vastly easier for the next one.

Ann Davison

The quote that opens this chapter pretty well captures Davison's zest for
life, and aptly characterizes all her varied "adventures" up to the moment she sailed from Plymouth, England—adventures she had usually
shared with her husband, Frank.

In the mid-1930s, after becoming an airplane pilot, she met and married
another pilot, Frank Davison. As World War II approached, they became
civilian flight instructors for fledgling Royal Air Force pilots. When war
came, they rented an island in a Scottish loch and became farmers, raising
crops and animals for market and commuting to the nearest town by
motorboat.

Fig. 8–1.
Ann Davison.
(Photo courtesy
Woman's Own)

After the war, Davison's husband revealed a long-buried ambition to make a long sea voyage and suggested they buy a boat and sail around the world. Always game, Ann agreed. They acquired a 70-foot ketch named *Reliance* (with a 9-foot draft) and for the next two years they worked like slaves, spending every cent they had—and some they didn't—completely refitting her.

Then came the day they realized they were overextended financially— badly so. Their creditors were howling for payment. Unable to face the thought of losing *Reliance,* with the ketch not complete enough to command a decent selling price, and with a sheriff's writ nailed to the mast— they did something incredibly rash. In an act of desperation, they slipped out of port and simply sailed off into the Atlantic. They were bound for the Caribbean, where they hoped to complete the vessel, pay off their debts, and have something in hand for another boat.

The sea was not kind. Although they gained some offing from the Cornwall coast, a series of southwestly gales drove them relentlessly back toward the land. After nineteen days of terrible hardship, *Reliance* was driven onto the rocks of Portland Bill, the treacherous promontory off England's Dorset coast. The Davisons took to the liferaft to save themselves. Again and again the raft was capsized in the raging seas, and Frank was killed by the frigid water. Somehow Ann clung to the raft for fourteen hours, finally was swept ashore, and managed to clamber up the rocks to safety.

In time she recovered from the shock, was taken in by friends, and began to reassemble her life. To support herself, she got a job in a nearby boatyard, learning to sand, paint, varnish, scrub boat bottoms, handle tools, and move boats around. It was the typical apprenticeship in a postwar English boatyard catering to wood boats—in the years before fiber glass.

While she worked there she took up her portable typewriter and—with her considerable writing skill—turned out a book about the *Reliance* episode. When it was accepted for publication, but before it had appeared, she sat down to her typewriter again and, in another year, wrote a second book, the story of Frank's and her three years on the Scottish island.

The first book paid off the *Reliance* debts, and the royalties from the second left her with money in hand to turn the dream she had shared with Frank into reality—sailing across the Atlantic.

Fig. 8–2. *Ann Davison in Nassau, Bahamas. (Photo courtesy Nassau Newspapers)*

Her first obstacle was that she didn't know how to sail. She found a teacher at Torquay, in Devon—England's "west country"—a retired ex-Royal Navy commander named Lund. After a couple of weeks of lessons, morning and afternoon, aboard his 18-foot daysailer, during which she had literally "learned the ropes" under his patient tutelage, she confronted her second problem. Hesitantly, she informed the commander—who had taught the subject for twenty years in the Royal Navy—that she wanted to learn celestial navigation. When he asked why, she told him. With typical British aplomb—no more than a raised eyebrow—he said, "Well, in that case, what you need to know is thus and thus . . . "

Now it was sailing lessons by day and navigation exercises in the evening—convenient, as she was boarding with the commander and his wife.

Once the solo voyage plan was out of the bag, Davison was free to begin looking for a suitable boat, and Commander Lund became an enthusiastic member of her support team. One evening, when she was visiting friends in nearby Plymouth, she received a phone call from him. He told her he thought he had found the perfect boat. It lay in a boatyard just across the river from Plymouth. He urged her to take a look.

She asked its size and he told her 23 feet. "Too small," she said. "Come and see her," he urged. "She's just the ship for you. Practically new . . . diesel auxiliary. . . . " She liked that, as she had been hoping to find a boat so powered. "And the funniest thing," the commander continued. "What do you think she is called? *Felicity Ann!*"

"Oh, *no*," Davison replied. "I couldn't possibly own a ship with a name like that! Everyone will think I called it after myself." (They did, too.)

But the price was right, so she and the commander went to look her over. Davison: "As soon as I set foot on her I knew she was *right,* and that she was the ship for me. She was sympatico. She had a slightly aggressive air and the quality, distinguishable but indefinable, that spells reliability; adversity, I felt, would bring out the best in her."

A couple of weeks later, after a survey by the widely-known English sailor Humphrey Barton, the 23-foot *Felicity Ann* became hers.

The Hull

In the years before World War II, a small boatyard near Plymouth (the Cremyll Shipyard, run by the Mashford Brothers) built a series of four-ton "Thames Measurement" sloops. (This measurement, deriving from the tonnage description in chapter 6, produces a higher number than the displacement in nautical tons of 2240 pounds.) Davison reports that these small sloops were "handy, fast, and able seaboats." Just before hostilities started in 1939, a new hull was begun and planked up. Then war came, and "she was tucked away in a corner [of the boatyard] and forgotten."

In 1949, a man planning a singlehanded cruise to Norway came upon the sloop, bought her, and had her completed to his requirements. To make her suitable for canal work and passing under fixed bridges, he had her mast made hollow (the others were solid), of silver spruce, and, to facilitate raising and lowering, had it stepped in a hefty tabernacle on deck. To absorb the extra strain of this arrangement, the deck beams in the way of the mast were doubled in thickness. These were backed up, Davison reports, by "an angle-iron frame and steel knees."

This little ship was *Felicity Ann* as Davison found and bought her, with the following particulars: LOA—23'; LWL—19'; Beam—7'6"; Draft—4'6" (and 5' under full load); Displacement—not given, but approximately 6000 lbs. *(see below)*; Ballast—2000 lbs. (1700 in keel, 300 inside); Sail Area (working rig)—237 sq. ft.

The approximation of a 6000-pound displacement is, like other guesstimates in this book, based on noodling with numbers until a reasonable figure emerges. The 6000-lb. figure is based on an *assumption* that 2000 pounds

Fig. 8–3. Felicity Ann *hauled out at Fort Lauderdale, Florida. (Photo Courtesy Fort Lauderdale Daily News)*

of ballast is *about* 33 percent of total displacement. To test this number, we can consider other common Ballast/Displacement ratios for cruising boats. A B/D ratio of 25 percent is about as low as one would like to go in such a small hull, despite its heavy displacement. But any lower than 25 percent and *Felicity Ann* would not stand up to her sail area in any kind of wind. What's more, 25 percent would project a total displacement of 8000 pounds and from the beam of 7′6″ and photos of the sloop, it seems clear that she doesn't have that much heft. Choosing a B/D ratio between these two— 30 percent—would produce a total displacement of about 7100 lbs. That's possible, but she doesn't look even that heavy. Davison's remark that she was a four-tonner (Thames), suggests three tons true displacement and makes the guess of 6000 pounds sound reasonable.

In general, *Felicity Ann,* is a rather pretty—i.e., nicely proportioned— 23-foot sloop (Fig. 8–3). Only the fact that she has a canoe stern—a feature she shares with *Temptress*—will make her somewhat unusual to American eyes. Here's another of those many tradeoffs we've encountered: the reputedly more seaworthy qualities of the double-ended stern versus the loss of buoyancy, deck area, and stowage space aft. Still, for the singlehander like Davison—or Allcard—these drawbacks were of small moment.

Unfortunately, we have no plans of *Felicity Ann,* so photos must serve. Fig. 8–3 provides an excellent profile view and, with Davison standing beside her sloop, reveals *Felicity Ann*'s considerable draft, the underwater profile, the rudder shape, and the cabin proportions to the whole.

There was a heavy guard rail at the sheer line, shod with a metal rubrail —probably bronze. The bulwarks, painted a darker color, look about 5 inches high—and are rare on a boat this size. She was painted without a boottop, and it seems likely that the waterline had been raised quite a bit, since Davison noted that the draft fully loaded for sea was five feet.

The Deck

With no plan available we must turn to the photos in Figs. 8–1, 8–2, 8–4, and 8–5 for a sense of the deck. First off, the side decks seem a bit narrow—probably to give reasonably good space in the cabin—but not unduly so.

Starting in the bow (Fig. 8–5), we see a handsomely fabricated stemhead fitting, probably bronze, which provides attachment points for twin headstays and a roller for the anchor rode. A samson post completes the foredeck fittings. There may have been a chain-stop mounted on the stemhead, as *Felicity Ann* used chain for a rode; if she had a windlass, it's not visible in any of the photos.

None of the six photos included here (or any of the others in Davison's book) have any visible sign of a forward hatch—however small or hidden

Fig. 8–4. Felicity Ann *under twin-staysail rig.*

by foredeck clutter—so the main companionway must be the only entry below.

The mast is stepped just forward of the trunk, in its husky-looking tabernacle (Fig. 8–4). Overall, the foredeck comes off as a good place to work the rig or ground tackle—although several photos show a good bit of "spaghetti" lying around on it. In fairness to Davison, the pin rail at the base of the mast appears to be so low that even neatly coiled halyards could not hang from it.

Next aft is the trunk cabin, with three portholes on each side and none in the forward end. The trunk is in nice proportion to the hull, considering that almost any trunk on this small, slim hull might look bulky.

The cabin sides merge directly into the cockpit coamings, and these are even higher than the trunk sides. This was not the original design but modifications made for Davison's crossing *(see Deck, below)*. The after end of the cockpit is equally unusual. Where the three coamings meet—sides and after end—they have been given a top to form a box. This provides several benefits: 1) protection for Davison and the tiller—which passed through the box—from seas breaking aboard; 2) extra support for the permanent gallows frame; and 3) a "ready" locker for items Davison needed at the helm during the sailing day. This "box" is reminiscent of the cockpit shelter on Allcard's *Temptress* but turned end-for-end. The high coamings obviated the need for weather cloths on the lifelines. The ready locker is a fine idea—in fair weather. But if the sloop took water over the stern, everything in it would be soaked by the water sloshing through the tiller slot (Figs. 8–2, 8–4, and 8–6), inundating Davison's cigarettes, and she's smoking in three out of the seven photos.

As evident in two photos (Figs. 8–1 and 8–2), the cockpit has a bridge deck and the companionway is fitted with doors. Fig. 8–1 also shows both the *original* coaming and the new one, as well as a small mushroom vent just outboard of the cabintop grab rail—which was located over her bunk.

Whatever the merits of this deep, boxed-in cockpit—and the psychological benefits to a tyro sailor must have been considerable—the fact is that if filled by a sea, all the water from the top of the coamings down to the seat-bridgedeck level would pour down into the cabin before the scuppers could go to work. If the doors were closed, that would slow it down a bit, but it would leak below nonetheless until Davison could bail or pump it out down to seat level. In the list of modifications made *(see below)*, Barton suggested that the hatch opening be made smaller, but that was reluctantly discarded as too complicated and expensive. Perhaps drop-slides could have been added, in addition to the doors, but they were not. Doors were quite common and widely accepted as "standard" in British boats those days.

As part of the Barton modifications, a pulpit with stanchions and double lifelines was fitted. Their unusual height is quite visible (Figs. 8–3 and 8–5). They were 2½ feet high because, as Barton told Davison, "Anything less than thirty inches is useless."

Not provided in *Felicity Ann*'s original construction, but insisted upon by Barton, the cockpit was rebuilt to be "watertight and self-draining." Another Barton recommendation was the addition of a cockpit dodger, partly visible in Fig. 8-2 and quite clear in Fig. 8-6. This is the first of this now ubiquitous item we have seen. Studied closely, it seems more semipermanent than quickly convertible—as they are today. They were a rarity in 1952.

A close look at the photos in Figs. 8-2 and 8-6 reveals that the original boom crutch (see Fig. 8-3) had to be modified after the mast was shortened *(see Rig)*, obviously because it was no longer high enough to catch the boom. Instead of tearing out the old one and starting over, the boatyard simply fastened a lighter pipe frame to the after side of the original gallows frame.

To the original strengthening of the cabintop already described, Barton insisted that a pair of steel straps be added "to strengthen the coach roof." Just where they were fitted is another puzzlement. Certainly, the cabintop was not torn off so these straps could be let into the upper face of the cabintop beams, so they must have been attached to the underside of these beams, probably on a diagonal, further to distribute the compression stresses from the deck-stepped mast. If this seems like redundancy to a fault, perhaps it was, but Barton shared the view of Smith's father and was skeptical of the newfangled idea of a mast stepped on deck—still experimental in 1952. There was not much engineering data available on which to base strength requirements, so he wanted Davison to err, if at all, on the side of too strong.

Cabin

For an idea—even a vague one—of the cabin layout we must depend totally on Davison's description. She reports that it was different than the earlier sloops in the series, saying: "The cabin was very simply laid out for single-handed sailing, with a settee bunk to port, a head discreetly hidden forrard amidships, and a table-locker and galley [occupying] most of the starboard side of the cabin. There was a zinc-lined [watertight] locker under the bunk and another, unlined, under the galley. Forrard of the head was the chain locker and a wide open space for the stowage of sail bags, etc."

For the voyage, and as one of Barton's further suggestions, a twenty-five-Imperial-gallon water tank was fitted under the cockpit sole, to supplement a ten-gallon one already fitted. In addition, Davison carried two dozen one-quart aluminum bottles, which she considered her "emergency" water supply, for an all-up total of fifty-nine gallons.

Under the influence of Barton's suggestions, Davison had a field day below decks. She says, "I visualized sailbags and paint pots being flung about in an inextricable confusion without anything to restrain them, so I had lockers put in on both sides (of the hull) from the head forrard."

The Rig

Once again, not having a sail plan, we must rely on photos and Davison's remarks for the details of the rig, and trust no important item is overlooked.

Fig. 8–5. Felicity Ann *during trials, with reduced rig.*

A quick glance at the photos might suggest that *Felicity Ann* is a typical (of the day) Bermudan sloop—what Americans call a Marconi sloop. But in fact, she has a ⅞ rig in the fore-triangle. (Actually, it's between a ¾ and a ⅞, but closer to the latter.) Today, of course, we rarely see anything less than a masthead rig, except in daysailers. The age of the aluminum mast, which made the masthead rig technically simpler to achieve without really complicated rigging, still lay in the future.

The sail inventory, as described by Davison, included the following canvas sails: working main and jib and genoa, plus "a spare mainsail of very heavy canvas, a storm trysail and a storm staysail [jib]." All these were mildew- and water-proofed, and dyed blue.

Before departure, at the urging of Barton, she added twin staysails (Fig. 8-4) and all the extra stays, booms, guys, and sheets to set up and control them. These sails, too, were canvas, but not dyed. (Here we can add another bit of information from a different source, Humphrey Barton's book *Atlantic Adventurers,* published two years after Davison's voyage and now out of print. In it Barton quotes extensively from letters Davison wrote

191

him along her passage track, describing many details not included in her own book. Henceforth, this extra information will simply be noted as coming from "Barton's book.")

From Barton's book we learn that after his supervision of modifications had ended (he was a partner in the prestigious firm of J. Laurent Giles, surely one of the ranking yacht designers of all times, which had undertaken the redesign of *Felicity Ann*'s rig) and Davison was working on her own again, she had a brainstorm: she had a second storm jib cut, exactly the size of the one that came with the boat, and planned to set this pair as her "small" twin staysails, in boisterous tradewind sailing.

Barton's initial rig alterations—insisted upon for a tyro sailor on an Atlantic crossing—was to cut down the mast by no less than 6 feet, and to shorten the boom by 8 inches. These two changes, of course, required the mainsail to be recut. So, while the total working sail area of the sloop was noted above as 237 square feet, from Barton's book we learn that the area at departure was only 183 square feet. (That fact largely explains *Felicity Ann*'s slow passage. The boom was solid, of Columbian pine, and was fitted with bronze, worm-gear roller-reefing.)

Another Barton alteration was total replacement of the sloop's original standing rigging with new stainless wire of the next larger diameter—no sizes given. This was, he told Davison, mandatory for an ocean crossing with a deck-stepped mast. And although *Felicity Ann* did not have it at departure, by the time she reached the Caribbean the standing rigging was festooned with baggywrinkle.

A rig feature especially worth noting was the double sail track on the mast, one for the mainsail, the other for the storm trysail. The trysail slides could be slipped onto its track and be ready for instant hoisting upon lowering the main, thus ensuring control at all times. By keeping way on the sloop, she remained responsive to the helm. This wasn't a brand new idea in 1952, but it was probably a wise rigging choice for Davison.

Another, equally good feature was the double headstays, which allows the same quick sail change described above between the working and storm jibs. Being able to get off the foredeck quickly, especially when it's heaving like a bronco, is good for the crew's morale.

As for the arrangement of the running rigging, not yet mentioned, it is more complicated than we see on a comparable sloop today. First, there are twin headstays, balanced by the permanent backstay. Next, there are a pair of lower shrouds on each side, starting at the base of the lower spreaders and ending—well spaced fore and aft—at the deck (see Fig. 8–6). After that, a single upper shroud on each side, each beginning at the base of the upper spreaders, passing over the outboard ends of the lower spreaders and reaching the deck between the two lower shrouds (Fig. 8–4). Finally, a pair of diamond stays, one on each side, that begin at the masthead, pass over the

Fig. 8–6. *Ann Davison departing Plymouth, England. The sloop is well below her marks. (Photo courtesy A.H. Lealand)*

diamond spreaders (Fig. 8–4) and end just above the lower spreaders. This latter staying, of course, is designed to insure necessary stiffness to the top of the mast, since the "upper shrouds" don't reach to the masthead.

All the shrouds end at "rigging screws" (turnbuckles) at the deck. These, in turn, are attached to chainplates that must be internal, as there is no sign of them on the topsides in any photo.

Running Rigging. As noted earlier, the halyards, (apparently of manila, but not specified), ended at a pinrail on deck. These included two for the headsails, rove through blocks hung at the root of the diamond spreaders, and a masthead sheave for the main halyard. The topping lift looks like it is wire; it starts at the masthead and runs halfway down to the boom, where it ends in a small block; from there it is completed by a rope "tail" that is fastened to the end of the boom, runs up and is rove through this block, and runs back down to a cleat near the end of the boom, thus giving the helmsman a 2:1 advantage when adjusting the boom height. This is just barely discernible in Fig. 8–4.

As for sheets, the jib had two, each single-part, as this sail overlapped the mast. They ran down each side to a bullet block on deck—in a straight line with the jib's miter seam—and then aft to their cleats, which had been transferred to the outside of the new coamings. This is pretty clear in Fig. 8–5.

The mainsheet setup is seen most clearly in Fig. 8–2. It is the "double-ended" arrangement described in an earlier chapter. First, there is a double block hung from the end of the boom. On deck, there are three blocks, all singles: the center one is mounted on a traveler so it can slide back and forth. The other two are swivel blocks fastened to the deck to port and starboard, sited to have a fair lead to their cleats on the new coamings, which were abaft the jibsheet cleats. The sheet lead can almost be seen in its entirety in Fig. 8–2, rove as follows: from the port cleat, through the port swivel block, up through one sheave on the boom block, down through the single block on the traveler, up through the *other* sheave on the boom block, down to the starboard swivel block, thence forward to its cleat.

With the really small sail area of the rig—the original and especially the reduced one—there was no need for winches.

Engine

The diesel engine that so pleased Davison was a 5-HP Coventry-Victor, once a common name to the British and those who read English yachting magazines. The same can be said of other English engines—such as the Stuart-Turner. Today, one suspects that the Volvos, Sabbs, and Yanmars have had as much impact on the British boating market as they have upon the American, for many of the old familiar engines in both countries have disappeared.

The engine was installed under the bridge deck, with a ten-gallon fuel tank fitted under the cabin sole. In addition, Davison carried a dozen two-gallon cans of diesel oil, which were stowed around the boat—for a total of thirty-four gallons.

Let's estimate a fuel consumption of one quart per hour (quite possible on such a low HP engine). If run at half speed, producing 2.5 HP, then—using the most common formula of $\frac{1}{10}$ gallon per HP, per hour—it would burn .25 of a gallon, or one quart per hour. This would allow *Felicity Ann* to run for 136 hours. Her Speed/Length Ratio of 1.0 (modest) should produce a speed of 4.36 knots; but, as she was a full 6 inches below her designed waterline, we'll cut that back to 4.0 knots and give her an *assumed* range under power of 544 miles.

If the above fuel consumption figures seem too low, and we recalculate at one-third gallon per hour consumption for the same speed, the range would drop to 408 NM. Either way, Davison could afford to run the engine at least occasionally to power out of a flat calm in hopes of finding wind. Returning to the comment that *Felicity Ann* was overburdened, Fig. 8–6 shows just how deeply loaded she was. The sloop in this photo is under sail, but the engine is also running. *Felicity Ann* is on the starboard tack, but Davison has not shifted to the port jib sheet—a lapse attributable to the fact that this photo was taken during the excitement of her departure from Plymouth, under the eyes of many friends, the Mashford boatyard crew, the local press, and even a photographer from *Life* magazine.

Shortly before her departure, "The Coventry-Victor Co.," Davison reports, "on learning that one of their engines was bound across the ocean in [the] charge of a feather-headed female, sent post-haste their chief maintenance engineer to overhaul the engine and make sure it was correct to the last split [cotter] pin, and provided a handsome bunch of spares." In her engine's behavior, Davison was fortunate, for it performed well all the way across.

Stores and Gear

Davison took an offhanded approach to listing such things except for a few, precisely described, since her narrative stressed sailing rather than technical details. But some specific items emerge from her casual remarks.

Bilge Pump. As built, *Felicity Ann* had a bilge pump fitted into the cockpit. Davison felt one wasn't enough, saying, " . . . bilge pumps have been known to choke, and I reckoned that when you want [one] you want [it] more than anything else on earth and are not likely to count the cost." So she had another fitted, down in the cabin.

Compass. "The installation of the compass," she says, "an ex-RAF surplus grid type, gave us a bit of a headache. It had to be visible from the cockpit, out of the way, protected, but away from [ferrous] metal. It was eventually put in gimbals and screwed to a shelf in the cabin on the aft port bulkhead, through which [a window was cut so it] could be viewed from the cockpit."

Medical Kit. She took a surprisingly small stock of medical items, remarking, "Medical supplies were reduced to Dramamine, Vegamin (pain killer), benzedrine . . . bandages, common sense and a reliance upon normal good health."

Navigational Instruments. As publicity inevitably mounted about her proposed voyage—the first-woman-ever angle—unsolicited sponsorship in kind began to come her way. The Tissot Watch Company presented her with a wrist watch, presumably of very high quality; another company sent her an alarm clock; and, "an ex-Merchant Service officer," Davison reported, "himself fitting out for a round–the–world votage, sent a chronometer watch in gimbals." She doesn't mention her sextant, but we know she had one, a gadget she viewed with some suspicion. (In fact, she sailed all the way to the Canaries by dead reckoning and only took up celestial on the long run to the Caribbean.) In Las Palmas she bought a stopwatch to keep exact time for her celestial. By arrival in the Caribbean, she was an old hand at taking sights and doing the related arithmetic.

Batteries. A motor company in Plymouth sent her a supply of assorted batteries for her radio and flashlights.

Radio. We know from the above that she had a receiver, but there are no other details.

Cabin and Navigation Lights. Her running lights were on light boards affixed to the shrouds, but only Fig. 8–6 shows this. We don't know if they, and the cabin lights, were kerosene or electric (or both), because Davison doesn't say whether her engine was hand- or electric-starting.

Paint and Varnish. The British Paints Company sent her a full supply of these and remarked somewhat wistfully in their accompanying letter that they were "always doing this and no one ever got anywhere, but you never know." This time, they were rewarded by Davison's success. This was a real budget saver, as she did all her own painting and varnishing.

Food. The Heinz Company donated six dozen cans of "self-heating" soup. To heat up one of these soups, she merely had to peel off an adhesive strip from the top of the can, touch a match or cigarette end to the flammable material underneath, and, by the time it burned out, the soup was hot. (A great idea, but where are they today, when we still need them?)

As for other foods carried, we have again a maddening lack of detail. Davison notes that "the book says a person needs three pounds a day of food (for a healthy, active man leading an outdoor life)," and that she "worked out a beautifully balanced diet, proteins, carbohydrates and (other) stuff on this basis, only to discover . . . that my whole system revolted against such arbitrary regulation." All we know is that she took a variety of food, including such odds and ends as "a tin of sausage, chocolate, pepper, coffee."

At Las Palmas in the Canaries, Davison purchased citrus fruits, bananas, tomatoes, onions, fourteen pounds of potatoes, and three dozen eggs. The two really interesting items bought there were bread rusks, baked for her by a friend's cook, which Davison kept in a sealed biscuit tin to keep them fresh. The other item was *"Gofio,"* kernal corn that is first baked and then ground and can be eaten as is with milk and sugar.

Spares. From one of Davison's diatribes about the multiple details and hard work that precede an ocean voyage, and especially from her plaintive but humorous remarks about being a slave to lists (every time you cross off an item, you add two more), we do get a haphazard inventory of "things taken." Of lists, she says, "Once you buy a boat you start making lists, and as long as she, or any other boat, is in your possession, you go on making lists. I daresay once having acquired the habit, it is yours for life."

From her many lists we learn that she carried: engine spares, bo'sun's gear, paint, extra fuel, two fisherman's anchors (weights unknown), running lights (if not permanently installed, they must have been kerosene burning), rope, wire, blocks, shackles, nuts and bolts, screw eyes, cup hooks, copper tacks, cotton wool (for cleaning), batteries, radio spares (tubes?), vitamins, an extra logline, canvas for patching sails, etc.

Cruising Track

Britons have a phrase that seems perfectly to capture the art of casual cruising: "pottering about." It conveys an image of lazy, enjoyable weekends or vacation cruises, sailing tidal waters ("swatchways"), sounds and coastal waters, bound by no fixed schedule, anchoring every night in some sheltered spot, sleeping and eating aboard and taking the weather, ports, people, and sights as they come.

Ann Davison's cruise was something like that, pottering her way across the Atlantic to the Caribbean, though not of her own choosing or liking. Among the obstacles she faced were her own inexperience and a nagging doubt that "she could do it all," a certain fear of the sea, and arguably one of the worst summers on record for dependable tradewinds.

Yet she did it, despite her fears, and if courage is properly defined as bravery in the face of acknowledged fear, she was truly courageous. Her low daily averages pale into relative insignificance when set beside her accomplishment.

Here are *Felicity Ann*'s ports of call from Plymouth, England, to New York City:

Plymouth, England . . . Douarnenez, France . . . Vigo, Spain . . . Gibraltar . . . Casablanca, Morocco . . . Las Palmas, Canary Islands . . . Dominica, B.W.I. . . . Antigua . . . Nevis . . . St. Thomas . . . Nassau, Bahamas . . . Miami, Florida . . . Fort Lauderdale (mast unstepped) . . . Boynton Beach . . . Jupiter . . . Fort Pierce . . . (anchored between) Melbourne and Eau Gallie . . . Daytona . . . Marineland . . . Amelia City . . . Sea Island, Georgia . . . Beaufort, South Carolina . . . Charleston . . . Georgetown . . . Bucksport . . . (via Cape fear River to) Morehead City, North Carolina . . . Pongo River (anchored) . . . Belhaven . . . Alligator River (anchored) . . . (via Albemarle Sound to) Portsmouth, Virginia (mast restepped) . . . (offshore via Sandy Hook to) Atlantic Highlands, New Jersey . . . Bayonne . . . New York City (Coast Guard Pier 9, at the Battery). So, there she was at Pier 9, nineteen years after *Cimba*'s departure from the same spot.

Sailing Performance

Because of *Felicity Ann*'s slow crossing, with few days to analyze or extol, we'll take a different approach to this section. First a couple of general comments, summing up the voyage from England to the Canaries, with some speculations on the "why" of the slow crossing, and then, to capture the day-by-day voyage as Davison experienced it, some fragmentary notes taken from her log entries.

Coast-Hopping Southward. Following Barton's suggestions, Davison took a port-hopping route south along the French and Spanish coasts. The idea was to learn to handle the boat at sea in varied weather and still be able to duck into a port for rest or repairs when she needed them. After weathering three days of rough weather in the Channel, she had to be towed into Dournenez, France, by a French trawler because she was exhausted, the sloop was taking water, and the pumps were clogged. In all, she weathered three gales in this early period. She used her sea anchor for the first and only time —then the rode chafed through and she lost it. *Felicity Ann* was rolled onto her beam ends in one of the gales, but Davison handled the necessary sail reduction and pumping, gaining confidence with each new hazard conquered. At Vigo, Spain, she had a repair done on the upper crosstress. Whatever doubts about her ability to complete the voyage remained, her visits to Spain, Gibraltar, and Casablanca were so enjoyable that her morale batteries were charged with new enthusiasm and resolve. This was a very slow passage, but by the time Davison reached the Canaries, she had developed enough confidence that she knew she would go on.

The Slow Crossing. The reasons for this are basic and familiar in any sailing, anywhere, even daysailing in protected waters: 1) The sloop was grossly overladen, being six inches below her designed waterline; 2) The rig had been cut down drastically, from 237 to 193 square feet; 3) Davison had no deep-water experience and, in fact, had done minimal previous sailing at all; 4) The winds were fluky all the way across: Davison often complained in her log that they were "too much or too little" and that the trade winds seemed to be unusually unreliable that year.

As to the overloading, that was both unfortunate and unnecessary. It's hard to conceive that a 23-footer couldn't carry enough stores, water, and fuel for a one-person crew without being overloaded. Second, surely Barton's rig reduction was excessive, being just shy of 20 percent. Here again is one of those tradeoffs, a buffer against Davison's inexperience versus acceptable sailing performance. Arguably, the rig reduction was the main cause of the slow passage and her dangerously exhausted condition on arrival. If that's so, is there a *real* safety factor in a short-rigged boat?

Regarding Davison's inexperience, there's no question but that she was a much better sailor at the end, in both sail changing and navigation; but, she was worn down by the length of the voyage. Finally, she had atrocious luck with the trade winds that summer of 1953, as the daily mileage figures *(below)* reveal.

One point bears additional discussion: that *Felicity Ann* could have made the crossing with a lighter load. After all, *Nova Espero* did so—and the comparison is instructive. Deck gear, rig, equipment, tools, and personal possessions must have been very nearly equal on both boats—or even favored *Felicity Ann* in the ratio of load to displacement. The critical difference lay in the weight of the extra person aboard *Nova Espero,* plus the weight of his food.

It seems to break down this way: on the yawl, one extra person (150 lbs.), plus his food for 100 days ($2\frac{1}{2}$ lbs. per day $\times$ 100 = 250 lbs.) for a total of 400 lbs. (No water carried for him.) Aboard the sloop, Davison did carry water (45 gallons $\times$ 10 lbs. per gallon = 450 lbs.) and presumably 250 lbs. fewer of food. Total: only 50 lbs. more than the much smaller yawl. Yet *Felicity Ann,* at three tons, is *three times* the displacement of *Nova Espero,* or very nearly so. Or, allowing for underestimating the yawl's displacement, and overestimating the sloop's, *Felicity Ann* is easily twice that of the yawl. Take the ballast comparison: 800 lbs. for *Nova Espero* and 2000 for *Felicity Ann.* It's still a puzzler, as the heavier boat *should* have been able to carry a virtually equal load with a yawn of indifference. Whatever this may lack as a final answer, it underlines for all of us the importance of proper loading for a voyage and the effect of improper loading on sailing performance.

As for the everyday reality of the passage, we turn to Davison's log. It tells a complete and unvarnished story of *her* voyage. We pick up these fragmentary excerpts (as she did in her book) at the end of the second week out from the Canaries. (The figures in parentheses after each date are the days at sea out of Las Palmas.)

Dec. 3 (13): 0750—Up since before dawn doing odd chores. Considering having only one meal a day. Trade winds blowing quite fresh. Feeling not so good these last few days. Don't know why—eyes bothering, sore from salt and glare, and I don't think last night's crack on the head from the boom helps much. Will have to wait for this to ease down before trying to raise twin staysails. . . . 1630—One hell of a sea got up. Reefed and changed to storm jib. *FA* [as Davison calls *Felicity Ann*] carries a lot of weather helm, which makes steering very hard work. She fights all the time to turn up into the wind. . . . 1955—Hove to for night. Very tired.

Dec. 4 (14): Have been troubled since 0400 by dysentery again. Feeling lousy in consequence. No sign of wind abating either. . . . 1900—Heave to. With best will in the world cannot steer more than 12 hours at a stretch.

Dec. 5 (15): 1040—Spent since dawn setting up twin staysails. Quite a task. . . . 1140—Making only 3 knots under this rig. But it is blowing quite hard and . . . I think it is wiser to stick to these two small jibs than put up the big ones. . . . 2340—Lying to. Have utterly failed to get the twins self-steering. Must sleep. Beat.

Dec. 6 (16): Surfaced at 0645 feeling absolutely scuppered. . . . Get tired more quickly and for less effort this trip [beyond the Canaries]. . . . Getting worn down, or appalled at the enormity of the distance? If the twins won't self-steer either, this is going to be a long, slow passage. Sore throat. . . . 0815 —Big twins up. Pulling like a couple of horses . . . Blowing F.5. . . . Spent all day dickering with the twins and getting *Felicity Ann* to steer herself. Succeeded after drilling and sawing away part of the cockpit coaming so that the sheets leading from the booms did so [without friction].

Dec. 7 (17): Ship steered herself through the night and put 45 on the log. The motion is fierce, very quick and erratic [but] at last feel we are getting somewhere. . . . 1200—Took [rest of] day off and read whodunits. Feel better for rest. [With a deep draft—5′—a narrow beam—7′6″—and a heavy keel —2000 pounds—*FA* must have had a wicked motion.]

Dec. 8 (18): Surfaced at dawn to find log reading 818. This is *joy*—to have her sailing whilst I sleep. Leap out like an enthusiastic chicken farmer counting eggs. . . . 1200—Day's run, 76.

Dec. 9 (19): Surface dawn as usual. Delicious morning. F.3 winds. No cloud. Hot sun. Fixed Primus and went to town with fried potatoes and eggs. . . . Passed empty rum bottle. Who are we following? 1200—Day's run, 76.

Dec. 10 (20): 1200—Day's run, 74. 1000 just registered on log. One-third of the journey done. . . .

Dec. 11 (21): Three weeks at sea. Blew up F.7 since sunset yesterday and still blowing F.6. Very overcast and damp. Ship steering herself well, but motion wicked. . . . Day's run, 86.

Dec. 12 (22): Cooked enormous breakfast of french fries, apples, and eggs. The motion never really settles down. Takes over an hour and a half to prepare and eat breakfast, a very exhausting procedure. 1200—Day's run, 70. Hot and sunny.

Dec. 13 (23): Day's run, 70.

Dec. 14 (24): 1200—Day's run, 41. Managed to get a slight croak on the radio last night. Fading badly. Suspect battery is going to peter out. Hot, humid cabin is no storage place for dry cells. Read *Riddle of the Sands* second time on this trip and nth time since first doing so. . . . 1800—Utterly becalmed. Have taken in log line, it having grown barnacles again.

Dec. 15 (25): 0015—Lighter from SW; hardly enough to fill sails; but why *SW!* 1200—Day's run, 81. Take time off to cook sausages and peas for lunch. For which I feel better, thank you. I must eat more often.

Dec. 16 (26): Squalls all night. Continuous lightning and heavy rain. 0500—Deemed it wiser to reef and change jibs. Wind *still* SW. And more squlls to come. Very disappointing. Had to dismantle twin rig completely. . . . 0645—Under way. Filthy morning. Clouds low and black. Wind screaming. Waves hissing. Wind SW, F.8. Have no alternative but to heave to. . . . 1150—Everything eased down. . . . 1600—Here we go. More squalls. Rising seas. Now dark. Lightning all round us. Terrifying.

Dec. 17 (27): Wind went round to E this morning at 0600. But all that fearful weather . . . is coming back. Am afraid squalls would blow out those light twins if I put them up. . . . 1000—Squalls broke up and passed over without a fuss. Spend an hour getting twins up and then discover wind has gone around to SW again. Sickening. Back to old fore-and-aft. . . . 1300—Wind SW, F.2. Lumpy seas, heavy cross swells. Very tiring. Making 2 knots. . . . 1745—No wind. What did I tell you? Heave to. . . . 2100—Had just gone to sleep when awakened by shriek of wind, and found . . . ship lying right over and lightning flashing all round. Reef down on wet deck tilted at incredible angle. Wind takes your beath away like an icy plunge. Work in dark as cannot hold flashlight and hold on as well. . . . Are we every going to get back to some nice Trades?

Dec. 18 (28): Four weeks at sea and not half way. . . . 1055—Running with reefed main and storm jib. Squalls blow up to F. 8. 1700—Heave to. Tired out and gybing as unable to concentrate any longer. Arm aches and hand trembles from strain of holding tiller. Yet, a comforting thought if I do go overboard, she would luff up and wait for me.

Dec. 19 (29): Wake up after really restful sleep, cook and eat breakfast. 0950—Took out worn ends of mainsheet. Made baggywrinkle—the ocean cruiser's best friend—all morning. 1245—Have just taken a look at the bottom . . . *covered* with barnacles. This in only 4 weeks. So much for copper paint. [This makes three English boats in a row with serious fouling problems in an Atlantic crossing.] Another factor to slow us down. 2355—A most unrestful night. Twins started flogging . . . had to turn out to readjust sheets . . . colossal struggle.

Dec. 20 (30): Surface feeling pretty washed out. Log only registers 1368 and yet it was blowing smartish during the night. Only 35 [NM] since yesterday noon—19½ hours. This is serious. Bloody barnacles!

Dec. 21 (31): Squalls started again at 2200 and continued throughout with heavy rain. 0815—Just finished breakfast. Make a rule to have this before anything else, [or I] overlook eating altogether. Never feel hungry. . . . Generally, meals mean time off at expense of progress—which I begrudge. Rarely have energy to fix anything at night and would rather sleep anyway. . . . 1355—Close hauled again. . . . Rigged boom guy, which is a vast improvement to peace of mind. In these seas . . . the boom swings like a crazy pendulum, trying to demolish the gallows frame—and me if I am handy. . . . 1630—Exasperated. . . . Torrential rain. . . . Soaked to skin. . . . I am going below and it can do what it likes. Disgusted.

Dec. 22 (32): Disappointed—wind *still* SW. Cooked breakfast, made baggywrinkle. 1100—Wind pulling around to W. We are making 1 knot. Am making northward in hopes of finding the Trades. 1800—Reefed down. . . . Unnecessary, of course, but I don't want to turn out in the night to reef in a squall.

Dec. 23 (33): Fooled again. You take a chance and get a wind fit to blow the anchors off an admiral's buttons; you reef and nothing happens. Quiet night, but sleep fitful and nightmarish. . . . Suffer much from thirst these days. It is very hot and everything I do makes me sweat inordinately. The water temp. is around 80° and the boat is virtually floating in a warm bath, so the cabin is not only hot but humid. I have only to sit on the settee to have sweat running off me. . . . So I am thirsty. But water is limited. . . . 1115—Start motor. Must put a few miles on the clock. . . . 1500—making 4 knots. Blazing hot day but [no] wind. . . . 1915—Stop engine, 31 miles further on the way. Calm night; half moon; very beautiful.

Dec. 24 (34): Another quiet night, which fills me with suspicion. [Later:] Wind suddenly rushes in from SE with rain squalls. 1050—The bottom is solid with barnacles now. . . . Topping lift is going to unravel itself and there is nothing I can do but watch, it being . . . way up out of reach on the permanent backstay. By light of day I see several more strands have gone in the main halyard. . . . 1500—Back painful [which] makes the simplest task [a] most exquisite torture. . . . 1600—I have been making intensive researches into the *Ocean Passage Book;* wind charts, etc., to see where I could possibly have gone wrong, but I am no wiser. The Trade Winds *ought* to be blowing here and why they're not, God knows. They can't have read the book, which says they blow steadily from NE through SE according to the time of year, never more than 6 knots and never less than 3, and they blow 365 days a year.

Dec. 25 (35): What a Christmas! I feel acutely lonely, saddened, dispirited, desolated by a sense of absolute isolation. . . . 1925—Start motor. 1125—Stop motor. Until we run into the Trades shall run motor two hours daily. This . . . gives my morale a much-needed boost and adds some miles to the day's crawl. . . . Figure we are making point-eight knots. Heat is stupendous. . . . 1415—Start motor; so calm, can't resist. 1615—Stop motor. Really, it has been a beautiful day and my back is much better.

Dec. 26 (36): 0400—A knockdown squall struck ship. . . . 0915—Oh, what a beautiful morning—black as your hat as far as the eye can see. Thunder, lightning and no wind to speak of. 1200—No sight, no sun. 1455—Raving wind on port quarter and away we go furiously on course 308°. 1725—Heave to. Conditions superficially a little better.

Dec. 27 (37): 0630—Quiet morning. Sea calm. Wind, very light from W. 0920—Usual chores. Put up main, or rather, take out reef. . . . Put up working jib [mostly] to dry it out. 0930–1130—Run engine. Healthy following swell but no wind. 1225–1425—Run engine again, but now have only two cans of fuel, which must conserve for landfall. 1715—*FA* still ambles along . . . and I continue with my lifework—making baggywrinkle.

Dec. 28 (38): 0030—Must sleep, so heave to. 1635—Wind barely noticeable. 1815—No radio either. Tried out spare battery, but that is flat, too. Don't know that I have ever felt lower.

Dec. 29 (39): Beautiful dawn, and now at 0800, just enough movement of air to keep us going at half a knot. 1715—Sun glides down in golden splendour and another day of light wind . . . comes to an end.

Dec. 30 (40): 1200—We have sailed close-hauled all morning with a SW wind of F. 3–4. It is very, very hot. 1835—Today we have advanced at the

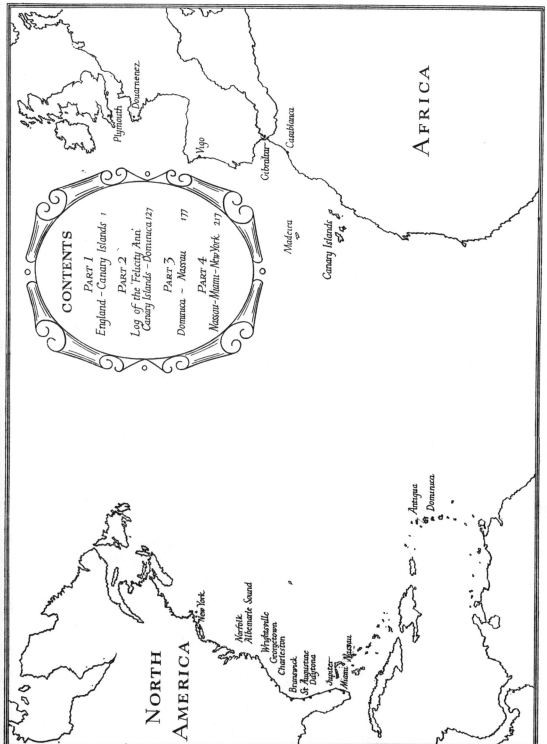

CONTENTS

AFRICA

Plymouth
Douarnenez
Vigo
Gibraltar
Casablanca
Madeira
Canary Islands

NORTH AMERICA

New York
Norfolk
Albemarle Sound
Wrightsville
Georgetown
Charleston
Brunswick
St Augustine
Daytona
Jupiter
Miami
Nassau
Antigua
Dominica

Fig. 8–7. Felicity Ann's track across the Atlantic.

rate of 1 knot. . . . Made a queer batter from 1 spoonful of *gofio* and 2 spoonsful of dried egg and ate the result with margarine and brown sugar, and liked it very much indeed. Sail until 2245, then go below to warm up. Lightning all around . . . getting increasingly nervous and restless. . . .

Dec. 31 (41): 0600—Surface reluctantly after wretched night. Although not the least bit hungry, am preparing breakfast, which is the only protection against apathy and despair. 1700—Heave to, absolutely beat. Today touched an all-time low.

Jan. 1 (42): Woke at 0600, absolutely scuppered—not having rested at all. 1800—Heave to . . . after running all day with reefed main and small jib. Seas were heavy and swells monstrous, 30 feet at best. If this is a Trade Wind it has returned very stern and forceful after a Christmas vacation. . . . Regret not being able to use this wind but too exhausted to go on.

Jan. 2 (43): 1000—After breakfast, shook out reef and put up working jib. . . . Don't know what to do about this nervousness. I feel dizzy most of the time and am at the mercy of uncontrollable emotional impulses. The least little thing can delight or distress beyond measure. . . . I have wept more in these last few days than . . . in my whole life—and for such trivial things as failing to light stove on one match.

Jan. 3 (44): Calm this morning and now at 0730 it promises to be very hot. 0830—Glassy calm. 1200—Longitude works out to 45°W. I do hope this is true. 1730—After a sweltering day . . . I am all set for one of those super squalls they do so well out here.

Jan. 4 (45): Fooled again. Quiet night. I put up the twins once more and now at 0925 we are under way. If you can call it that. . . . 1200—Wind is only F. 1. 1700—Wind still light but swell coming from N—if only it doesn't go round to NW.

Jan. 5 (46): A nice smart wind got up during the night and we bowled along until dawn, when it began to drizzle in a most English fashion and the wind abated to leave us rolling in a brisk chop. 1100—After making that entry, wind blew up again . . . a good F. 6 all morning, with F.7 in the gusts, and *FA* fairly romped along. Tiller was very stiff and I hit upon the notion of greasing the tiller slot in the aft coaming—which seemed to be the cure. 1200 —Too rough for a sight and horizon is obscured by waves.

Jan. 6 (47): Restless, anxious night as wind and seas continue high. . . . The twins [kept] having flogging bouts and I could visualize them blowing out any minute. 1200—Day's run, 87.

Jan. 7 (48): Another harassing night. Seas savage this morning. Noon— Day's run, 95. [This is the best of the voyage.]

Jan. 8 (49): Seven weeks at sea. A more restful night but maybe I am more tired—if that's possible—and care less. 0900—Have had to make a new decision regarding landfall. [I] can carry on like this and go to Barbados, or put *FA* back [under] fore and aft rig and make for Antigua as originally planned. But if I put up the main and jib again, it means steering and only half a day's progress against *Felicity Ann* steering herself for 24 hours—days on end. So Barbados it is. 1200—Day's run, 94.

Jan. 9 (50): 0850—Observed position 15–00 N., 50–08 W., which is more like it. 1200—Day's run, 94. [A sequence of respectable daily runs—and 90-plus is respectable for *Felicity Ann*—prompts a look at Davison's position on the chart, and suggests she had done three-quarters of the passage before she found any decently consistent trade winds.]

Jan. 10 (51): Don't know why the motion seems worse in the morning; maybe one has to get used to it every day. 1200—Day's run, 85. 1345—If this position is correct, we are only 420 miles from Barbados. Broached last bottle of brandy, opened last tin of cigarettes, and finished last of potatoes for breakfast. So we had better be only 420 miles from Barbados. 1615—Have painful sty on eye.

Jan. 11 (52): Wretched night. Hardly any sleep, as eye was painful and had to keep bathing it; this morning, it was a most sordid sight. Wind got up during the night, *Felicity Ann* driving like a scalded cat, and the motion was worse than ever—if that's possible. 0900—Got a fairly reasonable sight and it appears we are fairly walloping up the distance to Barbados. 1200—Day's run, 95.

Jan. 12 (53): 0350—An awful night. Awake and on watch most of the time. Squalls really bad and twins flog violently, yet every time I get set to take them in, it eases off. Two hours sleep, from 0600–0800. . . . Woke up to find *FA* running too hard. . . . She is now lying-to, without any canvas. 1200—Day's run, 92. Blowing a gale now with F.9 in gusts. Running before it under storm jib. No sign of any let-up. 1800—Pack up. Lying to quite comfortably. . . . There is nothing you can do with these top-heavy waves; if they get you, they get you. . . .

Jan. 13 (54): Slept some last night; I was dead-beat and I would have slept through atomic warfare. 0850—Breakfast almost an insuperable task, but managed pineapple juice, omelet and coffee, simple enough, but by the time I had finished I was drenched with sweat and worn out. 0950—Started running under storm jib with wind on starboard quarter. . . . 1820—Folded up for the night. . . . A new hazard: with the decks being constantly wet, the paint put on before we left is slippery as all get-out, and I cannot get a foothold on it at all. It is my fault. I should have seen that it was mixed with pumice before it was put on as I usually do, but I didn't, so now I am paying for my carelessness.

Jan. 14 (55): It blew worse than ever during the night with very bad squalls and some shocking knockdown waves. I lay on the cabin sole, jammed [in] there by a couple of sailbags, on top of the big fisherman anchor, and fretted about the compression strain on the mast. Now, morning, it's as bad as ever. I cannot bear to look at the fury of the ocean. 0840—Under way [again]. Wind F.9. Running under storm jib, jittering. *FA* lying to, 2 warps trailing astern. What it is blowing now I am in no state to judge.

Jan. 15 (56): Eight weeks at sea, the maximum time I expected to take for the crossing. Fortunately, it is much quieter this morning. 0800—Got sight which gives position approximately 175 miles from Barbados. 0945—Raked up some energy . . . and got under way. 1200—Day's run, 13. Heavy squalls. . . . 1600—Heave to on starboard tack. 1700—Heartened & encouraged by most perfect rainbow I've ever seen. . . . 2100—Here we go again, blowing hard as ever. Had to turn out & take in another reef. . . . *FA* pitching wildly. . . . Wherever we make a landfall, Hell, Hull or Halifax, it will do me.

Jan. 16 (57): 0200—Each night seems worse than the one before. . . . This is the hardest hundred miles of the voyage. 0700—Dreadful night. . . . Have just had a self-heating can of malted milk. These cans have been a godsend in bad weather. . . . 1000—Barometer rising. . . . 1315—Sky clear at last . . . heat scorching . . . but conditions eased somewhat. Tried to make griddle scones & although they turned out all right, I just couldn't eat. . . . We are advancing steadily toward Barbados. If only we can hang on. . . .

Jan. 17 (58): 0710—Awakened by a fierce squall.
I do believe we have made a landfall!

And so she had—Barbados, her goal—but she was not to anchor there for another six days! The tail end of her transatlantic passage became a nightmare. Although she had sighted Barbados, she was not close enough to enter the harbor at Bridgetown before darkness. So, she hove to for the night, only to discover in the morning that she had been driven into the Caribbean, west of the island, and now faced a hard beat to return to it. Utterly discouraged, living on coffee, vitamin pills, and benzedrene, she had to stay at the helm most of the next three nights, dodging the heavy ship traffic that swirled around the islands.

Her eyes were extremely sore from salt and sun glare (she was seeing double out of her left eye), and she was down to her last dregs of strength —and rum. Now that she had successfully crossed the ocean, she felt she now could ask for help. So, she raised the international code V flag ("I require assistance," somewhat less urgent that the full distress signal), and twice fired rockets at passing ships—but none responded. She ran out of cigarettes, winds grew heavier, and now, if possible, she concluded almost disbelievingly that the waves and motion were worse there in the Caribbean than in the ocean. On Jan. 20 (61) she wrote in her log, "Am stupid with fatigue and my thinking is warped."

She hove to once again off an island she had tentatively identified as Grenada, only to discover on Jan. 21 (62) that it was St. Lucia. By Jan. 22 (63), as a result of heaving to for food and sleep, she found that once again she had been driven west of the island. Emotionally unable to face a beat back, she now decided to carry on to her original destination, Antigua. During the six days between landfall and arrival, sea conditions were so bad that one day a wave broke over *Felicity Ann* and fell into the open hatch, soaking everything below; another day the motion was so bad that she had to make a "hasty" sea anchor out of a canvas ditty bag and ride to that for many hours—this after making oil bags, filling them with lube oil, and streaming them over the side in a vain attempt to calm the seas.

At last, on Jan. 23 (64), she passed between Martinique and Dominica, five days after first sighting land. Then, the next day, she decided that holding out for Antigua was merely being stubborn, and now, "two islands south of it," she headed for Dominica. At 0720 on Jan. 24 (65), she started the diesel and powered into Prince Rupert Bay, where she anchored off the town of Portsmouth. By early evening she had been cleared by customs. Then: "I sat in the cockpit watching the lights of the little village spring out like fireflies in the deepening dusk, and listened to the jungle chorus of humming and drumming and ringing in the green-mantled mountains, which were quickly losing their identity in the dark velvet of the tropical night. I had no desire to go ashore. . . . "

She did go, of course, the next morning. After resting for several days, and getting used to the land again, she sailed again, taking four months to work her way up the island chain *(see Cruising Track)* until she reached St. Thomas. There, she jumped off for a thirty-day ocean passage north to Nassau, Bahamas, arriving in May, 1953. From there she headed west, cleared U. S. Customs at Miami, had the mast lowered in Fort Lauderdale, and then made the 1500-mile trek up the Intracoastal Waterway. At Norfolk, Vir-

Fig. 8–8. *Ann Davison and* Felicity Ann *at the 1954 New York Boat Show.*

ginia, on the Intracoastal, she met the peripatetic Edward Allcard. Arriving at New York City, she and *Felicity Ann* were a highlight of the New York Boat Show in January 1954.

One evening during the show, when she was standing near her sloop, staring at it and recalling the cruise, two men with typical "Noo Yawk" accents stood near her, reading the sign that announced her feat and expressing disbelief that anyone would "do a crazy thing like that" in so small a boat. Then, suddenly aware of Davison standing near them, one of them turned, grinned, and said: "Don't get any ideas, honey."

The irony of that remark is the ultimate accolade for Ann Davison.

I feel there is something almost sacred about building a boat. It is a difficult thing to explain, but I have found that other boatbuilders have shared this feeling. It is almost like creating a living thing; a boat seems to have a character all her own.

—John Guzzwell
Trekka Round the World (1963)

John Guzzwell

John Guzzwell was raised on the English Channel island of Jersey, son, grandson, and great-grandson of men who made their livings from the sea. His grandfather was an owner of fishing smacks that harvested the sea for fish. His father, coming along as the Age of Steam began, elected to go to sea as an engineer aboard one of the new steam trawlers that were then, early in this century, beginning to replace the vast fleet of sailing trawlers. For a number of years, he sailed all the oceans of the world in commercial steam.

In the 1930s, married and living on the Channel island of Jersey, John Guzzwell, Sr., decided after several years ashore that it was time to take his family cruising. He had a 52-foot gaff-rigged ketch built and, with his wife and son aboard—young John was three—and an island man as crew, he sailed to South Africa and back in a cruise that consumed almost a year. Settled once again on Jersey, he found the ketch was too big for sailing local waters, so he sold it and replaced it with an 18-foot cutter named *Try Me*. It was in this boat that John Guzzwell, Jr., learned to sail. Living on an island, most of his days were spent in, on, and around the water—and boats.

"When war was declared in 1939," Guzzwell says, "it seemed for a while that peaceful Jersey would escape the maelstrom. . . . " That illusion lasted only a few weeks, and many islanders queued up to escape to England in small coasting vessels. Guzzwell's father felt these slow, unarmed boats were too vulnerable to strafing by the *Luftwaffe*. Reasoning that a small sailboat would not be an inviting target, he decided to attempt the 80-mile crossing in the family's small cutter. Three times the family sailed from the island, carrying only a few possessions, and on each attempt they were turned back by gales. Four days later, German forces landed on the island and all English citizens were interned for the duration of the war. For a time, conditions were tolerable as the Guzzwells were permitted to live in their own home. Then the German army moved a portion of the internees to a prison camp

Fig. 9–1. *John Guzzwell on his return to Victoria, B. C., Sept. 12, 1959.*
(Photo courtesy Irving Strickland, Victoria Daily, B.C. Times)

in Wurzbach, Germany. It was two and a half years before the Allied
victory in Europe won the Guzzwells their release; in that period, Guzzwell's father's health was broken, and he died in 1948. During the prison
camp years Guzzwell was taught celestial navigation by his father and began
an apprenticeship in carpentry.

After liberation, Guzzwell and his mother emigrated to South Africa, where they lived for two years, during which he completed his carpentry training. He found himself growing increasingly restless, with a deep longing to see the world. Wherever he wandered, he felt, so long as he had his box of tools, he could earn his living. With these thoughts driving him, he sailed by ship from South Africa to England.

It's difficult to imagine a more auspicious set of credentials for a young man about to set off on a cruise around the world: a youth spent around boats, an ability to sail, superior carpentry skills, a knowledge of celestial navigation, and a box of boatbuilding tools.

After spending the summer of 1952 in England, he moved again, this time to Canada, settling in Victoria, British Columbia, in March, 1953. There, he rented a room, got a job, and, to save money, did his own cooking and washing. It would not be long before he would be able to start building a small yacht.

For a design, he turned to one of the world's most respected naval architects, J. Laurent Giles & Partners. He sent off a set of requirements to the Giles office in Lymington, England. A flurry of letters flew back and forth between client and designer, and some months later a set of plans arrived. They were for the 20′6″ yawl shown in Fig. 9–2.

When built by Guzzwell, named *Trekka,* and launched and sailed around the world between July 1955 and September 1959, the yawl became the smallest boat ever to circumnavigate—until an 18-footer, *Super Shrimp* (chapter 13), replaced her in the record books.

The Hull

Trekka is not a conventional yawl—that is, with her reverse sheer and reverse transom, she certainly was not in 1953. Guzzwell's requirements to the Giles office were for a "an ocean cruiser that was strong, light, and small." It's too bad we don't have a body plan for her (as we did for *Nova Espero*) to see what similarities might exist between the two, but the profile plan shown in Fig. 9–2 certainly suggests that both yawls share a similar buoyancy of shape and that *Trekka* has good carrying capacity for her size. We can see the similarity of the two in these figures:

	LOA	LWL	Beam	Draft
Nova Espero	20′0″	16′0″	6′3″	2′10″
Trekka	20′6″	18′6″	6′6″	4′6″

If we make a few imaginary changes to *Trekka*—plumb the transom from the deck line (minus 6 inches), subtract 3 inches from the beam, and change the sheer from reverse to conventional, we have a hull very much like *Nova Espero,* at least in general shape. The displacements are close, too: *Nova Espero* (by my estimate), 1 ton and *Trekka* (from Guzzwell), 1.5 tons. The draft is the one marked difference. If we fudge a bit for convenience and call *Nova Espero*'s 3 feet (loaded), then *Trekka*'s draft is 50 percent greater, suggesting a much stiffer boat under all conditions and, with that much more lateral plane, a boat with superior windward ability.

To look at it another way, if *Nova Espero* had her 800-pound ballast keel hanging on a fin keel with a total draft of 4'6", she would certainly show an improved performance. It's a simple principle of physics that if you lengthen a lever arm, its counteractive power against the force on the other end—a sail rap-full of wind—is greatly increased. This is not to denigrate *Nova Espero*'s design characteristics, for each of which the Smith brothers had a rationale; it is merely a passing comparison. The Smiths particularly had their reasons for selecting a 2'10" draft—the ability to give with the blows of the sea in a gale. Finally, the two boats had virtually identical cabin layouts, demonstrating that not much variation is possible when working with that size, cubic volume, and shape. Despite these apparent similarities, they truly were different boats, *Trekka* being a sterling performer and reeling off, as we shall see, some really stunning daily and weekly mileages.

The keel was a ⅜-inch steel plate with two large iron castings bolted to the bottom edge (Fig. 9–2), but Guzzwell does not mention the weight of either the plate or the castings.

In underwater profile, *Trekka* had a modern shape, especially for 1953, although fin-keelers had been around for decades in small numbers. The rudder is especially interesting in light of today's many fin-keeled boats. The skeg and rudder-blade assembly were first built of steel but later changed to wood, and the rudder is balanced.

With his plans in hand, Guzzwell was ready to start building. First, he rented a 32- × 16-foot storeroom next to a fish-and-chips shop. When he discovered he would have to loft the lines, he bought a book to learn how to do that. (He made a mistake on the first try, so he had to start over, the full job taking a week.)

The first job was to laminate an oak keel, which required a temperature of at least 70 degrees for the glue to set. As the temperature of his storeroom was only 45 degrees, he got permission to do the job in the boiler room of the local YMCA. As the oak strips were already cut, this job took only twenty-four hours—a friend helping—and Guzzwell was able to carry the completed keel back to the storeroom.

The hull was designed on a bulkhead-framing system (Fig. 9–3). With these bulkheads remaining in the hull once they were set up at their appropriate stations, the longitudinal stringers and steam-bent oak frames went in next, creating an extremely strong skeletal structure. Planking followed, Guzzwell using 9/16-inch red cedar strakes, and Fig. 9–4 shows what a superb

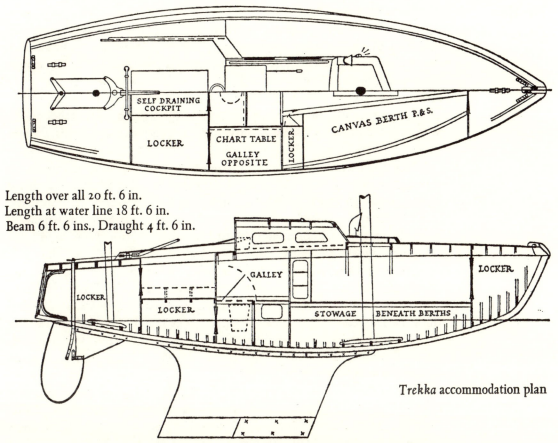

Length over all 20 ft. 6 in.
Length at water line 18 ft. 6 in.
Beam 6 ft. 6 ins., Draught 4 ft. 6 in.

Trekka accommodation plan

Fig. 9–2. Trekka: *Deck/Cabin Plans and Inboard Profile. (Photo courtesy J. Laurent Giles and Partners)*

job he did. Equally interesting is the perfect shaping job done on the oak stem, as anyone who has done wood boat construction will acknowledge.

When the hull was planked up to the turn of the bilge, Guzzwell invited a group of weight-lifters from the Y, who had expressed interest in his boat, to have a look. Once they were there, admiring his work, it was an easy matter to persuade them to lift the hull and turn it right-side up. (Beyond the humor of this little gambit, it says much about the all-up weight of *Trekka*'s hull.) Then Guzzwell finished the planking up to the sheer. Next, there were 3000 rivets to be peened over roves. For this job, Guzzwell again had the help of a friend. The insistent tap-tap-tap of the hammer for days on end did not make them popular with the restaurant patrons next door.

213

Laminated deck beams came next, followed by a ⅜-inch marine plywood deck that was glued and screwed to the deck beams. Next, the deck was fiber glassed, another job that made Guzzwell persona non grata with his next-door neighbors. They even reported a gas leak, and a serviceman arrived on an emergency call, only to track down the cause as the heady aroma of polyester resin. Up to the completion of the deck, Guzzwell had been working full time, having taken time off from his job, but now he was called back to work and only had evenings and weekends for the boat.

Nevertheless, near the end of August 1954, only nine months after lofting the lines, *Trekka* was skidded out of the door, trucked down to the harbor, lifted by crane for her keel (fabricated elsewhere) to be bolted on, and then gently plopped into the water. Through that autumn, Guzzwell built the masts and booms, and the simple cabin interior. Nine months to launching, working mostly alone, is a professional building schedule.

With the first sign of spring in 1955, the masts were stepped and Guzzwell spliced his own stainless steel standing rigging. Finally, he bent on the new suit of working sails and took *Trekka* out on trials. The first thing he learned—to his great pleasure—was that his yawl "would steer herself to windward quite easily and just as well as I could do." This was no small matter, as *Trekka* was the first of her class, and there was no book on her performance characteristics.

The profile of the hull—especially the rudder, skeg, and keel—are quite clear in Fig. 9–3. As built, *Trekka*'s specifications were: LOA—20′6″; LWL —18′6″; Beam—6′6″; Draft—4′6″; Displacement—1½ tons (3360 lbs.); Sail Area—184 sq. ft. (working rig).

The Deck

The upper plan in Fig. 9–2 shows the deck pretty well, but five features deserve mention. The first is the small size (especially narrow) of the trunk cabin, which starts abaft the mainmast. This was a rather important design decision by Laurent Giles, as a hull with a 6′6″ beam must grasp every opportunity to create the best possible foredeck for sail changing and anchor work. This space will never be luxurious on such a small hull, but the smaller trunk certainly helps. Further, the reverse sheer delivers a good percentage of the added interior cube that a raised-deck boat would provide; this is especially important, because the deck and topsides do not meet at a right angle but are joined by a slanted ramp that joins deck and topsides. This feature, probably aimed at reducing windage and the apparent topside height (note in the photos that it's painted a different color), has not yet been built in Fig. 9–4.

Fig. 9–3. Trekka: *The yawl in frame.*

Fig. 9–4. Trekka: *All planked up.*

215

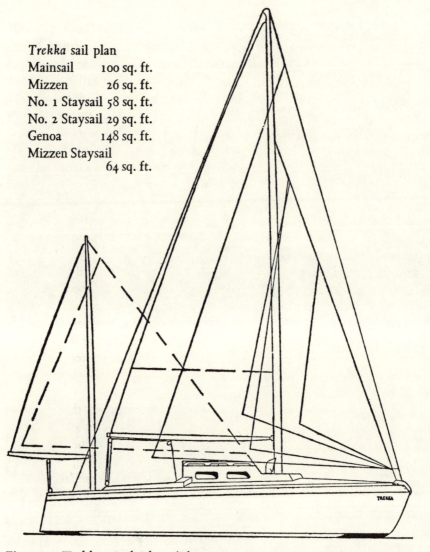

Trekka sail plan
Mainsail   100 sq. ft.
Mizzen   26 sq. ft.
No. 1 Staysail 58 sq. ft.
No. 2 Staysail 29 sq. ft.
Genoa   148 sq. ft.
Mizzen Staysail
                64 sq. ft.

Fig. 9–5. Trekka: *Sail Plan. (Photo courtesy J. Laurent Giles and Partners)*

Second, the two dorade ventilators are unusual in that they sit on a wood tunnel that stands free of the cabin, extending forward like a blunted arrowhead. If you look closely at the profile drawing in Fig. 9–2, you can trace the route of the fresh air flowing into the cabin: into the cowl vents, forward to the baffle (the scuppers that drain off water that enters are not visible but are there), then around to the centerline, where it flows down into the cabin between the two berths.

The running lights were mounted on this wood tunnel, which provided Guzzwell with a handy, watertight way to run his wires back to the battery.

Third, there is the steering arrangement. Although Guzzwell calls *Trekka* a yawl, the rudder post being abaft the mizzen, Americans would label her a ketch. (The British however, prefer to determine the ketch/yawl designation by the area of the mizzen. I believe they call it a yawl if the mizzen is less than 25 percent of the working sail area. With the mizzen mast standing between the rudder post and the only position the tiller could occupy, some method was needed to transfer tiller movement to the rudder. This was accomplished with an English development, a "Braine Gear," first used in the 1930s on model sailing boats, then later adapted successfully to cruising vessels.

Fourth, the cockpit, unlike *Nova Espero*'s, is self-bailing, the helmsman sitting on the side decks just inside the low coaming. The foot-well is quite small, to hold as little water as possible, and is sited well forward to keep the helmsman's weight where it won't affect trim.

Fifth, a special accolade is due Guzzwell for his superb building job on *Trekka*. The quote that opens this chapter reveals his feelings about building a boat. When we examine Figs. 9–1, 9–3, and 9–4, we can see how the sentiment emerges as reality. The cockpit coamings and four cabin corners reveal not only mortise-and-tenon joints but dovetail joints as well—all of them as near perfection as one can determine from a photograph. The planking job in the lower photo of Fig. 9–4 speaks for itself—joiner work executed to master carpenter standards.

The setup of the stanchions and double lifelines, and the specially fabricated stanchion bases, are clearly shown in Fig. 9–1, and are probably by the same person who custom-made the stem fitting for the jibstay.

Finally, *Trekka* had a bridge deck (about 10 inches long) for added strength amidships, and as a place to mount the steering compass.

The Rig

The first point to be made about *Trekka*'s rig is that it was designed to let the yawl achieve optimum performance for her waterline length yet maintain perfect balance among strength of individual components, least possible windage, and lightness of parts. How well reality matched that expectation will be noted later.

Masts and Booms. Masts were hollow, of silver spruce, as already noted. Guzzwell doesn't say, but the booms probably were solid and of the same wood. Fig. 9–1 shows the entire mizzen set-up: one shroud to each side, cleats for topping lift and mizzen halyard (the lowest is for the main sheet), a light line that must be a flag halyard, and the two-block sheet arrangement, giving a 2:1 advantage—plenty for a sail of only 26 square feet. *Trekka* has a three-quarter rig, the jibstay terminating at the upper spreaders.

Standing Rigging. For a mast with upper and lower spreaders, the wires that keep the mast standing are as follows: twin headstays to the bow; a masthead and lower shroud on each side; twin standing backstays to the quarters (they can been seen in Fig. 9–1); a single shroud on each side of the mizzen mast, terminating at the deck.

All turnbuckles were the open-body type, and the chainplates were bolted to the outside of the hull.

Running Backstays. Unusual, but not unheard of, *Trekka,* although marconi rigged, also had running backstays that were made taut with Highfield Levers, an English hardware item. These were (flexible) wire stays, fixed at the upper spreaders, and running down to the deck, through the fairlead blocks, then aft to the levers. For those who have not seen these in use, they are quick to employ, as the helmsman simply grabs the handle (in its forward position), flips it back and down toward the stern, and snaps it down to the deck—against pressure—for the last few inches. And that is it. To release it when engaging another one, the helmsman simply lifts it up—against pressure again—and flips it forward. When a lever is lifted, the stay thus released has enough slack so that it goes forward and cannot be hit by the boom in a gybe. Here's yet another tradeoff, the slight bother of using the levers against the really stiff mast and headstay for windward work.

Running Rigging. The jib sheets are single-part, running aft through bullseyes (on deck amidships) to cleats on the outside of the coamings, port and starboard. Note, too, in Fig. 9–6, that the genoa had its own pair of bullseyes, mounted on the sloping ramp deck described earlier.

The mainsheet is rove through two blocks, a single with becket sliding on the traveler, and a double hanging from a pivoting tang at the end of the boom. It is rove as follows: from the becket up through one sheave of the double, down through the single, back up through the other sheave in the double, and then aft to its cleat on the mizzen mast.

The mizzen sheet is so simple, and so clear in Fig. 9–1, that it doesn't need description; apparently, its cleat is mounted low on the after end of the cockpit footwell.

Sails. They were of canvas, new at departure from Victoria, and were replaced partway around the world, at New Zealand, by terylene (dacron) sails shipped out to Guzzwell from England. This made *Trekka* something of a transitional boat between the two technological eras during her circumnavigation. Note that the sail plan (Fig. 9–5) shows a single deep reef in the main, but that in fact, Guzzwell had his sailmaker put in two lines of reef points (Fig. 9–6), and that the two upper battens are quite long—almost across the entire sail. Fig. 9–6, it may be added, shows particularly well-cut sails, setting perfectly as *Trekka* creams along on a close-reach or, perhaps, a beat. Worth noting, too, is that on such a point of sailing, be it ketch or

Fig. 9–6. Trekka *under sail*—*leaving San Francisco.*

yawl, the mizzen sheet is started and its boom lies at a different angle than the main boom to the centerline; anything else is a waste of effort.

Sail track was used for mainsail and mizzen, on both masts and booms. Halyards are flexible wire with rope tails, and there are winches only for the headsail sheets (perhaps solely used for the genny), mounted on the coamings (Figs. 9–1 and 9–7).

Twin Staysail Rig. Guzzwell doesn't give the area of his twins, but in use they are hanked to separate wire stays that lead from the upper spreaders to the foredeck, landing about midway between the stem and the ventilator coaming. To get them taut, each had its own Highfield Lever, these being visible in Fig. 9–6 just abaft the foredeck cleat. The rest of this downwind rig can also be seen in Fig. 9–7, its two booms pivoting off their fittings on the band around the mast, the sheets leading aft to blocks (the port block is *just* in view), thence to the tiller to control its movement and correct the course if the boat falls off too far in either direction. No guys running forward are visible, but they must be there (hidden by the twins) because, without them, if either sail was taken aback, it would quickly slap its boom back against the forward shroud on that side. Likewise, there don't appear to be any boom lifts—probably none were needed for sails of such small area.

One of the clever wrinkles applied by Guzzwell to his twin staysail rig was flying a small spinnaker above and forward of them, using the boom ends to tack down the corners of the 'chute. By doing this, he was able to sail with just one set of twins—of modest size—and use the spinnaker during the day in good tradewinds, lowering it at night to let the yawl sail herself under just the twins in the hours of darkness. This avoided the problems that plagued Ann Davison, changing back and forth from small to large twins, and deciding which ones to leave aloft at night.

The Cabin

There's not much to say about *Trekka*'s cabin, so much does it resemble *Nova Espero*'s, except to mention its minor variations: the small shelved lockers at the head of each berth and the boxed bucket (head) at the foot of the companionway, with access through the back of the box to the stowage area beneath the cockpit. The berths, of course, are quite narrow, as they must be with a 6′6″ beam—and had only canvas for a sleeping surface, a saving of weight and cost, and probably comfortable enough for a young man.

The bow and stern lockers are carbon copies of *Nova Espero*'s. In the trunk cabin sides there were a pair of fixed windows on each side, held in place (Fig. 9–1) by metal trim that appears to be stainless steel, these in turn

Fig. 9–7. *Guzzwell in the cockpit with twin staysails set. (Photo by John Guzzwell)*

sitting atop wood moldings routed out to take the glass. (There were no ports in the forward end of the cabin.) This extra complication allowed the glass to be larger than the cabin-side cut-out, thus insuring that the glass could not be shoved inward if struck by a sea.

Engine

For power, Guzzwell bought a 4 HP (English) Seagull outboard, which was clamped onto the stern when in use and was stowed in the lazarette the rest of the time. It was only used in dead calms or for entering harbors, Guzzwell notes, so he only carried four gallons of gas, also stowed in the stern.

Stores and Gear

During the months of building *Trekka,* whenever Guzzwell went to the market for groceries, he bought a few extra cans "for the voyage." By sailing time, he had 300 of them stowed in his room. He doesn't make much of his cooking and eating arrangements, except to mention a few foods he usually had on board: hot chocolate, butter, jam, condensed milk, eggs, pancake mix, porridge, coffee, and cornflakes. None of his meals were remarkably outside the standard fare we've encountered. For cooking, Guzzwell relied on the sailor's old reliable, the single-burner Primus, and he often used a pressure cooker for the previously mentioned benefits it offered.

My comments throughout about "simple fare" are not intended as criticism—far from it. Rather, I see a linkage between galley-menu simplicity and the best-conducted cruises.

As for gear, he lists only a few items that were crammed into his rented room prior to departure, such bo'sun's items as rope, paint, extra blocks, tools, etc. He used a sleeping bag at night.

For navigation, he had a large selection of charts, a sextant "bought at a junk shop," a patent log, a radio receiver, and a small wind-speed indicator. (Later, in New Zealand, he imported a "transistor" radio (receiver) from the United States, so he spans another two areas of technology, from vacuum tubes to transistors. We can assume he had all the rest of the navigational tools—parallel rules, dividers, etc. One other item was a pressurized kerosene lantern, which he tied in the rigging when sailing at night, apparently not using the regular navigation lights at sea. There was a gimbaled kerosene lamp in the cabin.

Guzzwell did not fit a water tank in *Trekka.* Instead, he purchased a dozen "two-gallon plastic chemical bottles," which he stowed in odd corners. This arrangement worked well, for Guzzwell remarks that when he was in remote harbors with no docks, it was much easier to row his plastic bottles ashore and fill them than to ferry water back and forth with a couple of containers to fill a built-in tank.

Speaking of "ferrying," Guzzwell departed Canada without a dinghy, simply because of his early assumption that *Trekka* was too small to carry one. But when he paused for sixteen months in New Zealand to go off on another boat, he returned to *Trekka* with a different idea. Taking careful measurements, he discovered that he could just fit a 5'6" dinghy on the cabintop and built one out of ⅛-inch plywood. The clever part, the part that made the idea work, was that the dinghy's transom was removable, permitting him to slither down through the companionway hatch. He fiberglassed it for strength and to keep its seams tight in the tropical sun. And, he fitted handrails to its bottom, which served as grabrails when it was inverted on the cabin top.

Guzzwell carried two anchors; we don't know the weight of the smaller one—probably the working anchor—but the heavier one was a 27-pounder, type not given.

A Major Refit

The sixteen months away from New Zealand in the Cape Horn attempt aboard *Tzu Hang,* while *Trekka* was stored in a friend's shed in the town of Russell, gave Guzzwell other ideas for improvements, changes he felt were worth time, money, and effort for the benefits to be derived on the rest of the voyage.

Since the steel fin keel had been unbolted so the hull could be skidded into the shed, Guzzwell had the ideal conditions to fiber glass the hull, "something," he says, "I regretted not doing when she was being built." The hull was completely dry now, so it was easy. First, he removed the oak garboard strakes—which had become badly checked—and replaced them with new ones of mahogany. (He felt that the glass would adhere better to mahogany, and in this he was right, as polyester resin does not adhere well to oak, though epoxy does.) Then, with the hull canted at a 45-degree angle, he glassed each side, after first removing the paint with rotary and orbital sanders.

While he waited for the various coats of resin to dry, Guzzwell painted the cabin interior, made new cockpit coamings, and fabricated laminated oak knees to replace a set of steam-bent ones that provided the inside backing pieces for the chainplate bolts. Next, he made a new rudder of mahogany to replace the steel one, which had rusted badly. This was another saving in weight aft, directly below his position at the helm.

In the meantime—this work consumed four months—the new suit of terylene sails mentioned above arrived from England, along with the new radio from the United States. Guzzwell turned next to the spars, sanding and varnishing them with several coats.

The final job was to dig the keel out of the sand, where it had been left to inhibit rusting, clean it down to bare metal as best he could, and apply a couple of coats of "rust preventive" paint (zinc chromate), followed by two coats of anti-fouling. He gave the deck and topsides two coats of enamel: light blue for the hull, with white on the ramp and deck to keep the cabin cool in the tropical sun.

One of the last technical jobs in Russell was to attach a fitting to the yawl's tiller that made her self-steering on any point of sailing with the wind forward of the beam. This fitting allowed Guzzwell to attach the mainsheet to the tiller so that when *Trekka* wandered off course, pressure from the mainsheet made the necessary correction.

At Whangerei, Guzzwell's next-to-last stop in New Zealand—before sailing to Auckland to pick up his new sails and radio, and heading across the Tasman Sea to Australia—he bought himself new oilskins and sea boots, several more plastic bottles for water and, just before departure, fresh vegetables and bread.

At his first port in Australia, Coff's Harbor, Guzzwell had *Trekka* lifted out with a crane onto a dock and did a bottom scrub and paint job. (He repeated this job—this time tiding out while leaning against a wharf—at Thursday Island, just before heading into the Indian Ocean.)

As he entered Torres Strait, heading toward the Indian Ocean at about latitude 11° S., temperatures became horrendous—98° in the cabin and 20° higher out in the cockpit. With only twenty-four gallons of water aboard, he found himself drinking a half-gallon a day—a considerable increase over his normal consumption—and realized he would have to protect himself from the heat, despite being something of a sun worshiper. With the twin staysails steering *Trekka* and the spinnaker flying above them (to do the pulling), Guzzwell found he could set his awning on the main boom for sun protection. In addition, he doused himself with buckets of sea water several times a day.

In Durban, South Africa, after the swift Indian Ocean crossing, Guzzwell notes, *"Trekka* was in need of some attention and I spent several days repainting and varnishing until she looked more like her former self." At the local yacht club, which had made him a guest member, he made a small teak table for the cabin, which could be attached to the mast at sea and stowed away while in port.

At Cape Town, he laid in a large supply of canned goods for the passage up to the South Atlantic. Members of the yacht club gave him two six-gallon plastic jugs to supplement his water supply. Finally, he put two coats of varnish on the mast and was given a batch of charts by the club's secretary.

At Cristobal, Panama Canal Zone, Guzzwell tided out again to scrub and paint the bottom—this time it being especially important, as he faced a Pacific run to Hawaii of 5400 miles. When he reached Honolulu, the yawl was hauled out again for the same job. Since his last run rould be 2600 miles to Victoria, B.C., he also painted the topsides and deck and had a local sailmaker repair his oilskins, as he now faced both chilly and wet weather in the North Pacific.

Cruising Track

Guzzwell departed Victoria on July 10, 1955, and returned on September 12, 1959. Deducting the sixteen months in which he sailed aboard the *Tsu Hang,* his circumnavigation was completed in 34 months.

Ports of Call: San Francisco, California . . . Hilo, Hawaii . . . Fanning Island . . . Apia, Samoa . . . Vavau Island, Tonga Islands . . . Russell, New Zealand . . . Motu Arohia Island . . .Tutukaka . . . Whangarei . . . Auckland . . . Coff's Harbor, Australia . . . Trial Bay (anchored) . . . Cape Moreton (anchored) . . . Brisbane . . . (Various anchorages northward along the Great Barrier Reef—only major towns and places listed) . . . Gladstone . . . South Molle Island . . . Townsville . . . Cairns . . . Cooktown . . . Thursday Island . . . Keeling Cocos Islands (Indian Ocean) . . . Rodriguez Island . . . Mauritius Island . . . Durban, South Africa . . . Port Elizabeth . . . Plettenbergs Bay (anchored) . . . Mossel Bay (anchored) . . . Cape Town . . . Jamestown, St. Helena Island . . . Georgetown, Ascension Island . . . Bridgetown, Barbados . . . Cristobal, Canal Zone . . . Transited Panama Canal ($2.16 fee paid) . . . Balboa, Canal Zone . . . Honolulu, Hawaii . . . Becher Bay, Canada . . . Victoria, B. C.

Sailing Performance

Since Guzzwell's book, *Trekka Round the World,* is very much in print after two decades *(see Bibliography),* and the story of sailing *Trekka* is so well told by her skipper, this section will concentrate on summarizing the truly remarkable performance the yawl achieved and trying to draw some instructive conclusions.

But first, and briefly, two vital considerations: the yawl's behavior in heavy weather, and her numbers.

During trials, Guzzwell learned that his boat would steer herself reliably, hands off, when the wind was forward of the beam. This is by no means automatically true of fin-keel boats. But her heavy-weather behavior was of even greater concern, and this Guzzwell learned soon after departure from Victoria, when he encountered his first gale. As the winds increased and the waves mounted, Guzzwell lowered the jib and main, left the mizzen standing, and streamed his sea anchor.

He reports: "She lay about 75° off the wind, and had a most violent motion. This obviously was not the answer, for *Trekka* was complaining bitterly about this treatment. Finally, she decided to do something about it and broke away from her sea anchor. [Here's *that* problem again!] We immediately lay beam on the seas, and, though it may sound dangerous, she was far more comfortable." The sounds down in the cabin—where Guzzwell was jammed into his bunk—were worse than the motion, but by the time the gale blew itself out, he knew he had a viable way to manage the yawl in storms. With slight variations to meet specific conditions, this approach worked the rest of the way around the world.

Now, to *Trekka*'s numbers, with a special note: her S/L table *(below)* has been carried beyond the boat's hull speed of 1.34 to an S/L ratio of 1.5, in order to cover the speeds *Trekka* actually achieved; and, observe that *Trekka* does not reach 6 knots until she is up to a S/L of 1.4.

Here are the highlights of *Trekka*'s world cruise:

Trekka: Speed/Length Ratio			
(WL = 18′ 6″ $\sqrt{18.5}$ = 4.30			
S/L × $\sqrt{WL}$ =		Speed (knots) × 24 =	NM (1 day)
1.0	4.30	4.30	103.2
1.1	4.30	4.73	113.5
1.2	4.30	5.16	123.8
1.3	4.30	5.59	134.2
1.34	4.30	5.76	138.3
1.4	4.30	6.02	144.5
1.45	4.30	6.24	149.6
1.5	4.30	6.45	154.8

Upon departure from Victoria, it took Guzzwell thirteen days to sail south to San Francisco, as he ran into much "miserable" weather and was reluctant to push the boat too hard until he knew her better. The passage was so helter-skelter that he does not mention any daily runs.

(For cruising sailors afflicted with *mal de mer*—and who don't think it's funny—it may be some comfort to learn that Guzzwell was seasick every time he left port, usually for three days.)

En route to Hawaii, *Trekka* reeled off 95 miles on the first day out and 103 on the second (that's S/L 1.0). At the end of ten days, the yawl had covered 700 miles. In the calm of the next five days, she notched only 120 miles. The verdict still was not in. Then the wind returned, and in the next week they logged 741 miles—with a best day of 134 miles—S/L 1.3. In another day's sailing, the mountains of the islands were in sight, the twin staysails having been up for thirteen straight days.

Guzzwell and *Trekka* sailed among the islands for four months in company with the Smeetons aboard their 49-foot auxiliary, *Tzu Hang*. Then, on March 4, 1956, both vessels were off again, on an 1100-mile passage almost due south of Hawaii to Fanning Island. *Trekka* completed it in fourteen days, an average of 78.5 miles a day—not very impressive, but this run included the fluky wind systems and currents that run in bands on either side of the equator.

The next jump was to Apia, Samoa. *Trekka* took fourteen days to cover the 1200 miles, with an average of 85.7 miles—a slight improvement, though the S/L ratios for both passages were under 1.0.

Now bound for Russell, New Zealand, Guzzwell stopped to rest briefly at Vavau Island in the Tongas, sailed again, weathered his first gale in many months, and, reaching into more southern latitudes, found himself wearing his heavy wool sweater by day and sleeping under a blanket at night. One day of this passage, *Trekka* registered 120 miles—about S/L 1.15. Otherwise, he provides no details of this passage.

Now Guzzwell joined the Smeetons aboard *Tsu Hang* for the Cape Horn attempt mentioned earlier. They sailed to Australia, spent four months refitting the big ketch, and sailed east across the Pacific through the Roaring Forties until they were approaching the Chilean coast. There, *Tzu Hang* was capsized by a gigantic rogue wave that wiped the deck clean—taking both masts, the doghouse, and both skylight hatches, and leaving the hull half full of water. Their survival was a near-miracle. How they achieved it, built a jury rig, and sailed to Coronel, Chile, is told in two chapters in Guzzwell's book and in full, fascinating detail in Miles Smeeton's book, *Once Is Enough (see Bibliography)*.

Upon returning to New Zealand, Guzzwell completed the major refit to *Trekka* already described and continued his voyage westward, for the first time really committed to making his cruise a circumnavigation. After sailing to Australia, he headed north inside the Great Barrier Reef. In the final stretch of this passage, *Trekka* gave Guzzwell a striking demonstration of what she could do in strong, favorable winds. Guzzwell's words capture it best:

> Of all the sailing along the Great Barrier Reef, I remember the day's run from Lizard to Berwick Island best. The wind was blowing a steady 25 knots . . . and even without her mainsail *Diana* [a 40-foot gaff cutter sailing in company with *Trekka*] began to pull away. [*Diana*] was using two big headsails boomed out and her mizzen, while *Trekka* had her usual staysail and main up. It would have been impossible for me to set the spinnaker in these conditions by myself, but I thought that I might be able to set the masthead genoa and boom the staysail out with one of the twin booms. *Trekka* was doing six knots as it was, and I had to be quick on the foredeck to get the genoa hanked on and hoisted before she came up into the wind or gybed, but all went well, and I reached the tiller just as the sail filled. *Trekka* hesitated a brief moment, then like a racehorse that has the bit between his teeth, she bolted towards the fleeing *Diana*. In a series of fantastic surfs on the curling waves, when her speed must have gone beyond 10 knots for seconds at a time, *Trekka* tore through the water at a rate that left me gasping with excitement. I found that by throwing my weight forward at the right moment it was possible to get her surfing on practically every wave and, using these tactics, it was not long before we caught *Diana* and came up under her stern.
>
> At this moment, *Trekka* caught a wave and began to surf down the face of it . . . I was certain we were going to disappear down *Diana*'s companion-way . . . then at the last moment we sheered away, just missing her transom as we rushed past. Waiting for the right moment, I ran forward to the foredeck in the same manner surfers in Hawaii do on their large boards. This had the

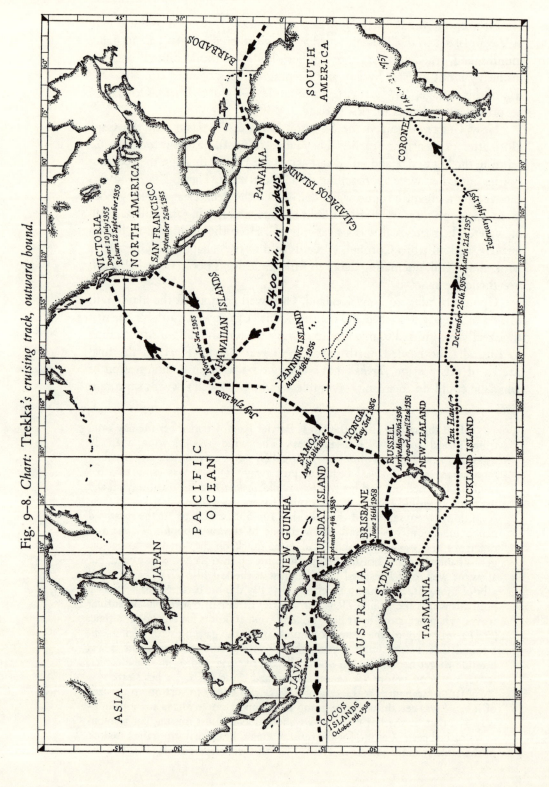

Fig. 9–8. *Chart: Trekka's cruising track, outward bound.*

BARBADOS

SOUTH AMERICA

1957

NORTH AMERICA

CORONEL (Chile)

VICTORIA
Depart 10 July 1955
Return 12 September 1959

SAN FRANCISCO
September 26th 1955

PANAMA

GALAPAGOS ISLANDS

February 14th 1957

5400 mi. in 62 days

December 26th 1956 – March 21st 1957

November 3rd 1955

HAWAIIAN ISLANDS

FANNING ISLAND
March 18th 1956

Tzu Hang →

AUCKLAND ISLAND

July 27th 1955

PACIFIC OCEAN

SAMOA
April 18th 1956

TONGA
May 3rd 1956

RUSSELL
Arrive May 30th 1956
Depart April 21st 1957

NEW ZEALAND

JAPAN

NEW GUINEA

THURSDAY ISLAND
September 4th 1958

BRISBANE
June 16th 1958

SYDNEY

ASIA

JAVA

AUSTRALIA

TASMANIA

COCOS
ISLANDS
October 9th 1958

228

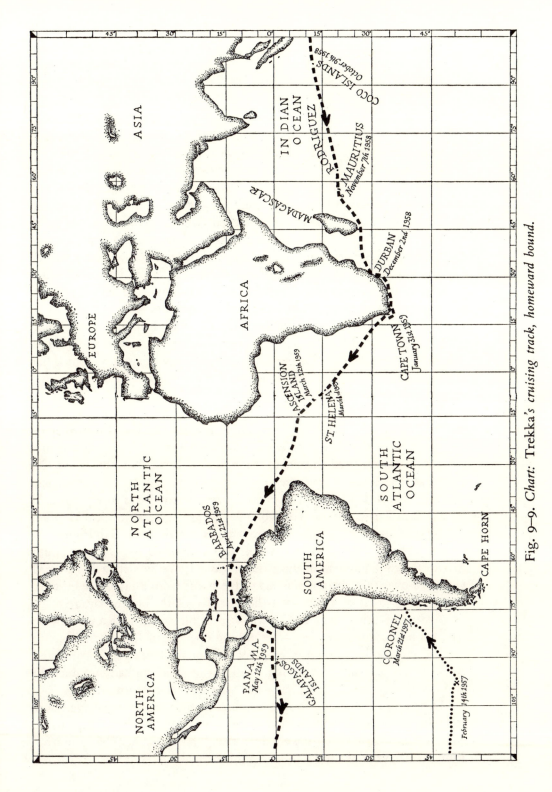

Fig. 9-9. *Chart: Trekka's cruising track, homeward bound.*

229

effect of making *Trekka* stay on a wave even longer, and soon we had left *Diana* a long way behind. At three o'clock in the afternoon, *Trekka* was anchored behind Berwick Island, having covered the 43 miles from Lizard Island at a speed of just under seven knots; this, I think, was the fastest sailing she ever did.

That speed—call it 6.9 knots—for a full day would have netted 165.6 miles, and represents a S/L ratio of better than 1.6. That's really impressive for even part of a day, but equally impressive sailing lay just ahead.

Departing Thursday Island on her eastward course across the Indian Ocean, *Trekka* was ready to show her skipper what she could really do, and for sustained periods. On the 2800-mile passage for Thursday Island to the Keeling Cocos Islands, she at once notched two consecutive daily runs of 115 miles (S/L 1.1+), following with a skein of outstanding days (S/Ls in parentheses): 98 (under 1.0), 118 (1.1+), 125 (1.2+), 133 (almost 1.3), 125 (1.2+), 120 (1.1+), 127 (1.2+). The 133-mile day added up to 146 miles with its helping current of 13 miles, but Guzzwell only counted the mileage made good *sailing* when recording his daily averages.

In that first week, *Trekka* ran 845 miles and, with helping current, made good 910 miles. What's especially impressive is nine straight days with just one under 100 miles, and that one only two miles shy. It also says something about the consistency of the southeast trades in the Indian Ocean at that time of year.

There, in what Guzzwell considered the "best ocean" for sailing, *Trekka* made the first 858 miles from the Keeling Cocos in seven days, for an average of 115 miles per day. It was on this 2000-mile run to Rodriguez Island that Guzzwell "standardized" his use of the spinnaker flying above the twins. On arrival at Rodriguez in seventeen days, seven and a half hours, the average was 111 miles a day (about 1.1). This, Guzzwell says "was surely a record for a boat of *Trekka*'s size." The worst day's run in that period was 81 miles.

Next, Guzzwell carried the government mail from Rodriguez to Mauritius Island and, after two weeks there, departed for Durban, South Africa. The high moment of this passage was a day on which *Trekka* logged 132 miles over the bottom, *plus* a 23-mile boost from a favorable current, for an all-up total of 155 miles—the best day of the entire voyage.

Between Durban and Cape Town—a difficult stretch with a worldwide reputation for rotten weather—*Trekka* had one day of 100 miles, which is not bad considering the series of gales and squalls Guzzwell encountered (which prevented him from flying a full suit of sails, and had him ducking into coastal achorages several times to wait out foul weather).

Departing Cape Town for the South Atlantic, Guzzwell averaged over 100 miles a day with the twins and spinnaker set, and of this passage to St. Helena Island, he said, Guzzwell liked that kind of passage "very much." After three days of rest and sightseeing (of particular interest was Napoleon's exile home, "Longwood"), Guzzwell was ready to sail again. He left on March 5, 1958, and reached Ascension Island on March 12—an average of about 100 a day for the 700 miles.

En route to Barbados, *Trekka* once averaged 108 miles for four straight days, and arrived at the Caribbean island, 3000 miles off, in thirty-seven days. She crossed to Cristobal, Canal Zone, in fourteen days (1200 miles). Once through the canal, at Balboa, Guzzwell faced the longest passage of the circumnavigation, both in days and in miles—to the Hawaiian Islands. After that, the last leg, from those islands to Victoria, was in the nature of a "short hop," except that it is almost invariably dominated by windward sailing.

The 5400 miles from Balboa to Hawaii took sixty-two days, and the final stretch to Victoria and home, thirty-five more, with *Trekka* arriving on September 12, 1959, the smallest boat ever to circle the globe.

Because the first part of Guzzwell's voyage, in the Pacific, was dominated by island-hopping, and the second half, across the Indian Ocean, South Atlantic, and Eastern Pacific to his home port, contained the longer and more impressive runs, it may be of interest to recapitulate *Trekka*'s cruising achievement in tabular form, from Thursday Island to Victoria:

	Days	Miles
Thursday I.—Keeling Cocos Is.	28	2800
Keeling Cocos Is.—Rodriguez I.	17½	2800
Rodriguez I.—Mauritius I.	7	700
Mauritius I.—Durban, S. Africa	20	2000
Durban—Cape Town	(incomplete figures)	
Cape Town—St. Helena I.	16	1700
St. Helena I.—Ascension I.	7	700
Ascension I.—Barbados	37	3000
Barbados—Cristobal, C. Z.	14	1200
Balboa, C. Z.—Honolulu	62	5400
Honolulu—Victoria, B. C.	35	2600
	243½	22,900

These figures produce an average of 94.4 miles day, and while a quick glance might dismiss that as unimpressive, a closer look reveals otherwise. First, the average is over a distance of virtually 23,000 miles—almost the circumference of the earth—and, second, in a boat of such modest displacement (1.5 tons) and short waterline (18'6"), sail reduction or sail changing occurs much sooner than on a boat of, say, a 25-foot waterline length, which most of us would consider small.

A wind increase of only 6 to 8 knots might very well call for corrective action by Guzzwell: While *Trekka* might be comfortable and sailing efficiently under full working rig in 16 knots of wind, at 22 to 24 knots the motion and angle of heel might easily call for a "first reef" to be rolled into the mainsail—particularly as the seas got up. Yet in the same conditions, the 25-foot waterline boat might *just* be reaching her top performance and would be bothered only marginally by the increased motion. There is certainly a difference in reaction between *Trekka* and a 25-footer to such a small increase of wind.

The shorter and smaller the boat, the luckier (with weather) the skipper must be, and the harder he must press every swift-sailing opportunity, all day, every day, to achieve maximum performance. Although *Trekka*'s 23,-000 miles netted an S/L ratio of under 1.0, her large number of 100+ mile days points to the excellence of her hull and rig design and calls for a second accolade—after the one for his building job—to be extended to Guzzwell for his sailing ability.

If someone with a computer and a penchant for playing with numbers were to program about twenty-five circumnavigations (of closely comparable length, with the data going into the computer as raw passage times), factor in the waterline length of each boat (the working LWL for those with longer-than-average overhangs), and combine these to produce a ranking based upon equalized specifications—rather than just by fastest sailing time —when the computer spit out its list, I would bet the best sextant ever made that *Trekka* would place in the top five cruising boats of all time—not counting round-the-world races, of course.

Guzzwell's Afterthoughts

Proud as he was of his splendid little vessel, Guzzwell was not blind to her shortcomings, principal of which was her cramped living accommodations. He frequently mentions the frustration of wanting to return hospitality extended to him by other crews and not being able to have more than one person aboard because of limited sitting space. Indeed, looking at the cabin plan, one wonders how he pulled on his pants in such quarters.

So it's no surprise that by the time he returned to his hailing port, Guzzwell had formed a picture of his "ideal" boat for such a cruise as he had just completed. Here are his particulars:

1) Light-displacement hull, 25- to 30-feet LOA; 2) draft, 5 feet, for efficient windward work; 3) cutter rig (here he departs from Smith-Violet in his final verdict on the yawl rig); 4) *some* standing headroom, at least in a small doghouse; 5) vane self-steering system; 6) low-horsepower diesel engine, hand-starting; 7) no electricity aboard—kerosene lamps and stove; 8) no water tank; plastic bottles for water supply; and 9) above all, simplicity throughout.

This may appear at first glance like a considerable advance over *Trekka*, but analysis reveals that Guzzwell has focused most of his "changes" on cabin comfort (space), more waterline for greater speed, a vane to reduce the tyranny of the helm, and a "more efficient" rig—also for improved performance. Otherwise, he sees all mechanical systems as simple ones or does without them—just a hand-starting diesel—and no electricity at all, anchor rigged for instant release, rig set up for maximum singlehanded efficiency, etc.

As it developed, Guzzwell married, sailed back to Hawaii with his new wife, had twin sons, sold *Trekka*, and went to England, where he built a 45-foot cutter in which the whole family returned to the South Pacific. But it is *Trekka,* the 20-foot yawl, that put John Guzzwell's name permanently into the record books, for his outstanding voyage around the world, as the smallest boat ever until 1982.

10. *Humming Bird*

One day I sat down at my desk at the oil company where I'd been working as a draughtsman for the past six years and wrote several letters. They were all to American yacht designers, enquiring what it would cost me to have designed a small ocean-going yacht, in which I hoped to cross the Atlantic to England. . . .

Before this I had looked through dozens of yachting magazines . . . in hopes of finding a suitable set of plans for the boat of my dreams; but I'd had no success. . . .

At that time I'd read almost every book on ocean cruising I could lay my hands on, by such famous men as Slocum, Gerbault, Robinson, and the present-day English singlehander, Edward Allcard—whom I was lucky enough to meet before our Atlantic crossing.

I was not rich, but in the six years which I'd spent planning for the voyage I'd managed to put aside something for the day when I'd start on the boat that was to take me away from the rat-race of everyday life: "One day I'll get out of this hum-drum existence, even if only for a short time; and my way will be by sailing an ocean in a small boat—alone, if needs be. For surely this can't be all there is to life: There must be something more, somewhere."

—Harold LaBorde
An Ocean to Ourselves (1962)

AUTHOR'S NOTE: In the end, it was not an American designer but an English naval architect who provided the plans for *Humming Bird,* which LaBorde built and sailed across the Atlantic. While there is no intention in these cruising tales to favor the home builder over the skipper who buys his or her boat, *Humming Bird* stands as a prime example of the simplicity of approach that so often flows from slimness of bankroll. If there is a hidden motive behind including her in this collection, it is to persuade the younger crew that with simplicity as a starting principle, a suitable cruising boat *is* attainable.

Harold LaBorde and Crew

At sixteen, LaBorde built his first boat, an 11-foot cat-rigged dinghy, which he named *Lark.* His second boat was a 16-foot Snipe-class sloop named *Whip,* which he raced regularly in Trinidad's local racing association events. In *Whip* he introduced his girlfriend, Kwailan, to sailing.

Then, after two seasons of sailing and racing *Whip,* LaBorde, his best friend, Buck (full name, Kelvin "Buck" Wong Chong), and a third friend joined forces and built an 18-foot Rebel-class daysailer. LaBorde had sold *Whip* to purchase the materials for the new boat—christened *Revenge* at launching.

Fig. 10–1. *Harold LaBorde.*

In a somewhat daring cruise, the three young men sailed the open sloop ninety miles from Trinidad north to Grenada, where they spent eight days sightseeing, and then sailed home—to be hailed as heroes by the local newspapers on their return. Such a success, although a limited one as LaBorde saw it, simply stirred the embers of his blue-water ambitions into a flame of desire. In Buck he felt he had someone who would join the big venture—if he could—but Kwailan was another case entirely.

She was now no longer just his girlfriend but his fiancée, and *her* dream encompassed not an ocean cruise but marriage, home, and children—four of them. If Kwailan had aborted the cruise, it would not have been the first time that, sad to relate, the woman in a man's life put the quietus on such a dream. But she was not yet his wife, and LaBorde was convinced that when she saw his finished boat, she would change her mind.

He was now in the midst of an exchange of letters across the Atlantic with an English naval architect, Philip Goode, who had agreed to design a boat to LaBorde's requirements. A few months later, when the ketch was started, Kwailan accepted a good-paying job in Venezuela. When she left Trinidad, that seemed to be the end of their romance. But, when she returned home on vacation some months later, she was staggered by the size of the hull; at the plans stage it had looked tiny to her, and she had blanched at the thought of crossing the Atlantic in a 26-footer. Ultimately she decided to sail, but only as Mrs. Harold LaBorde, and so they set the wedding date for a few weeks after her contract ended in Venezuela, by which time, LaBorde promised, the hull would be ready for a honeymoon cruise.

With Buck the situation was different. LaBorde knew Buck had been keen on the project for years, but he could not just assume Buck would— or could—go. So one day, before the final plans arrived, he put it to Buck directly, explaining that building the boat might consume all their spare

Fig. 10–2. *Kelvin Buck Wong Chong.*

Fig. 10–3. *Kwailan LaBorde. The tiller shape is clear in this photo.*

time for as much as two years, that they might encounter terrible weather in the crossing—real danger—and that Buck would have to help with costs by contributing money for his own food and for a return passage, as he, LaBorde, would be spending his last cent to get the boat built.

Buck's response was the stuff of Frank Merriwell, the classic answer from a best friend: "Harold, all my life I've wanted to do something big, something to make my children—if I ever have any—proud of me. But right now I can't say whether I can go with you. I'll certainly help you all I can with building the boat; when the time comes, we'll see."

When the time came, Buck sailed.

The Hull

The plans LaBorde received from Philip Goode revealed a transom-stern ketch, a hard-chine hull with the following dimensions: LOA—26'9"; LWL—22'0"; Beam—9'0"; Draft—4'6"; Displacement—6000 lbs.; Ballast Keel—1800 lbs. (concrete and iron); Inside Ballast—400 lbs. (approximate); Sail Area (working)—300 sq. ft.; Headroom—4'6"

On January 1, 1958, LaBorde, Buck, and Kwailan started the first job on *Humming Bird:* lofting the lines. As LaBorde was on a very tight budget, he missed no opportunity to avoid what he considered unnecessary costs. A dozen or more times during the building, he found ways to save money— but he never skimped on an item he considered vital to safety. He seems to have been guided by the motto "Extra strong is barely good enough." Beyond his approach, he was building his ship in a tropical climate, where, though rain was frequent, he could build outdoors. This he did under a shelter of tropical materials, free for the gathering, a shed erected on a rent-free site. Even today, the tropics offer many economies to the backyard builder.

To do the lofting job, LaBorde needed a sheet of heavy paper 30 by 10 feet to lay down the lines full size. He considered using ¼-inch plywood, but having no further use in the boat for that thickness, he rejected the idea. Instead, his father, who worked in a printing plant, got his son eight pieces of heavy, waterproof paper in which rolls of newsprint were delivered; LaBorde pasted them together with fish glue—and had his full-size lofting sheet for nothing. The three friends spread it out on the ballroom floor of the Port of Spain Aquatic Club, of which they were members, and, with LaBorde directing the operation—not really a mystery, as his job as a draftsman gave him an easy familiarity with blueprints: scaling off dimensions, fairing lines, etc.—laid down the lines. It was just an extra-large mechanical drawing to him. Laying down the lines took several days, then he and Buck were ready to start boatbuilding.

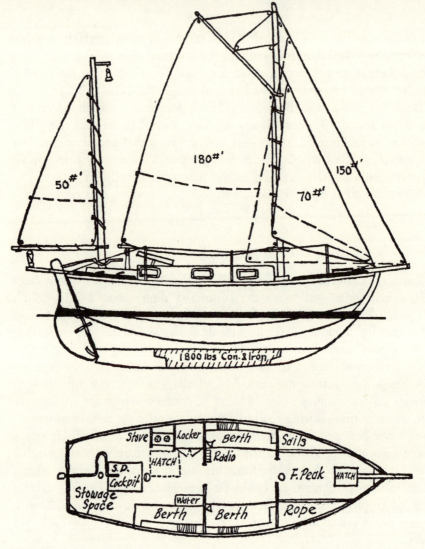

Fig. 10–4. Humming Bird: *Sail Plan and Cabin Plan. (Drawing by Harold LaBorde)*

The first job was the keelson, and LaBorde had already found, in a local lumber yard, the perfect balk of timber for that, 12 inches by 12 inches by 24 feet long. It lay at the bottom of a pile of heavy stuff, and LaBorde had to grease the palm of the foreman to have it dug out, but a week later it was delivered to the Aquatic Club. Here they would construct all the hull components until hull assembly began. During this period, work went on only evenings and weekends, as LaBorde was still at his job.

With the Keelson timber chocked up, Buck and LaBorde went at it with all their wood-cutting tools. But they made scant progress. One day a local shipwright, nicknamed Daddie, who had drifted over to watch the amateurs at work, laughed at their efforts. Annoyed, LaBorde asked what was so funny.

The man, said, as LaBorde tells it: "What happen to you young people? Can't you see you usin' de wrong tools for de job?" LaBorde asked what he meant, and Daddie replied, "Man, don't you know de firs' tool a shipwright must have is an adze? I will get mine and show yuh somet'ing'." He was back in a few minutes with a "murderous looking" weapon and gave the two young men a lesson in its use. Two days later LaBorde bought his own adz, and thereafter shaping the keelson progressed swiftly.

The next job, in February 1958, was to find the right curved piece—or pieces—for the stem. LaBorde scoured the lumberyards for a hardwood but had to settle for two curved pieces of a local wood named *cyp,* not a true hardwood but strong enough, LaBorde felt. Even after he had the lumber mill saw off both faces, it still netted 5 inches by 5 inches. He and Buck cut a scarf in each and joined the two pieces with glue and six ¼-inch galvanized carriage bolts.

During these first weeks, Kwailan frequently worked with them, but then she received the attractive job offer from nearby Venezuela, and off she went. Emotionally, it was a hard moment for LaBorde, for he now felt all his persuasion had failed to convince Kwailan to join the cruise. But, both of them apparently believing that "true love will find a way," they agreed to remain engaged.

LaBorde and Buck turned to the deadwood assembly, cutting and fitting the pieces, and then connecting them to the keelson with heavy galvanized bolts, all faying surfaces being well bedded with red lead. It was genuine, old-fashioned shipbuilding procedure.

The last job before hull assembly could begin was making the 2-inch by 4-inch pitch-pine frames. This went fairly smoothly, as the shape could be taken directly off the full-size Body Plan on the lofting sheet. They merely had to mark and cut the correct angles on the side and bottom frames and fasten them together with heavy gussets of *cyp* on both faces of the chine angle—glued and bolted. Wherever these frames were to be joined across the boat by an unbroken deck beam, they fitted it at this point. To guarantee a uniform deck curvature, LaBorde made a plywood template, scribed each deck beam, and had the curved beam cut by the sawmill—a great saving of time. When cut, these deck beams were joined to the topside frames with *cyp* gussets, also glued and bolted (Fig. 10-5).

Now they were ready to move to the building site. As it was April 1958, and summer heat was fast approaching—95 degrees was usual—LaBorde decided they and the hull needed protection from the tropical sun. He and Buck cadged some long timbers for posts from the local Bauxite Transfer Station, set them in the ground, framed out a roof, and then hired a local

Fig. 10–5. Humming Bird *in frame.*

character nicknamed Benzine (it was rumored that in the absence of rum, he would drink *that*) to cut 500 fronds from nearby coconuts palms and thatch a roof. Beyond the sun protection, it kept the rain off the boat's skeleton.

On Sunday, April 22, 1958, LaBorde and Buck started on the hull construction. One standard practice followed throughout was that every piece was liberally sloshed with creosote before it was joined to another. First, the heavy stem-piece was plumbed and squared and bolted to the keelson. Next, the horn timber, with the transom of 1-inch-thick pitch-pine already fastened to it (its shape taken off the Body Plan), was erected on the aft end of the keelson. To complete the ketch's spine they fitted the apron to the stem—the member to which the hull planking is fastened. It was made of six pieces of pitch-pine, each ½ inch thick and 8 inches wide (2½ inches wider than the stem itself.) These pieces were laminated right onto the inside of the stem with resorcinol glue and clamps, then through-bolted. The projecting edge was cut to a bevel to accept the plywood planking.

On July 30 they began the difficult job of bending in the chines. These were also of 2-inch by 4-inch pitch-pine. Once the chine "corners" were notched to accept the chines, LaBorde realized how difficult it would be to bend such heavy pieces (we recall Pidgeon's struggle with them), so he decided to have them ripped lengthwise, and laminated the chine of two

1-inch thicknesses. The amount of on-edge bending required can be visualized when we realize that when they had the first laminate lag-bolted into the stem, it extended toward the stern at such an angle that it touched the ground amidships. By the two-piece approach, they were able to force each length into its frame notch, glue it, clamp it, bolt it, and move on to the next. In all, the chines took a month to complete, and each was stronger than if put in as one piece.

The sheer clamps were next, generally the same kind of job but easier, as the on-edge bends were gentler. By this time the palm-frond roofed had dried out, and though still adequate for sun protection, it was not for rain, so they had several batches of resorcinol glue ruined by tropical showers.

During this period, April into May, LaBorde and Buck also fitted *Humming Bird* two bulkheads (Fig. 10-4, bottom), a job much easier done, of course, before the planking went on, as they could work while standing between the frames. These bulkheads, of ¾-inch pitch-pine, provided the interior structure for fitting bins, berths, bookshelves, and the galley.

Ballast Keel. Now LaBorde faced a project that had been his *bête noir* since he had begun his correspondence with Philip Goode. He had first told the designer he wanted a lead keel so he could cast it himself and save money. For this plan, he had the cost-cutting idea of extracting lead from old car batteries, and for several weeks he and Buck had scrounged around for them, buying a few but getting most of them free. LaBorde had estimated that he might get as much as twenty pounds of lead from each one. (This collection job had started even before the final plans had arrived.) At twenty pounds per battery, LaBorde knew he needed 150 batteries to reach the designed keel weight of 3000 pounds.

When they had collected about sixty batteries and had pounded them to pieces with a sledgehammer, picked out the lead, melted it in a heavy pot over a bonfire, and weighed the lump, they found that they were getting only four pounds of lead from each battery. At that rate, LaBorde calculated, he would need 750 batteries. Considerably discouraged, he wrote to Philip Goode asking for a new solution.

Goode's answer was to the point: Would they consider using a keel made of concrete and scrap-iron, if Goode designed it for them? The answer was yes, and with this they were off and running again. LaBorde knew he could buy the scrap, but as always his impulse was to see if he could get it for nothing. The answer materialized on the Port of Spain waterfront. Wandering along the commercial wharves one day, LaBorde came upon a work crew cutting the rivets off an old dredge with oxy-acetylene torches, leaving the ground littered with rivet heads. He asked the port authorities if he could have them if he gathered them and took them away. Reluctantly —more puzzled by the idea than opposed to it, even after LaBorde had explained his use of the heads—they agreed.

It was a sweaty, back-breaking job in the blazing tropical sun, and it took three days. By the time LaBorde had finished, the area was picked so clean that he had to resort to any odd fragment he could find to reach the required weight; but, he had his ballast. A friend transported it to the building site in his light truck—nearly breaking the truck's springs in the process. With 1800 pounds on hand—the original 3000 pounds had been reduced to a 2200-pound keel (1800 of scrap and 400 of concrete) and 400 additional of inside ballast—LaBorde could begin. This type of ballast keel, admittedly a poor man's special, is rarely used, even by backyard builders, but is more successful than usually given credit for in cruising circles.

They started on it in September 1958, by building a mold of "cheap, local timber," whose inside dimensions were 11 inches wide by 18 inches high by 13 feet long. The sides were strongly braced to prevent bulging when the pour was made. As LaBorde reports, "Holes had already been bored in the floors of the boat [and through the keelson and deadwood, too, of course], to accommodate seven galvanized bolts of three-quarter inch diameter." He continues, "[W]e then made a sort of basket consisting of one-half-inch diameter steel rods and chicken wire; pieces of galvanized pipe were also set in the mould [vertically] in positions exactly corresponding to those of the keel-bolt holes. The entire reinforcing basket was made one-inch smaller all round so that the iron would be well protected from rust by the shell of pure concrete."

The cement mixture (to me "concrete" suggests cement mixed with gravel, but there is no gravel in a "concrete" keel) was made by a mason nicknamed Tall Boy. The mix proportions were "three parts stone dust [not sand] to one part cement, mixed with water to a stiff paste." When the mix was ready, the three men began to fill the mold: first a layer of the mix, then a layer of rivets, with all three of them pounding the mold box with heavy hammers to drive out air and prevent large air spaces from forming bubbles, and so on until the box was filled. The final layer was cement, smoothed off with trowels. At the end of the day, they wet down the top and covered the whole thing with wet burlap bags. (A month later, when they broke off the mold box, they found a perfectly smooth ballast keel, ready for painting.)

With the help of friends, then, they maneuvered the new keel under the keelson, using levers to raise it, end by end, and sliding blocks of wood under it until it was snug against the keelson. Then they drove well-greased galvanized bolts up through the ballast, the deadwood, keelson, and floors, where the nuts were tightened over large washers—a job completed in one long day of work.

Finally, they were ready to plank the hull. Although Goode had designed it with developable surfaces so it could be planked with plywood, he had recommended carvel planking. However, LaBorde, still thinking of

Kwailan off in Venezuela, and hoping to change her mind, felt the completed hull would be a powerful persuasion and chose the plywood option, which would go on faster. For this he decided the best was the only sensible choice, and he purchased high-quality marine plywood. He was convinced that this would not ultimately cost more than carvel planking—pitch-pine being locally available at modest prices—because the time and money saved by avoiding the extra fastenings and the caulking of the carvel planking would make the two options about equally expensive. The bottom was to be ¾-inch plywood and the topsides ½-inch. With *Humming Bird*'s frames only 18 inches center-to-center, he visualized an extremely rigid hull.

For this job, which LaBorde felt was beyond the ability of himself and Buck working alone, he hired a young boatbuilder named Reynold Saxon —a wise decision, as it turned out. They started on the topsides first. As each piece of plywood was marked, cut, and fitted, they fastened it to the frames with resorcinol glue and a special type of galvanized nail with spiral rings that rotated as it was hammered in and held like a screw. As each piece of plywood went onto the frame, Reynold planed a chisel edge on both faying surfaces, slathered each face with glue, nailed on the new one, then backed the joint with a glued-and-nailed butt block.

Although this may appear a rather rudimentary building technique, when we consider the closely spaced frames and deck beams and all parts being glued and nailed, the hull actually was extremely strong and rigid, with few seams to cause trouble. It's still a good approach for a backyard builder, especially if the hull bottom is fiber glassed for water-tightness up to the LWL, to provide teredo protection in tropical waters. A boat like *Humming Bird* might last, with proper maintenance; if built with marine plywood, twenty-five years.

When the topsides were complete, the work crew turned to construction of the cabin trunk, framing in the cockpit and planking the decks—these latter being plywood and fitted with a thick layer of paint between them and the deck beams. Of these relatively few plywood joints in the entire hull, none leaked except one small pesky spot behind a frame up in the forepeak area. This was maddening to LaBorde on the cruise but was kept up with by daily pumping.

On December 13, 1958, LaBorde jotted in his Work Log: "Have finished deck, cockpit and cabin top to date and after a coat of priming paint, will start putting on bottom in ¾-inch ply." The bottom planking had been left to last because, as LaBorde notes, if it had gone on any sooner, the bilges would have filled with sawdust and shavings—a mess at very least—not to mention the possibility of the risk of rot starting when rain water soaked such building debris.

The bottom panels to be connected to the stem required enough bend that they caused considerable trouble to put in—as anyone knows who has tried to bend three-quarter ply—until Reynold made a saw-slit down the middle of each wedge-shaped piece. Knowing how, they had a much easier time with the second bow piece. The rest of the topsides was routine work. Before Reynold moved on, there was one more major job: the rudder.

This is a prime example of LaBorde's overkill approach when it came to strength. Reynold built the rudder of a single piece of 2-inch-thick pitch-pine. This was reinforced by boring holes right across the blade and driving ⅜-inch galvanized rods, well greased, through them. Then cheek pieces, also 2-inch pitch-pine, were bolted to the rudder head to stiffen it against the twisting action of the tiller, which slipped into a slot in the rudder head. Finally, the rudder hardware. Goode had specified ⅝-inch pintles. To LaBorde, this seemed skimpy, so he went to his drawing board and designed a new set with 1-inch pintles.

When the foundryman took a look at the dimensions on the drawings, he raised his eyebrows and asked how big the boat was.

"Twenty-seven feet," LaBorde replied.

"Using pintles *one inch* in diameter on a twenty-seven-foot boat! Are you expecting a hurricane?"

"Yes," LaBorde answered. End of conversation.

When LaBorde picked up the gudgeons and pintles a few days later, they weighed forty pounds. And when they were attached, it took the three men to lift the rudder into place. At sea in a gale some months later, LaBorde merely lay in his bunk and smiled when he thought about the rudder.

The Deck

There was, as LaBorde says himself, nothing unusual about the deck. The side decks were only about 6 inches wide, barely more than the width of the lifeline stanchion bases (Fig. 10-6). Up forward there was a foredeck hatch that opened at its forward end—ventilation in good weather. The mainmast passed through the foredeck just forward of the trunk and was fitted with a "boot" visible in Fig. 10-9. That photo also shows a toerail 2½ to 3 inches high. The stanchions, three to a side, were 36 inches high, with a single lifeline at the top, and these were tied into the main and mizzen shrouds. Neither the decks nor the cabin top were covered by anything but paint, yet they remained completely watertight.

The cabin had three 10-inch by 14-inch deadlight windows in each side of the trunk, merely for light. They were well bedded in paint and secured with moldings; they didn't leak, either. Despite the somewhat rough-looking joiner work, the ketch was dry below.

There were no cowl vents anywhere on deck, as LaBorde feared that in a big storm they might be swept off and endanger the ketch.

Fig. 10–6. Humming Bird *just after launching.*

One of the most interesting deck features—considering the cabintop as part of it—is the companionway hatch. LaBorde was so determined to have a dry boat below that he placed the hatch in the cabin top only, just to port of the centerline, with no threshold or drop slides. In addition, the hatch was the double-coaming type, virtually leakproof. This added to general structural strength, as the after-most cabintop beam was unbroken from side to side; and, the bridge deck just below it had two full-width beams right across the ship.

Consistent with this feature, the cockpit was small. The footwell measured 3 feet long by 2 feet wide by 2 feet 6 inches deep and was drained through the stern by two 2-inch scuppers connected by hoses to the transom.

Certainly the oddest item on deck is the tiller, visible in use by Kwailan in Fig. 10-2, and in the sketch view of the outboard profile in Fig. 10-4. Fabricated of 1-inch steel stock, it was Goode's solution to the same problem faced by Guzzwell on *Trekka:* The mizzen mast was located *between* the rudder and the cockpit. Rather than specify a Braine-type gear, Goode

245

adopted a simple but unorthodox idea: a tiller that curved around the mizzen mast. With a U-turn in its middle, it could swing "through" the mast and still give the helmsman a full arc of rudder movement 45 degrees on either side of the centerline. (More than that only produces braking action.) It was odd-looking but never gave a moment's trouble.

The Rig

As for the rig—especially the sails—it was spared the close scrutiny given everything else by LaBorde in his quest for economy. Early on, he had considered making the sails himself but decided that was a poor economy as the sails were the only driving force on the ketch and the ultimate arbiter of performance. In a tight spot, he felt, they might decide whether the boat got out of trouble or not. So, he had them made by England's Carter & Cranfield, the sailmaker that had cut the sails for his three previous boats.

They were ordered during the hull construction period and were made of the very best quality Egyptian cotton—a very heavy cloth for the working sails and a lighter cloth for the genoa. There was also a storm jib that LaBorde acquired locally. The areas were: Mainsail—180 sq. ft.; Jib—70 sq. ft.; Mizzen—50 sq. ft.; Genoa—150 sq. ft.; Storm Jib—30 sq. ft. The total area with the genny in use was 380 sq. ft., adequate but not exceptional for light-weather conditions. The mainsail had one set of reef points, and although the sail plan shows the same arrangement for the jib and jigger, LaBorde apparently had these eliminated as these two sails had areas of only 70 and 50 square feet.

The spars, of course, were made by LaBorde and Buck, but finding the right wood for the mainmast was impossible in Trinidad, so LaBorde imported a 27-foot long, 8-inch by 8-inch spruce log from Canada. When it arrived by ship on February 21, 1959, they made 1-inch offcuts on all four sides and glued them together to make the mizzen mast and two booms. Like most of *Humming Bird*'s specs, the spar dimensions were robust: Mainmast —6 inches in diameter, 22 feet above the deck; Main boom—15 feet long; Gaff—9 feet long; Bowsprit—27 inches beyond the stem; Mizzen mast— 4 inches. Reynold returned to help in this job, each spar being heavily sloshed down with linseed oil. From start to finish the spars took three weeks, including fitting the copper chafe bands on the masts where the booms and gaff jaws would rest.

Standing Rigging. A pair of ⅜-inch galvanized wire shrouds were fitted on each side of both main and mizzen, each one ending in an open-body or pipe turnbuckle, followed by about 8 inches of galvanized chain, which in turn, was shackled to its chainplate. LaBorde wanted to splice the shrouds himself, a job he knew how to do do, but he was now so pressed for time

Fig. 10–7. Humming Bird *sailing in the Windward Isles.*

with the honeymoon cruise looming ahead, he had the job done by a local
rigger, a friend who charged him nothing. The chainplates were as robust
as anything else on *Humming Bird*—¼-inch mild steel, 2½ inches wide,
about 18 inches long and each fastened to the hull with four ⅜-inch bolts.
When the shrouds were done, Buck rubbed them down with white lead and
tallow and wrapped them with a fine marline.

247

Running Rigging. Mostly manila, with some terylene (dacron), as revealed by the line just forward of Kwailan in Fig. 10-3, and another on the foredeck in Fig. 10-9. All cleats were handmade and screwed or lag-bolted to masts and coamings.

Halyards. For a basic, straightforward rig like *Humming Bird*'s, the halyard schedule was utterly simple: Mizzen—two-part, running through a block hanging from the masthead; Main—throat and peak halyards in the standard fashion of gaff-rigged sails, probably with the same block arrangement as we saw in Pidgeon's *Islander;* Jib & Genoa—two-part halyards for each, rove through single blocks hung from the mast at the heights shown in Fig. 10-4.

Sheets. These were equally simple: Mizzen—a two-block arrangement between boom and deck, running forward to a cleat in the cockpit. Jib—as this sail overlapped the mainmast, it had double sheets, each running aft to its cleat on the cockpit coamings. Genoa—same arrangement as jib. As a guess, the genoa sheets probably were rove through the blocks on the forward mizzen shrouds, port and starboard, which can be seen in Figs. 10-2 and 10-3.

The main boom and gaff jaws were held against the mast by a cheap and trouble-free method: parrel straps, which may have been used all the way up the mainsail luff, to judge by Fig. 10-9, which shows one such strap above the boom jaws. This photo also suggests that the mainsail was roped all the way around—except, probably, along the leech. The sail plan in Fig. 10-4 indicates that the sails were laced to their booms and masts, and this seems to be the case, with the exception of the mainsail.

For anyone who has not sailed with laced sails, that utterly cheap and highly reliable method (I used this method aboard my 37-foot ketch), to know it is to love it. The lacing can be of really cheap line—even polypropylene—as the load imposed on it, unlike track and slides, is automatically distributed over the entire length of the lacing.

The moment you cast off the halyards, the weight of the gaff causes the whole lash-up to sag about a foot, and the lacing instantly slackens; each loop around the mast increases in size, and since there are no projections on the mast there is nothing to snag the lacing loops as they slide down. The sail comes down easily, even with the wind aft of amidships. Sometimes you have to yank on the leech to force the gaff peak down level with the jaws so the weight is distributed evenly and brings the gaff down against the friction of the peak halyard blocks—but that's nothing to do with the lacing. In *Humming Bird,* it appears from Figs. 10-3 and 10-7, the lacing may have been dispensed with on the mizzen boom—just tack and clew lashings, adequate for a sail that only does real work when the wind is on the beam or aft of it, and a bellying effect makes the sail more efficient.

En route to their departure island of Antigua, LaBorde and Buck stopped for a few days at Bequia, where LaBorde had a local sailmaker make him a new mainsail of flax (he doesn't indicate why he needed one so soon), plus a storm mizzen, a storm jib and a sea anchor.

The Cabin

We can cover the cabin briefly, as LaBorde had neither time nor money to fit any real amenities. Once the essentials were in, that was it. The cabin plan in Fig. 10-4 shows the layout: a forepeak for stowage, the main cabin with two berths for the LaBordes (the port one next to the radio for LaBorde), bookshelves outboard, and the quarterberth aft for Buck, opposite the galley. There was stowage all around—aft under the cockpit on either side of the water tank, in the food locker beside the galley, and under the berths.

Being West Indians from an island covered with brilliant tropical flowers and surrounded by the turquoise sea, the crew of *Humming Bird* did not lean toward a dark interior but toward familiar hues, so Buck painted the cabin thusly: Overhead, white; bunks, light blue; bulkheads, pink. LaBorde notes that it was always cheerful below decks, even on a gray day.

Gear, Stores, and Refitting

As one might expect, *Humming Bird*'s economy cruise across the Atlantic was accomplished principally by doing without in the equipment department. "Essentials only" was the guiding principle.

For water, LaBorde fitted a 30-gallon tank under the cockpit in the space that would have been occupied by an engine if he had been able to afford one. This was a good location for 300 pounds of water, down low in the boat.

In the galley, Kwailan—who did most but not all of the cooking—had a two-burner kerosene stove that was fitted in a niche in the galley, with a shelf above and a bin below. Cruising through the Windwards, LaBorde eventually gimbaled it for her. She had a mixed bag of pots and pans, but one of the most important items was her pressure cooker—an item that keeps earning high marks from long-distance sailors.

There was a kerosene riding light (there were navigation lights too, but LaBorde rarely used them at sea), an ex-Admiralty sextant purchased secondhand, a shortwave radio receiver to get time ticks from WWV, plus the usual navigation tools and charts. For binoculars, good ones being beyond the budget, LaBorde made do with a pair he picked up for ten shillings, and for keeping the ship's DR position, he imported a patent log from England.

In the bo'sun's department, the bilge pump was a massive model that LaBorde picked up secondhand; its capacity was reported not as strokes per gallon but as one ton of water in seven minutes!

Humming Bird's anchor can be seen on the foredeck in Fig. 10-8, a fisherman's type of about 25 to 30 pounds. It appears to have a manila rode, but the boat also had, as a storm anchor, a 40-pound Danforth with 45 fathoms of chain as a rode. LaBorde designed an 8-foot prom dinghy, and he and Buck built it of plywood. It fit exactly between the main hatch and the mast.

After the launching of the boat on June 7, 1959—by flatbed truck to the harbor and by crane into the sea—the newly married Mr. and Mrs. Harold LaBorde went off on a ten-day honeymoon cruise to Grenada. Buck went along as crew, much to the consternation of family and friends, who viewed this arrangement with raised eyebrows. But then a local boy planning to be the first West Indian to cross the Atlantic didn't fit Trinidad's conventional mold, either.

On their return the newlyweds and Buck returned to their jobs, working on the ketch evenings and sailing on weekends. *Humming Bird* was moored in a cove right outside their bedroom window—in the home of Harold's parents—and they checked it the first thing upon arising every morning. This was idyllic, but the departure date was fast approaching, and they still did not have anywhere near the amount of stores needed for the voyage.

Then LaBorde's father " . . . came up with a brilliant suggestion: 'Why not write to some of the firms in the city, asking for foodstuffs and other things in return for advertisement?' " It was worth a try, LaBorde decided, so Kwailan typed "about a hundred letters" to local companies.

Much to everyone's surprise, within twenty-four hours they had their first response, a letter offering cases of "tinned milk and carrots." Another company gave them a Bulova watch, which functioned accurately all the way across for their longitude calculations, and more items followed: rum, biscuits, film, beer, marine paint, rope, medicines, lifebelts, and the two-burner Primus kerosene stove. English friends gave them a large quantity of plastic bags (used to store their canned goods), and a yachtsman presented LaBorde with a collection of shackles and turnbuckles he didn't need.

In November, LaBorde resigned his job. As a parting gift at the farewell party, his office friends gave him a large Thermos bottle—an item blessed by the watchkeeper on many nights afterward. Although his job had symbolized entrapment in a humdrum life, LaBorde nevertheless had a lump in his throat when he bade the office staff goodbye.

Christmas 1959 came and went, and during the holiday period, the company that had launched *Humming Bird* by crane plucked it out again, gratis, so LaBorde and Buck could repaint the bottom and topsides. A radio receiver was finally located locally, a German model that ran on a 9-volt battery; a friend fitted it with a pair of earphones so that LaBorde could pick up his time ticks even when reception was poor.

Early in January 1960 Buck arrived at the boat one evening with exciting news: at last he knew for certain he was able to sail with them; his boss had given him a four-month leave of absence.

As the days dwindled down to departure date, fitting-out accelerated. A friend who owned a grapefruit farm contributed 300 of the fruit, still green, which were stowed in the lazarette. A few days later they used the dinghy to move aboard "cases and cases" of the food that had been collecting in the LaBorde house. While this is not a complete list, it gives a good idea of foods they carried: fresh eggs, coffee, sugar, rice, tea, cocoa, fruit juice, custard, canned fruit, corned beef and other tinned meats, sardines, baked beans, potatoes, flour, dried nuts, candy, and one large salted cod.

At the bon voyage party on January 29, 1960, there were more gifts: a hot-water bottle "for cold nights at sea" from LaBorde's aunt, and a complete set of international code flags from a friend. Local customs officers attended the party, to make certain that none of the guests dipped into the rum given as gifts by local Port of Spain merchants—as no duty had been paid on it.

Then, at last, LaBorde and Kwailand rowed the dinghy out to the ketch for the last time in home waters. They would sail northward at a leisurely pace through the Windward Islands and be joined by Buck at Antigua in time for the crossing.

In spite of all the work already done, LaBorde had many more small jobs to do during the northward cruise: At Grenada, he bought some airtight tins, painted them with aluminum paint, and used them to store all their perishable dry foods. At Bequia he had the above-mentioned flax sails made. While waiting for them he browsed the waterfront shops and made a useful purchase—a pressure-kerosene Tilley lamp of English manufacture—and picked up the required fittings to install the massive bilge pump.

Sailing on, the LaBordes visited some of Harold's relatives on St. Vincent. Here he purchased some lumber and carried it as deck cargo to St. Lucia, where he paused long enough to build additional sail and gear bins in the forepeak. Then he took the time—at last—to fit the big Vortex bilge pump.

Six weeks out from Trinadad, *Humming Bird* reached English Harbour, Antigua, and here they remained completing the final jobs before the Atlantic. Reasoning that an 8-foot pram could not serve as a lifeboat for three people, LaBorde swapped it with an English sailor just arrived from England for better lifejackets, distress flares, rope and a good bo'sun's knife. During all this, Kwailan went on shopping sprees by taxi to a town fourteen miles away, buying several more cases of canned food, boxes of chocolate bars, 200 green mangoes, and 20 dozen eggs; these they greased with white vaseline and replaced in their cartons; only *one* of them went bad by the time they reached England.

(A cruise like this, to Antigua, of three months' duration, is an ideal way to conduct a shakedown voyage. Living aboard day-in, day-out allows one to check out living arrangements, provides trials and testing of the rig— and time to correct deficiencies—and tests the stowage plan while the crew still has time to make modifications. A long coastal cruise ought to be a self-imposed prerequisite before any blue-water voyage.)

Buck arrived at Antigua in mid-April, bringing LaBorde's last-minute requests: galvanized jerricans, extra tools, two fruitcakes from LaBorde's mother, and a batch of their favorite calypso records. With Buck's help, LaBorde immediately tackled a new job: With *Humming Bird* in the water, they shifted all the inside ballast to one side of the keelson, causing the ketch to heel that way, and then painted the opposite topsides from the dinghy, reversing the procedure late that day and finishing just before sundown. Another day they fitted toerails to the foredeck, a job that had not been done before launching.

While they were in Antigua, they became friendly with Edward Allcard, who was there chartering his newly rebuilt ketch, *Sea Wanderer,* to raise funds for his voyage to South American waters and for a try at Cape Horn. Allcard gave them a 25-gallon water tank he didn't need and, with the 30-gallon tank under the cockpit, and two water casks they carried— one of which is visible next to Kwailan in Fig. 10-3—*Humming Bird* had an all-up capacity of 100 gallons for the voyage.

Their final purchases at the island included several gallons of paraffin (kerosene), new oilskins, a couple of coils of rope, and "the thousand and one things which must be carried on such a voyage." Last-minute fresh foods put aboard included several stems of bananas, a couple of dozen pineapples, and two "very large pumpkins."

Kwailan, skilled at Caribbean cuisine, prepared fairly elaborate dishes all the way across, stretching the supply of fresh foods all the way to the Azores.

By this time, *Humming Bird* was noticeably down on her marks—she had, after all, only a 22-foot waterline—but if that was to cause any early loss of performance, LaBorde felt that they would soon eat their way back to the designed draft. (In fact, Kwailan gained twenty pounds on the voyage!) Ship and crew were now ready for the Atlantic.

Voyage Track

Humming Bird departed Antigua on May 16, 1960, arrived at the Azores on June 21, departed there July 1, 1960, and reached Falmouth, England on

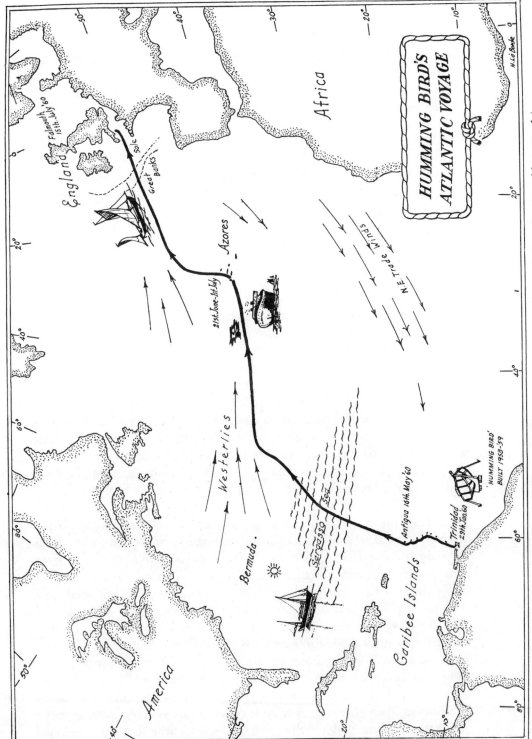

Fig. 10-8. *Chart: Humming Bird's track across the Atlantic. (Chart by Harold LaBorde)*

253

July 15, 1960. From the start at Port of Spain, Trinidad, the ketch made the following ports of call: St. Georges, Grenada . . . Tyrell's Bay, Carriacou . . . Admiralty Bay, Bequia . . . Kingstown, St. Vincent . . . Castries, St. Lucia . . . Fort de France, Martinique . . . St. Pierre, Martinique . . . Portsmouth, Dominica . . . Bourg de Saintes, Saints Islands . . . Anse à la Barque, Guadaloupe . . . English Harbour, Antigua . . . Horta, Fayal, Azores . . . Falmouth, England.

Sailing Performance

For the first week out of Antigua, the weather was fairly mild and progress slow—which didn't bother *Humming Bird*'s crew very much because they all suffered from seasickness for several days, Kwailan taking the longest to recover.

On the second day out, May 17, LaBorde tried a sextant sight at noon but made a botch of it. When plotted, "I found, somewhat to my amazement, that we were apparently somewhere in the mouth of the Orinoco River. At these disastrous results I felt rather concerned. . . . " When Buck asked about their position, LaBorde "mumbled something about the sextant needing adjustment." That day, too, they passed Barbuda, lying just north of Antigua. The wind, freshening from forward of the beam, caused LaBorde to lower the mizzen, and he was pleased to note that, under jib and main, *Humming Bird* sailed herself without a fuss.

Later that day they were overtaken by squalls, and LaBorde found himself wishing he had purchased a barometer. The day was further distinguished by the discovery of the small leak up forward, under a frame, that was to "weep" for the entire voyage and frustrate them with the required daily bailing. It was too inaccessible to caulk and too slight for the bilge pump intake to manage. But it was an annoyance rather than a danger.

The fourth day they had more squalls and reefed the main for the first time. They made a botch of this job, too, and soon after eliminated the lashings that had secured the foot of the mainsail to the boom. Sailing with the mainsail loose-footed made it much easier to reef. On May 21 they were surrounded on all sides by thunderheads, but winds were light and they had easy sailing all day. That night, and into May 22, they encountered their first gale. LaBorde was on watch after midnight and, as the winds picked up and swung into the south, he carried on too long. Suddenly steering became very difficult, and *Humming Bird* was hove down with the main boom nearly dragging in the water. He shouted for Buck and Kwailan, who came tumbling out on deck. Kwailan took the tiller while the two men struggled mightily for nearly a half-hour to get the main down and lashed to its boom; then *Humming Bird* rode easier. Shortly afterward, they hove to for the first time under the jib, and then went below to get dry and take to their berths. It was the first big lesson of the voyage, and LaBorde vowed never to wait so long again to reduce sail. The shock of this incident subdued them all for several days.

The need for caution at sea was repeated two nights later, when LaBorde was again on watch. He was standing at the edge of the cockpit (relieving himself) when the ketch gave a lurch and threw him backward across the deck until his neck hit the opposite lifelines. His shout of surprise brought the crew on deck in a rush, and when he explained what happened, Kwailan began a voyage-long habit of pestering both men to hook up their lifelines whenever they were on deck alone.

At the end of ten days, LaBorde got his celestial navigation under control, and records his first three daily runs: two days of 10 and 12 miles (in near calms), then one of 37 miles. On May 25 it climbed to 55 miles, on the 26th, to 85 miles, followed by a run of 80 miles on May 27. Here we might pause to take a look at *Humming Bird*'s numbers:

Humming Bird: Speed/Length Ratio $(WL = 22'\ \sqrt{22} = 4.7)$			
S/L $\times$ $\sqrt{WL}$	=	Speed (knots) $\times$ 24	= NM (1 day)
1.0	4.7	4.70	112.8
1.1	4.7	5.17	124.1
1.2	4.7	5.64	135.4
1.3	4.7	6.11	146.6
1.34	4.7	6.30	151.2

After discussing three boats in a row with waterlines under 20 feet, it's clear how a few extra feet qualifies a boat to achieve a 100-mile day while only sailing at an S/L ratio of 1.0. Despite this, *Humming Bird* covered that distance only a few times, probably because her beam of 9 feet is considerable for a 22-foot waterline, she was heavily loaded (1000 pounds of water in a boat of 6000 pounds displacement), her working rig of 300 square feet is somewhat scant for her displacement, and the wetted surface is considerable in this type of hull.

LaBorde's route plan, worked out with several of the ocean-crossing sailors he had met in Antigua, was, in his own words:

Up till [now] our course took us generally northward, roughly in the direction of Bermuda. The reason for not heading directly for England was that, if we did, we'd be beating against the Northeast Tradewinds for hundreds of miles; after that, we'd have a slant through the Sargasso Sea, with all its calms and squalls.

The best course lay, therefore, in sailing north for about a thousand miles, crossing the Northeast Trades and the Sargasso Sea at right angles. By the time we reached [the latitude] of Bermuda, we should have picked up the Westerlies, which should then blow us eastwards across the Atlantic. In planning this route we consulted the [U. S.] *Wind and Current Charts* for the period May to August.

At the end of two weeks at sea, their seasickness was gone, they were used to the motion, and they were settled into their sea routine. Kwailan was producing a succession of delicious meals and, because she had this extra work, was standing only one two-hour watch during the hours of darkness. As they reached northward on their route, they encountered squalls frequently, but now their sail handling was smooth, so lowering or reefing the main became routine.

On May 30 they managed 100 miles in just over a day—twenty-six hours. The next day, they passed a freighter that came closer to investigate. They shouted to her bridge to report them to Lloyd's of London, as they had made the arrangement to have such sightings relayed to their parents, but apparently they were not understood, for no sighting report reached Port of Spain.

By the end of the third week at sea, LeBorde was wearing four sweaters on night watch—but he acknowledged that, to a West Indian, anything below 75 degrees was considered cold.

In the fourth week, during a calm, Buck and LeBorde went over the side for a swim and found, to their pleasure, that the bottom was still completely clean—a sharp departure from the experiences of *Temptress, Nova Espero,* and *Felicity Ann* on the same track, although they sailed it in the opposite direction. Can it be that sailing from cold water to warm stimulates growth of barnacles and weed, and sailing the other may inhibits it?

LaBorde and Kwailan celebrated their first wedding anniversary at sea on June 7 with a special meal she prepared. Being half-Chinese, she had brought along Oriental ingredients for it—a huge bowl of chop suey that included dried squid, duck and mushrooms in soy sauce, with fried rice; for dessert, fruit cake, lychee nuts, and custard, topped off with a bottle of Martiniquan wine that had cooled in the ocean for half a day at the end of a line. For this occasion, LaBorde got *Humming Bird* to sail herself all day on the starboard tack, with sheets started and the tiller lashed.

By now they were at 34°30′ N. latitude, well north of Bermuda, and LaBorde was disgusted: the wind charts showed a predominance of westerlies for that part of the ocean, and they were being plagued by easterlies—a complaint all to often heard from blue-water sailors going both ways across the Atlantic.

One calm day, Buck and LaBorde shifted all the internal ballast—as they had for topside painting—and scrubbed the bilges, flushing them with seawater afterward. LaBorde didn't say why this was needed, but one suspects the bilges had an accumulation (perhaps a fragrant one) of food scraps, construction debris, and rust from the internal ballast. In this period, LaBorde notes that to get their position each day, he relied entirely on a noon sight (probably what the overwhelming majority of ocean voyagers depend on) and did not attempt any star sights. Standing watch alertly, you can count on making your first landfall safely by picking up lights; or, you can avoid an arrival in darkness by slowing down after your penultimate noon position—to insure making your landfall in daylight.

As Capt. Robert P. Beebe, USN (Ret.), the wartime navigator of the USS *Saratoga* and author of *Voyaging Under Power,* who has trained many navigators, says, "The only sight that really counts is the one you make the day *before* arrival." The soundness of this observation is borne out by an experience LaBorde had halfway across the ocean. He realized one day, while getting his time-tick from WWV, that he had been taking the time from the wrong instant in the announcer's time count. It worried him, until he realized all the accumulated error—if any—was corrected by the one plot, that day, in which he used the correct time. The same, of course, is true of all other errors: they're not cumulative but instantly solved with the first sight that is accurately shot, calculated, and plotted.

Late in the fourth week, they spoke a ship whose captain confirmed their position as 35° N.–53° W.—*almost* halfway between Bermuda and the Azores. They finished the week with two daily runs of 70 and 90 miles—nothing to brag about but, nevertheless, reasonably respectable. At least they got a sense of progress from the fact that they were about at the eastern edge of their chart and were almost ready to break out the new one for the eastern half of the Atlantic.

The fifth week delivered intermittent rain showers and squalls—like the fourth week—but, in between, produced some favorable slants of wind, of good force. They reeled off two consecutive days of 140 and 138 miles—S/L ratios of better than 1.2. On June 16 the Azores lay only 390 miles off.

On the seventeenth *Humming Bird* faced gale-force winds, and LaBorde decided the best choice was to heave to. They did so, and he reports, "Soon we had the mainsail well reefed down and *Humming Bird* hove-to on the starboard tack, lying about 50° to the wind and sea. In this manner, she made almost no movement forward and, consequently, rode the sea very well." For the rest of the night they took to their berths, but by morning the wind and seas had increased to such a degree that even the working jib was too much sail area. LaBorde hooked on his lifeline and worked his way forward to the foredeck to change over to the 30-square-foot storm jib. Unfortunately, his cost-cutting impulses did not pay off very well this time, as he had not bought piston hanks for this sail but had substituted eight shackles

—perhaps the ones his English friend had given him. As a consequence, between dashing aft to cling to the mast every time Kwailan shouted that a large wave was bearing down on them, and having to tighten each shackle with a pair of pliers, the job took quite a long time. Still, it was a gale on a sunny day with billowing clouds. After watching the 20-foot waves slide under them from the safety of the cockpit for a while, they all retired to their bunks to read and try to forget the storm outside—which was possible except when large waves crashed right over the ketch.

At 0300 on June 18—LaBorde's birthday—the gale blew itself out, and by daylight they were sailing again. Kwailan cooked LaBorde a special birthday lunch—sardine cakes fried in butter with white sauce, potatoes, black-eyed peas, and peanut punch, with custard and fruit for dessert.

On June 20 LaBorde got a good sight that put them sixty miles from Fayal. That afternoon, two motor vessels passed them, which they took to be island fishing boats. In darkness early that evening, LaBorde was on watch, suffering those pangs of anxiety known to all first-time navigators: whether or not the Azores—any one of them—would appear off the bow in the next few hours. And then—was that a light blinking up ahead? He scrambled halfway up the mast and looked again: "I saw the unmistakable blink-blink of a lighthouse! LANDFALL!" For the rest of the night, the three of them sat in the cockpit, sailing on in a light breeze, discussing what they would do in port—and polishing off a bottle of muscatel.

The next day, they ran into calms and did not make it into port, but that night, June 21, 1960, in darkness and with the navigation lights lit for only the second time in the voyage, they accepted a line from a small Portuguese fishing boat and were towed into the port of Horta, Fayal Island. They "dropped the hook in six fathoms" and were cleared by port officials only an hour later.

Humming Bird remained in Horta for nine days, during which the crew rested, went sightseeing, and found that thirty-six days at sea had so weakened their land legs that they were exhausted each time they returned to the ketch. But there was time to give the boat a thorough cleaning, to reeve new main and jib halyards, and to fill the water tanks. And, of course, for Kwailan to lay in another healthy supply of stores for the final leg of the voyage.

On July 1, 1960, they sailed again, first north for about 500 miles, then northeast on the westerlies. On the fourth they were only 85 miles out—not much progress for three days of sailing. LaBorde had hoped to complete the 1300 miles to Falmouth in fifteen days, as Buck had only a bit more than a month to reach England and return to his job in Trinidad. As if in answer to their need, the wind picked up sharply that night and blew all the next day, so that by noon they had notched the best day's run of the voyage—150 miles, an S/L of 1.34. LaBorde notes that this was attained with a

Fig. 10–9. Humming Bird's *landfall: Cornwall, England.*

favorable current setting northeast at a rate of 1.5 knots—worth 36 free miles. For the rest of this passage, LaBorde notes, "Our course no longer took on that erratic look it had done when we first left the West Indies; that day's runs were almost in a straight line, . . . and much longer."

They suffered considerably from cold as they gained each degree of latitude, not only because it was so unlike their Caribbean climate but also because, despite its being July—as everyone knows who has been out on the water—the sea wind is really chilly when the sun goes down, even on a summer day.

Despite a gale that blew for the next three days, they managed to keep sailing and hold to their course. When the storm intensified, they took all sail off her, and even under bare poles they ran before it at 3 to 4 knots. It was tricky steering, keeping *Humming Bird* dead before the wind, but only once did they broach and take a knockdown—a scary few minutes when the cockpit was filled before they got *Humming Bird* straightened out and running before it again. On the third night of the gale, they hove to as LaBorde felt it was too risky to attempt the demanding steering in darkness.

The next morning, the gale had abated and they raised sail again. At noon, LaBorde got a good sun sight and announced that England was only 300 miles off—suggesting strongly that the three days of stormy weather had produced three 100+ days. On July 12 they had gale force winds again, and on the thirteenth they saw increased shipping traffic bound in and out of England. On July 14 a large liner passed close by in the morning of a "perfect sailing day," unexpected because of the forbidding stories they had heard all their lives about English weather. At noon, a sun sight put them ten miles west of the Scilly Isles. LaBorde estimated they should sight Bishop's Rock Light at 1500, but at that hour they saw nothing. Then a few minutes later, Kwailan shouted:

"I can see it, a light grey tower, on the port bow!"

The rest of the voyage into Falmouth was routine. *Humming Bird* was in England.

II. Seraffyn

Anyone can go cruising. That is, anyone who really wants to, and does three things: First, decide that you are going, that nothing is going to stop you, and that from that moment on all your time and effort will be directed toward your goal. Second, accept the fact that it may take four or five—even ten—years of preparation before you actually cast off your mooring lines and sail. And third, be prepared to evaluate what size boat you really need to live comfortably. You have to list necessities and make sure you don't include needless luxuries that only absorb time and money. . . .

Choose a modest, simple yacht, one you can afford (and still have money in the bank), a yacht you can handle easily, and you'll find real cruising comfort—mental and physical.

—Lin & Larry Pardey
Cruising In Seraffyn (1976)

AUTHOR'S NOTE: I got acquainted with Lin and Larry Pardey by letter in—if memory serves—the spring of 1975. At the time I was the editor and publisher of Seven Seas Press, a small nautical publishing company whose philosophy was practically indistinguishable from the four themes of this book, and which aimed at showing *more* people how to do *more* cruising by jettisoning the mistaken notion that a heavy cargo of technological gear was mandatory to pleasure and success.

I knew the Pardeys' series of cruising articles then running in *Boating* magazine. In their letter to me, they proposed that they write a cruising cookbook, but I saw a much better story in them—the story of their cruise. From their letter it appeared that such a book had not yet been started.

To jump ahead, in 1976 *Cruising in Seraffyn* appeared under the Seven Seas imprimatur, became a major selection of the Dolphin Book Club, and was the first big success for my company. In the next several years, three more books on the Pardeys' circumnavigation were brought out by the publisher of this book, and Lin and Larry wrote two other books *(see Bibliography)* and built a 29-foot "big sister" to *Seraffyn,* designed by *Seraffyn's* architect, Lyle C. Hess.

Through the weeks that we worked together on the final draft of the book —they were briefly in the United States—I became more and more impressed with their approach: their cutter itself (no engine, no electricity), the philosophy under-lying their cruise—which I felt was the true driving force behind its success—and the documentation they had collected along the way that amply "proved" that for many—perhaps most—cruising people, the smaller boat got you cruising sooner, kept you at it longer and cost you less to do it, without significant loss of safety or comfort. In making such a choice, the data suggested, your cruising track was less strewn with the shoals of high initial cost, the reefs of technological complex-ity, the coral heads of high operating expense, and the sandbars of excessive physical demands.

Their figures showed clearly how the people on smaller boats kept cruising longer and spent less—without any loss of cruising satisfaction. A cruising partner of mine once put the same idea in a catchy phrase: "We have no luxuries aboard, but all necessities are at a luxurious level." That might have been a motto for the Pardeys, for in spite of some things they did without (and didn't really miss), they lived well on their cruise: strong, simple first-class equipment that worked all the time because it was manually operated, a good stove on which Lin produced first-class meals, wine and cheese and other native delicacies offered by the foreign ports they visited, good berths for proper rest, many restaurant meals ashore they could not have afforded if an engine and electronics had been installed, and a well-matched hull and rig that performed almost flawlessly under their expert handling.

This chapter covers just the first part of their circumnavigation—the building of *Seraffyn* and their cruise from California to England. Their book on this leg of their long cruise and the three later ones covering the rest of their long voyage are currently in print *(see Bibliography)*.

Lin and Larry Pardey

*L*arry Pardey knew, from the time he was a teen-ager in high school, that he would someday acquire his own "ideal" boat and sail off on a long cruise. For the next seven years in Canada, his native country, he bought, rebuilt, and sold—each time at a profit—a succession of boats, and served as paid hand and later skipper aboard large yachts. Then, in 1964, with an impressive amount of boatbuilding and sailing experience under his belt, he headed south to California to seek his dream ship. None of the used boats he saw met his requirements, so he spent three and a half years building her —*Seraffyn*.

He was working as skipper on a large yacht when he spotted *Seraffyn*'s prototype, *Renegade,* and knew instantly he had found her. Unfortunately, *Renegade* was not for sale, but through her first owner, Hale Field, he found his way to the gaff cutter's designer, Lyle Hess. From extensive meetings with Hess emerged Larry's variant model—the same hull but a number of other changes. As soon as the modified plans arrived from Hess, Larry was ready to begin building.

He had finished lofting the lines and was shaping the keel timbers when he met Lin. She had been a music major in college—not too long before —and soon they were a "crew," working together on the cutter, although Lin always insisted that until she met Larry she had "never heard of" a cruising yacht. (Years later, when I chided her for such an obvious exaggeration, she so vehemently insisted it was true I had to believe her.)

It would be eminently worth describing the building of *Seraffyn*— expecially for those who appreciate details of fine wood boat construction

Fig. 11–1. *Lin and Larry Pardey aboard* Seraffyn. *(Photo courtesy the Pardeys.)*

—but lack of space to cover it adequately, and the fact that the full story is in their book, makes it necessary to summarize that job and discuss only the cutter's special features.

The Hull

Seraffyn's hull was based on the lines of England's Bristol Channel Pilot cutters. These working boats had, over a century and a half, evolved as close to perfection as they were ever going to get. For their work, they had to be heavy, burdensome, seaworthy, and seakindly. Beamy and short-ended, with a strong sheer, they were really more boat than their LOAs would suggest, and this was the model upon which Lyle Hess based his new version. A good many owners of contemporary yachts up to 32 feet LOA might be chagrined to find that their displacements are appreciably less than the smaller, 10,000-pound *Seraffyn*. While some of these (especially the fin-keelers) might outperform *Seraffyn* under certain sea conditions, they almost certainly would not over the broad range of weather encountered on a long voyage—especially not with the seakindly comfort offered by *Seraffyn*.

When Larry Pardey was still a boy and gradually farming a mental picture of his ideal boat, he decided it had to have three things, regardless of any *other* compromises he might have to make: good windward performance, teak decks, and the ability (dimensions) to carry a hard dinghy on deck.

When he ultimately sat down with Lyle Hess to work out the specifications of his cutter, one of the first things he wanted—a departure from the more traditional gaff rig seen on this type hull—was a Marconi rig. This choice was made to achieve his first requirement, good windward performance. (He had decided, years earlier, that there would be no engine, so his safety would depend on the cutter's ability to beat out of a cul-de-sac.)

A second change was a switch from a cast-iron ballast keel to lead. (The keel was made in their backyard building site by Lin and Larry—melting down 3000 pounds of scrap lead in an old bathtub and releasing it into a heavily reinforced mold, then bolting it to the deadwood with one-inch bronze bolts.)

The hard dinghy requirement was met, too, when Larry found a 6'8", 55-lb., round-bottom, lapstrake fiberglass sailing pram. When set in its chocks, it fitted above the trunk cabin and provided just enough room for Lin and Larry to slip through the companionway beneath it.

As for the cutter's construction material, that too was foreordained—wood; Larry is a superb shipwright. As he says, "I knew I wanted the method of construction that would be repairable anywhere in the world, so I chose the traditional wood-and-bronze method because you can usually find these materials in the most remote places."

Fig. 11–2. Seraffyn: *Isometric drawing of the hull. (Plan courtesy Lyle C. Hess.)*

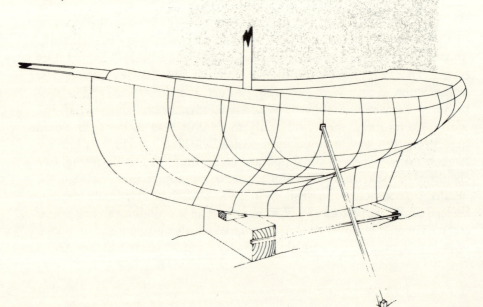

Specifications: LOA—24′4″; LWL—22′2″; Beam—8′11″; Draft—4′8″; Displacement—10,686 lbs.; Keel (lead)—2700 lbs.; Sail Area (working)—461 sq. ft.; Prismatic Coefficient—.535; Displacement/Length Ratio—296; Pounds/Inch Immersion—630 lbs.; Sail Area/Displacement Ratio—15.29.

Scantlings: Keel Timber—6″ × 12″ × 16′ long. This narrowed at the after end until it was 2¼″ wide under the heel of the rudder. *Planking*—Mahogany, 1⅛″ thick, copper riveted. *Sheer Clamps*—each 26′ long and made of two pieces of mahogany, scarfed together to net dimensions of 2½ × 4″. (One of them, slowly drawn into place by Larry with a Spanish windlass, was just about to be fastened when it shattered into four pieces, so it was back to square one; the other one went in without mishap.) *Deck Beams*—white oak, 1⅞″ × 2¼″, reinforced with bronze tie rods between cockpit carlines and sheer clamp, which were held in place with clench rings. *Deck Planking*—1¼″ × 1⅞″ teak, nibbed into the Honduras mahogany covering boards.

At the end of two years' work—about 2000 hours—*Seraffyn* was ready for her "whisky plank" party, a traditional shipwrights' bash to celebrate the shutter plank going into the hull and closing it up from keel to rail.

Fittings. These were bronze throughout. During the hull construction, all bronze bolts were made by Larry, cut to size from rod stock, and threaded himself—at a considerable saving over store-bought bolts. Then, when the Pardeys' foundryman advised them that he would be pouring bronze for their fittings, they went to the foundry with a new batch of hand-carved patterns that had been collecting and spent the day watching the process: setting the patterns in the molding sand, pouring the molten bronze, the hardening, the new fittings being withdrawn, knocking off the rough edges, and being "tumbled" into finished castings. Larry's comment on this is a valuable tip for any backyard builder: "Bronze casting makes good sense: If you make your own patterns, you get handsome, noncorroding hardware items that suit your boat exactly and cost less than galvanized iron fittings."

Despite being of wood construction, *Seraffyn* is unique among the boats in this book in having sawn frames. As it is virtually impossible to buy naturally grown crooks of white oak, sawn frames are accomplished today by doubling up futtocks (shorter curved sections, bolted together so that each joint between sections is overlapped by the one next to it by an unbroken section). For these, Larry used Philippine mahogany. Taking off the bevels on these frames so the planking would lie flat is a job for a master shipwright, as the bevels' accuracy depends on the care taken when laying down the lines at lofting time. In this system, not all frames are sawn, as there are two intermediate frames of steam-bent white oak between each sawn set, the steam-bent ones being 1½ inches square.

Stem, Stern Post, and Horn Timber. Laminated of white oak and then rabbeted to take the hood ends of the planking.

Bulwarks. These were something special aboard *Seraffyn,* as so few boats today have this handsome and practical feature. The Pardeys waited many months before their lumberyard received a shipment of mahogany containing boards that were "at least" 27′4″ long and 10 inches wide," so that Larry could get each bulwark out of a single piece. Fitted, they were 8 inches high and, being fastened to oak stanchions that were let into the covering boards, had continuous 1-inch scuppers that threw off a load of seawater on deck in just seconds. This arrangement, as seen in Fig. 11-1, offers great advantages when sailing, as it is easy to attach blocks anywhere along the bulwark simply by using a strop of nylon webbing—giving an infinite number of positions along the deck to suit any desired sheet lead.

The isometric drawing (Fig. 11-2) reveals the real beauty of the hull—seemingly without a single square foot of hull surface that is not curved, and showing that special grace of a vessel with tumblehome aft and a bold sheer.

Load-Carrying Ability. As noted above, the cutter had a cargo capacity of 3000 pounds. Larry notes that this permitted them to carry 50 fathoms of 5/16-inch chain (330 pounds), three anchors of 22, 25 and 33 lbs. (80 pounds), 50 gallons of water (500 pounds), tools (let's say 125 pounds), personal possessions, spare parts, odds and ends of wood and metal for repairs, the dinghy, and a three-month supply of canned and dried foods. So much for the oft-repeated remark about "such a small boat." (Just the four items listed add up to 965 pounds.)

The cutter's cost, in time and money, added up to 4200 hours of labor spread over three and a half years (1965–68) and $7765. in materials and fabrications by other craftsmen. (One must add that this dollar amount is now twenty years old and probably triple that today.)

Finally, a comparative look at two boats, *Humming Bird* and *Seraffyn,* just because they happen to stand cheek by jowl in this book, and because although they're at opposite ends of the spectrum of boatbuilding sophistication, they have enough specification similarities to make the comparison instructive:

	Humming Bird	*Seraffyn*
LOA	26′ 9″	24′ 4″
LWL	22′ 0″	22′ 2″
Beam	9′ 0″	8′ 11″
Draft	4′ 6″	4′ 8″
Displ.	6000 lbs.	10,686 lbs.
Ballast	2600 lbs.	2700 lbs.
Sail Area	300 sq. ft.	461 sq. ft.
Bldg. Time	18 months	42 months

What appears to be a batch of remarkably close numbers—except for displacement and sail area—reveals why the objective data from engineers so rarely tell the whole story where esthetics and performance are concerned and illuminates, too, why there is still as much art as science in designing a yacht.

While acknowledging that *Humming Bird* was conceived, designed, and built as an economy boat—with hull shape and rig selected to achieve that end—and giving full marks to Harold LaBorde for realizing his transatlantic dream by displaying the dedication described by the Pardeys at the opening of this chapter—we can nevertheless look for reasons that explain the marked disparity in the two miles per day (MPD) averages, with *Seraffyn*'s excellent ones showing up in her performance section, below.

First, despite her 8′11″ beam on a 24′4″ hull, *Seraffyn* has finely modeled lines with wine-glass sections—lines that are inherently faster. Second, although *Seraffyn* is 4000 pounds heavier, giving her more heft to drive her through the water, she has the greater sail area, the added ballast, and the deeper draft—especially for windward work—to do the job. On a long tradewind run, *Humming Bird*'s gaff rig might improve her relative performance (gaff mainsails being pretty good at running), but *Seraffyn*'s spinnaker (1000 square feet) was a powerful puller, and its pole was often used to boom out a headsail—often the genny—as Lin and Larry were never loathe to work their rig when the wind served—from any direction. Third, *Seraffyn*'s cutter rig, with its single mast, was simply more efficient in general than *Humming Bird*'s ketch rig with its two sticks, which meant more windage, while its working sail area was cut up into smaller areas. Consider this: the cutter's working rig was 50 percent greater than the ketch's. Fourth, despite LaBorde's considerable sailing experience as a youth, this was matched by Pardey, who also had considerably more offshore experience. Over a long voyage this translates into higher miles-per-day averages.

The Deck

The after section of *Seraffyn*'s deck, principally the cockpit, is shown in Figs. 11-1 and 11-3, which also reveals the generous proportions of the side decks—with Lin and Larry sitting on them crossways. The same portion of the deck is show diagrammatically in Fig. 11-6, along with the cabin plan.

One clever idea is that the two quarter-berth cushions *exactly* fit the cockpit well *(see Cabin, below)*. Fig. 11-1 shows that aft, everything is nicely proportioned and robust: the steering vane, "Helmer" (vane itself not visible), the handsome boom gallows, the bronze lifeline stanchions, the curved tiller, the breadth of the footwell (4 feet), the kerosene running lights at the forward end of the trunk, the fit of the 6′8″ dinghy atop the trunk, the "bottomless" box forward of the trunk (holding the propane and water

Fig. 11–3. *The Pardeys in* Seraffyn's *roomy cockpit.*

tanks), the 8-inch-high bulwarks, and, finally, the channels on the topsides to broaden the shroud base. (Note, too, the man-overboard and anchor lights hanging on the gallows stanchions.)

Fig. 11-3 further reveals the roominess of the cockpit, easily as large as on many seagoing 30-footers, and an important part of the "living" space —for dining, especially—in warm climates.

Up forward (Fig. 11-5) there is the above-mentioned foredeck hatch and good standing room for working the rig and ground tackle. In the bow, note the bronze anchor windlass, the bowsprit with its stemhead roller, and 25-pound CQR plow permanently stowed there, ready for instant use. One rarely seen but highly appreciated item was the bronze-flanged deck prism —with one over the galley on the port side and two more over the forward bunk.

The Rig

Seraffyn's sail plan is shown in Fig. 11-4, with the following sail areas: Mainsail—200 sq. ft.; Jib—156 sq. ft.; Staysail—105 sq. ft.; Genoa (150 percent)—396 sq. ft.; Spinnaker—1000 sq. ft.

SAILS					
	MATERIAL	LUFF	FOOT	LEACH	AREA
MAIN	7 OZ. DAC.	30'-0"	13'-0"	31'-9"	200□'
JIB	7 OZ. DAC.	33'-0"	16'-0"	22'-6"	156□'
STAYS'L	7 OZ. DAC.	22'-3"	10'-4"	20'-3	105□'
GENOA 150%	6 OZ. DAC.	33'-0	25'-6"	31'-6"	396□'
STORM TRYS'L	8 OZ DAC	12'-0"	10'-9"	18'-0"	63□'

Fig. 11–4. Seraffyn: *Sail Plan. (Plan courtesy Lyle C. Hess.)*

Fig. 11–5. Seraffyn *under sail.* (Photo: Tom Nibbea)

We have progressed three-quarters of a century from *Spray* to *Seraffyn,* from one technological era to another in boat construction, and the latter boat's wood-and-bronze construction is something of a throwback. For the standing rigging Larry Pardey chose the benefits of stainless steel wire because he was able to, and did, splice it himself. (Two years later he was disgusted to find rust on it and, testing it with a magnet, found it had attractive qualities, so he sent to England for all new stainless wire and respliced all of the standing rigging.)

Spars. All of spruce and made by Larry, the mast hollow, while the boom, bowsprit boomkin, and spinnaker pole are solid.

Halyards. Dacron, handled by two bronze halyard winches on the mast. Sheets also dacron, with sheet winches on deck aft.

Seraffyn did not have a twin staysail rig but used poled-out headsails to balance the main when running. This may seem an odd omission for a sailor of Larry's obvious sailing experience, but we must remember that *Seraffyn* sailed around the world *eastabout,* not on a tradewind route. At their departure from California, the Pardeys' guiding theme was "as long as it's fun," and their first sailing goals were the Caribbean and the U. S. East Coast. By the time they reached Virginia—with a circumnavigation by no means decided upon—they had sailed too great a distance to backtrack to the Pacific for a tradewind voyage around the world. (The world-voyage decision, in fact, was not made until they had reached the eastern Mediterranean and weighed the alternatives of Suez and eastward against returning to Gibraltar for a westward crossing of the South Atlantic.)

The really significant point about *Seraffyn*'s rig is that she carried a very large sail area for the displacement. This is desirable for a pure cruising boat, which spends a preponderance of time in light winds, but the feature is hard to come by except in the custom boat. This may have caused more frequent reefing aboard *Seraffyn,* but there was less sail changing. With her full working rig aloft, she would more often reach her hull speed of 6.31 knots (S/L 1.34) when winds exceeded 15 knots—say about 20. Even in light airs, her genoa of 396 square feet and spinnaker of 1000 square feet would keep her moving at respectable speeds.

The Cabin

The cabin plan in Fig. 11-6 pretty well shows the layout below, though not in great detail. The head, located forward, was not fitted; instead, the Pardeys adopted the "bucket and chuck-it" approach. This was probably acceptable then in most of the world outside the United States, but its legality has narrowed considerably since they first sailed off two decades ago.

The top-opening icebox to starboard, with a flip-down chart table above it, holds 100 pounds of ice and is well enough insulated that the ice lasts about nine days.

Not obvious but highly unusual is that Larry did not build a single drawer in the boat. His reasoning is that besides being a time-consuming job during construction, the drawer framing sharply reduces stowage space. So he fitted top-opening bins throughout. (About three cubic feet of the overall stowage space is devoted to the tools with which he had built the boat.)

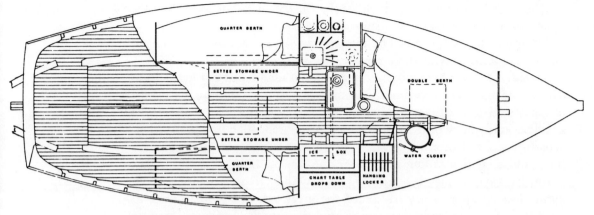

Fig. 11–6. Seraffyn: *Deck/Cabin Plan. (Plan courtesy Lyle C. Hess.)*

A special feature of *Seraffyn* is the two "honeymoon" berths. One double is in the forepeak. Though smallish, it was made possible (remember the LWL is only 22 feet) by the absence of an engine, which makes the area under the cockpit available for seven bags of sails and the water tank. The other double is in the cockpit, described above.

Finally, the galley merits special study (Fig. 11-6). First, the Pardeys departed from the more conventional choice of a kerosene stove and chose a three-burner propane stove with oven. Second, it is sited athwartships— possible because of the 8′11″ beam. Both feel strongly that this position for the stove, well bolted down, is far superior to the gimbaled stove parallel to the keel. Their reason is that a boat's rolling motion is worse than its pitching, and that even in gimbals a stove may throw the boiling contents of a pot onto the cook. (They met two women who were severely burned this way and heard of a third who was so badly burned she had to be evacuated to civilization by helicopter.) With the stove set athwartships, an extra-heavy lurch in the midst of rolling will throw a pot's contents to port or starboard. Even this risk can be virtually eliminated by use of deep pots, high stove rails, and good pot clamps. Further, the deep sink, just an arm's reach from the stove, provided Lin with a handy "bin" in which to place a full pot if Larry yelled a warning or if she were suddenly needed on deck.

Otherwise, Larry fitted a maple drain board in place of the usual formica. The sink was gravity-fed from the ten-gallon tank in the box on deck, which in turned was filled from the tank under the cockpit with a jerrijug and siphoning hose. This is the essence of simplicity-cum-convenience—running water at the sink, but only dependent upon a simple transfer pump. There was also a below-water-level tap for sea water, used for washing dishes and cooking vegetables. And for Lin, 4′10″ in height, this galley provided full headroom within the trunk and put everything within arm's reach.

In the forepeak, an eight-gallon kerosene tank sat atop the chain locker, with copper tubing running to a petcock in the main cabin—a neat, easy, fast way to fill the cabin and navigation lights. As Larry says, " . . . filling lamps in a rough sea with a can and a funnel will exasperate even the most patient sailor."

By any standard, *Seraffyn*'s cabin was well ventilated. In Larry's words: "Ventilation is the life blood of a wooden boat and vital to the comfort of the crew. Air flow on *Seraffyn* is provided by a cowl vent forward, a hatch over the double bunk, a four-way opening hatch over the galley with glass in it for light, four 4-inch by 7-inch opening ports in the cabin sides, the companionway hatch, and sliding doors at the foot of each quarter berth which allow air to flow through the bunks and below the cockpit."

For light, the cutter had four kerosene lamps with extra-large smoke bells to protect the overhead even at large angles of heel.

The quarter berths provided snug, safe, and comfortable sleeping at sea, the forward double only being used in port and the cockpit double when at anchor in fair weather.

The two small settees, inboard of the quarter berths, are a real conve-

Fig. 11–7. *Lin Pardey in* Seraffyn*'s galley. (Photo courtesy the Pardeys.)*

nience. They provide each berth occupant with a bin for personal clothing, a seat for pulling on shoes or boots, and, with the dining (and typing) table pulled out from under the cockpit and set up with its folding leg, luxurious seats for just Lin and Larry when eating, or seating for another couple aboard for a meal.

Finally, it's a rare boat today whose complete interior is brightwork—teak, oak, mahogany—but that was so on *Seraffyn*. Beautiful and traditional shipbuilding woods, each covered with four to five coats of varnish, hand-sanded between coats—this was just one time-consuming job tackled by Lin, not to mention the 4000 wood plugs she glued into the hull. The interior, though darker-hued than most boats today, nevertheless had its good points —it is highly resistant to dirt and finger marks and easier to clean when it does get dirty. The cost of such a finish, of course, is sanding and varnishing every four or five years. Still, to judge by today's auxiliaries, nothing seems to satisfy a boat owner like teak.

Stores, Gear, and Refits

Navigation. The Pardeys had the minimal list: leadline, taffrail log, compass (mounted to starboard in the after end of the cabin), sextant, chronometer, and oil navigation lamps. One of only two electrical gadgets aboard was the Zenith Trans-Oceanic radio receiver. Used for getting weather reports, time-ticks, and short-wave radio entertainment, it performed reliably throughout. The other electrically operated item (also using D batteries) was the stereo casette player, and it—as if to confirm their distrust of things electrical—gave constant trouble; fortunately, it was not critical to the safe operation of the ship. The rest of the navigator's department contained the usual plotting tools: *Pilot Charts*, *Light Lists*, the current *Nautical Almanac*, *H. O. 214 Tables*, *Sailing Directions*, *Ocean Passages for The World*, and "charts for every port from California to the Panama Canal."

The windvane was built by Larry—with a bit of outside fabrication—and operated by actuating a trim-tab in the trailing edge of the rudder. This is our first boat to have vane steering, although they were in rapidly widening use by 1968, when the Pardeys sailed from California. (None of our last three boats, right up to 1980, had a vane.)

Just before departure from Newport Beach, the Pardeys went on their last serious shopping trip, for items practically unavailable in Mexico: sail needles and twine, stainless steel shackles, books, wine, and canned butter. And of course, they bought enough canned and dried foods to last three months. In all, 3000 pounds of food and gear disappeared into *Seraffyn*'s lockers—including a comprehensive medical kit.

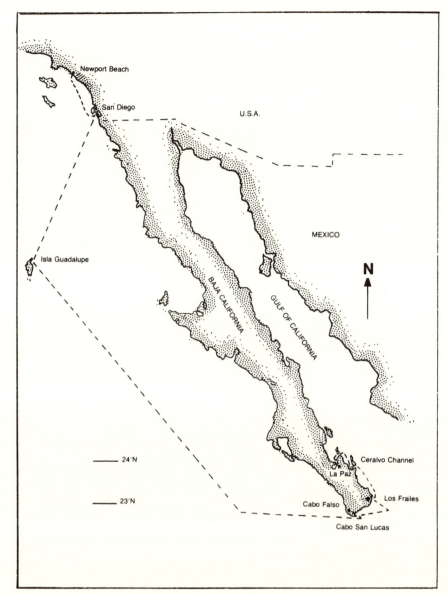

Fig. 11–8. *Chart: Newport Beach, Calif., to LaPaz, Mexico.*

At Guaymas, Mexico, their first mainland Mexican port, they did a job that was unique to *Seraffyn* among all the boats in this book and possible because they had no electrics. They emptied it out—every single moveable item—and then, as Lin describes it:

> With a hose and bucket of soapy water, we scrubbed *Seraffyn* from chain locker to stern post, flushing down the soap and dirt [with fresh water] as we

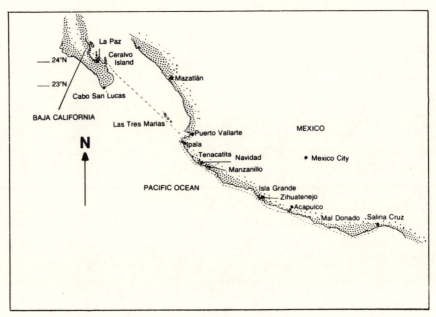

Fig. 11–9. *Chart: LaPaz, Mex., to Salina Cruz, Mexico. (Charts courtesy Seven Seas Press.)*

went along, and pumping the bilges as she filled. We inspected every inch of the boat as we dried it out with a chamois. Then we returned everything to its place, checking each item before putting it back aboard. Things such as paint cans with only a half-inch of old paint were chucked out; our rubbish heap was staggering. We polished our oil lamps and trimmed the wicks. Larry inspected the rigging from truck to deck. Then, after three days of varnishing the exterior brightwork, we had a new boat.

This routine they followed religiously twice a year, and besides the gain in cleanliness, the big bonus was the removal of sea salt from below decks. Salt, being a hydroscopic agent, gets below in great quantity despite all efforts to prevent it, and thereafter it constantly absorbs moisture from the air, leading to mustiness below, mildewed clothing, rust on ferrous metals, and general clamminess that increases discomfort of humid days. With a semiannual flushout, the Pardeys avoided this annoyance.

At LaPaz they began the first of several yacht delivery jobs (to California). On one of them, with their return air fare paid, they arrived back at *Seraffyn* carrying a twenty-five-pound CQR anchor—which Larry had sworn to buy after two anchoring mishaps with their twenty-two-pound Danforth (first coral and then a net caught in the flukes), either of which might have cost them the boat.

At Acapulco, where large supermarkets were again handy, they laid in stores to replace what they had consumed in almost a year of cruising Mexican waters—during which they had sailed 3600 miles.

In Puntarenas, Costa Rica, Larry contracted to do a big repair job, rebuilding a 48-foot sportfisherman that was "suffering from dry rot." When he had finished—taking four months—their cruising fund had been given a healthy shot of cash. During that period Lin "put three coats of varnish on everything, painted the bulwarks, the cove stripe and the bowsprit." After six months in Costa Rican waters, they hauled *Seraffyn* for fresh bottom paint and restocked the food lockers.

At Balboa, in the Canal Zone, Lin bought a small turkey in the U. S. Commissary. Then, sailing on a broad reach back to the Las Perlas Islands, she put it in the oven. By the time they were anchored in the lee of Contadora Island, the bird was roasted. Sitting in the cockpit, they gorged themselves on a traditional Thanksgiving dinner: turkey, dressing, gravy, candied yams, cranberry sauce, mixed salad, mince pie, and coffee. Such meals weren't an everyday occurrence aboard *Seraffyn,* but they illustrate that the "sacrifices" others imagined they suffered on so small a boat were more imagined than real.

Back again at Balboa, they had the radio checked out and the chronometer rated. For the canal transit (fee: $4.83), they borrowed an outboard and Larry jury-rigged a bracket for it on the boomkin. On the Atlantic side— a good source of fitting-out supplies—they spent a week at the Panama

Fig. 11–10. *Chart: Santa Cruz, Mex., to Panama.*

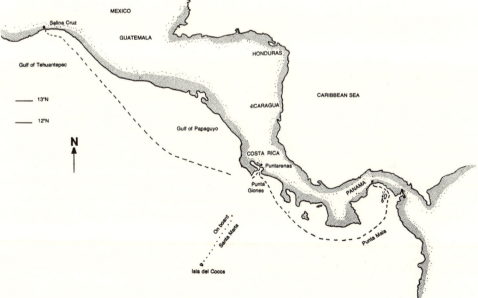

National Yacht Club, where they scraped the teak decks, and Larry sewed a third set of reef points into the mainsail—a decision dictated by the fact that they were facing virtually all windward work in the Caribbean. Just before departing they put aboard a locker full of duty-free stores.

At Cartagena, Colombia, *Seraffyn* was anchored in a small lagoon with a tidal range of only twenty inches, but they were able to keep the cutter standing on her keel with lines running out to anchors set to port and starboard. The tidal ebb was just enough to let them scrape off the original enamel paint boot-top and a swath of bottom paint, apply three coats of creosote, and then repaint this band around the hull with anti-fouling and a new boot-top.

At Kingston, Jamaica, they hauled again, this time at the Royal Jamaica Y. C. (made temporary members to enjoy this privilege) for just a day to scrub and paint the entire bottom.

At Miami's Dinner Key Marina, one day while they were away, *Seraffyn*'s channels were deeply gouged when the cutter was bashed against a dock during one of the frequent squalls that swept the area, but Larry was able to grave in a new piece and repaint it in one long day of work. Here, too, he got another repair job on a mast that further fattened their cruising fund. And while they were in Miami, more yacht delivery jobs came their way.

In Urbanna, Virginia, they removed *Seraffyn*'s mast and rigging and stored her afloat in a waterside shed through the winter of 1972–73. Larry got a job at the boatbuilding yard in Urbanna, and several more delivery jobs came along. Working weekends, they stripped the cutter bare and flushed her out again. Lin took up writing boating articles and had the thrill of selling the first of many subsequent articles—which provided more "freedom chips," their name for cruising funds.

Over that winter they also: 1) stripped and revarnished (six coats) the mast and boom; 2) repaired the dinghy seats; 3) spliced the new stainless wire from England; 4) had the propane tank repaired; 5) purchased charts from Virginia via Bermuda across the Atlantic to England; 6) stripped the hull to bare wood and repainted it; 7) varished the hatches and bilges; 8) gold-leafed the name on the transom; and 9) painted the blue bulwark trim. In all, this major refit consumed almost 500 hours of working time and $400 for materials. By Larry's estimate, the cost of this work in a boatyard at then-current hourly rates would have been nearly $3000—another example of how the smaller boat, capable of being maintained by its owners, lowers costs and keeps you cruising longer.

Just before departure from Virginia, they took on stores: a 20-pound turkey (a gift), 100 pounds of ice, 25 pounds each of onions and potatoes, 144 fresh eggs, fresh meat, and fruit.

At Norfolk, just before jumping off for Bermuda, "A friendly but very busy sailmaker was kind enough to let us sew up a new vane cover on his machine." And then they were off.

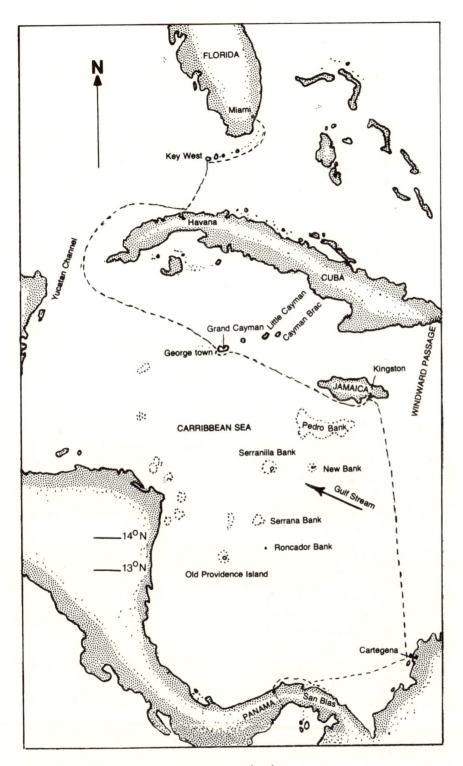

N

FLORIDA

Miami

Key West

Yucatan Channel

Havana

CUBA

Grand Cayman Little Cayman Cayman Brac

George town

Kingston

JAMAICA

WINDWARD PASSAGE

CARRIBBEAN SEA

Pedro Bank

Serranilla Bank

New Bank

Gulf Stream

14°N

Serrana Bank

13°N

Roncador Bank

Old Providence Island

Cartegena

San Blas

PANAMA

Fig. 11–11. *Chart: Panama to Miami, Florida.*

279

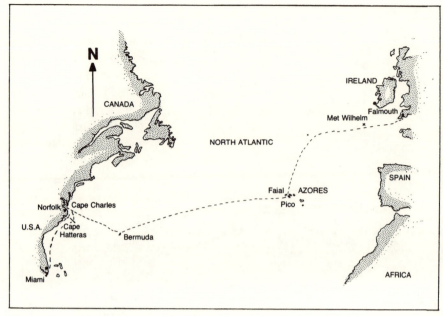

Fig. 11–12. *Chart: Miami to Virginia to England.*

During a month at Bermuda (they had planned to stay a week), they sailed as crew in local dinghy races, went sightseeing, and enjoyed living at anchor in the open harbor of St. George's. In one of the curious coincidences that occur in the remarkably small world of the cruising fraternity, when the Pardeys sailed as crew in a keel boat race, the skipper was Laury Brangman, almost certainly a relative of the Fred Brangman who recut *Cimba*'s mainsail (chapter 5).

Just before the Atlantic crossing, Lin put aboard the following stores: green tomatoes and lemons (individually wrapped in newspaper), four cabbages, six cucumbers, and more onions. They still had eight dozen eggs left from Virginia, which were turned over every day and which lasted a total of three months. They also found canned Camembert and Brie and filled their various tanks with water, propane, and kerosene.

On the day they sailed from Bermuda, late in the afternoon, Lin discovered that the kerosene tank in the forepeak was leaking—a crack in the solder around the filler pipe. With the crack spurting kerosene at every surge of the boat, no way to stop the leak, and kerosene the only fuel for their lamps, Larry decided there was no choice but to put about. In three and a half hours they were back in harbor. The resoldering job was completed the next day—removing the tank was the hardest part—and they sailed again. Their next port was Horta in the Azores, and then it was on to Falmouth, England.

Seraffyn's ports of call: Newport Beach, California . . . San Diego . . . Isla Guadaloupe, Mexico . . . Cabo San Lucas . . . LaPaz . . . Isla Espiritu Santo . . . Isla San Francisquito . . . San Everisto . . . Rancho los Delores . . . Aqua Verde . . . Escondito . . . Isla Carmen . . . Loreto . . . Isla Coronados . . . Santispac . . . Mulege . . . Isla San Marcos . . . Santa Rosalia . . . Guaymas . . . San Carlos . . . LaPaz . . . Isla Ceralvo . . . Puerto Vallarta . . . Ipala . . . Tenacatiti . . . Navidad . . . Manzanillo . . . Isla Grande . . . Zihuatenejo . . . Acapulco . . . Salina Cruz . . . Puntarenas, Costa Rica . . . Panama City, Panama . . . Balboa, Canal Zone . . . Las Perlas Islands . . . (transit canal) . . . Colon, Canal Zone . . . Portobelo, Panama . . . Isla Grande . . . San Blas Islands . . . Cartegena, Colombia . . . Kingston, Jamaica . . . Georgetown, Grand Cayman Island . . . Key West, Florida . . . Miami . . . Urbanna, Virginia . . . Cape Charles (anchored) . . . Norfolk . . . St. George, Bermuda . . . Horta, Fayal, Azores . . . Falmouth, England.

Performance

One of the first indications of *Seraffyn*'s superior sailing ability was demonstrated while the Pardeys were still cruising the Gulf of California. One night, sailing on a beam reach with a following sea, they were "practically surfing" as they roared along toward the lights marking the entrance to Guaymas. Taking two shore bearings in the moonlight, Larry later confirmed that they had held a speed of 7 knots for several hours. So, with that first concrete example, we should look at her numbers:

Seraffyn: Speed/Length Ratio			
(WL = 22' 2" $\sqrt{22.2}$ = 4.71)			
S/L	$\sqrt{WL}$ =	Speed (knots) × 24 =	NM (1 day)
1.0	4.71	4.71	113.0
1.1	4.71	5.18	123.0
1.2	4.71	5.65	133.4
1.3	4.71	6.12	146.9
1.34	4.71	6.31	151.4

So, the 7-knot reach turns out to be an S/L ratio of 1.5. Twenty-four hours at that pace would notch 170 sea miles, but of course such numbers are just the stuff of sailors' dreams.

At Ipala, Mexico, in the Gulf of California, they raced a 34-foot Block Island ketch (with a 10-foot longer LWL) over a 12-mile run to Tenacatiti and beat her by 12 minutes.

Sailing along the coast from Mexico to Guatamala, they ran into a gale and decided to try their sea anchor for the first time. It was an 9-foot-diameter nylon parachute with a trip line. At first it jerked the bow up into the wind, but a few minutes later the cutter's head began to fall off. They tripped the chute, hauled it in, and discovered that the trip line was completely twisted into the shrouds. Setting the chute again, this time without the trip line, they found it now worked fine—reassuring for any future serious need ahead.

Sailing past the Las Perlas (Pearl) Islands en route to Panama, *Seraffyn*'s log recorded 6 knots (S/L 1.25) for several hours.

Departing Portobelo, Panama, and now facing constant windward work to Jamaica and beyond, Larry retuned *Seraffyn*'s rigging. As Lin reports, "In the Pacific most of our sailing had been off the wind, so the rigging had been left slack to ease any strain on the hull and get better downwind performance. Now Larry tightened the shrouds until the mast stood perfectly straight."

Under triple-reefed main and staysail they beat from Cartagena, Colombia, to Kingston, Jamaica, a distance of 480 miles to windward, and averaged ninety-five miles a day—exceptional sailing for a boat with a 22-foot waterline, especially as they kept at it for five days!

After a couple of months in Miami, tired of the hot, muggy weather and the seemingly constant stream of hurricane warnings issuing from the radio (it was September 1972), they sailed north to the Chesapeake, covering the 800-mile northward beat to windward in exactly eight days—an even more impressive example of the cutter's windward ability—this time 100 miles a day.

Once in the Atlantic en route to Bermuda, they caught perfect conditions one day—a beam reach in strong winds—and for several hours creamed along at 6 knots under double-reefed main and staysail only. On the second day out they recorded a 24-hour run of 112 miles—S/L 1.0.

After their two-day delay in departing Bermuda, once *Seraffyn* was fairly into the Atlantic, she really showed her ability to sail. For the next fourteen days Lin and Larry did not have to touch the vane, "Helmer," as it steered the cutter at speeds that hardly ever dropped below 5 knots (S/L 1.1). Here are six nonconsecutive days in the passage to the Azores, with the S/Ls in parentheses after each day's run: 138 (1.23), 120 (1.07), 130 (1.15), 130 (1.15), 120 (1.07), and 128 (1.14). Six days over 100 miles is quite impressive, but even more so is the fact that *Seraffyn* covered the 1900 miles in 15 days, 18 hours, or 15.75 days—an average of 120.6 miles a day. Outstanding! Most larger boats, crossing the Atlantic *westward* under the push of the tradewinds, would be satisfied with such runs.

Fig. II–13. Seraffyn *sailing past Denmark's Elsinore Castle. (Photo courtesy Tom Nibbea.)*

Seraffyn's final leg was 1180 miles from the Azores to England, but the Pardeys had to sail 1412 miles to cover that distance. It didn't start well. They were completely becalmed for twenty-seven hours just outside the Azores, a period nearly half as long as all the hours they had yet been becalmed—sixty-five—in their first three years of cruising. Then the winds returned.

Seraffyn reeled off two twenty-four-hour runs of 115 (1.0) and 125 (1.1), then the wind backed into the north and the next four days only produced 60, 62, 40, and 60 miles—S/Ls not worth noting. (These four days show again how easy it is to kill off a good passage average and drop it below S/L 1.0, and reinforces the point of how impressive a 100-mile day really is.) Then, any chance of a good passage to England was spoiled by a gale that kept them hove to for thirty hours.

On arrival in Falmouth nineteen days out of Horta, the passage looked this way: 1180 miles (rhumb-line distance), average—62.1 MPD, or 1412 miles (actual distance sailed), average—74.3 MPD. If, just out of curiosity, we drop out the one rare day of total calm (twenty-seven hours) and the one and a quarter days (thirty hours) of gale, the above figures improve to 70.4 and 84.2 MPD.

Seraffyn had reached England after her first cross-ocean passage, ready for jaunts to Scandanavia, the Mediterranean, and points east, in what would become by November 1980 one of the rare and commendable eastabout circumnavigations.

Rope Ends

The Pardey book is full of useful wrinkles for the would-be cruising person wondering if such a voyage is practical and possible. A sampling:

- "We have to work about three months a year to pay for cruising in a twenty-four footer. If we went to a thirty-five footer, we'd be working four or five months for money, plus an extra month of work on the boat. . . . "
- Of the hundreds of boats they met, only thirty-two had been cruising for longer than a year.
- Their survey questionnaires revealed that it cost an average of 25 percent over the purchase price to prepare a boat for long-distance cruising.
- Their total monthly cruising expenses (1975) were $300 to $340.
- Cruising expenses jump sharply the second year out as maintenance increases: a mandatory haul-out in an expensive port, serious engine repair, a new sail, replacement of a lost anchor, etc.

Not evident in this factual, data-oriented report, in which the focus has been on the details of hull, rig, and gear and the crew's approach to the cruising realities, is the vital aspect of the Pardeys' mental approach to their circumnavigation: From the time they cast off in California, their guiding principle, as I mentioned earlier, was to keep sailing "as long as it's fun." They stuck to this self-imposed rule, and the result was a circumnavigation that in spirit resembled Harry Pidgeon's much more than those of so many post–World War II contemporaries, for whom the ocean crossing is "the thing" and who either return immediately to terrestrial pursuits or congregate with other yachties in some foreign port for months, even years on end.

In sailing on and on to discover the ever-new fascinations that foreign countries and people can provide, Lin and Larry were not, of course, absolutely unique, for they met many cruising couples who shared their approach, but they were, as their four books amply reveal, part of that select group that knows how to experience a long voyage with a special zest for every part of it.

STRANGER ON THE DOCK (*after several minutes' silent inspection*): *Uh . . . that's a nice boat you've got there, Mister. Taking some kind of cruise somewhere?*

THE CAPTAIN (*painting a hatch cover*): *Well, yes. As a matter of fact I'm sailing to West Africa.*

STRANGER: *West Africa! You must be kidding. That's some voyage. Are you alone?*

CAPTAIN: *No, I'm taking my family—wife and two kids.*

STRANGER: *You're taking your family all the way to Africa on that boat? It's a little small, isn't it? Aren't you afraid?"*

(The conversation continues until the Stranger finally remarks that he wishes he could do the same.)

Wistful strangers on the dock are not rare in this world. Almost every American harbor we entered produced a few. In some the procession seemed endless, my disclaimers and explications a nightly ritual. It's surprising how many American males long to play Jack London and run away to sea. Well, why not? Voyaging is one of the very few occupations remaining in this modern world whereby a man can go where he pleases, do what he wishes, be what he will. The life is certainly attractive, yet pitifully few dockside dreamers ever realize their Great Ambition. What's the problem? Is breaking away all that difficult? I suppose it must be, or more would succeed."

> —Matt Herron
> *The Voyage of Aquarius* (1974)

AUTHOR'S NOTE: This is the first boat in the collection about a *family's* cross-ocean voyage, and the only steel boat. My own years with the steel ketch White Seal pitted a ten-year wood boat owner against the needs of a vessel about whose maintenance I was monumentally ignorant. Two years later I was extolling the virtues of steel boats so loudly and often that I had become a pest to cruising friends. A phrase picked up about that time, from somewhere—familiar but not referring to steel boats—was "To know it is to love it." For me, that was true.

It seems that most of steel's detractors (in print) are out of date regarding the newest technology for preventing rust and electrolysis in steel boats. As to cost—where a one-off boat, as most steel boats are, is under consideration—since the first fuel crisis in 1973, fiber glass boats have made quantam leaps in price, because the materials are petroleum derivatives. During the same period steel prices have only risen at the normal rate of inflation. If construction cost is a major factor, as it usually is, steel deserves serious consideration.

As for strength, there is simply no comparison with any other boatbuilding material, in any respect *(see table below)*. Steel so out-performs all the others, in all measurable properties, that it's no contest. The only explanation for there not being thousands more steel boats is unfamiliarity with the material, an unreasoning fear of rust and electrolysis, and a scarcity of steel boat builders.

The Herrons

*T*here were four of them, Matt (father), Jeannine (mother), Matthew (son), and Melissa (daughter). All got equal billing as authors of their book, because all contributed to its writing.

The decision had been made—the family was going to sail *Aquarius* from New Orleans to West Africa. The reasons were personal, but not that uncommon among cruising families. Matt Herron described the feelings he shared with his wife that led to the decision:

> In a very real sense *Aquarius* was [our] access to a new medium, a sea change I had searched for to restore balance in a life I felt was going soft with comfort and routine. I hoped, somehow, to replace the secondhand experiences, the emotion-by-proxy that had so deadened the taste of life for me in modern electronic America, to replace it with a series of primary encounters between my family, the sea and whatever people the sea might bring to us. It was a romantic idea; I realized that. I wanted to explore hardship and tranquility, touch new coastlines, gaze at unfamiliiar faces, put out questions in an uncharted world and wait for answers to filter back through the circuits of experience.

Aquarius was docked at Eagan's bayou boatyard, about 80 miles from the Herrons' home in New Orleans, and the voyage plan was beginning to unfold with the first tentative steps of fitting out. Whenever Matt Herron was not busy with a magazine assignment—he was a free-lance photographer who worked for many of the national magazines—he would drive the 160-mile round trip to put in a day of work on the sloop.

Then hurricane Camille was born in the Caribbean.

The storm had been tracked for several days, with constant radio and television warnings about its progress up into the Gulf of Mexico. It struck on August 17, 1969. Early that morning Matt raced out to Eagan's yard to see what, if anything, he could do to save his boat. In those low-lying coastal regions it is not unusual for storm tides to rise 20 feet above normal levels —and this hurricane had incredibly high winds. When it struck, Camille had winds of 200 MPH in the New Orleans area, and at Eagan's yard they reached 150 MPH.

Until mid-afternoon that day, Matt worked feverishly against the storm's approach, bracing railroad ties against the hard chines of his sloop. He attached lines to the rails, port and starboard, and ran them out to a telephone pole one way and a massive dredge the other—with a prayer that *they* would ride out the storm. By late afternoon it was raining heavily and the wind was rising. There was no more time and nothing more he could think of to do. So he took refuge in the Eagan's brick house to stand a

Fig. 12–1. *Matt and Melissa Herron. (Photos courtesy Matt Herron.)*

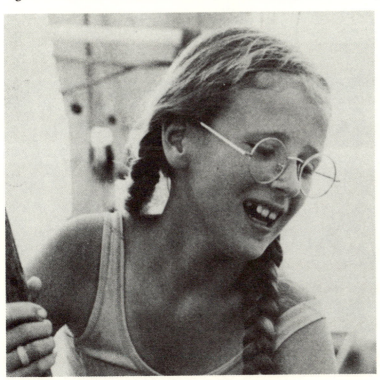

Fig. 12–2. *Jeannine and Matthew Herron.*

hurricane watch with the family, the yard workers, and a few others, like himself, trying to save their boats.

For several hours, as darkness fell over the bayou, the rain fell in great gusting sheets and the wind rose to heights Matt had never before experienced. "Insane fury" sounds like a cliché, but nothing else comes close to describing it. No one dared venture out of the house to see what was happening in the yard. Occasionally Matt would step out onto the partial protection of the porch and aim two flashlight beams in the general direction of his sloop—where he could just make out that one railroad tie under the stern was still standing.

During the night the huddled group in the house heard great shrieking sounds outside: Was it just the wind, or was Camille destroying the yard buildings and all the boats? At one point, while Matt watched, the needle on the kitchen barometer dropped right off the scale. Near dawn, the rising waters of the bayou had crept to within a few feet of the front steps. Matt began marking each new high-water mark by placing a stick in the mud. They were still moving Eagan family possessions to the upper floor when the water stopped rising.

In the gray dawn an hour later, the wind now finally dropping, they went outside. The machine shop—a 40 × 60-foot all-steel building, with the yard's heaviest equipment jacked up and chocked 12 feet above the floor, and with two heavy diesel engines hanging by chains from the 8-inch steel I-beam rafters—was gone without a trace!

Yet, there, standing alone in a corner of the muddy yard, the railroad ties washed away but the two lines still holding, *Aquarius* stood up square on her keel! It must have seemed to Matt Herron like an omen.

Jeannine Herron, a research biologist with all her class work complete for a Ph.D., had just finished four years of work in the lab and lecture hall, while concurrently caring for her family. Now, worn down and needing a change, and with the firm promise of a research job at an institute in California—in two years' time—she found herself thinking that the voyage was exactly what she wanted and needed.

Matthew and Melissa were in school. One familiar refrain their parents heard whenever they discussed the voyage with friends was the thought that —horrors!—they were going to take their children out of school for a year. Both parents, college educated, were confident the correspondence courses they planned to teach their children (used by many cruising families) would be more than adequate—not to mention the much broader education both children would receive from the cruise. At departure, Matthew was thirteen and Melissa, eleven; only she among the four Herrons had grave reservations about going, but these dissipated in time.

This was the Herron crew as the fitting-out for the voyage began in earnest.

The Hull

Aquarius was a design by Al Mason, one of the preeminent naval architects in the United States and perhaps the very best delineator of plans when he is at the drawing board. The design first appeared in *Rudder* magazine's March 1946 issue, under the name *Intrepid.* Mason—two editions of whose design book I had the pleasure of publishing, in 1974 and 1976 —never sold the design himself but licensed the plans on a royalty basis to *Rudder,* where it appeared in the magazine's plans catalogue for over thirty-five years. As designed, she was a hard-chine steel sloop with these dimensions: LOA (designed)—29'; LWL—24'; Beam—9' 6"; Draft—5'; Displacement—15,000 lbs. (est.); Sail Area—350 sq. ft. (est.).

She has a transom stern with outside rudder, and the ballast is in the keel cavity. Matt didn't specify *Aquarius*'s type, but it can be lead or scrap steel, set in tar, cement, or resin. (*White Seal* had 5000 pounds of boiler punchings set in tar.)

The Herrons purchased *Aquarius,* the sloop having been built in somewhat modified form from Mason's original. It was put together in Canada by Jerry St. Jacques, a carpenter who taught himself to weld and then built three boats at once, selling two to pay for his own. He moved his new wife aboard and sailed down the East Coast to Miami, where they lived aboard at dockside quite happily, until they had a daughter and began to feel a need for more space. The Herrons arrived at this psychological moment, bought her (christened *Atria*), renamed her *Aquarius,* and moved her around to New Orleans.

We don't have many specific details on the hull, but one this size usually has ⅛-inch bottom and topside plating—sometimes ³⁄₁₆-inch on the bottom —and a keel trough of ½-inch sides and ¾-inch to 1-inch bottom. The good feature of using lead ballast encapsulated in such a keel—starting with that heavy piece of one-inch steel on the bottom—is that it usually permits the trough to be only about half-full to meet the ballast requirement, and that allows the water tank(s) to be set atop the ballast in the trough, adding to the ballast effect down low and freeing the usual water-tank space elsewhere for added stowage.

Jerry St. Jacques made some basic changes in the design as he built *Aquarius:*

- Instead of the transom stern, he extended the hull lines aft two feet and produced a counter stern, which increased the designed LOA from 29 to 31 feet. This required that the rudder be shortened and carried up through the hull (Fig. 12–4). The prop, instead of being in an aperture, extended aft beyond the top of the rudder blade. In doing this, St. Jacques apparently tried to compensate by increasing the rudder area, but

Fig. 12–3. *Matt standing on* Aquarius's *pulpit. Note the toerail-bulwark, welded directly to the deck.*

he apparently overdid it, so Matt had to cut it down before departure. That's easy with a steel rudder (it is *not* with a wood or fiber glass one, both of which are internally reinforced). All you do is scribe a line, cut off the excess with a torch, and grind the new edge smooth.

- The second major modification was to give the sloop a masthead rig. (We don't know if he made any other adjustments—such as a stronger mast—to compensate for this change.)
- Matt notes: "The carpentry work was superb, every detail solidly made and meticulously finished. Jerry lavished mahogany on the interior and the boat had an elegance not usually associated with steel."

- Before buying her Matt had her surveyed, and the report was that the welding " . . . was solid and plenty strong enough, although not handsome enough to please a master welder," but he concluded that was "Fair enough," as "Jerry was a carpenter, not a steel worker—but he built to last."
- Another interesting point, reminiscent of Larry Pardey's advice in chapter 11: "The hefty winches in the cockpit were homemade. Jerry himself cast them of silicone [*sic*] bronze and they worked quite nicely."
- But on the other hand, " . . . the electrical system was an unmitigated horror: a tangle of household extension cord twisted together and wrapped casually with electrical tape, not a fuze in the boat. Most of the wiring lay in the bilges along with the storage batteries, ready to be drowned by the first influx of water."
- Finally, the sloop was anything but ready for sea. Matt notes that she "was lacking in one other important respect. She had spent most of her days idling at dockside and carried only the minimum gear for cruising —and almost nothing for ocean cruising."

An example of *Aquarius*'s early vulnerabilities: Out daysailing one day, all the crew and some friends were in the cockpit sipping wine—except Matt, who was below trying to repair the head. He gave a heave on his pipe wrench to tighten a plastic through-hull fitting, and it sheared off, the outside flange falling off into the sea and giving Matt a flash shot of golden sand beneath the boat before the sea gushed in. It was a merry few minutes until they got a wooden plug carved and hammered into the hole. *(See below for the solution to this weakness.)*

So began the frantic, rushed, list-making, frustrating, character-testing, and budget-busting period known as fitting-out.

Preparing for Sea

So much work was done we can handle it only as a list. It started seriously in September 1969, barely a month after hurricane Camille, and while the sloop was still at Eagan's yard—without water or electricity since the storm—and with no yard hands available for work on yachts, as they were still trying to put the yard back together.

Matt had firm ideas about condition and quality before departure:

I set a certain standard for these repairs [and modifications]. *Aquarius* must be strong enough to withstand any foreseeable disaster at sea. The mast and rigging must stand up to winds of at least hurricane force; the cockpit drains, hatches and other fittings must be such that the boat could survive a 360-degree roll-over and come up, if not unscathed, at least floating and intact. The battery case, for example, was built strong enough to keep the batteries from shifting or breaking free in a storm, or from dropping out if the boat rolled over. I didn't really expect to encounter any of these nightmare conditions, but I wanted to be ready for them. I felt we were resourceful enough as a family to handle any normal emergency, but I didn't want to expose us to needless dangers caused by equipment failures or lack of preparation.

It's not a bad idea to frame such a guiding statement *before* you start the horrendous job of preparing for a sea voyage, because when you have one, it serves as a quality yardstick to hold up against each job as you approach it—and it's likely to keep you from cutting corners when time and your temper grow short.

For the next several months the Herrons worked on their own in the yard, doing their own welding, spray painting, electrical wiring, and rigging work. Specifically, these jobs were completed:

Enlarged and replaced cockpit drains . . . Replaced all plastic through-hull fittings with welded-in steel collars . . . Fitted a strainer to the engine intake valve . . . Replaced an undersize bilge pump . . . Welded a steel reinforcement under a rudder gudgeon (probably the lowest one) . . . Welded a plate over a crack in the keel . . . Poured cement into inaccessible parts of the bilge where water could collect . . . Faired rough spots in the hull with epoxy compound . . . Fiber glassed both hatch covers and the masthead . . . Cut down the propeller . . . Installed a depth sounder . . . Rewired the engine and the entire boat, converting the electrical system from 6 to 12 volts and replacing the engine's generator with an alternator . . . Fabricated a steel battery box and welded it into the hull (*excellent idea!*) . . . Installed spreader lights . . . Built a fuse box with circuit breakers, a battery-condition indicator, a converter for charging batteries with shore power, and a knife-switch so that both batteries could be used together for ship's lighting or starting the engine . . . Rebuilt the marine toilet . . . Scraped and painted the mast and boom . . . Replaced the galvanized wire rigging with stainless steel wire . . . Rebuilt the masthead fitting . . . Recharged the fire extinguishers . . . Spray painted the entire boat with a five-part metal boat paint system.

By March 1970 these jobs were complete and the sloop went back into the water. The Herrons moved her to the Southern Yacht Club in New Orleans to eliminate the long drive back and forth from their home, and the work continued through April and into May. The pressure to finish mounted by June 1970 and the approach of a new hurricane season. Their plan had been to depart New Orleans by June 1 in order to reach Florida's East Coast in time for a July-August Atlantic crossing.

At New Orleans the work continued at an even faster pace, as the next list of jobs completed *(below)* demonstrates. Matt remarked, "If we had known all that was involved from the beginning, we might have passed over the entire voyage." The final batch of jobs:

Made grab rails for the cabin top and interior . . . Built a "self-draining" [*double coaming*?] forward hatch . . . Built a cover over the main hatch . . . Built and installed lifelines and bow and stern pulpits . . . Installed radio-telephone and aerial . . . Cleaned and painted the [gasoline] tank, painted the engine, and installed a fuel line cut-off valve . . . Installed an engine compartment ventilation system and bilge blower . . . Fitted two new fifteen-gallon water tanks . . . Designed and ordered a storm jib and twin staysails and made a mast tang for a new inner forestay . . . Made an extra spinnaker pole . . . Built a binnacle for the compass . . . Installed self-steering vane . . . Added a mooring cleat to the foredeck . . . Built an icebox in the cockpit and put extra shelves in the galley . . . Added shelves in the hanging locker and head . . . Built a cockpit locker, a cabin table, and racks along the hull sides for canned goods and put a partition in the lazarette . . . Sewed sail covers, cockpit covers, a cockpit awning, and courtesy flags for all the countries of West Africa.

That's an awesome worklist, but there was no escaping it, because, as Matt notes, the sloop had been dock-bound for years, barely cruised, and was not ready for sea. These jobs done by the Herrons remind me of a remark made by a cruising friend, Carl Vilas, author of *Saga of Direction* (Seven Seas Press, 1978) who has owned only two boats in well over a half-century of cruising! (They were a 20-foot keel catboat—twenty years —and the 33-foot cutter *Direction*— 1946 to 1984.) Carl says, "When you get a new boat—even a used one—it takes you at least three seasons of sailing to get her fitted out to suit your own cruising style."

Steel Boat Construction

The inclusion of *Aquarius* in this book prompts some remarks about steel boat construction that would otherwise be inappropriate but may be of special interest to skippers contemplating a custom cruising boat and of at least passing technical interest to owners of nonsteel boats.

- The strength of a steel boat so far surpasses that of any other construction medium as to make any comparison meaningless; against steel there's no contest. This is not to say that steel has no vices, just that its virtues are impressive—especially collectively. For example, in the table below, the only material even approaching steel's strength is aluminum. But that medium, to me, loses some of its attraction by being much more expensive than steel. It's lightness, however, makes it very attractive for racing boats.
- Beside the inherent strength of steel itself, a welded steel boat is what marine engineers and naval architects call a monocoque structure; that is, its entire hull is a single continuous unit. Welding does not join two

Ultimate Strength of Various Boatbuilding Materials

Material	Tensile Strength	Compression Strength	Modulus of Elasticity
			(10^6)
Ferro–Cement	1690 psi	12,225 psi	1.3
Douglas Fir	2150 psi	1550 psi	1.6
Structural Steel	60,000 psi	60,000 psi	28.9
Aluminum (6061–T6)	42,000 psi	32,000 psi	10.0
Fiber Glass	11–30,000 psi	17,000 psi	1–2.0

steel plates with a joint, like glue; rather, it makes two steel plates into one, and the welding line is no weaker than the original plates on either side. A steel boat is like a lobster, its "skeleton" being its exterior shell. Steel boats have very little internal framing to begin with, and when steel boats are built over a jig—especially if they are double- or triple-chine construction—they can be built with virtually no framing at all. In fact, most of the framing in even a single-chine boat serves to define the shape until all the hull plating is welded together. A wood boat, on the other hand, is more like a whale, with a true internal skeleton of fairly robust dimensions and an outer skin of wood to keep out the water.

Fiber glass boats share many of these monocoque properties, with the hull, deck-cockpit-cabin unit, headliner, and hull liner molded as separate units and then bonded into the hull, either mechanically (bolts) or chemically (fiber glass and adhesives) or both. The hull liner, with its shaped interior furniture (berths, settees, galley flat, etc.), is an innovation about ten years old, whereas fiber glass boats in general are over thirty-five years old. These hull liners—in addition to reducing building costs by eliminating costly piece-by-piece carpentry—materially contribute to hull stiffness and strength because at every point in on the hull where they touch and are bonded, they act as a skeleton and materially reduce the expanse of unsupported hull surface. Some of the best built fiber glass boats of today also have "hat section" stringers bonded into the hull in areas of greatest stress —suggesting that the latest FRP engineering data indicates that this type of monocoque structure does need additional internal stiffening. This points up the value of steel's strength factors shown in the table above, since that strength is largely in the skin.

Of course, one could overcome this fiber glass vulnerability by increasing the hull thickness to the point where it delivered the marine engineer's strength specification without internal stiffening, but that would add considerable weight and give a massive nudge to the cost because, as noted earlier, these products are petroleum derivatives. Or, you could take the newer approach and go to foam-core (or balsa-core) construction (two glass skins with an ultralightweight material between that so thickens the cross-section that it sharply increases strength factors with little additional weight.) But this is a trickier, costlier technology. However, there are welcome fringe benefits from core construction—excellent heat and sound insulation and, in smaller boats, a floatation property.

These points about fiber glass boats are made in the interest of being even handed while singing the largely unknown, or misunderstood, qualities of steel boats. So, in fairness it must be added that steel boats—the plating having high conductive properties—need insulation against the skin or they will sweat heavily in rapid changes of temperature—as FRP boats did before the introduction of hull liners.

The final, critical item of comparison is this: While the finished steel hull is a single unit, no part weaker than any other, the fiber glass boat's hull-deck joint remains forever a vulnerable juncture in the structure, despite the two bonding systems used. Without making a sweeping condemnation, even one failure in this critical hull-deck joint is too many, yet we read about such failures in the yachting press. There would be more of these horror stories in the magazines but for the fact that boat manufacturers are the advertising bread-and-butter of the magazines, and only a small percentage of owners so afficted can—or are keen to—tell their sad stories.

Another impressive feature of steel boat construction appears at this same hull-deck joint and is revealed by *Aquarius* in Fig. 12–3. She has toerails that appear to be simple upward extensions of the topsides but in fact are separate pieces of steel welded on top of the pipe (or bar) that forms the corner between deck and topsides. When this toerail—or bulwark—is welded in place, it's easy to weld on top of it a "caprail" of pipe. When this is done with a continuous weld (tack-welding may lead to rust at the unwelded sections), the structure is tremendously strong because the curves of both elements become a locked-in curve by the weldment.

On *Aquarius* the bulwark was about 3 inches high amidships, rising to 6 inches at the bow. Probably ⅛-inch steel, such a bulwark provides other benefits: 1. If you want a hawse pipe in the bow, simply cut an oval hole in the steel and weld in a large chain link—no other refinforcement being necessary; and, you don't need bow chocks. 2. You gain a solid base for stronger-than-usual lifeline stanchions; just weld a steel "socket" (a 6- or 8-inch pipe of the next larger size than your stanchions, with a Vee cut in the bottom to drain water) to the deck, bulwark, and caprail, and drop the stanchion into it; if you mangle a stanchion against a dock, just unreeve the lifelines and drop in your spare stanchion (the one you were wise enough to make up when you installed this system); a piece of pipe costs a pittance compared to the "gold-plated" stanchions in the catalogues. 3. The outboard face of the caprail goes a long way toward serving as an upper rubrail (the bulwark should be vertical, not follow the rake of the topsides); although not as strong as the lower rubrail, it will help considerably when being bashed against a dock and give good protection to the lifeline sockets. 4. You can cut as many scuppers in the bulwark as you want, thus providing as many attachment points for sheet-lead blocks as you need, and if all the scuppers don't provide enough points, it's easy to weld additional chain links to the top of the caprail, and any one of them will hold the biggest genoa. 5. Such a bulwark is so strong that chainplates are just rectangular pieces of steel—say, ¼-inch—standing on edge at right angles to the bulwarks and welded to the deck, bulwark, and caprail, with the lower outboard corner cut off to let water run down the deck. 6. While not as pretty as teak or mahogany, a pipe caprail is cheap, practical, less vulnerable to damage than wood, very strong, and requires only the same maintenance as the rest of the boat. 7. When I wanted some strong midship cleats for spring-lines on my steel ketch, I bought 6-inch galvanized cleats and welded them to the caprail, canted slightly inboard so they wouldn't be torn off on a dock.

To continue with steel's virtues: The prospective backyard builder, currently debating which construction material to select for the cruising boat that will take him beyond horizons, would do well to give serious consideration to steel, even if he now knows nothing about it. I suspect that most people in such a position are considering the familiar materials: if they like wood, then carvel or strip planking or perhaps marine plywood; if they lean toward fiberglass and the project is a one-off hull (I discount the skilled amateur who could, and would, build a wood mold and, after laying up a glass hull, sell off the mold to recoup his investment), then Airex foam core or C-flex construction; if a heavy displacement hull is in prospect, ferro-cement.

Steel deserves to be weighed as carefully as the others. The material is relatively cheap, as, not being a petroleum derivative, in the years since the first fuel crisis its cost has risen only the normal rate of inflation. Welding is not that difficult (it just takes patience and practice) and can be learned in an adult evening program at a local school or in a trade school course of about six weeks (sometimes given at night). Even today the complete outfit to do welding is not much more than $1000—a welding machine (requires 220 volts), a cutting torch, a good grinder, and personal gear like mask, leather gloves, chipping hammer, etc. When the boat is complete, one can sell all this and recover about half of the outlay—something commonly done. The only objection to using this approach with aluminum as well is that the material cost is high due to the great amount of energy used to manufacture it. And, welding aluminum is a good deal trickier than working with steel.

The Deck

The available photos of *Aquarius* don't provide any deck views, except for the cockpit and bow. The cockpit is more modern than in other boats in this collection, except for *Mahina* in chapter 14. It is the commonly seen length of about 6 feet or so (you could sleep on the seats in fair weather), with a bridge deck and companionway on the centerline. But let's start with the stern.

Aft, the deck is unbroken by a hatch, as the lazarette is reached by a door in the after end of the footwell—another of the many design choices: a smooth deck on which you won't crack a toe on a hatch that might leak in heavy weather versus a lazarette door that might leak if the cockpit is filled by the sea.

Moving back into the cockpit, we find two unusual and commendable design features: seats that are lower than the side decks (with high coamings for good back support and better spray protection) and a bridge deck that is higher than the side decks. The cockpit is scuppered. One of the nice things about a steel boat is that instead of using expensive bronze or vulnerable plastic through-hull fittings for scuppers, you simply drill a hole and weld a piece of steel pipe underneath for the hose. The strength and simplicity of this is offset by the care you must take to isolate bronze seacocks from the steel hull.

With steel boat construction, the cockpit footwell is really just a box hanging from seat edges, the bridge deck, and the after deck. It requires hardly any internal framing to hold it up, so the under-cockpit area is roomier and easier to crawl through and offers more storage space. However, if you forget that you own a steel boat, your knuckles, elbows, skull, and shins will always be carrying a bruise to remind you that there's no free lunch.

Aquarius has three seat lockers, the forward one on the starboard side being a well-insulated icebox.

The bridge deck is especially noteworthy for being higher than the seats. This puts the companionway threshold—about 4 inches higher—well above the side decks. Two drop-slides close it, and with one slide in place and the hatch closed, the cabin can have fresh air without much water getting below —even on a rainy day.

The lifeline stanchions appear to be installed as described above (that is, welded), but they have "loops" on the inboard edge of the sockets—for attaching blocks or fenders—so it is possible that the sockets are bolted-on bronze. Or, the builder was smart enough to crib the idea from the commercial type and weld on loops of steel rod. The lifelines themselves are double, of wire, and there is a place to open them amidships, port and starboard, for easy access to the deck.

The foredeck is laid out in a way I have always favored—no hatch to break its surface. Instead, the forehatch is installed in the cabintop (with its double-coaming, noted in the worklist, *above*). It seems to me this setup is far preferable to others for keeping the boat dry below. Even on a fine day, with only a mild breeze, if you have a deck-fitted hatch open for ventilation, sooner or later the bow bashes into a confluence of waves that sends one great dollop of sea over the bow and straight down the hatch.

The cabin trunk has a rather high crown—probably for headroom below—and just three nonopening rectangular windows, two in the after end of the trunk sides (above thesplit gallery), and one in the forward end of the trunk.

On the side decks, the Herrons occasionally carried jerricans of extra gasoline lashed to the lifelines, or in a special rack Matt built for them on the cabintop just before they sailed.

Up in the bow (Fig. 12-3), the bulwarks are higher, 6 inches, tapering up from about 3 inches amidships. Here we see the pulpit Matt made in New Orleans, the chain deck-pipe for the chain rode, the Danforth anchor, and a piece of split pipe (steel or plastic) in which the Danforth's shank rested —a permanent stowage set-up.

The Rig

We have no figures for the sail areas (none mentioned in the book), but an estimate of about 350–400 square feet seems about right for the working rig of mainsail and jib, increasing to about 450–475 square feet with the genny hoisted.

Aquarius had a wood mast of oval section, so it's likely—though not certain—that this was a solid stick, and the boom almost certainly was solid.

As the jib was overlapping, its sheets were handled by a pair of bronze sheet winches mounted on pedestals outside the cockpit coamings. Two more winches, for the jib and main halyards, were mounted on the mast.

The mainsheet had its track mounted on the after end of the bridge deck, and its car could ride nearly the full width of the cockpit. Just below the track, on the after face of the bridge deck (remember, it is higher than the seats), the mainsheet cleat was mounted. So the helmsman, with hand on the tiller, sat in the forward end of the cockpit, with the sheet and cleat just an arm's length away—very handy. Of course, hauling on the sheet means using both hands, but the skipper with a tiller soon learns to steer with his leg—or teeth—to leave both hands free. The main sheet itself is four-part, with two double blocks—one on the end of the boom, the other shackled to the car riding the track.

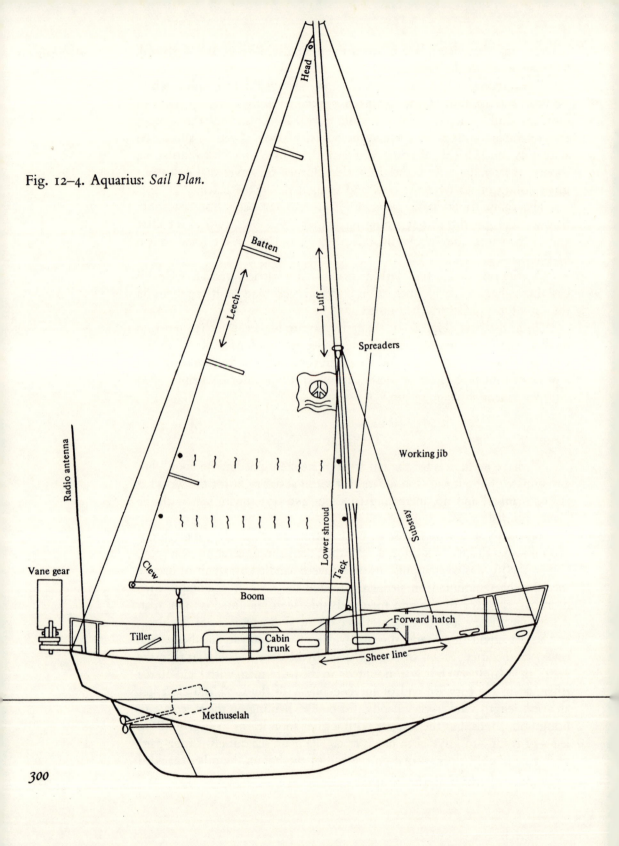

Fig. 12–4. Aquarius: *Sail Plan.*

Head

Batten

Leech

Luff

Spreaders

Radio antenna

Working jib

Lower shroud

Substay

Vane gear

Clew

Tack

Boom

Forward hatch

Tiller

Cabin trunk

Sheer line

Methuselah

300

As a guess, the main halyard ran over a sheave let into the masthead, and the jib halyard block hung from a tang on the forward face of the mast —with the backstay running off the after end.

Fig. 12-4 provides only the general proportions of the rig, but except for one omission (a line not completely drawn), it shows the standing rigging: jibstay and backstay, lower shrouds, upper shrouds passing over the spreaders (the top part of the upper shroud is the line not completed), and an inner stay, running to the foredeck and labeled "substay." This is the one unusual, but very practical, item of standing rigging aboard *Aquarius,* a wire whose upper end was permanently attached to the mast at the spreaders, with its lower end just lashed to the mast (or lifelines) in fair weather when the jib or genoa was in use. But in heavy weather, the lower end was shackled to the deck (probably with a turnbuckle or pelican hook) in the position shown. When set up, it provided a fine, inboard position for the storm jib, easier to set and lower in the heavy motion of a gale, and bringing the sail's center of effort aft a bit and closer to the hull's center of lateral resistance. This made the driving effort more efficient when sailing, and when the sloop was hove to under the storm jib, the bow would not be blown to leeward so readily.

Finally, there was a pair of twin staysails, which were set upon their own removable wire stays, whose lower ends were fixed to eyebolts in the foredeck just forward of the trunk cabin.

The Cabin

Though the cabin plan in Fig. 12-5 is a bit more representational than schematically precise, it gives an adequate sense of the layout below. The cabin is the first one we've seen that closely resembles the typical modern auxiliary. (The only change that would make it more so is a chart table opposite a port-side galley, but *Aquarius* didn't have the interior length for that.)

Fig. 12-5. Aquarius: *Cabin plan.*

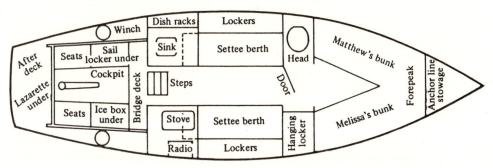

So, we find **V**-berths forward, the head opposite a hanging locker, midship settees, and galley aft, split to port and starboard. Note that the settees, to be sleeping berths, have their ends extending under the galley flats —an unavoidable overlap dictated by the 22-foot waterline.

Of the three lockers under the cockpit seats, the forward one on the port side was an icebox, and it may have been reachable by the cook when standing on the companionway steps.

As for sleeping arrangements, the children occupied the forward cabin and their parents the main cabin—with a door between for privacy.

The stowage space was the usual arrangement—in lockers outboard of the settees, under the bunks, in the bilges (canned and dried foods) and the batten racks mentioned above for storing canned goods against the hull outboard of the settee backs—plus the extra shelves noted earlier.

The Engine

The engine, according to Matt, was an ancient four-cylinder Graymarine gasoline model, probably 25 HP. When he wrote to the company and sent the serial number, he learned it was thirty-three years old! So they named it *Methuselah*.

The gas tank held fifteen gallons, but with extra jerricans the range under power was increased to 300 miles.

The engine gave them trouble several times during the voyage—water in the gas and a clogged carburetor—but each time they were able to solve the problem, and they kept it going all the way to Africa.

Stores, Gear, and Refits

Because *Aquarius* was so shy of cruising gear when they bought her, the Herrons had to make many gear purchases, including:

"Rope, blocks and deck tackle . . . Two Timex Quartz watches (to serve as chronometers) . . . Hand-bearing compass . . . Sextant . . . Charts . . . Zodiac inflatable dinghy . . . Personal safety lights . . . Flares . . . Gasoline-powered emergency pump . . . Radio direction finder . . . Shortwave radio . . . Radio-telephone . . . Spare anchor and 500-ft. rode . . . Binoculars . . . Stopwatch . . . SCUBA gear . . . Engine spares . . . Life jackets . . . Hand tools . . . Foul weather gear . . . Boat hook . . . Hand-held signal light."

The cliché has it that a boat is never done, and most skippers discover this to be one of cruising's basic truths. The trick, it appears, is to leave when all essentials are complete—experience being the arbiter of that—and finish the work along the way. That's what was finally done aboard *Aquarius,* between New Orleans and Fort Pierce, as follows:

Made bo'sun's chair (Biloxi, Miss.) . . . Installed depth sounder (Biloxi) . . . Made reefing gear for mainsail, calibrated compass, and made chip log (Panama City, Fla.) . . . Made baggywrinkle (Panama City to Azores) . . . Installed screens (along Okeechobee Waterway) . . . Made frame on cabin top for storing fuel cans and Zodiac (Fort Pierce) . . . Made engine crank (Bermuda) . . . Installed automatic bilge pump (Canary Islands).

The sloop carried two anchors, one of them a 22-pound Danforth with a 250-foot, ¾-inch nylon rode; the other one's type and weight were not given.

The running lights were electric; cabin lights, kerosene.

Jeannine took charge of stores and stowage, a job that will test the organizational ability—and sanity—of the victim. With ideas culled from books and cruising friends, and her own ingenuity, she did an outstanding job—considering the volume of food needed for four persons for four to five months, two of them children, for whom she included many "treats." Some examples of how she handled the job:

- At a railroad salvage outlet she bought "slightly dented" cans of food, sometimes in case lots, at a fraction of supermarket cost: catsup, pork and beans, wheat germ, canned fruits and juices, corned beef hash, raisins, honey, paper towels, soups, condensed milk, vegetables, etc.
- Helped by Matthew and Melissa, she labeled every can with a water-proof marker and then dipped it—first one end, then the other—in paraffin or varnish. With this system, even cans stowed in the bilges resisted rust, with only a few losses.
- For dried foods (flour, brown rice, cereals, etc.) she used one-gallon mayonnaise jars. After filling each jar, a "walnut-sized" piece of dry ice was put in the top (the carbon dioxide given off by this apparently displacing the oxygen that might have permitted bacterial growth). Each lid was screwed on, and the entire top of the jar was dipped in paraffin. She reports: "The dry ice did its work of preservation. Later, on the high seas . . . we would draw up [from the bilges] . . . plastic jars coated with the grease and *ick* of ten months of voyaging and, after scrubbing the outside, we would find the contents as fresh and delicious as the day it was packed. The wheat flour, which has a high oil content and usually spoils more quickly than white flour, was never rancid and we never found weevils."
- For egg storage, they used the same type of jar, packing the never-refrigerated eggs in rock salt after first smearing them with vaseline; they kept fresh for four months.

- Dozens of cans in rows were stowed outboard of the settee backs in the batten racks. When a can was withdrawn from the bilge, the entire row above it rolled down to fill the space. You sometimes see this setup in supermarkets.
- All told, the Herrons carried 150 books aboard—volumes on games, handicrafts and string figures for the children, plus science fiction for all of them, English, French, and Portuguese dictionaries, and a thesaurus. For his navigation, Matt had *Bowditch, Mixter,* several books by Eric Hiscock, and "various U. S. Hydrographic Office publications."
- To keep track of all these items, Jeannine notes that she created a stowage file but adds, "Unfortunately, no one could ever remember where we filed the file."
- To supply the medicine chest, they worked up a list from the late Paul B. Sheldon's *First Aid Afloat* and *How to Travel the World and Stay Healthy* by Drs. Doyle and Banta.
- Jeannine's canvas work included covers for the cockpit cushions and two large awnings that when laced together covered the boat from mast to backstay. Matthew cut up an old spinnaker and sewed a wind-sail that fitted in the forehatch to scoop air down into the quarters.
- Matt decided at Ft. Pierce that he wanted another adult in the crew for this first ocean passage, so he invited their good friend from New Orleans, Bill Seeman, to sail with them.
- The radio-telephone was added at the last minute—at Jeannine's insistence.
- For water, they had tanks of twenty-five, thirty-five, fifteen, and fifteen gallons, for a total of ninety gallons. With five aboard, that's eighteen gallons apiece; at a consumption rate of one half-gallon a day per person, any crossing of thirty-six days or less would cause no hardship.
- Matt ordered a steering vane from a boating magazine (in Fig. 12-4 it appears to be an English make called The Quartermaster). At first it didn't work, but father and son fiddled with it until it did.
- At Fort Pierce, Matt built a cabintop rack to hold extra jerricans of gasoline and the inflatable dinghy. Here, too, the twin staysails and storm jib arrived from their Biloxi sailmaker.
- At Bermuda, Matt had a machine shop make a hand crank for the engine, as one had not come with the boat, and sooner or later nearly every battery goes flat. He also bought a new battery and a watertight seal for the gas filler cap. The final job was replacing all the screws in the mast track with a larger size as, en route to Bermuda, a section of it had pulled free and Bill had to go up the mast to repair it.
- Bound for the Azores, Matt noted that "Some piece of gear is always breaking." Such as: One day the twenty-five-gallon tank ran dry and Matt found the surge in the tank had caused a crack near the bottom.

That was worrisome, but they were carrying "six to seven cases of fruit juice," which he regarded as the emergency water supply. Another job was fitting cheek blocks and cleats to the boom to speed up reefing, a job that would have been long since done had they cruised the boat for several seasons beforehand.

- Every day at sea they ran the engine to charge the batteries. One week out, the oil pressure had dropped ten pounds, but, coughing and rattling, it kept going all the way to Africa.

  Not a repair but certainly "morale maintenance" for the children, there were special events such as a treasure hunt concocted by Matt (prizes: balloons, Silly Putty, yo-yos) or a surprise batch of brownies by Jeannine.

- In the steward's department, they regretted taking only four dozen eggs; another time, they decided, ten dozen would not be too many, considering their many uses: atop corned beef hash, in pancakes and cakes, etc.

- Another food note: Halfway across, Jeannine, now recovered from seasickness, found she got much pleasure from baking bread in her pressure cooker (with an asbestos pad over the flame to prevent scorching the loaf). A cooking trauma occurred one day when the stove, with two pots of food on it, suddenly crashed to the cabin sole. Inspection revealed that the stove's swinging action had sawed off the pivot bolts.

- One important lack aboard *Aquarius* was a wet locker. In squally weather, Matthew complained, foul weather gear just lay on the sole because there was no other place to put it.

- At Horta, Azores, they repaired a cracked spreader and a broken cockpit seat and had a local sailmaker restitch the head of the mainsail to the lower part, which he did by hand.

- At Santa Cruz, La Palma, in the Canaries, Matt installed two mirrors below, one in the forepeak and the other on the door leading to it, which gave an illusion of greatly increased space. Final purchases there included fruit, vegetables, clothes for the children, and gasoline.

Cruising Track

From the departure at New Orleans, *Aquarius* stopped at the following ports and places: Lake Ponchartrain (anchored) . . . Biloxi, Mississippi . . . Panama City, Florida . . . (280-mile direct passage to) Egmont Key (off Tampa Bay) . . . (across Florida via) Okeechobee Waterway . . . Fort Pierce . . . Bermuda . . . Horta, Fayal, Azores . . . Tezacorte, La Palma, Canaries . . . Santa Cruz, La Palmas Island . . . Santa Cruz, Tenerife Island . . . Port Etienne, Mauritania, Africa.

Aquarius departed Fort Pierce, Fla., on Aug. 22, 1970—at least six weeks after the Herrons' planned departure date. On this pasage—to Bermuda—their friend Bill Seemann, who had given much useful advice during the fitting-out, sailed with them—an experienced sailor who had taught them a lot and helped build confidence on their first ocean voyage.

At departure, *Aquarius* had a strong southwesterly of about force 6, and this continued for several days, during which they logged 75, 75, 110, 130, and 125 miles. To see what this means (using an LWL of 25 feet instead of the actual one of 24 feet because of the counter stern), let's turn to the sloop's numbers:

Aquarius: Speed/Length Ratio							
(WL = 25' $\sqrt{25}$ = 5.0)							
S/L	$\times$	$\sqrt{\text{WL}}$	=	Speed (knots)	$\times$	24	= NM (1 day)
1.0		5.0		5.0			120.0
1.1		5.0		5.5			132.0
1.2		5.0		6.0			144.0
1.3		5.0		6.5			156.0
1.34		5.0		6.7			160.8

Another reason for altering the LWL (a 4 percent increase, but justified by the de facto LWL) is to noodle around with the exact square root of 25 (5) for the first time in this book. The sailor planning to have a cruising boat designed for him would do better to say to his naval architect at the preliminary meeting, "I require a sloop (cutter, ketch, etc.) of about fifteen-thousand pounds displacement, with a twenty-five-foot waterline mini-mum, as I would like to reach six knots when she is sailing at a Speed/Length ratio of 1.2" than merely to say, "I'd like a boat of about X feet with a cutter rig and preferably on the fast side." (That sounds a bit like L. Francis Herreshoff's quaint writing style, but you get the point.)

If the boat delivers such performance, in a breeze of say, 18 knots, you're working with a speed of 6 knots (S/L 1.2), and 6 is a nice number to work with in coastal navigation, as you know you're covering a mile every ten minutes—especially handy in fog. Even more important, if you tell your designer that reaching an S/L of 1.2 is important to you, he can immediately start thinking about other vital concerns—prismatic coefficient, dis-placement/length ratio, sail area/displacement ratio, for example—and begin reconciling these many factors that he must bring into esthetic and engineering harmony in the final design.

The passage to Bermuda was a "testing" for the Herrons, getting to know the boat's behavior under various sea conditions and, for Matt, perfecting his celestial navigation. All of them suffered some degree of seasickness, but it was Melissa, 11, who had the hardest time, for she had not wanted to go on the voyage and felt "outvoted" by the rest of the family; in time, as mentioned earlier, she became reconciled to it, especially as she lost her fear.

On September 1, 1970—ten days out of Fort Pierce—the sloop reached Bermuda, making the 860-mile passage at an average daily run of 86 miles —not an impressive average, but on the edge of respectability, considering the family's experience. One night, before Bill Seemann flew home, they all sat in the cockpit discussed cruising principles, finally arriving at a list that bears repeating: "1. Never trust anyone else to be competent [supervise the job yourself]; 2. Never leave anything unfixed; 3. Never go into a strange port at night unless you are sure of everything [anchor off or heave to until daylight]; 4. Never go anywhere without an engine crank [Matt: "It's foolish to trust batteries."]; 5. When in doubt, turn back to safe waters."

Just before Bill left, Matt, respecting his vast ocean-racing experience and acknowledging the family's tyro status, asked, "Are we ready to go?" Bill's response is sound advice for all beginning crews: "Yes, I think you're as ready as you could be, considering the lateness of the season and the time you've had to prepare. You've done a good job with *Aquarius,* and after sailing to Bermuda with you, I'm not worried about your ability to take care of yourselves. If there's one thing that still bothers me, I guess it's this: I don't think you have enough respect for the sea, and that's something you can only learn from experience."

Eventually Bill flew home, and *Aquarius* got a new crew member for the Atlantic crossing, a friend named Phil Stiles. Unfortunately, he had never been to sea, and ocean voyaging was not his cup of tea; sick most of the way with fever and a low-grade infection, he did his work but was miserable. It was a situation that recalls the old crusing adage, "Never sail with anyone you don't know very well." It was a disappointment for all hands.

Aquarius sailed from Bermuda on September 12, 1970, bound for the Azores, 1800 miles off. As predicted by a last-minute meteorological report, they had easterly winds for several days, and once again Jeannine was miserably seasick. Fortunately, the vane gear was now working reliably and Matt estimated that " . . . it has been relieving the helmsman about 70% of the time." Despite this, someone always stood watch during darkness. By the fifth day, Jeannine was recovering.

Six days out they were 345 miles ENE of Bermuda, averaging only 60 miles a day, in winds either easterly or fluky. On the eighth day out— September 19—they sighted a freighter, the *Freubel Asia,* and spoke to the captain by radio-telephone, got a position check, assured him they needed nothing, and sailed on. An hour later, they were bowling under a strong westerly, wing-and-wing under genny and main.

Matt acknowledged a tendency to delay reefing too long, carrying on in the hope strong winds would moderate, only to discover that the job is tougher and riskier later on—an outgrowth of not having had enough reefing practice before departure.

On September 21 the noon plot put them one-third of the way across with their daily average—for eleven days of sailing—now up to 73 miles, or 3 knots. (Matt provided few speed or mileage figures, so we must rely for this on the occasional remark.) One astute comment by him shows his grasp of ocean-cruising realities: "Experience has demonstrated that 100 miles in 24 hours is a very good daily run for *Aquarius.* Ninety miles pleases me very well, and yesterday's run of 115 miles caused the captain to dance gleefully on the foredeck." Amen to that conclusion, in spite of the fact that this distance was less than S/L 1.0 for *Aquarius*.

On September 24 Matt complains of having been "deadlocked in doldrums for almost three days. . . ." On one of them, "We logged [drifted] exactly eight miles." The weather was not laid on for a fast crossing. Another day, they ran under engine for three hours and notched only 33 miles in twenty-four hours.

They logged 115 miles on September 27 and on the next two days covered 121 and 125 miles (both S/L 1.0). On October 1, after covering only 70 miles in the previous twenty-four hours, they encountered a force 7 gale —from the west— and the barometer dropped to 29.70. Once again they waited too long to reef, and when they finally tackled it, the head of the mainsail was completely torn off the rest of the sail. Starting the engine, they powered back into the westerly wind while for three hours Matt sat on the cabin top, his safety harness snapped into a lifeline, and sewed the head of the sail back onto the rest of it.

When it was repaired, raised again (triple-reefed), and the storm jib set for the first time, they hove to for the first time ever and discovered what a joy that is compared to the previous wild motion, flying spume, and shrieking wind. After observing for a few minutes how their sloop was handling herself, they went below, closed the hatch, drank hot soup, and then crawled into their berths.

Familiar as this experience may be for many readers, heaving to was a rite of passage for the Herrons—a long-posed question answered with comforting certainty. By morning the gale ended, and Matt's fix showed that they had been driven between 85 and 100 miles southwest of their previous position.

The next two days netted them 110 miles each day, and then, on October 8—the twenty-seventh day—they sighted land—the high mountain on Pico Island. Late that afternoon they entered the harbor of Horta on the island

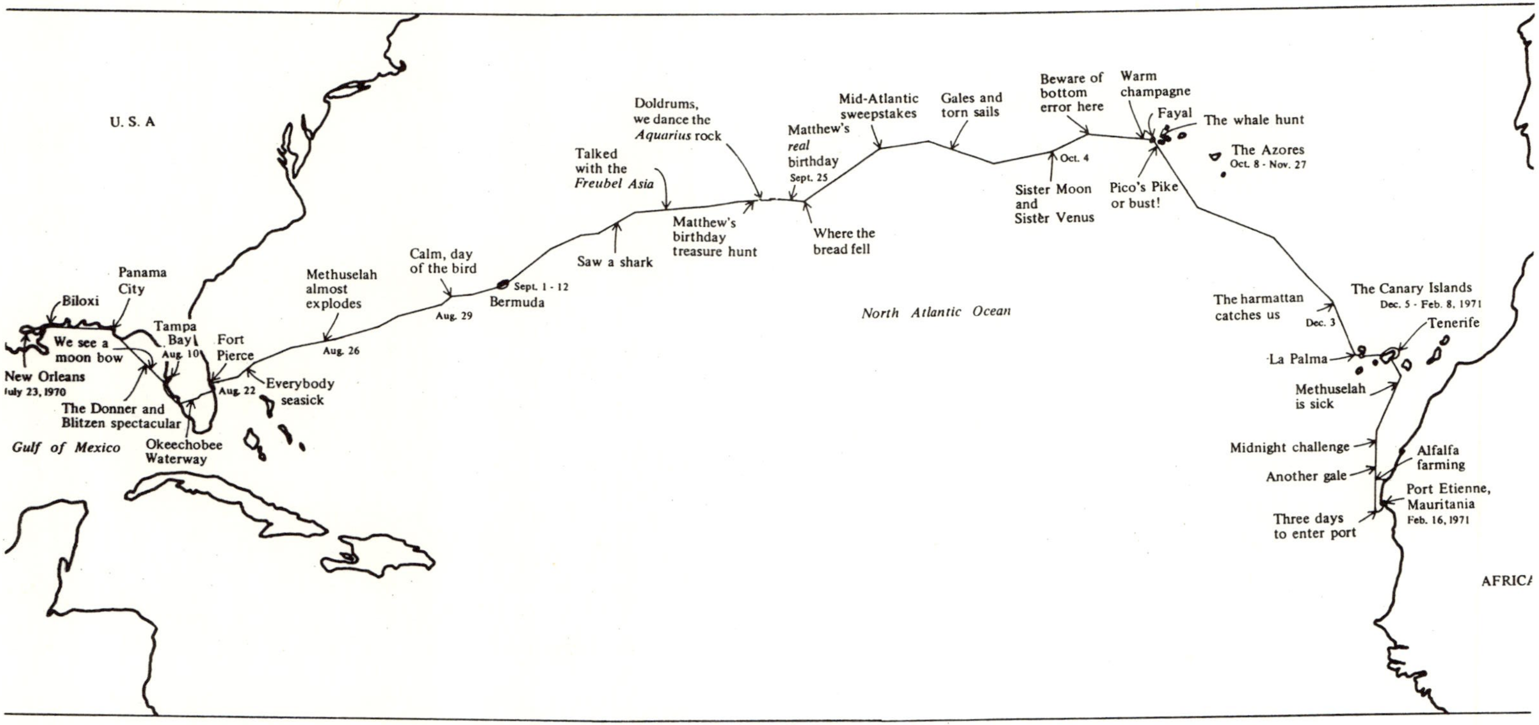

Fig. 12–6. *Chart: The track of* Aquarius *across the Atlantic.*

AFRICA

The Canary Islands
Dec. 5 - Feb. 8, 1971
Tenerife

Alfalfa
farming

Port Etienne,
Mauritania
Feb. 16, 1971

Methuselah
is sick

La Palma
Dec. 3

Midnight challenge

Another gale

Three days
to enter port

The harmattan
catches us

The whale hunt

The Azores
Oct. 8 - Nov. 27

Warm
champagne

Fayal

Beware of
bottom
error here

Oct. 4

Pico's Pike
or bust!

Sister Moon
and Sister Venus

Gales and
torn sails

Mid-Atlantic
sweepstakes

Matthew's
real
birthday
Sept. 25

Where the
bread fell

North   Atlantic   Ocean

Doldrums,
we dance the
Aquarius rock

Talked
with the
Freubel Asia

Matthew's
birthday
treasure hunt

Saw a shark

Calm, day
of the bird

Sept. 1 - 12
Bermuda

Aug. 29

Methuselah
almost
explodes

Aug. 26

U. S. A

Panama
City

Tampa
Bay

Fort
Pierce

Aug. 22 Everybody
seasick

Aug. 10

Biloxi

We see a
moon bow

The Donner and
Blitzen spectacular

Okeechobee
Waterway

New Orleans
July 23, 1970

Gulf of Mexico

309

of Fayal. Lest anyone think that ocean voyaging is only for the precious few, let it be recorded that *Aquarius* was the fifty-ninth yacht to arrive in Horta that season—and that was fifteen years ago!

Sailing 1800 miles in twenty-six days gave an average of 70 miles per day.

Now it was time for rest, sightseeing, and restaurant meals—and a serious reappraisal of their performance so far. Their conclusions: Because they had been "uptight" about the possibility of a long, slow voyage, they had been niggardly with stores (extra food treats would have helped morale) and water (a few gallons more used for personal washing would have improved personal comfort), and the sloop was really too small for a crew of five. The crowding problem was eased when Phil departed for a vacation in Europe.

After seven weeks ashore, on November 27, 1970, *Aquarius* sailed for the Canary Islands in a brisk northerly. (Matt had a copy of Slocum's book aboard and found the old master's description of *his* departure from Horta on July 24, 1895, particularly fascinating.)

For three days *Aquarius* averaged 110 miles a day on a generally south-east course. Then gale-force winds kept the sloop under reefed mainsail for seven days. Even in the southern reaches of the North Atlantic, November is not summer.

On December 6 at 0100, Matt was sleeping below in a rising gale—Jeannine on watch—when intuition suddenly snapped him awake and drove him up on deck. Peering into the misty gloom ahead, he made out "... a dim but unmistakable shape ... jagged, volcanic, towering. ..." It was the island of La Palma, about twelve miles off. They were driving down on it swiftly, with too much canvas aloft—again—having been disinclined to round up to reduce sail in the rising waves. They were lucky: Two hours later the wind dropped. At 0600 it was practically a dead calm in the lee of the island, where the Herrons anchored for a couple of hours to clean the boat from stem to stern and air all the damp bedding and clothing. On December 8 a fisherman named Tomás guided them into the harbor at Tezacorte.

After six days there, resting, they sailed *Aquarius* to Santa Cruz, the principal harbor and capital of La Palma, where they remained through Christmas. Then, on January 10, 1971, the sloop sailed again, "bound for another Santa Cruz, this one the main city on Tenerife." For this passage they were joined by a riend, Charles Rand, whom Matt called "an enthusiastic helmsman," and reached Santa Cruz twenty-four hours later.

On February 8, 1971, the Herrons departed for their ultimate destination, Africa, on a southward course that took them through heavy ship traffic. Matt noted that while they might sight six ships in a week during the crossing, here they frequently had six ships in sight at once.

Fig. 12–7. Aquarius *under sail in the Canaries.*

On the fifth day out they were overtaken by a force 7 gale but weathered it for twenty-four hours under storm jib and, successively, the first, second, and then third ("storm") reef in the mainsail, until conditions moderated.

At 1600 on February 14—the seventh day out—Matt's running fix put them "about 35 miles NNE of Cape Blanc, Africa—18 miles offshore." As the winds freshened and they approached the land, they were again carrying too much sail (the genny was up), with the waves becoming steeper and starting to break as they reached into shoaler waters in darkness. Matt decided to heave to on the offshore tack under storm jib until daylight—an operation that in these conditions, "took twenty or thirty minutes of the most violent effort. We finished drained and weary. . . . "

It had taken eight days to reach this position off Cape Blanc, and now it would take three more days to clear the cape and its off-lying shoals, turn east, and beat their way to windward, into the crook of land formed by the jutting cape and mainland Africa, and thus gain the precarious safety of a semiprotected anchorage for ore ships. This "harbor" lay a few miles from their intended destination of Port Etienne, Mauritania, and finally, by an all-family effort, they got the anchor down in nine feet of water, with one mooring line to the steel superstructure intended for mooring the ore ships and a second to a nearby trawler.

The Herrons were in Africa!

Postscript

Some months later, Matt again took a reflective backward look at the entire voyage, to see what he could distill from the experience—what they had learned, *what really counted*. These are the points he stresses: 1. Understand your motives. 2. Set realistic goals. 3. Be simple. In his words: "A lavish yacht is not a good cruising boat. It is expensive and its complex amenities will refuse to function after a few weeks at sea. . . . Simplicity saves." 4. Proceed in small steps. His argument: "If you have no experience afloat, or have only cruised in sheltered waters, don't try a world voyage the first time you venture beyond the breakwater." 5. Don't underestimate yourself. Matt: "We have within us reserves we can't even recognize until they are tested. Believe in them."

The Herrons may have qualified as beginners when they sailed, but by the time they reached Africa, *Aquarius* had a skipper who blended intelligence with experience to understand and apply Neptune's rules of the game.

13. Super Shrimp

The fact that my yacht Super Shrimp *has become—as far as I know —the smallest boat ever to circumnavigate the globe was not even a consideration when I left England so many years ago. I was not out to beat any record or do any daring deeds, but just to enjoy a rather adventurous way of life. The fact that I had no set plan or timetable was probably the main reason why I was able to complete the circumnavigation—having seen, in the course of my voyage, so many come to grief by trying to stick to a set route and set date.*

The small size of Super Shrimp *was dictated solely by my limited funds and my impatience to "get out of the rut." Having no idea of sailing, in fact, never even having set foot on a yacht before, I feel my choice of craft was very fortunate; I chose her by looking for what I thought was a strong and attractive shape. With my present knowledge, I feel I can say that the "Caprice" [class sloop], though not so roomy as many of her competitors, nor as hairy to sail, has a design a cut above the rest."*

—*Shane Acton*
Shrimpy (1981)

AUTHOR'S NOTE: The story of *Shrimpy*'s circumnavigation is included in this collection for two reasons: It took the "smallest-boat-ever" title away from *Trekka*, and Shane Acton showed a special talent for *enjoying* his cruise by getting out of it all the experience and pleasure each port had to offer. Some sailors cross oceans just for the joy of sailing or to prove they can do it, but Acton is a skipper who uses the cruise to expand his personal horizons by really seeing the world and taking enough time in each port to understand and enjoy what he sees.

Shane Acton and Crew

Shane Acton's first boat was a secondhand canoe, launched when he was twelve, so he was not totally without experience in boats. Nevertheless, he shares with Ann Davison a genuine tyro status and, with Harold La Borde, a desire to get out of a rut. Perhaps it was his dissatisfaction with life on land that led him to make such a *slow* circumnavigation and enjoy it to the fullest—like the Pardeys.

As a young man, he joined the Royal Marines, where he learned the handling of small craft, in such idyllic places as the Seychelle Islands in the Indian Ocean. After his tour of duty, his wanderlust took him roaming— to America and Europe—but each time he returned to his home in Cambridge, England, he found himself without a penny in his pocket.

Fig. 13–1. *Shane Acton and Iris Derungs.*

"That's when the idea struck me," he says. "If I had a boat and a visa I could just sail along to the next country!" So he got another in a long sequence of dull jobs, but this time he stuck to it until he had enough money to buy a small yacht. In has spare time, he read voraciously about small-boat cruising. Finally, with £500 in his pocket, Acton began searching for a small cruising sailboat—although he had never sailed in his life. He found her through an ad, lying in the owner's garage, and it was "love at first sight." Although ten years old, she had been beautifully maintained. Buying her took every cent in his boat fund, but he scraped up enough to have her moved to Cambridge by truck, where he launched her in the River Cam and immediately moved aboard. Soon after, despite the risk of "bad luck," he changed her name to *Super Shrimp,* but she was always called *Shrimpy.*

Some months later, when Acton had meandered across the Atlantic and

Caribbean and was at Cristobal in the Canal Zone, he sailed to the San Blas
Islands (which had been a favorite of the Pardeys). There he met Iris
Derungs, "a beautiful blonde-haired, blue-eyed Swiss girl who had rarely
even seen the sea, much less sailed on it, but who was quite an adventurous
person in her own right, having amongst other things, walked across the
Sudan by herself, living with any of the wandering Masai whom she met
along the way.. . . "

They had known each other only a short while when Iris decided that
she liked *Shrimpy* despite its spartan accommodations and was impressed by
the quiet competency of her skipper and his obvious enjoyment of the
cruising life. She signed on as crew and completed most of the remainder
the circumnavigation with Action.

The Hull

Acton's sloop was of the Caprice class, designed in 1957 by the widely
known English naval architect, Robert Tucker, who seems to have a special
knack for hard-chine hulls. (I say "widely known," and he is to those who,
like me, upon seeing one of his designs in an English yachting magazine
write instantly to the builder for a brochure.) *Shrimpy,* too, was a hard-chine
boat, built, like *Humming Bird,* of marine plywood.

One design characteristic sets her apart from every other boat in this
book: she is a twin-keel design *(see upper plan in Fig. 13–2 and isometric
drawing in Fig. 13–5).*

Specifications: LOA—18′ 4″; LWL—13′; Beam—6′2″; Draft—1′8″;
Displacement—2.10 tons (this figure must be Thames Measurement, as
Acton notes elsewhere that *Shrimpy* displaced 1.5 tons, or 3360 lbs.);
Ballast—500 lbs. (250 lbs. in each bilge keel); Sail Area—120 to 140 sq. ft.
(est.).

The hull and deck were built of ⅜-inch marine plywood, over white
oak framing. The cabintop and decks have considerable camber, not only
for roominess below but for the increased strength that derives from plywood being stressed into a curve: An inverted soup bowl will support much
more weight before breaking than an upside-down dinner plate.

There are a few frequently debated points about twin-keel (or bilge-
keel) boats. Adherents cite as advantages their extreme shoal draft without
the bother of a centerboard (and its potential for leaks in a wood boat) and
their ability to sit upright when aground. Critics points out that the penalty
for these virtues is increased wetted surface, which spoils sailing performance, especially in light airs. This argument, from both sides, is a classic case
of design tradeoffs in conflict—the cruising-performance advocate opting
for the single keel, and the cruising-convenience proponent seeing attractive
advantages in the shoal draft.

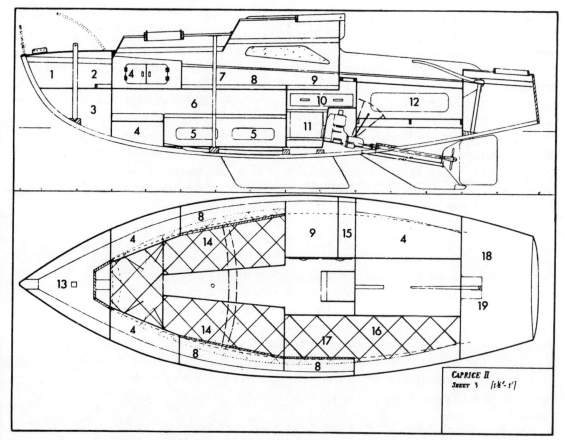

Fig. 13–2. Super Shrimp: *Inboard Profile and Cabin Plan. (Plan courtesy Robert Tucker)*

Under sail, the twin keeler does better than first impressions suggest. When heeled, the lower keel deepens the draft (and thus increases the lateral plane), while the upper keel (always *in* the water) is still exerting its righting force—with the aid of gravity. As for directional stability, the combined surface areas of the two keels and the skeg on which the rudder is hung are designed to provide enough area to ensure that the boat will go where you point her in any reasonable sea conditions. Almost any 13-foot-WL boat will hobbyhorse and make scant progress in a heavy chop.

The Deck

Figures 13–3 and 13–4 give a pretty fair impression of the deck layout. In both photos we can see the high camber mentioned above. Though the waist decks are narrow, making going forward in heavy weather a bit chancy, they had to be narrow if there was to be any decent sitting headroom below in a hull with 6′2″ a beam. Handrails atop the cabin would help when going forward.

The afterdeck is long for an 18-footer because the live weight of the crew is a considerable portion of the overall ballast, so designers insure that the crew can't concentrate its weight aft by making it impossible to do so. Fig. 13–2 shows a watertight bulkhead between the cockpit and the lazarette, but the drawing is of the Mark II version of this class; in *Shrimpy,* the Mark I version, this was only a partial bulkhead, ending at the top of the cockpit seats.

These seats look to be about 4 feet to 4 feet 6 inches long, not long enough for sleeping but comfortable enough, according to Action, to accommodate four when daysailing. The coamings, side and aft, are fairly high for comfort and spray protection. As built, *Shrimpy* did not have a self-bailing cockpit, but Acton corrected that later *(see below).*

The foredeck is somewhat different than the profile drawing in Fig. 13–2 —another variation between the Mark I and Mark II versions—as *Shrimpy* did not have the secondary trunk cabin forward, only a hatch in the

Fig. 13–3. Super Shrimp *in port.*

Fig. 13–4.
Locking up in
Super Shrimp.

foredeck, plus a robust samson post, homemade anchor chocks (no room for ground tackle below), and a long metal tang inboard of the stem, bolted to the deck and offering several holes in which to shackle the jibstay.

From just abaft the stem to the after end of the cockpit coamings, a toerail about 2 inches high was fitted, scuppered in about four places (Fig. 13–3) and interrupted where the shrouds connect to the chainplates, which are bolted to the outside of the hull.

The Rig

Shrimpy carried a pretty conventional sloop rig for her vintage, a smallish mainsail, made more so by the high boom position, so placed to protect the skulls of the cockpit occupants. The foretriangle is a three-quarter aspect ratio, with the top quarter of the mast stiffened by a jumper strut and stay, so that it could oppose the pull of the permanent backstay. With a rig of such modest proportions, there was no need for winches to handle either halyards or sheets.

Mounted outside the cockpit coamings were jam cleats—with bullseyes serving as fairleads—at about the middle of the coamings and, abaft of those, handmade wood cleats. Further aft there was a fairlead block, apparently for the genoa, so its sheets could run aft, then forward to the same cleats.

The mainsheet arrangement was utterly simple: a single block with becket hanging from a tang at the end of the boom, and another single block attached by a metal strap to the after cockpit coaming. The sheet lead was as follows: from the becket down through the lower block, back up through the upper block, then down again to a jam cleat mounted just inside the coaming. Handy, certainly, and the owner of such a small cruising sloop could hardly find a simpler, cheaper way to control his mainsail. The only thing it lacks, to my eye, is a traveler—perhaps a track mounted atop the coaming (with car)—a not very expensive modification. This would keep the boom lower when the sheets were well started, thus keeping the head of the sail from falling off, with a loss of driving efficiency when the wind is abaft the beam.

As a guesstimate, let's say the mainsail is about 80 square feet and the jib, about 40 square feet. From the pecked line on the sail plan (Fig. 13–5), it appears that the big genoa has a bit more area than the mainsail—say 100 square feet—so under main and genoa (if those estimates are reasonably close), *Super Shrimp* could set about 180 square feet of sail.

Now to the most interesting rigging wrinkle so far in this book, invented by the so-called beginner Shane Acton, whose cruise was run with as much enforced economy as any other reported here, except Fred Rebell's. What he invented was a single "running sail" that performed as twin staysails. He went to Penrose Sailmakers of Falmouth, England, and sketched out his idea (Fig. 13–6). As he describes it, it was a diamond shape with a bolt rope sewed up through the middle in a seam that "stood proud" of the sail by two inches. To this seam was sewn a row of piston hanks, which snapped onto the headstay. Then, an aluminum pole was lashed athwartships, its ends fastened to the two clews of the sail, from which sheets led after through fairlead blocks to the tiller. There, "resistor sheets" (probably shock cord) were lashed to each side of the tiller, to dampen its movement and prevent the running sail's two sheets from overcorrecting the helm when the sloop wandered off course. Finally, at a point about ten feet off the deck, a line ran from the aluminum pole to the mast to prevent so much pull by the sail that it might break the pole. (Note that the regular jibstay is abaft the stay on which this sail is set.)

Acton didn't say, but it appears that both sheets and halyards were of terylene (dacron) rope.

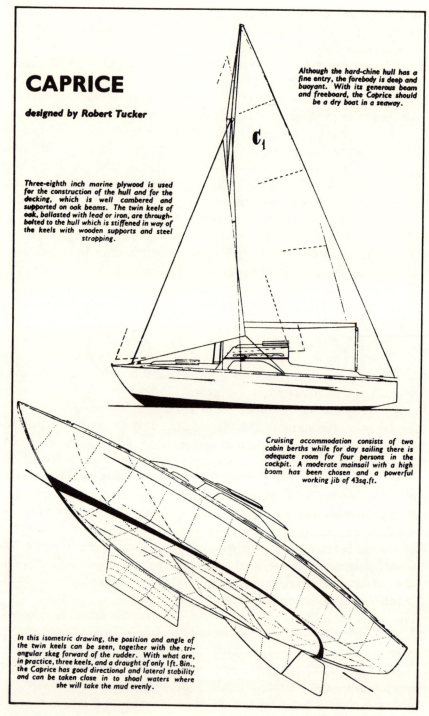

CAPRICE

designed by Robert Tucker

Although the hard-chine hull has a fine entry, the forebody is deep and buoyant. With its generous beam and freeboard, the Caprice should be a dry boat in a seaway.

Three-eighth inch marine plywood is used for the construction of the hull and for the decking, which is well cambered and supported on oak beams. The twin keels of oak, ballasted with lead or iron, are through-bolted to the hull which is stiffened in way of the keels with wooden supports and steel strapping.

C_1

Cruising accommodation consists of two cabin berths while for day sailing there is adequate room for four persons in the cockpit. A moderate mainsail with a high boom has been chosen and a powerful working jib of 43sq.ft.

In this isometric drawing, the position and angle of the twin keels can be seen, together with the triangular skeg forward of the rudder. With what are, in practice, three keels, and a draught of only 1ft. 8in., the Caprice has good directional and lateral stability and can be taken close in to shoal waters where she will take the mud evenly.

Fig. 13–5. Super Shrimp: *Sail Plan and Isometric Drawings. (Plan courtesy Robert Tucker)*

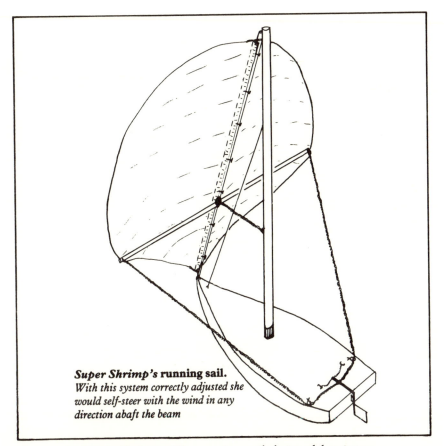

Super Shrimp's running sail.
*With this system correctly adjusted she
would self-steer with the wind in any
direction abaft the beam*

Fig. 13–6. Super Shrimp: *The running sail designed by Acton.*
(Drawing by Shane Acton)

The mast was stepped in a tabernacle on deck, a good feature in a boat
this small, making it possible to lower the mast quickly and easily—handy
in a dozen ways, especially when you poke into as many "gunkhole"
anchorages as *Super Shrimp* did, often at wild tropical islands, to ride out
storms. The easy ability to eliminate top hamper completely is awfully
valuable in a 18-foot sloop.

The Cabin

Below decks, Acton had what can only be called minimal space, yet the
cabin had no fewer than three berths, a galley, and several lockers. This is
visible in the cabin plan (Fig. 13–2, lower drawing), but it's worth noting
that the berths were narrow, as might be expected with a 6′2″ beam. (This
is often true in English boats, which tend to carry less beam than U.S.

auxiliaries.) Further, with a narrow beam and narrow side decks, anyone sitting on a berth is forced toward the centerline, so you might as well fill the under-deck areas with lockers, shelves, and cave bins.

The plan shows it all, but Acton had his own ideas for using the space, such as storing his water under the quarter-berth and converting the starboard berth into a chart table with storage space underneath.

Gear, Stores, and Refits

For water, Acton carried thirty one-gallon containers, which he calculated would last him sixty days. This weight was distributed between the quarter-berth and the starboard cockpit locker.

As the stove burned "paraffin" (kerosene), there was a five-gallon can of that fuel aboard, which also served the cabin lamps.

There was space for 120 cans of food, and Acton carried that many (varieties not mentioned) under the two settee berths, amidships. When he could get fresh fruit and vegetables, they were stowed forward under the foot of the settee berths. Finally, for dry-food storage, he imitated Rebell aboard *Elaine* and Jeannine Herron on *Aquarius* and purchased "twenty square Tupperware containers, which (were) stacked under the chart table."

For a "bilge pump," Acton used a reliable, unclogable bucket. When Suez Canal inspectors checked his "safety equipment," he held up the same bucket when they asked to see his fire extinguisher. He also carried red, orange, and white flares, and an inflatable dinghy with paddles.

In harbor, he says, "I used a small chemical toilet, but at sea this is impractical (have you ever tried?) and there is running water all around the boat anyway."

He's emphatic that his safety harness "was permanently attached to the boat and to me 24 hours a day, and I would suggest that anyone in a boat so small, and sailing alone, is an idiot not to do this." A wise rule, but there's a strong impression from many cruising tales that it is honored more in the breach than in the observance.

For celestial navigation, Acton carried the following: two compasses (one Davis plastic, one ex-army prismatic hand-bearing); radio receiver (Russian 8-band Vega Sebna); watch (Rolex Submariner); sextant (Ebbco plastic type); charts (he started with enough to get across the Atlantic and then "continually swapped with boats headed in the opposite direction"); books and tables (*Nautical Almanac*—a new one every second year, *Burton's Tables, Little Ship Celestical Navigation, Rantzen*). He concludes: "*Highly Recommended: Reed's Almanac* (1972 and 1980 only), 2 pencils, 1 parallel ruler. And that's all!"

When Acton got *Super Shrimp*, the galley had just the counter shown in Fig. 13–2 (no sink—the bucket again) with a single-burner Primus kerosene stove sitting loosely on it. (For his first meal at sea he had to cook out in the cockpit with the stove held between his feet.) To remedy this, in the Canaries Acton fastened the stove into a round bisquit tin (to catch spills) and then fitted pivot bolts to the tin for a set of "quick and dirty" gimbals.

Also in the Carnaries, Acton built a steering vane, which did yeoman service the rest of the way.

Super Shrimp did not have the inboard engine shown in Fig. 13–2 but used outboards, first a used English Seagull and later, when it "died" from old age and abuse, a new 5-HP Yamaha purchased in Australia. Jobs for both Iris and Acton in Australia also provided money for a new and better inflatable dinghy.

Acton lost the Rolex watch—a gift from the company—when the strap caught on a shroud, pulled it off his wrist, and plopped it into the sea. When he reported this with his regrets to Rolex some weeks later, they sent him another.

As for ground tackle, we know only that *Super Shrimp* had two anchors. One of them was a kedge (weight unknown) and 100 feet of chain, probably ¼-inch.

Despite the simplicity of his boat, Acton did more maintenance work than most other wood boat owners because his cruise lasted eight years, most of it in hot, humid tropical waters. Here's a summary of that maintenance, and other activity that reinforces the earlier chapters' impression of how much work is involved in a long voyage:

Canary Islands: Made stove gimbals and steering vane.

Mid-Atlantic: Cleaned radio to get it working again (a job he had to repeat) and varnished cabin sides.

Barbados: Chartered sloop to raise cash.

Cartagena, Columbia: Repaired sails.

Cristobal, Panama: Painted hull with free paint from International Paint Company.

Las Perlas Islands: Scrubbed and painted bottom.

Gorgona Island, Equador: Repaired sails and had holes in the deck patched—by murderers from the national prison.

Guayquil, Equador: Was inundated with gifts such as canned food, paint, dacron sailcloth, etc. after he appeared on a local TV show and the host *demanded* that his listeners help Acton complete his Pacific crossing. (Small boats make *big* impressions.)

Mid-Pacific: Mended steering vane and caulked a leak over Iris's berth.

Marquesas: Acton got a job loading copra onto the local trading schooner to raise badly needed cruising funds.

Cook Islands: At Rarotonga, Acton hired on as captain of a government boat and, while in port, modified the cockpit to make it self-bailing.

Australia: At Brisbane, received handsome fees for exhibiting *Super Shrimp* at several supermarkets and two boat shows. He left with an extensive collection of charts and a new dinghy. (NOTE: Stores purchased are not included here because Acton hardly mentioned such things.) In Jove, Australia, both got jobs, and Acton replaced the badly rusted keel bolts with new ones of stainless steel. He also purchased several hundred feet of new line.

Bali: Bought the Yamaha outboard.

Singapore: *Super Shrimp* got a free mooring in return for a lecture on the voyage to the yacht club members. A big addition here was new stainless steel chainplates.

Jeddah, Saudi Arabia: *SS* was warmly welcomed; Iris and Acton were wined and dined by the English community, and were given free gasoline for the outboard.

Red Sea Passage: The outboard broke down completely but in Al Wejh, Saudia Arabia, a local Arab mechanic fixed it for nothing—and threw in free spark plugs and oil!

Israeli waters: Thrown down on her topsides by a rogue wave, *Super Shrimp* suffered a split in the bottom, and Acton faced the most dangerous moment of the voyage. In a near-sinking condition, he dashed for shore under full sail and outboard power. Bailing with his trusty bucket as he went, he put *Super Shrimp* on the beach. There, he "blocked the hole with grease-covered bedding held in place by sawn-up bits of furniture used as wedges."

Cyprus: Acton had the sloop hauled out, made a proper repair to the split in the hull, and painted the bottom.

France: At Toulon, they got free use of an apartment, hauled out *Super Shrimp,* and completely repainted her. Just before entering the French canal system, the jib was badly ripped in a squall, so they spent a whole day anchored in the lee of a small island resewing it.

And that was it—nothing more than routine maintenance for the rest of the passage home.

Cruising Track

From her launching in the River Cam at Cambridge, *Super Shrimp* was sailed to Falmouth, where Acton lived aboard for six months while fitting out.

When he sailed from Falmouth, he visited the following impressively long list of ports and anchorages: Veana do Castelo, Portugal . . . Varzim . . . Lexioes . . . Aviero . . . Figueriro do Foz . . . Lisbon . . . Sines . . . Angrinha . . . El Yadida, Morocco . . . Safi . . . Las Palmas, Canaries (remained three months) . . . Gibraltar (navigated another yacht there)

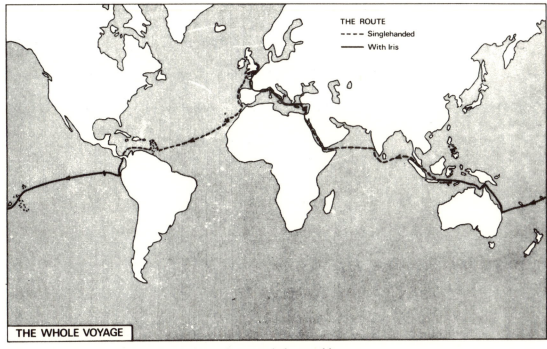

THE ROUTE
- - - - Singlehanded
——— With Iris

THE WHOLE VOYAGE

Fig. 13–7. *Chart:* Super Shrimp's *track around the world.*

. . . Las Palmas . . . Barbados, West Indies . . . (north and south through the Windwards, including) Antigua . . . Guadaloupe . . . Iles de Saintes . . . Dominica . . . Martinique . . . Canouan . . . Carriacou . . . Grenada . . . Curaçao . . . Santa Marta, Columbia . . . Cartagena . . . Cristobal, Canal Zone . . . San Blas Islands . . . Portobelo, Colombia . . . Cristobal . . . (transit) Panama Canal . . . Las Perlas Islands . . . Pinas Bay, Ecuador . . . Buenaventura . . . Gorgona Island . . . Manta . . . Salinas . . . (100 miles upriver to) Guayaquil . . . Santa Cruz Island, Galapagos . . . Post Office Bay, Floreana Island . . . Nuka Hiva, Marquesas . . . Takaroa, Tuamuto Archipeligo . . . Apataki . . . Papeete, Tahiti, Society Islands . . . Moorea . . . Huahine . . . Raiatea . . . Tahaa . . . Bora Bora . . . Avatiu, Rarotonga Island, Cook Islands . . . Suvarov Island . . . (back to) Rarotonga . . . Atiu Island . . . Atutaki Island . . . Palmerston Atoll . . . Niue Island . . . (several) Tonga Islands . . . Totoya Island, Fijis . . . Viti Levu . . . Suva . . . Aneitym, New Hebrides . . . Noumea . . . Brisbane, Australia . . . Sand Gate . . . Moolooba . . . Noosaville . . . Rainbow Sands . . . Fraser Island . . . Gladstone . . . Gould Island . . . Percy Island . . . (over 35 remote anchorages along the Great Barrier Reef, including these major ports and towns) Rockhampton . . . Mackay . . . Townsville . . . Cairo . . . Cooktown . . . (rounded) Cape York . . . Thursday Island . . . Prince of Wales, Island . . . (across)

Gulf of Carpentaria . . . Gove . . . (several remote anchorages en route to) Darwin . . . Sumba Island, Indonesia (their 21st country) . . . Sumbawa Island . . . Lombok Island . . . Bali Island . . . Jakarta, Java . . . (several remote anchorages along the coast of Sumatra and across the straits to) Singapore . . . (through straits to) Malacca, Malaysia . . . Port Swettenham . . . Pangor . . . Penang Island . . . Lang Kawi Island . . . (past the) Nicobar Islands . . . Port Galle, Sri Lanka . . . (past) Cape Cormorin, India . . . Cochin . . . Mangalore . . . Jibouti, French Somaliland . . . (into Red Sea to) Hamish Island, North Yemen . . . Port Jizan, Saudi Arabia . . . (several remote anchorages to) Jeddah . . . Port Yenbo . . . Al Wejh . . . Dhaba . . . (through) Tiren Islands . . . (into Gulf of Suez to) Elat, Israel . . . Suez, Egypt . . . (transit) Suez Canal . . . Port Said . . . (into Mediterranean Sea to) Larnaca, Cyprus . . . Symi Island, Greece . . . Rhodes . . . (through 15 Greek islands, mostly anchorages to) Athens . . . (transit) Corinth Canal . . . Delphi . . . Messina, Sicily . . . (north along Italian west coast to) Elba Island . . . Baie de Anges, France . . . Port Fos . . . (up Rhone River to) Arles . . . Port Sete . . . (across) Bay of Biscay . . . Rennes . . . St. Malo . . . (by canal across) Brittany . . . (across) English Channel . . . (in the Channel Islands) Jersey, Sark, Alderney . . . (back to) Barfleur, France . . . Calais . . . Ramsgate, England . . . Walton-on-Naze . . . Wells . . . Wash River . . . River Ouse . . . Denver . . . Cambridge.

This port list tops Harry Pidgeon's by a good bit!

Performance

This performance section will differ from the others, because Acton cared little for speed or mileage and provided little information about them. In fact, the only comment he made about speed was that *Super Shrimp* could make 5 knots. So, instead, we'll take a different tack, a mixed bag of Acton's impressions of foreign ports, including some widely regarded as tropical paradises.

First, though, a glance at her numbers, because Acton does provide some passage lengths by number of days:

Super Shrimp: Speed/Length Ratio			
(WL = 13' $\sqrt{13}$ = 3.6)			
S/L $\times$ $\sqrt{WL}$	= Speed (knots)	$\times$ 24	= NM (1 day)
1.0 3.6	3.60		86.4
1.1 3.6	3.96		95.0
1.2 3.6	4.32		103.7
1.3 3.6	4.68		112.3
1.34 3.6	4.82		115.8

Acton's 5 knots makes sense because the sloop's counter stern easily extends the effective LWL to 15 feet. Since the square root of 15 is 3.87, *Super Shrimp* could sail 3.87 knots at S/L 1.0 and reach 5.18 knots at S/L 1.34.

Here are some of the more specific details provided by Acton: "*Length of voyage:* 30,000 miles (approx.). *Duration:* 8 years. *Cost of navigational gear,* etc.: £50. *Amount of previous sailing knowledge:* nil. *Funds available for voyage:* £30. *Long legs:* the Atlantic (Canaries-Barbados)—40 days; the Pacific (Galapagos-Marquesas)—45 days; the Indian Ocean (Malaysia-Sri Lanka)—10 days; the Indian Ocean (India-French Somaliland)—28 days. *Pleasure gained:* incalculable."

Now, an assessment of some of his ports and passages:

Viana do castelo, Portugal: Acton found it rarely visited, suprising because it has a "simple" entrance, excellent protection inside, and courteous officials.

Lexioes, Portugal: " . . . a man-made commercial harbor just north of Oporto . . . not very interesting, but good mooring. . . . "

Lisbon, Portugal: " . . . turned out to be the most beautiful city I have ever seen." Overall rating of Portugal: A-1.

Morocco: He was fed and protected by local fishermen when he anchored off a deserted beach, was courteously treated by officials in El Yadida and Safi, and received great hospitality from private citizens everywhere.

Canary Islands: He waited out North Atlantic hurricane season in Las Palmas for three months but was greatly disappointed by the dirty harbor and unfriendly people. Nevertheless, life at anchor in the harbor and hob-nobbing with the other yachties was a pleasure.

The Atlantic Crossing: Day 6, 420 miles out (average, 70 MPD); Day 10, one-quarter or 750 miles out (average now, 75 MPD); Day 12, reached tradewinds and begins to use his special running sail; Day 15, rides out force 6 gale with only storm jib set; Day 25, halfway across (average now, 60 MPD); Day 33, speaks cargo ship *Ciudad Menzales* of Cartagena, Columbia, and assures captain he needs nothing; Day 39, sights land—Barbados, West Indies (final average, 76.9 MPD).

Not too shabby a performance for a 13- or 15-foot waterline.

Windward Islands: St. Lucia ("red tape") . . . Martinique (He put up a sign reading "Sailed single-handed from England" and "Please help me sail around the world" and immediately stopped looking for work, as the collection box under the sign was taking in £5 a day.) Of all these islands, he found " . . . the French ones are the best by any standards. . . . "

Curaçao: " . . . struck me as very European, very affluent, and very uninteresting. . . . "

Santa Marta, Colombia: Only there one day, but "the famous Colombia theives struck three times and I sailed out the same day—minus radio, watch and binoculars—in a very bad mood."

San Blas Islands: He enjoyed the friendly Cuna Indians on their islands and once he got so much food from them for an American dollar that he couldn't carry it all back to the boat.

Cristobal,: The anchorage was " . . . appalling, filthy water, very rough and exposed, and a good mile away from the only permitted landing spot."

Ecuador: Stopped at several remote ports: Pinas Bay ("snug anchorage"), Buenaventura ("a God-forsaken little town which lies about ten miles upriver from the sea, on a muddy island . . . covered with mangrove swamps and mosquitoes"), Gorgona Island ("a paradise"), Manta ("a modern but still attractive town"), Salinas (" . . . main seaside resort of Equador and sadly a copy of all the bad features of U.S. resorts and none of the good ones"), Guayquil (" . . . the red tape of South America that so many yachts have found so tedious and costly, melted away. Wherever we went, strangers smiled at us and wished us luck.")

Marquesas: Nuku Hiva ("We became enveloped in the sheer beauty of the South Seas. The people are kind, generous and beautiful. . . . " What depressed Iris and Acton was the negative impact of the government and the church upon the lives of the people.); Takaroa ("In the end we were driven from the island by swarms of flies . . . ").

Society Islands: Tahiti ("Well, once it was a paradise; it is now a 'rich men only' paradise and soon it will be a mess."); Raiatea ("fierce"); Tahaa ("small, dreamy"); and Bora Bora ("scenically startling"). "We spent two months in these islands and could easily have spent a lifetime."

Cook Islands: Rarotonga—"What impressed us most was the complete happiness of the children, so different from the sour, suburban kids of the European cities."

Fiji Islands: Approaching this island group, they encountered the most severe gale of the entire voyage. As Acton describes it, "Huge, steep seas and pouring, dense rain and too much wind for even the smallest sail! We just had to let *Shrimpy* drift around for a whole day in these coral-infested waters, completely at the mercy of the winds." It was a good time to have the shoal draft of a twin-keel boat, which *may* have saved them from a shipwreck in this instance.

Suva, Fiji Islands: "Bustling" Suva, Acton calls it, with things like traffic lights and elevators in the buildings. They thought it a "pretty little town . . . pervaded by the delicious small of drying copra," but it soon gave them a "claustrophobic feeling" and they pushed on.

Rena River, Fijis: This was an irresistible side trip, thirty miles up a jungle river under outboard power, until *Super Shrimp* began to bounce off the bottom despite her shoal draft. That night they were guests of a remote tribe at a feast: chicken, river fish, eel, taro, rice, breadfruit, coconut cream, and tea—a rare experience that resulted from Acton's unhurried approach to the cruise.

Now *Super Shrimp* was halfway around the world.

The 600-mile passage to Noumea, New Caledonia, was "the most frustrating sailing we've ever experienced." In spite of the weather charts calling for 70 percent easterly winds, they plugged into headwinds all the way. Disgusted by a week of scant progress, they diverted to Aneityum Island in the New Hebrides. There, for three days running, *Super Shrimp* arrived at the harbor entrance at sundown—just as the wind faded. Without an outboard (it had died), they drifted under bare poles—only to find, each dawn, they had drifted out of sight of land. On the fourth day, they were towed into port by a New Zealand yacht. They found the harbor " . . . one of the prettiest in the world" and the 300 islanders " . . . some of the gentlest, shyest, happiest of people."

Australia: Of Brisbane, Acton said, " . . . it was a beautiful place—as far as cities go. It took us a fair while to get used to all the noise and bustle after so long on tiny islands of the South Pacific."

The Great Barrier Reef: The cruise along this great, semiprotected stretch of coast was a period of easy sailing, few people met, and anchoring every night after a sail of twenty miles or so. In all, they anchored over thirty-five times.

Thursday Island: After rounding Cape York and turning east, they found this much-anticipated port disappointing: " . . . hot, dry and barren, no fruit, no flowers. The town uncared for, broken bottles and rubbish strewn all over the place—the whole gave an aura of decay. Surprisingly enough . . . the inhabitants seemed very . . . friendly despite their environment."

Crossing the Gulf of Carpenteria—a stretch of shoal water—Acton wasn't worried. He notes that the sloop's draft was 2 feet—which indicates the designed LWL of 1'8" was down 6 inches with the weight of two people and their cruising gear and stores aboard.

Gove, Australia: Acton celebrated his thirty-first birthday here, and the small town was a pleasant surprise: " . . . beautiful, perfectly protected anchorage. . . . " The Gove Yacht Club "turned out to be one of the smallest but also one of the best we have ever visited." Here, they both got jobs, bought a car to get back and forth to them, and completely refitted *Super Shrimp* while it was hauled out to wait out the hurricane season. On May 1, 1978, they sailed again.

Darwin: "The anchorage at Darwin Yacht Club left much to be desired, not well protected because of the huge tides . . . but the friendliness of the club outweighed [this] and we were soon made to feel quite at home." They sailed on June 10, 1978.

329

Indonesia: There were small adventures en route to Indonesia—rescuing a small motorboat off the coast of Australia and riding out another gale—and then anchoring in their twenty-first country with exotic sailing vessels crowding the harbor of the tiny port of Waingapu, Sumba Island. Ashore, they found " . . . life moving along at a slow, easy pace. No one gestured or asked for money; everyone was poor, but happy." At Bima on Sumbawa Island, and on Lombok Island, they climbed a mountain, enjoyed spicy-hot Oriental dishes with great mounds of rice, and were pleasantly surprised in Bali to find that tourism had not greatly spoiled these islands.

At Bali, Iris flew home to Switzerland to visit her mother and Acton now sailed singlehanded, headed northwest. (Iris planned to rejoin him in the Mediterranean.) Acton's route took him between Sumatra and the Malay Peninsula, and he anchored every night after a short sail. This island hopping plan was an unusual approach to crossing the Indian Ocean.

Singapore: An inauspicious beginning: "Obtaining a clearance was a cold, unfriendly and expensive business. . . . " At the yacht club moorings, raw sewage was flushed out into the harbor all around the boats. Island life, Acton found, was " . . . very fast, noisy and crowded." There was, as well, racial tension among the Chinese, Indians, and Malays who lived in the city's crowded streets. His conclusion: "My impression of Singapore was of a crowded noisy façade on a fast trip to hell; an interesting place to visit but no place to live."

Malaysia: Clearing customs was an easy procedure, as Acton's his landing pass valid for the entire country and open-ended. In Malacca he found " . . . people living at a [slow,] relaxed pace—as, indeed, throughout Malaysia. Though almost penniless compared to their affluent Singapore neighbors, they have, to my mind, a much richer life."

Lang Kawi Island: To Acton, pretty nearly the "perfect" tropical island: " . . . an awful lot of good and hardly any bad. . . . a perfect climate, calm blue seas, sandy bays and jungle hills provide a wonderful backdrop for the handful of villages and the single hotel on an island which, happily, has not yet been 'discovered.' "

On January 3, 1979, Acton started across the Indian Ocean, passing the Nicobar Islands (no stop) and crossing the Bay of Bengal.

Sri Lanka: "The end of a perfect sail has to have a perfect port, [and] Galle, Sri Lanka, was just that. . . . from the shore, shouts of welcome from . . . smiling faces. . . . flat, calm, well-protected waters overlooked by an old Dutch fort and a pretty little town."

India: Customs officials in Cochin, while "polite and correct," insisted on enforcing port charges "scaled for cargo ships . . . an astronomical figure for my overnight stay." This was finally reduced and Acton immediately rushed through the clearance procedure to escape from "Port Cochin's

jumble of red tape." Curiously, in Mangalore, he found " . . . no officials
to bother me and no charges to pay in this pretty little port." Of India,
Acton said, "I vowed I would return someday, for I had not seen nearly
enough of this huge, fascinating land."

Jibouti, French Somaliland: The town was " . . . dirty, hot, drab and
fearfully expensive. If it hadn't been for the friendliness and hospitality of
the local yacht club, Jibouti would have been unbearable."

Up the Red Sea: Here, again, *Super Shrimp* sailed only during the day
(about twenty-five miles a day average), and anchored nights, sticking to
the east—Saudi Arabian—coast.

Jeddah: " . . . dusty hot mass of blinding white concrete."

Saudi Arabia (mixed impressions): " . . . people sleeping on the streets
but watching color TV plugged into a handy street lamp. Any new gadget
which breaks down is thrown away for lack of repair facilities. . . . Empty
cans or packaging are just dumped anywhere you happen to be standing. . . . "

Yenbo: After weathering a 60-knot sandstorm and having the Yamaha
break down, he found this " . . . an uninspiring place" with "strict security
regulations. . . . no visitors allowed on the yachts. . . . searched every time
we left the port. . . . constantly under observation." Nevertheless, his
three-day stay there "was made very pleasant by a small group of English
families" who provided him with "free use of their bathrooms and swim-
ming pool."

Acton departed Saudi Arabia on May 15, 1979.

Tor, Israel: After experiencing the rigid conservatism of Saudi Arabia,
Acton was taken aback to observe Israeli women in micro-mini bikinis at
resort beaches.

Suez, Egypt: Officials wanted to refuse *Super Shrimp* transit of the canal
because she couldn't make 7 knots under her outboard but finally agreed the
sloop could be towed and reluctantly ignored her total lack of "standard"
safety equipment.

Port Säid, Egypt: The yacht club was "extremely generous and helpful."
When he wandered alone to look at the town, he "fell in love with it." It
offered "good vibrations—that indefinable 'something' which makes [a
town] ooze contentment and peace—despite poverty, traffic noise, and
congestion".

Cyprus: Arriving here after a solid week of beating to windward, Acton
found the Mediterranean " . . . very cold after the bathroom temperatures
of the Red Sea." He also found that " . . . throughout this inland sea, famed
for its clear, clean waters, I was never out of sight of . . . floating, man-made
debris." He sailed from here on July 14, 1979.

Greece: The passage from Cyprus was " . . . a slow, miserable affair. . . . the variable winds and confused, choppy seas of the Mediterranean were very uncomfortable compared to the long gentle swells and steady winds of the larger oceans." His real shock was to discover Greece had been spoiled by " . . . hordes of loud-mouthed, unclothed tourists, and especially by the status 'yachties' who barge their boats around. . . . exactly as they would their cars."

Rhodes: Acton found this island " . . . a heaving mass of humanity fighting desperately to get a photograph of something that did not contain a fellow tourist." But it was here, at least, that Iris returned! Visiting over fifteen Greek islands in the following weeks, they found these out-islands "expensive . . . intensely cultivated . . . highly populated . . . [with] primitively built houses . . . deserted now and . . . taken over by goats and donkeys."

Athens: "We were very unimpressed. . . . "

In the 250-mile crossing of the Ionian Sea, *Super Shrimp* weathered a gale and found the wind pattern to be "one day gale, one day calm and one day just perfect."

Messina, Sicily: "This dirty, oily harbour . . . made us . . . really miserable, until a local tugboat of jovial Italians beckoned us alongside and soon the whole crew was involved in Iris's washing . . . while we bathed [aboard and were] fed. . . . "

Sailing up along Italy's west coast, Acton was at the helm as dawn broke, and he spotted a scattering of objects floating on the sea ahead—sixty cartons of cigarettes. Some smuggler's jetsam was their gain, considering the price of cigarettes in Europe. This was the easy way to fatten a cruising fund.

Toulon, France: Here friends gave them a gala welcome, loaned them an apartment for the winter, and helped them find jobs, so they could refit the sloop for the final stretch to England.

In the spring of 1980 they lowered the mast and started up the French canals, " . . . a voyage of 600 kilometers and 118 locks" that they covered at about 20 miles a day.

In June 1980 *Super Shrimp* reached the English Channel again, sailing into the River Wash and from that to the Ouse River. At Denver, England, they took three days to rest and spruce up *Super Shrimp* for the triumphant arrival at Cambridge.

On the final day, the river banks were lined with cheering crowds throwing flowers to Iris. Reaching Cambridge, they stepped ashore to be met by the mayor and an honor guard of sea cadets—and the champagne flowed.

Acton's final words—a good guage of the pleasure he got from this long, slow circumnavigation, with its many stops at remote ports—catch his feeling of success exactly: "Yes—home is the sailor, home from the sea. *Super Shrimp* But we won't be staying for long."

Right! In 1984 Acton set sail again, this time to take *Shrimpy* up the Amazon.

14. *Mahina*

Since returning, I have met many people who have bought, or are saving to buy a 40- to 50-foot boat so they can cruise in comfort with the conveniences of home. These people often don't realize that for extended cruising they might ultimately be much happier if they were to settle for a smaller boat which would be paid off much sooner and have much lower operating costs.

Some definite advantages of a small boat are: [lower] costs to replace sails and hardware, lower fuel bills, lower moorage and port fees, less chance of theft, and a shallower draft that lets you into many places a larger boat can't go.

—John Neal
Log of the Mahina (1976)

AUTHOR'S NOTE: There are several reasons for including John Neal's sloop *Mahina* in this book. One, at 27-feet LOA, *Mahina* seems an ideal size for a singlehanded voyage, and she turned out to be just that whenever Neal sailed alone—although he usually had a pick-up crew aboard. Two, she is a stock fiberglass boat, a type otherwise underrepresented in this collection. Three, the Vega sloop (*Mahina*'s class), built by Albin of Sweden, has been available for about fifteen years now (both in the United States and the United Kingdom), so she will be familiar to many readers, enabling them to judge this cruise and Neal's conclusions against a known yardstick. Four, Neal sailed with minimum previous sailing experience but —it appears—swiftly reached perceptive conclusions about "what really counts" in offshore sailing; and, even more valuable for those of us who share his cruising ambition, he is trenchant and thorough in the details he provides. All these get close attention in the section on Gear, Stores, and Refits.

John Neal

*A*lthough *Mahina* had several different crew members on various legs of the cruise, Neal fitted out the boat for singlehanded cruising and several times sailed alone. Those who joined him at various points (no last names given) were:

"DJ"	Seattle to San Francisco
Diane	San Francisco to Hawaii
Cindy	Hawaii to Marquesas Islands
Ron and Tim	Samoa to Hawaii
Bruce	Hawaii to Seattle, Wash.

Essentially, Neal started his Pacific cruise on an impulse. He was living in Seattle, attending college at night and working by day, neither activity

Fig. 14–1. *John Neal aboard* Mahina, *in the Cook Islands.*

producing much satisfaction. "It just seemed time to try something new," he says. So he quit both occupations and, remembering how he had "greatly enjoyed" a backpacking trip to Hawaii some years earlier, decided to sail there. After buying *Mahina,* he began fitting out for the voyage and, to meet expenses, got a part-time job helping to build a 45-foot sailboat.

Neal was not totally without previous experience, as he had sailed a 20-foot sloop on Puget Sound for nine months, sometime earlier, though never offshore. Still, the smaller boat had given him some idea of what to look for. It appears that his choice was a good one, in spite of some structural problems.

The Hull

Mahina, the first "off-the-shelf boat" we've examined, has a traditional underbody, although her full keel is only moderately long. Her ballast is

Fig. 14–2. Mahina *under sail.*

encapsulated in the keel (and glassed over), and with a counter stern, she was tiller-steered. The fact that more than 1686 of this class were produced by Albin Marin AB says something about both the soundness of the design and the popularity of the boat itself.

Specifications: LOA—27′1″ feet; LWL—23′0″; Beam—8′0″; Draft—3′8″; Displacement—5070 lbs.; Ballast—2020 lbs.; Sail Area (working)—310 sq. ft.; Ballast/Displacement Ratio—40%.

Note that *Mahina*'s beam is somewhat less than we might find in a U. S. sloop of the same LOA, suggesting a hull form that might slip through the water a little easier than a beamier model. On the other hand, her transom is quite broad—more buoyancy aft to prevent squatting when the cockpit is full—of crew or seawater; and, a good way to work more space into what is essentially a light-displacement hull. In spite of her modest displacement, *Mahina*'s FRP layup schedule is not skimpy: topsides—$5/16$ inches; bottom—$7/16$ inches; keel—$1/2$ inch.

When she was designed—about fifteen or so years ago—she was given a low freeboard, probably for esthetic reasons. As a result, unless the trunk cabin was made somewhat high, the only way to achieve decent, but not full, headroom was to give the hull a virtually straight sheer. Some readers will question how much was gained, overall, by the low freeboard. Still, in her day she was a *modern* hull. Her ends are nicely balanced and her proportions are not unpleasing. She satisfied Neal, who knew as he began his search that he wanted a traditional underbody: "I had seen and heard of too many fin-keel boats losing rudders while gunkholing in coral [waters] or heavy seas. . . . Also, the fact that most full-keel boats can be balanced to steer themselves with self-steering gear is greatly in their favor."

The Deck

There is little to say about the layout once we have noted that, like *Aquarius, Mahina* has a "typical" deck layout of her design era—by which is meant the rather standard proportions of afterdeck, cockpit, bridgedeck, trunk cabin, and foredeck. She has a split pulpit forward (Fig. 14-2), a foredeck cleat, a trunk cabin that narrows considerably at its forward end to provide good footroom around the mast, lifelines and stanchions with weather-cloths attached to them abreast of the cockpit, a dodger at the forward end of the cockpit, and a stern pulpit. In the after deck, a hatch gives access to the lazarette.

The Rig

The Vega class, designed as a family boat, with no tricky, extreme, or demanding features beyond the skills of a cruising family (the cabin, laid out for four, is as traditional as they come), not only gained wide acceptance in Sweden but quickly became popular in the United States and United Kingdom. For such a market she naturally had roller reefing, a masthead rig (to take a big genoa in the light airs of summer), and a single set of spreaders. There was nothing *missing* in the rig, but it was designed for the minimum number of components consistent with building economy and safe operation; for example, a split backstay rather than the preferable twin backstays.

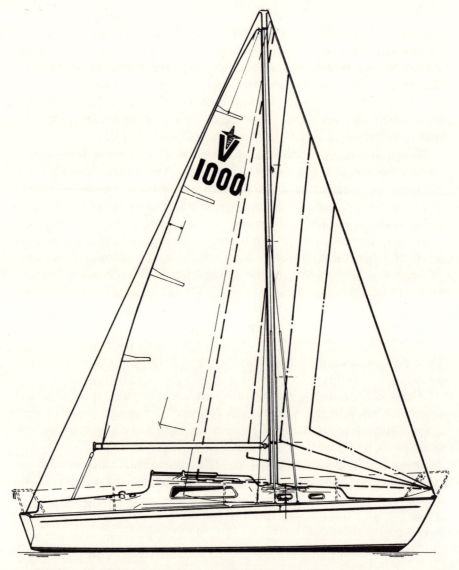

Fig. 14–3. Mahina: *Sail Plan. (Plan courtesy Vega Yachts)*

Standing Rigging: In addition to the split backstay, *Mahina* has a single headstay, twin lower shrouds on each side, from deck to the base of the spreaders, and a single upper shroud on each side, passing over the spreaders to the masthead. All shrouds end at stainless turnbuckles, and have *internal* chainplates which pass through the deck and are bolted to interior bulkheads. To prevent sail chafe, Neal fitted plastic "boots" over the turnbuckles and covered the wires with plastic sleeves.

Upon buying *Mahina,* Neal analyzed the rig and made these changes: 1) replaced the split backstay twin backstays; 2) replaced the forestay and upper shrouds with new stainless wire of the next larger size; 3) riveted to the mast (alongside the mainsail track) a second track, this one to take the storm trysail that was kept permanently attached to it ready for instant hoisting when Neal lowered the (reefed) mainsail; and 4) replaced rope and wire halyards with prestretched dacron line. There were a pair of winches mounted on the mast to handle the main and jib halyards.

Sails: Neal's mainsail and no. 1 jib were dacron, made by Ratsey, and came with the sloop. If any further proof is needed of dacron's vulnerability to sunlight—especially tropical sunlight—these two sails were stitched with red dacron thread, *all* of which rotted away. Neal had to completely restitch both sails during the cruise.

To these working sails he added a lapper, storm jib, and storm trysail, made by Seattle sailmaker Franz Schattauer. These sails, although a bit more expensive than the others, " . . . held up extremely well with almost no signs of wear in 15,000 miles." Neal doesn't mention the source or condition of his genoa. The two new storm sails had bolt ropes sewn all the way around, and the lapper had them on the leech and foot.

Most of the time on his cruise, Neal sailed with the mainsail single-reefed, because, he says, *"Mahina* is light and I don't like reefing. . . . " Apparently he felt this was a good decision, because on his return to Seattle, he had a new mainsail cut of tanned dacron, equivalent in area to the single-reefed original, with a straight leech and no battens.

One of Neal's standard routines was to go up the mast and inspect everything before every offshore passage. Proving that this was a worthwhile precaution, he twice found cracks in the aluminum spreader fittings. A failure there would seem to offer no better than a 50–50 chance to keep the mast standing, especially as the jolt that finally made the rig fail would almost certainly come in heavy going.

When using the storm trysail—which he did often because it was quick and easy to raise—Neal, lacking a boom gallows, strapped down the boom between the mainsheet and topping lift. He was quick to use the trysail for another reason—he felt it saved considerable wear and tear on the mainsail.

The Cabin

For the first and only time we have a cabin interior photo (Fig. 14-5) —not only have one but a good one, showing this sloop's traditional layout below.

Fig. 14-4 shows the arrangement, as traditional for a family cruiser as is the deck layout. Actually, for Neal's use, this boat might have been better if it had been laid out with three berths (one of them quartered), with the

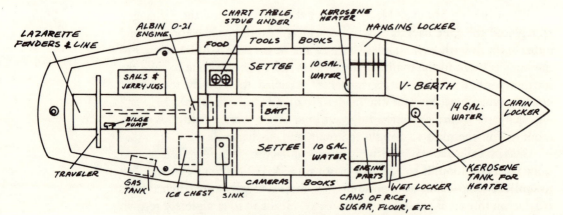

Fig. 14–4. Mahina: *Cabin Plan. (Plan by John Neal)*

Fig. 14–5. Mahina: *The cabin. (Photo by John Neal)*

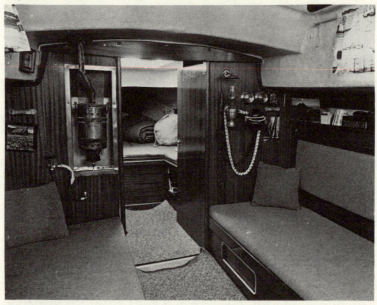

space of the fourth used as additional stowage space. Certainly a quarterberth layout is more suited to offshore use, but as Neal only once had three aboard, and one person was always on watch, they could hot-bunk the sleeping arrangement, so the two sleepers could use the saloon settees and avoid the motion of the forward cabin. As it was, Neal used that cabin for stowage, the bunks being untenable when sailing, anyway.

As for the galley, it was split into port and starboard counters because the fore-and-aft length of these two spaces was not great enough to hold a sink and stove on one side.

The decor is uncluttered, with lots of mahogany, both paneling and trim. Note the overhead grabrails, an extra touch of class. The upholstered settee backs swing down to reveal outboard stowage space, with bookshelves above. The cave lockers under the settees have never struck me as a great idea, their greatest virtue being economy for the builder, but in *Mahina*'s case, to achieve sitting headroom under the side decks, there was no other choice but to lower the settee heights and thus leave very shallow stowage space—not worth doors.

One last item to note—the mahogany plank spanning the main cabin bulkheads. This is the face-piece of the laminated beam—glass and wood —that supported the mast, which was stepped on deck. The near-collapse of this beam and a mishap to the rudder, were to challenge Neal's self-reliance to the utmost and point up the importance of being able to make one's own repairs when far from a boatyard.

The water tank (forward, under the V berths) held seventeen gallons.

The Engine

When Neal bought her, *Mahina* was fitted with a two-cylinder, 12-HP Albin Model o–21 gasoline engine. (His first preference was a diesel, but he couldn't afford one.) He briefly considered removing it and using the space for another water tank and extra stowage, but since the Albin was running, he decided to leave it in. If it died on the cruise, he decided, he could always remove it later. Having decided to keep it, he rebuilt it. When it was back in the boat, he added a fuel/water separator to the fuel line, but then the engine wouldn't work at all. Neal realized that with a gravity-feed gasoline tank, there simply wasn't enough pressure to force the fuel through the filter. So, he simply bought a rubber fuel line at an auto supply store and connected the fuel tank directly to the carburetor.

Fuel: Interestingly, Neal says he never had trouble finding gasoline in the South Pacific. With the present popularity of outbord motors in the islands, the supply schooners that serve even the most remote atolls now regularly carry supplies of gas.

The standard tank fitted in *Mahina* was made of copper and held five gallons, but Neal always carried two additional jerrijugs of gas, and the total of fifteen gallons gave him a range under power of about 180 miles. The Albin burned one-third gallon per hour for a speed of 4.5 knots.

Stores, Gear, and Refits

Neal covers this aspect of his long Pacific cruise very thoroughly, and his documentation of this part of it—keeping the boat going by solving all problems himself without depending on professional services—gives a good picture of a self-sustaining boat and a self-reliant skipper. First, a brief listing of his gear:

Wind-Speed Indicator. A hand-held model, calibrated to 50 knots.

Steering Vane. An RVG model, fitted by Neal, it was mounted on the afterdeck. As *Mahina* had a counter stern, the vane had its own small rudder. Like so many others, the vane was persnickety at the outset, but Neal's tinkering set it to rights and kept it going during the few times it gave trouble. (He makes a good case for carrying an assortment of wood, teflon, brass, bronze, and stainless steel for making repairs and modifications required by a vane.) Most skippers get to know this gadget so intimately they give it a name and can usually fix it if they have the means aboard. Once, Neal's vane broke down for an extended period, because of " . . . electrolysis caused by dissimilar metals under water . . . ," but he was able to keep sailing because *Mahina* steered herself when the wind was forward of the beam.

Commenting on self-steering systems in general, Neal noted that most of the ones he saw in the islands were the Aires model or "aires-type" (the wind presses the vane down, which actuates the lines that correct the helm, rather than the vertical type, where the wind turns the vane ("mast") on its axis, which makes the correction. Autopilots, he notes, are " . . . noisy, often break down and put quite a draw on the batteries." Finally, he said, "I met a couple of boats that used the small, cockpit-mounted auto-pilots with good success." (This type does use electricity but apparently puts a very low drain on the battery.)

Radar Reflector. Aluminum, hoisted aloft to the port spreader.

Life Preserver. A horseshoe buoy with safety light attached, in a bracket on the stern pulpit.

Ventilation. A pair of cowl vents fitted in the cabin top at the forward end of the trunk, plus the main and forward hatches.

Fire Extinguisher. A 2½-lb. dry chemical type mounted near the galley on the port side.

Compasses. The steering compass was mounted at the forward end of the cockpit, and Neal had another one in the cabin below—serving as a "telltale"—on the starboard main bulkhead. The other instruments visible in Fig. 14- are a matched pair of brass clock and barometer, what looks like a hygrometer for humidity readings, and a narrow gadget that appears to be an inclinometer.

Miscellaneous. Binoculars and flare gun.

Water Supply. The sloop was fitted with a fourteen-gallon tank up forward under the V berths. To this Neal added two ten-gallon flexible tanks, one each under the forward ends of the saloon settees. Of these he says, "I rarely rarely used the water in them—they were mostly for ballast [total, 200 pounds], making *Mahina* considerably stiffer in open water." (This confirms her light displacement sailing characteristics.) Neal also carried three five-gallon jerrijugs of water, which he stowed under the cockpit seats, as well as a varying number of collapsible plastic water containers. He confirms the opinion of John Guzzwell that when sailing in remote waters, it is much easier to replenish the supply when it is carried in a number of separate containers than to have only a couple of jerrijugs and have to make multiple dinghy trips ashore to fill large tanks. At sea, Neal found he used only one-third of a gallon per day. He rejected any thought of installing a water-pressure system because they " . . . waste water and are just one more gadget to break down." Another vote for simplicity.

Running Lights. The port and starboard lights were mounted on both sides of the split pulpit, and the white light on the mast was about seven feet above the deck, but Neal rarely used them at sea—feeling they would run down his starting battery. He preferred to have someone on watch in the cockpit and spot ships before they got close. On his return to Seattle he planned to replace these three lights with one of the new tricolor lights, mounted at the masthead.

Electronics. Until he reached Samoa, Neal's only electric item was a Zenith Trans-Oceanic, which he called " . . . an excellent quality radio, being hand-made in the states." He used it not only for weather reports and time signals from station WWV but for entertainment on the shortwave channels. This radio, for those not familiar with it, runs on shore power or eight D-cell batteries. Neal even used it for a rough-and-ready RDF, by holding it in his hands and rotating it until he got an approximate null from the station he wanted and then glancing at the telltale compass for a bearing.

As for radio-telephone, Neal felt that a VHF " . . . had very limited value for offshore cruising" and that single-sideband [SSB] sets are prohibitively expensive " . . . because you have to have a different crystal for every port you enter." Along the way, however, he became impressed with ham radio, so he ordered one for delivery at Samoa. He notes that it was " . . . no harder than VHF to install, and no costlier." Though he only carried one wet-cell battery, he found he "only had to run his engine 15 to 20 minutes a day to keep it charged to use the radio from one to two hours."

Depth Sounder. The one Neal carried " . . . had only a 100-foot range, which is just not enough." His plan is to replace it with a Coastal Navigator model, which has a 60-foot/60-fathom range, which he feels will be " . . . very helpful in picking up the 50-, 40-, 30- and 20-fathom curves during cruising on soundings." In a depth sounder, Neal prefers the older type of flashing dial to the digital readout because it can "spot" coral heads and reveal their depths—useful when anchoring in coral waters.

Speed and Distance Indicator. Mahina had a combination unit, operating off a small nylon paddlewheel mounted at the bottom of the transom. He preferred it to a unit that trailed a rotor that might be bitten off by a shark, on a line that might become tangled in his rudder or prop. His unit only consumed $\frac{1}{50}$ ampere and could also be run off flashlight batteries. The paddlewheel required occasional scrubbing in tropical waters to remove tube coral and insure smooth rotation.

Dodger. Neal had this fitted as one of his first modifications to *Mahina*. His first impressions was that it was only moderately sturdy as a hand-hold and that he would probably lower it as soon as he reached tropical waters. Well, it did collapse once when he fell against it, but he repaired it by cutting off the ragged ends of the aluminum tubing and slipping a stainless steel tube inside them. Thereafter, it stood the worst that he and the sea could throw at it—and he never again lowered it, finding it as valuable for sun protection as it was to deflect flying spray. In fact, he was so enthusiastic about it that he planned to have a permanent one of stainless steel tubing fitted upon his return. This and the cockpit weather cloths proved highly valuable, as most people don't appreciate—until they face it—the physical punishment weather can dish out, leading to fatigue and hypothermia.

Dinghy. Neal wished he could carry a hard dinghy on the cabintop, but there was simply no room for one (he had in mind an El Toro pram). Instead, he carried an Avon Redstart inflatable, lashed to the cabin top, with a CO_2 bottle wrapped up inside it, for instant inflation in the event of abandoning ship. For that possibility he carried a canvas bag in the cockpit filled with emergency supplies *(see below)*. Overall, the Avon was an extremely successful dinghy, especially going into island beaches through surf.

Emergency Kit. The canvas bag mentioned above held the following: waterproof Emergency Locator Transmitter, with a range of 200 miles, sending a signal on a frequency monitored by overflying aircraft; fishhooks, line, and a knife; compass; containers of water; space blanket for sun protection and collecting rainwater; a second piece of canvas for sun protection; seven "trail lunch" packets (beef jerky, candy bars, crackers, and nuts); an assortment of dried foods, ten cans of soup and fruit juice, vaseline, sunburn lotion, a book to read, pen and paper; one- and five-gallon plastic water bags, and masking tape to convert them into water stills if needed. In the cockpit were the above-mentioned water jugs, which could be thrown overboard as the Avon was launched and which, of course, float in salt water.

Stoves and Cabin Lamps. Kerosene was Neal's fuel throughout. For cooking, he used a two-burner Optimus stove with its own internal fuel tank—which burned for six weeks between fillings. He didn't have space on the galley counter to gimbal the stove—which also served as his chart table—so he lashed it down with shock cord. Sailing to windward, he put chocks under the leeward legs, and this worked unless it was very rough —when he used his Sea Swing stove with an Optimus kerosene burner mounted in it.

For light he had two brass cabin lamps, each with a smoke bell, plus a kerosene anchor light and hurricane lantern. Neal says, "I feel that kerosene is by far the most efficient and cheapest fuel. I averaged less than a gallon a month for the two stoves, the heater and five lamps during the past two-and-a-half years. Kerosene is available almost everywhere."

As for refrigeration, Neal never considered it seriously, saying, "I don't feel it's worth it to listen to the engine run for two or three hours a day for a refrigerator. The simplest thing is to get used to planning meals without the use of a refrigerator. This will mean shopping daily for fresh produce [which is fun] in areas that have it, and relying as much as possible on local foods."

Heater. A niche in the port main bulkhead held a sheet-metal, charcoal-burning fireplace when Neal bought *Mahina,* but he disliked the soot and ashes it produced, so he replaced it with a Taylor (English) pressure-kerosene heater. He notes: "The Taylor has proved much cleaner and easier to use. It has a two-gallon welded steel pressure tank with a small bicycle pump [that I mounted] under the V berths, and the two gallons will last day and night for about three days. Its biggest advantage is that it dries out the air very quickly." The Taylor has a stack and small smoke head projecting above the trunk, so the byproducts of combustion—especially condensation —are vented outside.

This was a successful item, and I'll second Neal's enthusiasm for the Taylor heater, as I lived with the identical model aboard my steel ketch for six years. My only problem with it was that I had a one-quart tank, and it would only burn about five and one-half to six hours before the pressure dropped and the flame went out. So, on many a chilly dawn I had to get up to repump the tank and relight the burner. Otherwise, it was a boon to autumn cruising. (There's no question that one should pay extra for the larger tank.) One other thing: These stoves and heaters—Primus type—both use the same burners, so either one can be cannibalized to keep the other going.

Provisioning. Neal had his own special approach to foods, growing out of current trends toward healthy diets—especially those that avoid chemical additives. He says, "I have avoided beef and pork for several years because I think there are healthier ways to get protein. Also, canned meats are expensive and often contain chemicals. . . . Instead of heavy meals, I've planned my [menus] to include rice, soups, fish, eggs, cheese, grain and bread, and vegetables and fresh fruit. . . . "

Some typical meals at sea: pancakes or french toast for breakfast, sea biscuits and peanut butter for a midday snack, and soup and canned vegetables mixed with rice for a dinner casserole, all of them quick and easy to prepare. One favorite meal was " . . . a can of tuna, a can of vegetables, and fresh sprouts grown at sea, [mixed with] mayonnaise." Neal found he could safely keep a jar of mayonnaise in the bilges for up to two months in the tropics without having it going bad.

When he bought *Mahina,* Neal removed the toilet and turned the head compartment into a large storage area, using it for off-season clothes, sleeping bags, camera equipment, and such stores as canned goods, dried foods, and staples.

Two galley items that proved especially successful aboard *Mahina* were Tang and Lemon Joy. The first not only served as orange juice but was used in small amounts to flavor the water supply, which often had an odd taste in spite of being safe; the detergent not only lathered well in sea water when washing dishes but served, in a pinch, as shampoo.

Cheap Stores. On a long cruise to remote islands one has to keep a sharp eye for bargains in food, and Neal turned up two good ones. At Rarotonga in the Cooks, he visited a local fruit cannery where he bought—shades of *Aquarius*—dented cans that could not otherwise be sold. For eleven dollars he got twenty-four cans of orange and pineapple juice, ten cans of fruit salad, and thirty of crushed pineapple. Two days later he went back and bought forty-eight more cans of the same items. Topping that coup in Rarotonga, he found a wholesale grocery store where he bought case lots of canned soup, butter (New Zealand made), vegetables, powdered milk, and oats. (It's worth checking your local community for such wholesale food outlets— they exist everywhere. I helped friends load up their ketch, *Childhood's End,* at wholesale prices—in case lots only—for a cruise to the Bahamas.)

Neal's other find occurred in American Samoa, where canned goods were very expensive. He went to the Burns-Phillips store—a New Zealand chain with many stores in the islands—and found these bargains: twenty-three dented cans of Campbell's Chunky Turkey soup at thirty cents each (usually eighty cents), and twelve one-pound cans of mackerel—also dented —at twenty-five cents apiece.

On the subject of expenses—both capital and operating—Neal provides an interesting note. One day while sailing between the Cooks and Samoa, he ran out of reading material, so he sat down and ran up his total investment to that point in *Mahina* and found he had spent $16,400, including the purchase price of the sloop and all modifications and additions. Remember, that was 1975.

As for running expenses, Neal kept records for over eighteen months and found he could " . . . generally get by on less than $100.00 a month for everything, including food, fuel, hardware, sail repair, and eating out occasionally." While that was more than a decade ago, it does point up the relatively lower cruising expenses of tropical islands compared with European ports.

The Broken Rudder

This problem Neal faced and solved gets a special section because it exemplifies the sort of self-reliance demanded on a remote-island cruise— or you may not finish it. En route to Palmerston Island in heavy going, *Mahina* was slammed down on her beam ends so hard that the rudder was pivoted violently across its arc and jammed under the port quarter so hard the tiller would not budge it. Neal was able to reach Aitutaki Island, using the vane's rudder, and then began a complicated process of repair.

Just to remove the rudder was a daunting task—and would have been impossible without his scuba gear—as he had to do the job underwater in a 4-knot current that made the water so murky he could see only a foot in front of his face. But, with the help of two native boys, he detached the rudder head fitting and managed to drop the eighty-five pound blade out of the hull.

On the beach he found the cause—the violent wrench to the rudder had broken the welds on the two rods that projected into the rudder blade at right angles from the stock. These welds broke, he concluded, because the rods were mild steel and the stock was stainless.

His first thought was a new rudder, so he cabled the United States for the cost. The answer came back in a few days: $120 for the rudder and $500 for the air freight to Tahiti—where he would have to go to pick it up. That eliminated the "simple" solution.

Next, with the help of the local padre, he twisted the steel stock out of the fiber glass blade. Then he went searching for someone on the island who could do a welding repair. Both the local mechanic and the airfield maintenance men *could* do oxy-acetylene welding, but both had been waiting for a shipment of oxygen for several months. By luck, one of these airport natives also did electric welding, and he did the repair, not only welding in the original rods but, at Neal's insistence, adding a 4-inch by 6-inch piece of $3/16$-inch steel between the two rods. With that additional bracing in place, Neal felt the rudder could take virtually any twisting force without separating the blade from the stock.

Besides supervising, Neal's main job was to work the blade back into the rudder, pack the blocks of fiber glass matrix he had chopped out of the blade back in around the rods and the new piece of steel, seal and bind them all together with polyester resin, and laminate three layers of new glass onto the outside to shut out water. And, of course, paint the rebuilt rudder with anti-fouling and fit it back into the boat.

Ground Tackle

This subject, too, deserves its own section, for two reasons: On an island cruise, you anchor most of the time, and Neal was unusually precise in describing his ground tackle. He says, "I carry four anchors . . . and consider this a minimum."

They were: a 25-lb. CQR with 60 feet of ⁵⁄₁₆-inch chain; a 22-lb. Danforth with 15 feet of ⁵⁄₁₆-inch chain; a 12-lb. Danforth with 65 feet of ⁵⁄₁₆-inch chain; and a 2½-lb. Danforth with 10 feet of ⁵⁄₁₆-inch chain (for the Avon inflatable, the chain being the same size as the others so it could be added to either big anchor when anchoring in deep water). Neal didn't specify how these anchors were designated, but it seems likely the CQR was his storm anchor, the big Danforth his working anchor, and the small Danforth his "lunch hook." Some readers may note the absence of a yachtsman's anchor, but this type really serves best in a bottom that is full of rocks, not where the holding ground is sand studded with coral heads, and that suggests the temperate zones, not tropical waters.

Although Neal carried several hundred feet of nylon line, he anchored exclusively with chain whenever possible, as the best protection against coral head chafe. When he did have to put out greater scope, he buoyed the nylon part of the rode to keep it off the bottom. He would have preferred to carry even more chain but comments, "I don't have all chain because it's expensive and would require buying an anchor windlass [also expensive]. It would also put too much weight up forward."

Finally, his most foolproof method of preventing anchor rode chafe in those waters was to dive down with his scuba gear and visually inspect how well and where the hook was set.

Underlining the advice of several sailors in this book, to take a fairly long cruise—even a coastal one—before heading out into blue water, it seems that one of the most valuable skills one can acquire is learning to anchor safely, day-in, day-out, in every type of bottom and in varying wind and tide conditions, and modifying one's gear and technique as suggested by these experiences.

Cruising Track

Mahina's ports of call: Seattle, Washington . . . San Francisco, California . . . Hilo, Hawaii . . . Marquesas Islands . . . Tuamotu Archipeligo . . . Society Islands (Tahiti, Moorea, etc.) . . . Cook Islands (Rarotonga, Aitutaki, etc.) . . . Palmerston Island . . . Pago Pago, Samoa . . . Christmas Island . . . Honolulu, Hawaii . . . Seattle, Washington.

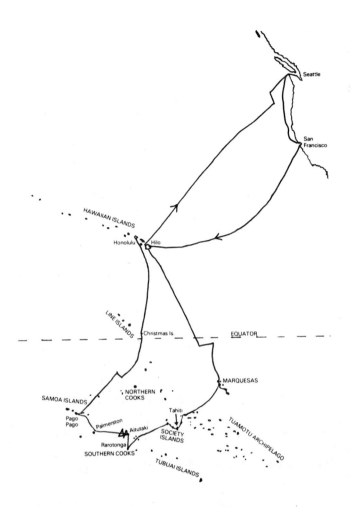

Fig. 14–6. *Chart:* Mahina's *track to the South Seas. (Chart by John Neal)*

Sailing Performance

Neal did not take special pains to record sailing speeds or distance covered, as, like Shane Acton, he sailed without a sense of urgency to reach any particular port in a hurry. But, as he departed with little prior sailing experience, he was naturally concerned with his sloop's behavior characteristics at sea, especially in heavy weather. So, as in several previous chapters, this section will concentrate on a few of Neal's most significant observations and conclusions. But, first, Mahina's performance—potential numbers:

Mahina: Speed/Length Ratio (WL = 23' √23 = 4.79)			
S/L ×	√WL =	Speed (knots) × 24 =	NM (1 day)
1.0	4.79	4.79	115.0
1.1	4.79	5.27	126.5
1.2	4.79	5.75	138.0
1.3	4.79	6.37	152.9
1.34	4.79	6.42	154.0

It was only five days out of Seattle that *Mahina* ran into a force 8 gale and Neal got his first chance to develop a heavy weather routine. (His friend D.J. was aboard on this passage.) As the wind was northerly, they first ran before it under working jib and single-reefed mainsail, and surfed at 8.5 knots under this much sail (as registered by log). Neal reports "everything was fine" so long as they were able to keep the stern squared to the following seas. Several hours later, as the wind and seas mounted, and they were growing tired, the sloop's speed put her in danger of pitch-poling and Neal decided they must slow down. He joined all the spare line aboard—490 feet of it—and trailed it astern in a long loop. This slowed *Mahina* to 6 knots.

But a few hours later the gale was approaching its peak, and both of them were really tiring from being wet and chilled, from the strenuous steering, and from the tension caused by an unending parade of ever-larger waves rearing up astern. Neal decided it was time to heave to and wondered how to accomplish that—never having done it before. He tried it under the storm trysail with the helm alee, and it worked. Then he and D.J. went below and tumbled into their bunks. With all the motion, it was difficult to stay in them, even with the lee cloths in place. Yet they remained hove to for nineteen hours, and at the end of that period the wind was still registering over 50 knots on Neal's wind-speed indicator. By mid-afternoon of the second day—after thirty hours hove to—the wind began to ease, and they began sailing again. Still, with the heavy slop left over from the gale, they could only raise the storm jib and storm trysail. In spite of their travail, Neal at least had acquired a vital piece of information—how *Mahina* could be hove to.

Bound for the Hawaiian islands out of San Francisco (Diane now aboard), *Mahina* reeled off her first 100-mile day (100.83 by the log), a great satisfaction to Neal. Now in warmer waters, the sloop's average speeds were more often 3.5 or 4 knots. But even 4 knots, it should be remembered, is a pretty fair pace, producing almost 100 sea miles if maintained for twenty-four hours.

This passage—August 4–24, 1974—was made in twenty days, and, using 2400 miles as the distance from northern California, we get an average daily mileage of 120 miles—a remarkably good performance. That's maintaining an S/L of 1.05.

After two months in the Hawaiian islands, during which he hauled out to paint *Mahina*'s bottom, Neal sailed again (this time with Cindy aboard) on October 22, 1974, and reached the Marquesas on November 14—2028 miles in twenty-three days, an average of 88 MPD. This slower daily average is probably a result of the fluky wind systems and calm belts that lie along either side of the equator. It was on this passage that Neal made the unsettling discovery that the tropical heat had warped both of his plastic sextants. Upon checking with other skippers at one of the islands, he learned that others had had the same experience and that his Ebco had acquired a 14-degree error. (Soon after, he had a friend back home ship him a regular sextant, and a Japanese Tamaya model arrived at Tahiti a few weeks later.)

While at Bora Bora in the Societies, a hotel owner showed Neal a scrapbook he kept, containing boat photos and comments by all the skippers passing through, and he told Neal that five of the recent entries had sunk since leaving, three of them by hitting the reef at Rarotonga in the Cooks. Recognizing a word to the wise when he heard it, Neal redoubled his efforts to achieve precision in his island-to-island navigation.

En route to the Cooks, he read up on the Fijis and Samoa and decided his next port of call would be the latter, as it sounded more enticing. Approaching Rarotonga, he sailed cautiously and, arriving safely, found it the "perfect island," with an ideal climate (80 degrees by day, 70 degrees by night), with beautiful mountains and beaches and friendly and helpful people. Another pleasant surprise was the price of food—one-third lower than in the Society Islands and the selection excellent, as it was imported from New Zealand rather than France.

His next island in the Cooks was Aitutaki, where he went through the rudder repair described above and where he would have remained through the approaching hurricane season except that there was no safe anchorage available. So, he sailed on to American Samoa. After the visit to Samoa, where he considered and then rejected the idea of selling *Mahina,* he prepared for the long voyage home—much of it to windward, especially from Hawaii on—by adding a Timex Quartz watch to his navigation gear, as a backup source in case something happened to the Zenith Trans-Oceanic. With two in crew aboard this time—Ron and Tim—he got food bargains at the Burns-Phillips store, had a new rudder-head fitting made of bronze by a local mechanic, made a repair to his Sea Swing stove—he anticipated having to use it often in the motion of windward sailing—and was ready to sail, after making his regular masthead inspection.

On the generally northward passage to Christmas Island, *Mahina* logged

100 miles a day for several days on end. But the startling change in *Mahina*'s homeward voyage was that Neal was in a whole new world of seagoing communications—he had installed the ham radio set. This gave him access to a remarkable if informal network in the South Pacific that enabled him to be patched in to U. S. telephones for calls to his family. Neal certainly represents a long stride technologically from chapter 1, Joshua Slocum and *Spray*.

Mahina's elapsed time from Samoa to Christmas Island was sixteen days, so she covered the 1415 miles at an average speed of 88.4 MPD.

After eight days at Christmas, Neal and his crew sailed again, and a week out *Mahina* recorded her best day's run of this passage, 140 miles (over S/L 1.2), repeating that distance the following day. Except for one calm day of only 36 miles, Neal reports no other figures on this passage.

In Hawaii, besides resting and replacing food stocks, Neal made one interesting, if noncritical, repair. He replaced the fastenings holding down the **V** berth flats up forward, using bolts with washers on both ends as a substitute for the original screws—all of which had been pulled out by the violent flexing of the sloop's bow while going to windward in heavy seas. This is an unusual structural problem. One is tempted to say "failure," but since Neal's two-year voyage probably represented twenty to thirty years of weekend and vacation cruising by the typical family for which this boat was intended, perhaps that's an unfair conclusion. That comment presupposes that most readers will agree that not *all* fiberglass boats are built to the rigorous demands of long-distance cruising. This is not intended to single out Albin for special criticism, as several of these Vega-class sloops have made Atlantic crossings, and the boats certainly enjoy a reputation for better-than-average construction.

A last-minute repair just before Neal's departure had to be made to *Mahina*'s mainsail—which split from "leech to luff" when daysailing. Finally, with a friend from home, Bruce, now sailing as crew, Neal sailed on August 8, 1975, bound for Seattle. The first day, *Mahina* covered 113 miles. Next, she notched 105 miles on August 14 and then twice logged 115 miles, on August 22 and 23—all four distances clustered around an S/L ratio of 1.0.

From August 26 to August 27 *Mahina* fought a force 7 gale, under just her storm jib and trysail to slow her down, but the stress on the hull was nonetheless enough to start delaminating the mast-support beam, already repaired once, and this, in turn, buckled the tops of the two main-cabin bulkheads. Fortunately, the weather eased and that situation deteriorated no further for the rest of the passage.

On August 29 Neal's noon sight revealed a run of 144 miles, and *Mahina* topped that the following day with a another of just under 145 miles! This is sterling performance, two days running of almost S/L 1.3, sailing throughout a twenty-four-hour period.

On September 2 at 0435 Neal sighted Cape Flattery, Washington. In near-calm conditions they closed with the land under power on and off all day and docked at a Crescent Bay resort at 1415. *Mahina*'s passage from Hawaii was outstanding—2446 miles in twenty-four days, a daily average of 101.9 miles. Light displacement helps such a performance, of course, and luck with weather plays its part, but *Mahina* and John Neal's sailing effort nevertheless rate a "Well done!"

Taking a retrospective look at the en voyage, Neal makes this remark, a pure echo of the Pardeys' advice:

> If you have the urge to go cruising, now is the time to go. However, before selling your house . . . take a little [cruise] and stick your nose out into the ocean for a few days to see if it is really for you. There have been too many sad cases of people leaving to go on a cruise they have dreamed [about] and saved all their lives for, only to [return] a week or two later and sell their boat because they weren't ready to handle the conditions [that called for] self-reliance where there is no Coast Guard to call. . . .
>
> I have come to a state of mind where I feel that the Pacific is an all-powerful being, and when she smiles, I go as fast as I can; when she is angry, all I can do is wait. I've learned a lot from her—about me, about her, and about life.

That final comment would probably earn an Amen from all the sailors in this book.

A Postscript from John Neal

In a recent letter from John Neal, I received these interesting comments about *Mahina*:

> The Vega Class sloop was never intended for extended offshore work. [After my cruise] I corresponded with the designer in Sweden, Per Brohall, and he was quite surprised to learn that a couple of Vegas had circumnavigated, and that I had put 18,000 miles on the boat in three years.
>
> After I wrote the book, I was planning to sail to Japan with *Mahina*, so I completely gutted her forward of the main bulkhead, put Airex foam and more fiberglass under the V-berth up to the waterline, and added some additional plywood stiffeners. Then I rebuilt the main bulkhead with a sawn oak beam and $2'' \times 4''$ posts carrying the mast compression down to a wooden floor I had epoxied on top of the keel. The end result was a stiff and "bulletproof" boat!
>
> I decided against sailing to Japan at that time, and instead took a delivery job—and ended up living in the Marquesas for a while.
>
> Back to the Vega. For one or two people on a budget, it's hard to beat; with just a little reinforcing, it's great. We actually had one 180-mile day, and five days in a row, did over 160 miles! It's a fairly light boat, with a somewhat flat entry, but is lots of fun to sail.

Bibliography

Acton, Shane. *Shrimpy*. Cambridge: Patrick Stephens Ltd. 1981.

*Allcard, Edward C. *Single-Handed Passage*. New York: W. W. Norton. 1950.

*_____. *Temptress Returns*. New York: W.W. Norton. 1953.

*_____. *Voyage Alone*. New York: Dodd, Mead. 1964.

Davison, Ann. *My Ship Is So Small*. London: Peter Davies. 1956. (1)

*Day, Thomas Fleming. *Across the Atlantic in Sea Bird*. New York: Rudder Publishing Co. 1911.

Guzzwell, John. *Trekka Round the World,* London: Adlard Coles. 1963.

*Herrons, The. *The Voyage of Aquarius*. New York: Sat. Review Press/ E. P. Dutton. 1974.

*LaBorde, Harold. *An Ocean to Ourselves*. New York: John deGraff. 1962. (2)

*Maury, Richard. *The Saga of Cimba*. New York: John deGraff. 1962. (3)

Neal, John. *The Log of the Mahina*. Seattle: Pacific Intl. Pub. Co. 1976.

Pardey, Lin and Larry. *Cruising in Seraffyn*. New York: Seven Seas Press. 1976.

_____. *Seraffyn's European Adventure*. New York: W. W. Norton. 1979.

_____. *Seraffyn's Mediteranean Adventure*. New York: W. W. Norton. 1981.

_____. *Seraffyn's Oriental Adventure*. New York: W. W. Norton. 1983.

*Pidgeon, Harry. *Around the World Single-Handed*. London: Rupert Hart-Davis Mariner's Library Edition. 1954.

*Rebell, Fred. *Escape to the Sea*. London: John Murray. 1939.

Slocum, Joshua. *Sailing Alone Around the World*. London: Rupert Hart-Davis Mariner's Library Edition. 1955.

*Smith, Stanley and Violet, Charles. *The Wind Calls the Tune*. London: Robert Ross Ltd. 1952.

(1) (2) (3) On a limited basis, these three books are available from Sailing Book Service, Clinton Corners, NY 12514.

RELATED READING

Culler, R. D. *The Spray*. Camden, ME: Intl. Marine Pub. 1978.

Slack, Kenneth E., *In the Wake of the Spray,* New Brunswick, NJ: Rutgers Univ. Press. 1966.

Smeeton, Miles. *Once Is Enough*. London: Rupert Hart-Davis Mariner's Library Edition. 1960.

Teller, Walter M. *The Search for Captain Slocum,* New York: Scribners. 1956.

Woas, Lee. *Self-Steering without a Windvane*. Newport, RI: Seven Seas Press. 1982.

*These books are, to the best of my knowledge, out of print.